GOSPEL REFLECTIONS AND PRAYERS

WHAT THE READERS SAY

"More than fifty years a priest and this is the book I've been waiting for all these years"
– Missionary Priest

"Your book takes a burden off my shoulder in preparing for our weekly gathering"
– Leader of a Parish Prayer Group

"We use your book for our prayer together every morning"
– Husband and wife, both retired

"He excels in pithy but thoughtful soundbites"
– Review in Intercom

"I use your book for my meditation every morning"
– Well-known apostle of charity

"These reflections are so visual that I doodle a picture at the bottom of the page"
– Self-confessed doodler!

GOSPEL REFLECTIONS AND PRAYERS

Daily Mass Readings

Silvester O'Flynn OFM Cap.

columba
BOOKS

First published in 2018 as
Homily Hints and Prayers by

23 Merrion Square North,
Dublin 2, Co. Dublin
www.columbabooks.com

This new edition, 2020

ISBN: 978-1-78218-374-7

Set in Kepler Std 10.5/14
Cover and book design by Alba Esteban | Columba Books
Printed by L&C, Poland

CONTENTS

PREFACE 07

Advent Hints

FIRST WEEK OF ADVENT 12

SECOND WEEK OF ADVENT 24

THIRD WEEK OF ADVENT 36

DECEMBER 17TH - 24TH 46

Christmas Hints | DECEMBER 26TH TO JANUARY 12TH 64

Lent Hints

ASH WEDNESDAY 102

THURSDAY AFTER ASH WEDNESDAY 104

FRIDAY AFTER ASH WEDNESDAY.................106

SATURDAY AFTER ASH WEDNESDAY............108

FIRST WEEK OF LENT...................................110

SECOND WEEK OF LENT 122

THIRD WEEK OF LENT 134

FOURTH WEEK OF LENT 146

FIFTH WEEK OF LENT 158

HOLY WEEK..170

Easter Hints

OCTAVE OF EASTER 180

SECOND WEEK OF EASTER 192

THIRD WEEK OF EASTER 204

FOURTH WEEK OF EASTER 216

FIFTH WEEK OF EASTER 228

SIXTH WEEK OF EASTER 240

SEVENTH WEEK OF EASTER 252

Ordinary Time

WEEK 1... 266

WEEK 2..278

WEEK 3.. 290

WEEK 4 302

WEEK 5...314
WEEK 6 326
WEEK 7...338
WEEK 8 350
WEEK 9 362
WEEK 10...374
WEEK 11 386
WEEK 12...398
WEEK 13 410
WEEK 14...422
WEEK 15...434
WEEK 16...446
WEEK 17...458
WEEK 18 470
WEEK 19...482
WEEK 20 494
WEEK 21...506
WEEK 22...518
WEEK 23...530
WEEK 24...542
WEEK 25...554
WEEK 26...566
WEEK 27...578
WEEK 28...590
WEEK 29...602
WEEK 30 614
WEEK 31 626
WEEK 32...638
WEEK 33...650
WEEK 34...662

PREFACE

"Speak concisely, say much in few words" (Sir 32:8).

These words were quoted by Pope Francis as advice on how to prepare a homily.

This book was written at the request of priests who have asked me when was I going to offer something on the Daily Mass Readings. They were familiar with my books on the Sunday Mass Readings, *The Good News of Matthew's Year; The Good News of Mark's Year; The Good News of Luke's Year; Sunday Seeds;* and *The Responsorial Psalms of Sunday* (all published by Columba Press).

People who come to weekday Mass like to get a thought for the day or some message of inspiration. The daily homilies of Pope Francis have a worldwide appeal. In many instances, time is a problem as people are under pressure to get to work or meet an appointment. The constraints of time are a challenge to come straight to the point with a clear message. Pope Francis has taken to heart the advice of Pope Paul VI to be simple, clear, direct and well adapted. I have attempted to follow these four directions.

Use simple language that anybody can understand. For instance, an Apostolic Exhortation can be called a booklet.

Have a clear message that can be summarised in one short sentence. If you have to qualify what you saying, you are losing power, like a slow puncture.

Direct, get straight to the point.

Well adapted, connecting the Word of God with the lives of the listeners.

This is the age of the catchy sound bite. Scripture is the inspired Word of the Lord. It belongs to all times. As Jesus said at Nazareth, "this text is being fulfilled today even as you listen". Pope Francis called the homily "a living dialogue between God and his people". The task of the preacher is to facilitate that dialogue by suggesting the connection between the written Word and life as we experience it, whether in the Church, in the world or in our own lives.

It is fascinating to listen to participants at a gospel Enquiry and to see how each one takes a different image, word or message. The American poet e. e. cummings wrote about four girls named Maggie, Millie, Molly and May who went down to the beach to play one day. Each one of them had a totally different experience as "it's always ourselves we find in the sea". That is exactly how the sacred Word can touch people in a very personal way. Through the inspired Word, God enables us to see life with fresh eyes, challenging, inspiring, consoling, questioning, shaping or directing.

I offer two short reflections on the daily Gospels. Each reflection can be read in about two minutes. The homilist may use either one or both. They are intended as homily hints. Many preachers want some idea or image that will act as a trigger to their own thinking. The best book is the one that inspires readers to do their own thinking.

The reflections lead into intercessory prayers connecting the Scriptures of the day with the needs of the Church and the congregation. The reader is encouraged to add prayers relating to other intentions such as a recent tragedy, exams, an anniversary, or prayers for the sick.

During Ordinary Time, I have rarely referred to the First Reading which has no direct connection with the Gospel. Furthermore, the First Readings follow the two-year cycle while the Gospels are on a one-year cycle.

With fewer priests available, many parishes will not have Mass every day. Where people take leadership of alternative prayer services, I hope this book will be a help to their reflections and prayers.

The seed is the Word of God and the rich soil represents those people with a noble and generous heart who have heard the Word and take it to themselves and yield a rich harvest through their perseverance.

LUKE 8:11, 15

This New Edition

For the new edition of this book I have changed the title from *Homily Hints and Prayers* to *Gospel Reflections and Prayers*. The idea of writing reflections on the weekday Mass Readings simmered in my mind for some time. There were a few false starts. Eventually the push I needed came in a request from Columba Books for *Prayers of the Faithful* drawn from the daily Scriptures. Writing began but soon I felt that the Prayers could not stand on their own so I added two short reflections as homily hints for the preacher. It came as a delightful surprise when many people, who never have to preach, told me how much they got from these reflections. The word Homily in the title probably deterred some likely readers from further investigation, so, for the second edition the title has been changed to *Gospel Reflections and Prayers*.

ADVENT

MONDAY

ISAIAH 2:1-5 | MATT 8:5-11

1. It's a pity that Advent has been devoured by the giant of commercialised Christmas. Advent is the season of hope – an invitation to get in touch with the winter experiences of life... spiritual darkness... illness... war... persecution... scandals... suicides etc. The constant prayer-word of Advent is COME. As long as there is Someone-who-is-coming there is hope. The Roman centurion begged Jesus to come to heal his servant. Jesus said, "I will come myself and cure him". Jesus is the Someone-who-comes. He comes to us in a special way in Holy Communion, the greatest source of spiritual healing. We join with the Roman centurion in saying, "Lord, I am not worthy that you should enter under roof". Holy Communion is not a prize for being good. It is a healing food to help us to be good.

2. Isaiah is the great prophet of hope during Advent. Today's First Reading comes from a time when Jerusalem was under threat of invasion. Isaiah urges the people to come to the Temple of God and to learn the path to peace. He offers wonderful images of a world at peace. Instruments of destruction will be beaten into agricultural implements, swords into ploughshares and spears into sickles. His words are inscribed at the headquarters of the United Nations. During Advent we come to God in hope for a better world.

PRAYERS

Let us invite the Lord to come to us in our needs. The Response to the prayers is: *"Come, Lord Jesus, come".*

For the Church, called to be the Body of Christ. May the Holy Spirit guide and support Pope *(name)* today and every day.
Come, Lord Jesus, come.

That the dream of Isaiah will be fulfilled when the weapons of destruction are changed into implements of cultivation providing food for those who are starving.
Come, Lord Jesus, come.

May the message of Advent bring hope to all who are experiencing a winter of the spirit.
Come, Lord Jesus, come.

That we might have a deep appreciation of what it is to receive the Lord in Holy Communion.
Come, Lord Jesus, come.

(Pray for any personal, local or topical intention)

O God, may this holy season of Advent enlighten our faith, strengthen our hope and inspire our charity, through Christ, our Lord. Amen

TUESDAY

ISAIAH 11:1-10 | LUKE 10:21-24

1. Isaiah is the voice of hope during Advent. In yesterday's Mass he spoke of the weapons of destruction being changed into implements for cultivating the land. We all long for a world without warfare. Isaiah promised that Someone-is-coming, a descendent of David's line, filled with the seven gifts of the Holy Spirit: wisdom, understanding, counsel, fortitude, knowledge, holiness and reverential fear of God. Then there will be reconciliation between traditional enemies... wolf and lamb... calf and lion cub ... panther and kid. Wars are the work of adults. A little child will lead us to peace, the child whose birth we will celebrate at Christmas.

2. Wars are the work of adults. Jesus found that people who thought they were clever rejected his ideals. But he was filled with joy by the Holy Spirit when childlike souls accepted the plan for life that he was revealing. In Advent we pray that nations will be reconciled in harmony and peace.

PRAYERS

Encouraged by the Word of God, we pray for peace.
Response: *Come, Lord Jesus, come.*

May the voice of the Church, appealing for peace, inspire all nations to live in harmony and peace.
Come, Lord Jesus, come.

May the grace of the Holy Spirit enable traditional enemies to be reconciled.
Come, Lord Jesus, come.

For families who are divided: may the grace of Advent reunite people so that Christmas can be celebrated in true peace and harmony.
Come, Lord Jesus, come.

"A little boy will lead them". May we accept the ideals of Jesus and live in harmony as brothers and sisters in the one big family of God.
Come, Lord Jesus, come.

   (Pray for any personal, local or topical intention)

God of mercy, help us to overcome our pride and hatred. Lead all nations to the way of peace. Through Christ, our Lord. Amen.

WEDNESDAY

ISAIAH 25:6-10 | MATT 15:29-37

1. Advent is the season of hope. Hope is the virtue that keeps us going through the dark seasons of life. The message of hope is based on the promises of what God will do. According to Isaiah, God will prepare a rich banquet for all people. God will destroy death forever. God will wipe away every tear and take away all shame. The Lord is our shepherd, there is nothing we shall want. Jesus felt sorry for the people and fed them.

2. Gandhi said that since hunger is such a widespread problem, the only acceptable way for God to come would be as bread. Despite our advances in knowledge and technology, the scandal of hunger remains. And there are the hungers of the spirit in loneliness, depression, suicide, the break-up of marriages, dependence on drugs. Jesus knew what he was doing when he chose bread as the embodiment of his presence with us. He is the Living Bread come down from Heaven.

PRAYERS

Jesus felt sorry for the people who were without food. So let us turn to him in prayer.
Response: *Give us today our daily bread.*

May the knowledge and technology we have nowadays be used to solve the problem of world hunger.
Give us today our daily bread.

As we plan for Christmas, may we avoid spending money on unnecessary luxuries and give generously to the organisations that help people in need.
Give us today our daily bread.

Many people suffer from hungers of the spirit. May we be more sensitive to their needs.
Give us today our daily bread.

The Lord has promised to wipe away the tears from every cheek. We pray for the consolation of people who are in deep grief and darkness.
Give us today our daily bread.

(Pray for any personal, local or topical intention)

Loving Father, as we recognise all the blessings we have received, may we be moved to share generously with those in any need. Through Christ, our Lord. Amen

THURSDAY

ISAIAH 26:1-6 | MATT 7:21. 24-27

1. The Lord is an everlasting rock. A house built on rock has a solid foundation. The rock is a symbol of stability and hope in the shifting sands of modern life. Is there anything to hold on to? Are we to change with every new fashion and current fad? Without the backbone of hope, people find it very hard to cope with any crisis. Today's culture has been described as liquid modernity. Liquid hardly suggests a solid foundation. But the person who listens to Christ's words and acts on them is building on an everlasting rock.

2. There is a huge difference between permissiveness and true freedom. Permissiveness wants no restrictions on what I want to do. True freedom is the inner strength to do what I ought to do, namely the will of our Father in Heaven. Permissiveness builds on the shifting sands of passion, feelings, peer pressure, popularity, or changing fashions. Freedom listens to the words of Jesus and acts on them. It builds life on an everlasting rock.

PRAYERS

The Lord is an everlasting rock. Let us pray to him in great confidence.

The first Pope, Saint Peter, was given a name which means *a rock*. May his successor today be a rock of fidelity inspiring the world with the message of Jesus.
Lord, hear us. Lord, graciously hear us.

May our lives always be guided by the teaching of Jesus.
Lord, hear us. Lord, graciously hear us.

We pray for those who seek direction and meaning in life. May Christ the Good Shepherd guide them along the right path.
Lord, hear us. Lord, graciously hear us.

We pray for people whose homes have been destroyed by war, earthquake, fire or flood. Lord, help them to make a fresh start in life.
Lord, hear us. Lord, graciously hear us.

   (Pray for any personal, local or topical intention)

O God, the Rock of Ages, you are the foundation of our hope. Hear the prayers we offer in the name of Jesus Christ, your Son, our Lord. Amen.

FRIDAY

ISAIAH 29:17-24 | MATT 9:27-31

1. Advent is the season of hope for healing. Isaiah, the great prophet of hope, offers hope to those areas of life where we are deaf and blind. "The deaf that day will hear the words of a book. And after shadow and darkness, the eyes of the blind will see." In the Gospel, Jesus touched the eyes of two blind men and restored their sight. There are many ways that we can be blind or deaf. Am I aware of the many blessings of my life? Do I appreciate the wonders of creation? Am I blinded by prejudice? Can I see anything good in certain people? Am I addicted to gossip? Am I deaf to the cries of the poor? Each one of us needs the healing touch of Jesus.

2. Helen Keller was blind and deaf from the age of eighteen months. When a friend came in after a walk in the woods, Helen asked her if she had seen anything special. "Not really," replied the friend. Helen was stunned. But that is just the way we are at times. God is all around us to be seen and heard. But we are spiritually blind and deaf. The poet, Gerard Manley Hopkins, wrote that all things are charged with God (like electricity) and give off sparks that speak of Him, if only we know how to touch them. Jesus knew the power of touch. He touched the eyes of two blind men and their eyes were opened. This Advent, may God open our eyes, our ears and our hearts to His coming.

PRAYERS

Let us pray with the Response: *The Lord is my light and my help.*

May the Church be true to its mission to be the light of the nations.
The Lord is my light and my help.

Lord, open our eyes to see your presence among us.
The Lord is my light and my help.

Open our ears to the wisdom of the Good News.
The Lord is my light and my help.

We pray for those who are physically blind or deaf, may the Lord compensate them with great spiritual sight and hearing.
The Lord is my light and my help.

(Pray for any personal, local or topical intention)

We offer up all our prayers in the name of Jesus Christ the Lord.
Amen

SATURDAY

ISAIAH 30:19-21. 23-26 | *MATT 9:35 – 10:1.6-8*

1. All this week, Isaiah has given us great images of hope. Today he speaks of the bread of suffering and the water of distress. And he refers to God as our teacher. Suffering can be a school where God teaches us valuable lessons. Suffering can break through our pride and make us humble. It brings us to our senses, gives us a bigger perspective on life. Suffering makes us appreciate how much we depend on others. It helps us to be more compassionate with others who are suffering. C.S. Lewis wrote, "God whispers to us in our pleasures, speaks to us in our conscience and cries out to us in our pain. It is his megaphone to arouse a deaf world".

2. Jesus travelled from village to village proclaiming the Good News and curing all kinds of diseases and sickness. He sent out the Apostles to extend his mission and healing. He felt sorry for all who were feeling lost and dejected. In our day there is a huge harvest of souls who are in great spiritual distress. But the labourers are getting older and fewer. There are very few specific intentions for which Jesus asked us to pray. There are many distracting voices leading people away from God's calling. That makes praying for vocations all the more necessary.

PRAYERS

Jesus had compassion on the people because they were like sheep without a shepherd. So, let us pray.

May the powers of teaching and healing which the Lord bestowed on the first Apostles be manifested in the Church today.
Lord, hear us.

Pope Francis pictured the Church as a field hospital for all who are wounded in the battlefield of life. May the Church be a source of hope and healing for people who are spiritually wounded.
Lord, hear us.

The harvest is rich but the labourers are few. We pray that many men and women will hear God's call and respond generously.
Lord, hear us.

For all who are suffering deeply: may their suffering be a school where they are spiritually enriched.
Lord, hear us.

(Pray for any personal, local or topical intention)

God of compassion, hear the prayers we offer in the name of Jesus Christ, your Son, our Lord. Amen.

MONDAY

ISAIAH 35:1-10 | *LUKE 5:17-26*

1. Advent is about the coming of God. Isaiah proclaimed to the people who were in exile in Babylon that there is hope. "Look, your God is coming, vengeance is coming, the retribution of God; he is coming to save you." It will be a time of liberation. The eyes of the blind will be liberated from darkness; the ears of the deaf unsealed; the lame shall leap like a deer and the tongues of the dumb sing for joy. Centuries later Jesus recalled the words of Isaiah to describe his own mission of liberation. The greatest liberation is from the guilt of sin. For those who rejected the claim of Jesus, he proved his divine power by enabling a paralysed man to stand up and walk. When we meet Jesus in the Sacrament of Reconciliation, we are liberated. We too can stand up and walk. We go home praising God.

2. The man on the stretcher was physically paralysed. There are many ways that we might be spiritually paralysed. Too much self-examination can result in paralysis by analysis. Spiritual paralysis can be caused by the burden of guilt, or the legacy of past failures. Fear or anxiety can cripple us. The voice of Jesus is strong: "I order you: get up: pick up your stretcher and walk."

Get up. Pick up. And walk.

PRAYERS

Jesus came down to our world to save us and lift us up. So, we have the confidence to pray.
The Response is: *Come, Lord Jesus, come.*

May the Church be an oasis of hope and mercy for all who feel spiritually paralysed.
Come, Lord Jesus, come.

For people who feel totally defeated by any addiction. May they learn to hand over their weakness to the Saviour who will lift them up to begin a new life.
Come, Lord Jesus, come.

May all of us be like the stretcher-bearers as our faith carries the needs of the sick to Jesus.
Come, Lord Jesus, come.

For people who are physically incapacitated: may the grace of God give them wonderful spiritual help.
Come, Lord Jesus, come.

(Pray for any personal, local or topical intention)

God of mercy, come to us this Advent, take away our fears and anxieties. Through Christ our Lord. Amen

TUESDAY

ISAIAH 40:1-11 | MATT 18:12-14

1. Isaiah has news of great hope for the exiles in Babylon. A new ruler there has a new policy and the Jews will be allowed to return to Jerusalem. So, prepare the way of return. Isaiah's imagery of the roadworks can guide our preparation for an Advent confession. What crooked ways must I straighten? What low valleys must be filled up... low faith, low prayer, low esteem for others? What hills must be levelled... pride, superiority, looking down on others? Prepare a way for the Lord.

2. "Here is the Lord coming with power, his arm subduing all things." Jesus came with divine power to subdue all evil spirits. He came as the shepherd feeding his flock, gathering lambs in his arms. Each individual is important to him. When one who has gone astray is found, it gives more joy to Heaven than do the ninety-nine others who did not stray. Pope Francis extended God's care for the sinner to include people who are trying although they cannot yet make the full break from sin. A small step, in the midst of great human limitations, can be more pleasing to God than a life which appears outwardly in order but has never faced great difficulties. Jesus came to give hope to the sinner.

PRAYERS

Encouraged by the Word of the Lord, we pray.

May the Church be the servant of God's love and mercy, welcoming back the lost sheep and giving hope to the sinner.
Lord, hear us.

May this holy season of Advent prepare us spiritually for Christmas.
Lord, hear us.

For all who feel helpless in dealing with their addictions and problems, may they hear the voice of the Good Shepherd calling them home.
Lord, hear us.

Let us pray for those who are sick, and for people who feel very lonely at this time of year.
Lord, hear us.

(Pray for any personal, local or topical intention)

O God, whose heart is full of joy at the return of a sinner, hear our prayers in the name of Jesus Christ, your Son, our Lord. Amen.

WEDNESDAY

ISAIAH 40: 25-31 | MATT 11:28-30

1. During Advent we think of God coming to us. But we should also think of our coming to God. Jesus invites us to come. "Come to me all who are heavily burdened and I will give you rest." He paints the picture of a pair of oxen harnessed together. Pull in harmony together and the burden is light. Pull at a different pace or angle and the pain is sharp. Jesus invites us to his pace and angle ... he is gentle and humble of heart. Come and pair up with him and you will find rest for your souls.
   Young men may grow tired and weary, youths may stumble, but those who hope in the Lord renew their strength, they put out wings like eagles.

2. Today's Responsorial Psalm can lift us up on eagles' wings.

   Listen again to these beautiful lines.

   Never forget all his blessings. He forgives all your guilt. He crowns you with love and compassion. The Lord is compassion and love, slow to anger and rich in mercy. He does not treat us according to our sins nor repay us according to our faults. My soul, give thanks to the Lord.

PRAYERS

The Lord invites us to come to him when we feel weary and overburdened.

May we learn how to walk the road of life in union with Jesus. May we be like him who is gentle and humble of heart.
Lord, hear us.

We pray for those who feel totally exhausted by the burdens they carry. May they find peace and new strength with the Lord at their side.
Lord, hear us.

For those who have stumbled and fallen: may they accept the hand of God reaching out to them.
Lord, hear us.

(Pray for any personal, local or topical intention)

O God of mercy and compassion, may we never forget all the blessings you bestow upon us. Through Christ, our Lord. Amen

THURSDAY

ISAIAH 41:13-20 | MATT 11:11-15

1. The Gospel readings for the next week focus on John the Baptist, the Advent man whose mission was to prepare the way for the Lord. Like many of the prophets before him, he was subjected to violence because his preaching challenged the powers-that-be. John suffered martyrdom because of his moral teaching. Are we prepared to stand up for our moral ideals? We may be mocked. We may have to swim against the current of very biased media. The opposition is violent because the sick eye cannot stand the light: the sick stomach cannot stand even the smell of food: and the sick soul reacts violently against godliness. Prepare a way for the Lord. But it may not be easy.

2. Draw strength from Isaiah the prophet of hope. The Jews got the news that they could return to Jerusalem from their exile in Babylon. However, the task of rebuilding Jerusalem and restoring the land would be difficult. Isaiah gives them assurance of God's help. "I am holding you by the right hand: I tell you, 'Do not be afraid, I will help you'."
Today's Responsorial Psalm will give us courage.
"The Lord is kind and full of compassion. Slow to anger and rich in mercy."

PRAYERS

All of us who received the light of Christ at our Baptism are called, like John the Baptist, to prepare a way for the Lord. Let us pray with the response: *Come, Lord Jesus, come.*

May the Church always proclaim the ideals of God's Kingdom, the sacredness of life, peace, truth, sharing and compassion.
Come, Lord Jesus, come.

For all who are persecuted or mocked for standing up for their Christian beliefs, may the Lord's grace support them.
Come, Lord Jesus, come.

For all who are going through a difficult time. May God's promise of support sustain them.
Come, Lord Jesus, come.

(Pray for any personal, local or topical intention)

Almighty Father, sustain us by your grace to be faithful to your Kingdom at all times. Through Christ, our Lord. Amen.

FRIDAY

ISAIAH 48:17-19 | MATT 11:16-19

1. There are two ways of offering correction to people: a strict correction, or a gentle appeal to do better. Stick or carrot. The threat of punishment or the promise of a reward. John the Baptist favoured the strict approach. His style of life was penitential. Jesus took up the more gentle approach. Each approach was correct in its own time. Some people needed to hear John's stern warning, whereas other people responded to message of mercy and hope which Jesus favoured. "Wisdom is proved right by her actions." Wisdom knows when to be strict or when to be gentle.

2. There are some people and you couldn't please them. Come and dance with me. No! Okay, let's play funerals. No! John the Baptist's penitential approach? No thanks! What about Jesus? Scandalous the way he mixes with sinners, a glutton and a drunkard.
   There are some people and you couldn't please them.
   Where do you stand?

PRAYERS

As we prepare for Christmas may we be guided by the wisdom of the Holy Spirit.
The response is: *Come, Lord Jesus, come.*

May the Church be guided by the wisdom of the Holy Spirit in knowing how to balance strict rules with gentle mercy.
Come, Lord Jesus, come.

When we have to offer correction to somebody, may the Holy Spirit guide us.
Come, Lord Jesus, come.

May we be humble enough to accept correction or guidance from others.
Come, Lord Jesus, come.

For those who find fault with everything. May they be less stubborn and more flexible in their thinking and behaviour.
Come, Lord Jesus, come.

(Pray for any personal, local or topical intention)

O God, fill our hearts with joy as we prepare for Christmas, the birth of Jesus, your Beloved Son, our Lord. Amen

SATURDAY

ECCLESIASTICUS 48:1-4. 9-11 | MATT17:10-13

1. Elijah was the most charismatic of the prophets. There is no account of his death but he was carried up to heaven in a fiery chariot. People expected Elijah to come back to prepare the way for the Messiah. Jesus identified John the Baptist as the person who performed that task. We think of prophets as foretellers of the future. But their principal mission was to reveal to people the message of God in their present situation. They revealed how God was correcting, punishing, inspiring, consoling or promising a better future. A true prophet enabled people to see God at work in the situations of life. They prepared the way for the Lord.

2. John the Baptist was identified by Jesus as a true prophet in the tradition of Elijah. He inspired people to wash away their sins and undertake a life of justice and truth. He prepared people for Jesus. He pointed to Jesus as the one who should be followed. Who are the prophets, the inspirational people of our times? Obvious examples are Saint Teresa of Calcutta, Saint John Paul II, Nelson Mandela, Martin Luther King. Can you think of anyone who has been an inspiration in your life? Who has been a source of great blessings? In the Sacrament of Baptism you were anointed with the oil of chrism to show that you are united with Christ as king, priest and prophet. Each one of us has a mission to help others to be more aware of God's presence and action in their lives.

PRAYERS

As we prepare for the celebration of Christmas we pray.
The Response will be: *Come, Lord Jesus, come.*

We thank God for the prophets of past ages who inspired and challenged people with God's message. May the Church of our times be blessed with inspirational leaders.
Come, Lord Jesus, come.

The great prophets like Elijah, John the Baptist and Jesus were persecuted. May the prophets of our day be sustained by God's grace to withstand criticism and opposition.
Come, Lord Jesus, come.

May the witness of our lives be an inspiration to others.
Come, Lord Jesus, come.

May we resist the commercial pressures of Christmas and focus on the real meaning of the birth of the Saviour.
Come, Lord Jesus, come.

   (Pray for any personal, local or topical intention)

O God, may the light of the coming of your Beloved Son free us from the darkness of sin. Through Christ, our Lord. Amen

MONDAY

NUMBERS 24:2-7. 15-17 | *MATT 21:23-27*

1. Jesus was questioned by the chief priests and leaders about his authority to preach. Authority is having a hard time today. It is regarded as an invasion of my rights. One night on a radio chat programme, three priests were being interviewed about their lives. When one of them mentioned the stress of preaching, the interviewer suddenly changed tone. "Who gave you the right to tell others how to live?" The answer is not about the right to preach but the responsibility to proclaim the message that has come from God through the teaching of Jesus Christ. The word *authority* is an extension of the word *author*. Authority in the Church is not about exercising power. What it means is the responsibility to be faithful to the Christ, the author of our faith.

2. In our First Reading we meet with Balaam. He is known as the man with the far-seeing eyes. He foresaw that a star from Jacob's descendants would arise to lead the people. We recognise Jesus as that guiding light. Advent is a time to look ahead, not only to Christ's coming at Christmas but also to Christ's final coming at the end of life. The digital watch is suited to the mentality of many today. The digital watch gives the present time to the exact second but it shows no past and no future. Blink and the figure has changed. People who live only in the present moment are easily broken. Having no sense of the past, they lack richness of memory to support them in a present crisis. Worse again, they lack the sense of future to give hope when all around them collapses. We need the big picture of life. We need Balaam's far-seeing eyes. With God in our picture there is always hope.

PRAYERS

As we are challenged by the words of Scripture, let us pray.
The response is: *Come, Lord Jesus, come.*

May the authority of the Church be seen as the responsibility to remain faithful to Jesus Christ who is the author of our faith.
Come, Lord Jesus, come.

May our political leaders exercise their authority by working for justice and peace, for the protection of life and for the welfare of all our people.
Come, Lord Jesus, come.

May our preparation for Christmas ensure that the birthday of the Saviour will be the centre of our celebrations.
Come, Lord Jesus, come.

May Jesus, the Star of Jacob, be the guiding light of our lives.
Come, Lord Jesus, come.

   (Pray for any personal, local or topical intention)

Heavenly Father, hear our prayers in the name of Jesus Christ, our Lord. Amen.

TUESDAY

ZEPHANIAH: 3:1-2.9-13 | MATT 21:28-32

1. When Jesus spoke about people making their way into the Kingdom of God, what did he mean? He was referring to the people who were buying into his ideals. In popular language, they were getting the hang of what he was about. The parable of the two sons contrasts the sinners who had said "No" to God, with the religious leaders who fancied that they had said "Yes" to God. However, the Yes-men were so self-righteous that they were actually saying "No" because they were rejecting Jesus. But the sinners were saying "Yes" by being open to the message of John the Baptist, a pattern of true holiness, and to Jesus. John and Jesus gave hope to the sinners. They believed in mercy and mercy is the essence of the Gospel.

2. The objection is made that there can be too much emphasis on mercy with the result that sin is not taken seriously. "Sure, won't God forgive me." The Latin word for mercy is *misericordia*, meaning a compassionate or suffering heart. The Irish word *trócaire* is an exact translation of the Latin. The person who is close to the feelings of the heart of God is very much aware of sin. Many of the saints wept for their sins. If you want to know what sin is, ask the saint, not the sinner. In the words of Cardinal Walter Kasper, "mercy is the essence of the Gospel and the key to Christian living."

PRAYERS

As we draw closer to Christmas let us prepare our minds and hearts to welcome the Saviour of the world.
The Response is: *Come, Lord Jesus, come.*

May our religious leaders inspire the world with the ideals of Jesus for the reign of God on Earth.
Come, Lord Jesus, come.

May we always say "Yes" to God's teaching, not only in word, but also in action.
Come, Lord Jesus, come.

Let us pray for those who are a long time away from confession. May the celebration of Christmas touch their hearts with the desire to celebrate God's mercy in the Sacrament.
Come, Lord Jesus, come.

May Christmas be a time of reconciliation and peace for families that are divided.
Come, Lord Jesus, come.

(Pray for any personal, local or topical intention)

God of mercy and compassion, hear the prayers we offer in the name of Jesus Christ, your Son, our Lord. Amen

WEDNESDAY

ISAIAH 45:6-8. 18. 21-26 | *LUKE 7: 19-23*

1. John the Baptist was imprisoned by Herod in a remote fortress. Locked up, not knowing whether he would be released or murdered, his thoughts were negative. Doubts set in. John had predicted that the one coming after him would wield an axe to cut down fruitless trees – in other words, a time of strict judgement and punishment. What was Jesus doing? Where was the axe? John was impatient. "Are you really the one who is to come or should we look for another?" Jesus told John's messengers to look at what he was doing. His ministry of healing and liberation was exactly what prophets like Isaiah had predicted. Jesus brought hope and renewal of life. "The Good News is proclaimed to the poor. Blessed are those who do not lose faith in me."

2. Blessed are those who do not lose faith in Jesus. We might add: Blessed are those who do not lose faith in the Church he founded. Many people find their faith shaken by the uncovering of scandals in the Church. Add in the constant negative brainwashing by hostile media. A modern parable. Think of the huge difference between an orange and a potato. One mouldy bit on the orange and all the juice is contaminated. If there is a bad spot on a potato, this can be removed and the rest is perfect. The Church is more like the potato. Yes, there are black spots but the overwhelming majority of Church members are good, continuing to work for the Kingdom of God on Earth, worshipping God, working for justice and peace, improving the quality of life through education, health care, feeding the hungry, bringing consolation and hope. Blessed are those who have not lost faith in the Church.

PRAYERS

After listening to the Word of God, we pray.
The Response is: *Come, Lord Jesus, come.*

May we never lose faith in Jesus. May this Advent be a season of growing in faith.
Come, Lord Jesus, come.

Since the time of Jesus, the Church has been outstanding in works of mercy. May the Church in our time be blessed with people who make the world a better place to live.
Come, Lord Jesus, come.

As we think of John the Baptist in prison, we pray for all who have been arrested because of their religious beliefs.
Come, Lord Jesus, come.

Let us pray for all prisoners, that their time in jail will bring them closer to God.
Come, Lord Jesus, come.

   (Pray for any personal, local or topical intention)

Heavenly Father, may our celebration of the birth of the Saviour prepare us for eternal life. Through Christ, our Lord. Amen.

THURSDAY

ISAIAH 54:1-10 | *LUKE* 7:24-30

1. Beware of the man of the one book. The ways of God are not confined to one way, one book, one novena never known to fail, one apparition. John the Baptist brought people to conversion through a strict lifestyle and penitential living. Jesus followed a different approach, the way of gentleness and mercy. Jesus expressed his admiration of John as an upright man who brought many people to conversion. "Of all the children born of women, there is no one greater than John. Yet the least in the Kingdom of God is greater than he is." This is no reflection on the personal sanctity of John. Rather, it is a statement that the age of the Messiah is so much greater than the time of preparation. At Christmas we will celebrate the coming of the new age of grace in Jesus Christ, the Saviour.

2. Today's First Reading, from Isaiah, tells how the people who had abandoned God were punished for a brief time. "I did forsake you for a brief moment, but with great love I will take you back. In excess of anger, for a moment I hid my face. But with everlasting love I have taken pity on you. My love for you will never leave you and my covenant of peace with you will never be shaken." The penitential way of John the Baptist was a preparation for the covenant that united Heaven and Earth in marriage, at the coming of the Son of God in human flesh.

PRAYERS

Enlightened by the teaching of Scripture, we pray. The Response is:
Come, Lord, Jesus, come.

As we prepare to celebrate the birthday of the Saviour, we pray that we will be spiritually ready to welcome him.
Come, Lord, Jesus, come.

John the Baptist was an upright man who did not sway with every passing breeze. Under the wise guidance of Pope *(name)* may the Church always be faithful to the teaching of Jesus Christ.
Come, Lord Jesus, come.

May the Holy Spirit guide us in discerning the right balance between strictness and mercy.
Come, Lord Jesus, come.

May those who find Christmas a lonely time discover the everlasting love of God which is greater than any human sorrow.
Come, Lord, Jesus come.

(Pray for any personal, local or topical intention)

O God of everlasting love, prepare our hearts for the coming of the Redeemer, Jesus Christ the Lord. Amen.

FRIDAY

ISAIAH 56:1-3. 6-8 | JOHN 5: 33-36

1. In John's Gospel the role of the Baptist is to serve the mission of Jesus. The Baptist recognised his role in his humble words: "He must increase, I must decrease".
   John was a lamp: Jesus was the light.
   John was the voice crying in the wilderness: Jesus was the Word.
   The lamp serves the light. The voice serves the Word.
   John the Baptist is the humble role model for the Church at the service of the Lord. We are here to serve.

2. The First Reading, from Isaiah, was addressed to the Jews who had returned from exile in Babylon. They set about restoring the nation and rebuilding the Temple. Restoration of the Temple was one task but the restoration of their faith was a greater challenge. Isaiah set before them three pillars: have a care for justice; act with integrity; welcome foreigners who want to join them in serving the Lord and honouring his name. These three pillars are as valid today as they were in the past: justice, integrity and a warm welcome to foreigners.

PRAYERS

Inspired by John the Baptist's humble service of the Lord, we pray.
The Response is: *Come, Lord Jesus, come.*

May the Church be a community, united in Christ, serving the
ideals of the Kingdom of God on Earth.
Come, Lord, Jesus come.

John the Baptist was a witness to the truth. May the example of
our lives draw people to the light of Christ.
Come, Lord Jesus, come.

May God bless the work of all who serve Christ in feeding the
hungry, caring for the homeless, and in other works of charity.
Come, Lord Jesus, come.

May we overcome any racial prejudice by welcoming foreigners,
especially people who were forced by war or persecution to leave
their homelands.
Come, Lord Jesus, come.

(Pray for any personal, local or topical intention)

Almighty God, Father of all, hear the prayers of your people gathered in prayer in the name of Jesus Christ, our Lord. Amen.

DECEMBER 17ᵀᴴ

GENESIS 49: 2. 8-10 | MATT 1: 1-17

1. Television programmes which trace somebody's genealogy usually uncover some skeleton in the cupboard, some forgotten scandal. The legal genealogy that Jesus inherited through his foster-father, Joseph, was no different. There were some holy people there but also some notorious sinners, adulterers, warlords and men of violence. The legal background of Jesus was a mixture of good and bad. He came to reform sinners, so he stepped into human life as we know it. The Letter to the Hebrews says that it was essential that he should become like us so that he could become a compassionate and trustworthy high priest for our relationship with God, able to expiate the sins of the people. He mixed with sinners and gave them hope. The name he was given was Jesus, the one who saves.

2. Five women are mentioned in this male genealogy and there is a question mark over each one. Tamer misled her own father-in-law so as to have a child and heir. Rahab was a prostitute. Ruth, the great-grandmother of David was a Moabitess, from outside the Jewish family. Solomon was the offspring of an adulterous relationship between David and the wife of Uriah. The biggest question mark is attached to Mary. How could a virgin bear a child? Unlike the other forty-one generations, the evangelist avoids saying that Joseph fathered Jesus. Since Jesus already existed he did not need to be fathered. The divinity of the child of Mary necessitated the virgin birth.

PRAYERS

In the light of the Gospel let us pray.
The Response is: *Come, Lord Jesus, come.*

As followers of Jesus Christ we have inherited the Jewish faith. Let us apologise before God for persecution of Jews. And may we be free from any racial discrimination in thought or action.
Come, Lord Jesus, come.

Let us be grateful for our forebears who have passed on life and faith to us down through many generations.
Come, Lord Jesus, come.

May the parents of today pass on faith to their children.
Come, Lord Jesus, come.

As we think of Mary carrying her child, we pray with all expectant mothers for a safe delivery and a healthy child.
Come, Lord Jesus, come.

(Pray for any personal, local or topical intention)

Heavenly Father, we offer all our prayers in the name of Jesus Christ, our Lord and Saviour. Amen

DECEMBER 18TH

JER: 23:5-8 | MATT 1:18-24

1. About Joseph we know very little but what we do know is very important. He was a man of honour, sensitive, compassionate and prayerful. Joseph and Mary were betrothed but not yet fully married. A child conceived after betrothal was regarded as legitimate. But Joseph knew that he was not the father of the child that Mary was carrying. By the letter of the law, he was obliged to let this be known. But he knew Mary well enough to accept that there was something here that he did not understand. So he decided to break off their contract very quietly. Being a prayerful man, he was attentive to the message of the angel which explained everything to him. As foster-father of Jesus, he was provider and protector of the Holy Family. He is patron of the Church and of workers. Many of the saints had great trust in him as provider for their needs.

2. Two beautiful names... Jesus and Emmanuel.

   Jesus – the one who saves. He saves us from the guilt of past sins by offering total forgiveness. His saving power reaches towards the future by strengthening our good resolution. "Go and sin no more."

   Emmanuel – God is with us. It is the last line of Matthew's Gospel: "I am with you to the end of time."

   Two names to be treasured. Two names to be repeated lovingly in prayer.

PRAYERS

We thank God for Saint Joseph, patron of the Universal Church.
The Response is: *Come, Lord, Jesus, come.*

As Joseph was once the protector and provider for the Holy Family, may he always protect and provide for the universal family of the Church.
Come, Lord Jesus, come.

Joseph worked as a carpenter to provide for Mary and Jesus. May all fathers provide for their children. May no fathers neglect their children.
Come, Lord Jesus, come.

The name of Jesus is very precious. May we never dishonour it. May this sacred name be the centre of our prayer.
Come, Lord Jesus, come.

Jesus is Emmanuel, God with us. May the prayerful repetition of this name fill us with confidence in God's presence.
Come, Lord Jesus, come.

(Pray for any personal, local or topical intention)

God, our Father, we offer all our prayers in the name of Jesus, Emmanuel. Amen.

DECEMBER 19TH

JUDGES 13:2-7. 24-25 | *LUKE 1:5-25*

1. John is a beautiful name. It means "God is gracious". Gracious refers to grace which is God's free gift, a gift that was never merited, never earned or deserved – a gift coming only from the love of God – a gift pure and simple. Elizabeth was barren. Her husband, Zechariah, was also getting on in years. Any hope of a child was receding with the years. Now it seemed that they were beyond hope. But never underestimate the power of the Holy Spirit. Advent is the season of hope. With the Holy Spirit there is always hope. John's name reminds us that God is gracious and full of surprises.

2. John was later known as the Baptist. Baptism means having a bath, having a good scrub. John the Baptist might be called John the Washer. His forceful preaching drew people to repentance and then he gave them God's washing. It should be part of our preparation for Christmas to have a thorough soul-washing in the Sacrament of Confession. For many people, it is a once-a-year ritual, but a very important one.

PRAYERS

The name, John, reminds us that God is a gracious giver. So let us pray with confidence.
The Response is: *Come, Lord Jesus, come.*

May the grace of the Holy Spirit enable the Church to show the loving face of God to all people.
Come, Lord Jesus, come

When it seems that our situation is beyond hope, may we never underestimate the power of the Holy Spirit.
Come, Lord Jesus, come.

For all who have lost hope. May the God of surprises break through their darkness.
Come, Lord Jesus, come.

Let us pray for people who, for one reason or another, dread the thought of Christmas. May God surprise them with the gift of joy.
Come, Lord Jesus, come.

(Pray for any personal, local or topical intention)

Gracious God, hear our prayers offered in the name of Jesus Christ our Lord and Saviour. Amen

DECEMBER 20TH

ISAIAH 7: 10-14 | LUKE 1:26-38

1. "Hail, full of grace, the Lord is with you." Mary is full of grace because there is no trace of sin in her. There is nothing in her to resist God's grace. But for the rest of us there are many little ways that we are not fully in compliance with God's grace. Our past sins have left a residue of damage in our characters, like clouds blocking the full splendour of God's grace. Hence we are greeted at Mass with a petition: "The Lord be with you". This is a petition that we might grow in compliance with God's grace. The fullness of Mary's union with God is expressed in her response to the angel: "Let what you have said be done to me".

2. The Church venerates Mary as the perfect model of faith. Mature faith is ever searching for greater understanding. Both Zechariah and Mary asked a question of the angel of Annunciation, but there was an important difference in the nature of their respective questions. Zechariah asked, "How can I be sure of this?" This question was one of doubt which originates in ME... how can I be sure? Mary's question was, "How can this come about since I am a virgin?" Mary did not express any doubt but she was searching for a greater understanding of what God was doing. This was the question of mature faith, searching for greater understanding. Theology has been described as faith searching for an understanding. Mary is venerated as a model of mature faith.

PRAYERS

The angel Gabriel assured Mary that nothing is impossible to God. Full of confidence, we pray.
The Response is: *Come, Lord Jesus, come.*

Through the angel Gabriel, you brought the message of salvation to Mary. May the celebration of Christmas bring great peace and joy to the world.
Come, Lord Jesus come.

As Mary sought a greater understanding of God's mystery, we pray that the searching minds of theologians will lead us to a deeper faith.
Come, Lord Jesus, come.

We pray for all who wrestle with doubts. May they move beyond the limitations of their own minds to accept the wonders of God's mystery.
Come, Lord Jesus, come.

The angel told Mary not to be afraid. We pray for people who dread Christmas. May the birth of the Saviour bring them great peace and joy.

(Pray for any personal, local or topical intention)

Pour forth your grace, O Lord, that we to whom the incarnation of Christ, your Son, was made known by the message of the angel may, by his passion and cross, come to the glory of his resurrection. Through Christ our Lord. Amen.

DECEMBER 21ST

SONG OF SONGS 2:8-14 | *LUKE 1:39-45*

1. When Mary visited Elizabeth, she was carrying Jesus in her womb. She was also the bearer of the Holy Spirit. At her arrival, Elizabeth also is filled with the Holy Spirit. And in the power of the Spirit she recognises the threefold blessedness of Mary. "Of all women you are most blessed" because she is chosen to be the mother of the Lord. "Blessed is the fruit of your womb." Mary is providing Jesus in her womb with his human flesh and blood. Thirdly, "Blessed is she who believed that the promise made to her by the Lord would be fulfilled." Elizabeth was deeply aware that her husband, Zechariah, had doubted the promise of the angel. Mary was the bearer of the Holy Spirit to Elizabeth's house. Years later, her presence with the apostles as they prepared for Pentecost, was very significant. The mystery of the Visitation anticipated Pentecost.

2. The child in Elizabeth's womb danced for joy. We usually think of John the Baptist as very stern and strict. However, the writer, Isaac Powers, wrote about John in a very different light. He called him John the Dancer. John's future mission would be to prepare the way for the Lord. It all began when he danced in his mother's womb the moment Mary greeted Elizabeth. Elizabeth picked up the music and celebrated the blessings of Mary. Mary completed the concert in her canticle of joy: "My soul glorifies the Lord, my spirit rejoices in God my saviour." It was John the Dancer who prepared the way for the Lord.

PRAYERS

As we reflect on the visit of Mary to Elizabeth, we are moved to pray. The Response is: *Come, Lord Jesus, come.*

Mary was uniquely blessed by the Holy Spirit, anticipating the birth of the Church at Pentecost. May the Holy Spirit powerfully guide the Church at all times.
Come, Lord Jesus, come.

As Mary responded to the needs of Elizabeth, may we be willing to help people who need our help.
Come, Lord Jesus, come.

The child in the womb of Elizabeth danced for joy. We pray for the health of all unborn children.
Come, Lord Jesus, come.

As we honour Mary and Elizabeth we pray for all expectant mothers.
Come, Lord Jesus, come.

(Pray for any personal, local or topical intention)

Gracious God, as you blessed Mary to be the mother of your Son in his humanity, continue to bless the Church in bringing Christ to the world today. Through Christ our Lord. Amen.

DECEMBER 22ND

1 SAMUEL 1-24-28 | LUKE 1:46-56

1. There are two parts to the Magnificat. In the first part, Mary lifts up her soul to praise God for the blessings bestowed on her. Holy is His name. Her contribution has been her emptiness. She was a good receiver. Many people know how to give but not how to receive. There are no barriers like self-importance, self-sufficiency or pride. When we honour Mary, it is God we honour. She reminds us that anything she received has come from God. "All generations shall call me blessed." The Church in its Evening Prayer repeats the Magnificat to praise and thank God for all the graces and blessings bestowed by God throughout the day.

2. The second part of the Magnificat anticipates the teaching of Jesus. She celebrates the mercy of God, the compassionate heart which feels the pains of people. Tyranny, domination, pride of heart and the selfish use of money will all be turned upside down as God hears the cry of the poor. Mary's Magnificat anticipates the ideals of the Sermon on the Mount. One might say that Jesus inherited his values from his mother.

PRAYERS

Inspired by the canticle of Mary we turn to God in prayer.
The Response is: *My soul glorifies the Lord.*

May our souls be filled with praise of God as we recognise the blessings bestowed upon Mary and on the Church.
My soul glorifies the Lord.

May we recognise that when we honour Mary, we are honouring God who is the source of all blessings.
My soul glorifies the Lord.

With Mary we pray for a world of justice and peace and for a fair sharing of the world's resources.
My soul glorifies the Lord.

May Christmas be a time of peace and joy for all our families.
My soul glorifies the Lord.

(Pray for any personal, local or topical intention)

O God, the giver of every good gift, we praise and thank you for all the graces conferred upon Mary. Through Christ, our Lord. Amen.

DECEMBER 23RD

MALACHI 3:1-4. 23-24 | LUKE 1:57-66

1. When relations and friends heard that God had shown such great kindness to Zechariah and Elizabeth, they shared their joy. Pope Paul VI recommended three steps towards joy ... giving, seeing and believing. Being obsessed with our own comforts is what Pope Francis called 'slow suicide'. It is in giving that we receive. The second step is in seeing; being open to the wonders of the world; seeing people through eyes that focus on goodness; being positive; avoiding prejudice and negative criticism. The third source of joy is believing. What a wonderful faith we have... the mercy of God, the presence of the Lord in the Eucharist, the power of the Holy Spirit, the promise of Heaven, the lives of the saints. The list is endless. May our Christmas be full of giving, seeing and believing. Then it will be a season of great joy.

2. Zechariah had lost the power of speech when he doubted the promise of the angel that they would have a child. He asked, "How can I be sure?" When his son is born, he fully accepts what Gabriel had promised. He resists the advice of the relations and insists that the child be given the name that the angel had told him. As a reward for obeying the divine instruction, his power of speech returned. When we allow doubts to fester in our minds, we lose the language of faith and prayer. May Christmas bring us a refreshing in our faith.

PRAYERS

As we are very close to Christmas, we pray for peace and joy.
The response is: *Come, Lord Jesus, come.*

The birth of John the Baptist was an occasion of great joy to all friends and relations. May our celebration of the birth of Jesus bring families together in peace and joy.
Come, Lord Jesus, come.

May the message of Christmas inspire all nations to work for an end to all warfare.
Come, Lord Jesus, come.

For people who dread Christmas for any reason. May they receive the joy of the Good News.
Come, Lord Jesus, come.

That there will be no bad accidents or acts of violence this Christmas.
Come, Lord Jesus, come.

(Pray for any personal, local or topical intention)

O loving God, you graciously answered the hopes of Elizabeth and Zechariah. Kindly hear our prayers offered in the name of Jesus Christ, our Lord. Amen

DECEMBER 24ᵀᴴ

2 *Samuel* 7:1-5. 8-12.14.16 | *Luke* 1:67-79

1. Blessed be the Lord, our God. He has visited his people and redeemed them. It is good to step aside from the hustle and bustle of Christmas Eve to focus a while on the centre of Christmas. The feast of Christmas was promoted to counteract the excessive orgies of the pagan festival of midwinter. Have we forgotten Christ and gone back to orgies of spending and gorging ourselves on eating, drinking and television? On the eve of Christmas, welcome this time to reflect. Pause, be still, put aside the cluttering so as to appreciate the wonder of Christ's coming. Blessed be the Lord, our God who has visited his people to redeem them.

2. Why did Jesus come to us? Because God so loved the world that he sent His Son in human form to save us. The Canticle of Zechariah called it the tender mercy of God, the loving-kindness of the heart of God. Jesus comes like the rising sun into winter's darkness. He gives life to those who sit in darkness and in the shadow of death. He guides our feet into the way of peace. As once he was born of Mary, may he be born afresh in your faith, your hope and your loving-kindness.

PRAYERS

Blessed be the Lord our God who has visited his people to redeem them.
The Response is: *Come, Lord Jesus, come.*

Let us pray that people will push aside the distractions of Christmas so as to ponder on what the coming of Christ really means.
Come, Lord Jesus, come.

As we reflect on Christ as a light coming to a world of darkness, may we renew our commitment to follow him.
Come, Lord Jesus, come.

May Christmas inspire all nations to turn away from war and to work together for justice and peace.
Come, Lord Jesus, come.

May Christmas be a time of family joy, for extending the hand of forgiveness, and for renewing friendships.
Come, Lord Jesus, come.

   (Pray for any personal, local or topical intention)

Merciful Father, you sent down your Beloved Son to save us from sin and darkness. Listen to the prayers we offer in the name of your Beloved Son, Jesus Christ, our Lord. Amen.

CHRISTMAS

DECEMBER 26TH

Saint Stephen

ACTS 6:8-10; 7:53-59 | MATT 10:17-22

1. The martyrdom of Stephen comes as a jolt on the first day after Christmas. The name, Stephen, means a crown. Saint Stephen is honoured as the first martyr to receive the crown of glory. The word *martyr* originally meant a witness. Stephen was a witness to Christ in life and death. In his life he was filled with grace and power by the Holy Spirit. He was chosen as one of the seven deacons who assisted the apostles in preaching and the distribution of alms. He was a witness to Christ also in his dying. He too prayed for his persecutors and, like Jesus, he gave up his spirit to God. The graces of the earthly birthday of Jesus prepared the way for the heavenly birthday of Stephen.

2. Christmas is a time for exchanging gifts. An ancient Christmas prayer celebrates the great gift of Christmas. "O wonderful exchange. The Son of God came down to earthly life so that we might be lifted up to share in heavenly life." Stephen drew the benefit of that wonderful exchange by receiving heavenly life. Just before his death, Stephen, filled with the Holy Spirit, gazed into Heaven and saw Jesus standing at the right hand of God. "I can see Heaven thrown open, and the Son of Man standing at the right hand of God," he cried. Just as the death of Jesus was redemptive, so also the death of Stephen drew down graces for other people. One of the people who plotted the death of Jesus was soon afterwards converted. We know him as Saint Paul. The blood of martyrs is the seed of Christians.

PRAYERS

On the Feast of Saint Stephen, we celebrate the wonderful exchange by which Jesus exchanged heavenly life for earthly life so that we might receive heavenly life after earthly life.

Stephen was the first martyr. May the Christians who are being persecuted in our time be filled with the consolations of the Holy Spirit just like Stephen.
Lord, hear us.

Stephen, like Jesus, forgave those who were persecuting him. May we receive the grace of the Holy Spirit to forgive those who have hurt us.
Lord, hear us.

The blood of martyrs was the seed of Christians. May the heroic witness of the martyrs of today move their persecutors to conversion of life.
Lord, hear us.

We remember all those who were lonely on Christmas Day. May the Holy Spirit be the source of their consolation.
Lord, hear us.

(Pray for any personal, local or topical intention)

O God, in the wonderful exchange between Heaven and Earth, Stephen was raised up to share in divine life. May he be an inspiration to all of us as we pray in the name of Jesus Christ, our Lord. Amen

DECEMBER 27TH

Saint John, Apostle and Evangelist

1 JOHN 1:1-4 | JOHN 20:2-8

1. Saint John is depicted in Christian art as an eagle. The eagle is reputed to be the only creature that can look directly into the light of the sun without damaging its eyes. More than the other evangelists, John looks into the life and light of the Blessed Trinity, Father, Son and Holy Spirit. He writes: "No one has ever seen God: it is the only Son, who is close to the Father's heart, who has made him known. The blinding light of God has been filtered to our limitations through the human nature of Jesus Christ. If we want to know what God is like, keep on looking at the human life of Jesus. "The Word was made flesh and dwelt among us"."

2. The First Letter of John was written after his Gospel in order to clarify or affirm parts of the Gospel. John testifies to the authenticity of what is recounted in the Gospel. We heard... we have seen with our own eyes... we have watched and touched with our hands the Word who is life. This is our subject. We saw and we are giving our testimony, so that you might be in union with us, as we are in union with the Father. At Christmas we celebrate the coming down of the Son of God to human life so as to lift us up to share in eternal life. "I have come so that you may have life, and have it to the full."

PRAYERS

Inspired by the insights of John's writings, we are moved to pray.

Jesus came as the light of the world. May the Church continue to bring the light of Christ to all nations.
Lord, hear us.

He came to his own but many did not accept him. We pray for the enlightenment of non-believers, especially among our own family and acquaintances.
Lord, hear us.

To all who did accept him he gave power to become children of God. May we grow each day in the power of our Baptism.
Lord, hear us.

Jesus is the way, the truth and the life. May we follow his way, know his truth and flourish with his life.
Lord, hear us.

(Pray for any personal, local or topical intention).

O God, you so loved the world that you gave your Beloved Son to lead us to salvation. Graciously hear the prayers we offer in his name, Jesus Christ, the Lord. Amen.

DECEMBER 28TH

The Holy Innocents

1 JOHN 1:5 – 2:2 | MATT 2:13-18

1. Today is a day to pray for children. The picture of the dead body of a little boy washed up on the Mediterranean shore shocked the world. The shock lasted a few days but the persecution and forced migration continue. Joseph, Mary and the infant Jesus were migrants too. Children in the womb are being deprived of the right to life. One child dies from starvation every ten seconds. Immature fathers constantly destroy their children's childhood. The prophet Jeremiah wept for the children who were taken off to exile in Babylon. "A voice was heard in Ramah, sobbing and loudly lamenting: it was Rachel weeping for her children, refusing to be comforted because they were no more." The Holy Innocents are part of the Christmas story because Jesus was entering into solidarity with all who are victims of injustice... including children.

2. It is only in Matthew's Gospel that we read about the massacre of the children and the flight into Egypt. Matthew, a Jewish Christian, wrote to prove to his fellow Jews that Jesus was the fulfilment of what we call the Old Testament. He wants to show the parallels between Jesus and Moses. Moses was born in Egypt, and that is where the child Jesus was brought. The Egyptian Pharaoh ordered the massacre of male children just as Herod did in Jesus' time. Moses escaped the massacre and so did Jesus. Moses grew up to become the liberator of his people from slavery. Jesus liberated people from sin. Moses received the covenant and the Law from God. Jesus inaugurated the new covenant and brought the Law to fulfilment in the Sermon on the Mount. Matthew is appealing to his fellow Jews to recognise Jesus as the new Moses – leader, liberator and lawgiver.

PRAYERS

On the Feast of the Holy Innocents let us pray especially for children.

May the voice of the Church be heard defending the right of children to life and to quality of life.
Lord, hear us.

May there be no more killing of innocent people through warfare, forced migration or starvation.
Lord, hear us.

We pray that people who are forced to migrate will receive a Christian welcome in their new land.
Lord, hear us.

We pray for the protection of children from any form of abuse.
Lord, hear us.

(Pray for any personal, local or topical intention).

God, our Father, look kindly on your children and protect them from all harm, in the name of Jesus Christ, your Son, our Lord. Amen.

DECEMBER 29TH

1 JOHN 2:3-11 | LUKE 2:22-35

1. "You see this child: he is destined for the fall and rising of many in Israel, destined to be a sign that is rejected – and a sword of sorrow will pierce your own soul too." Saint John Paul II called these words a 'second annunciation'. They tell of the historical situation in which Mary's Son is to accomplish his mission, in misunderstanding, rejection and sorrow. Mary's journey of faith would bring her to the foot of the cross. Her heart was pierced with the sword of sorrow as she looked at the body of Jesus in her arms, battered and bruised. Mary is our model in the journey of faith, experiencing light and darkness. She did not have clear light on everything that would happen. When Jesus, at the age of twelve, said that he must be busy about his Father's affairs, Mary and Joseph did not understand. But she stored up these things in her heart and pondered on them. She never doubted, but her faith accepted what she did not understand. Mature faith may not understand everything but is always certain. Blessed John Henry Newman said: "Ten thousand difficulties do not make one doubt". Mary is the model of faith for all of us, pilgrims on the road of life.

2. Simeon welcomed the child Jesus as a light to enlighten all nations. In today's First Reading, Saint John reminds us that we walk in the light of Christ only if we obey the commandments. To disobey the commandments is to walk in darkness. At the birth of Jesus, "the night is over and the real light is already shining". Love is the way of light but whoever lives in hatred is still in the dark, not knowing where he is going because it is too dark to see. Hatred is manifested in violence, vengeance, malicious talk and deliberate neglect of others. But to follow the way of Jesus is to walk in the light.

PRAYERS

Let us join with Mary and Joseph in presenting our prayers to God.

At the presentation of Jesus in the Temple, Mary and Joseph, in thanksgiving, offered their child to God. May we offer ourselves to God's service every day.
Lord, hear us.

Simeon rejoiced at meeting the Saviour of the world. We pray for all who are searching for meaning and direction. May the Holy Spirit guide them to the light of Christ.
Lord, hear us.

After seeing the child Jesus, Simeon said that he was ready to die in peace. May our faith prepare us to meet the Lord in peace.
Lord, hear us.

We pray for all mothers whose hearts are pierced with sorrow and anxiety because of the behaviour of their children. May Mary, comforter of the afflicted, sustain them in their sorrows.
Lord, hear us.

(Pray for any personal, local or topical intention).

O God, our heavenly Father, hear our prayers presented to you in the name of Jesus Christ, your Son, our Lord. Amen.

DECEMBER 30TH

1 JOHN 2:12-17 | LUKE 2:36-40

1. Christmas, to a great extent, centres on children. It is good to recognise the presence of two senior citizens in the story, Simeon and Anna. They are models of the beauty of prayerful old age. They have aged gracefully. Their lives are led by the Holy Spirit. Their happiness is to be in the temple of God's presence. They know that the circle of life is almost complete and that they are close to the point of returning to their beginning. And they are at peace.

2. Anna was the daughter of Phanuel, a name which means the face of God. As children inherit facial resemblance of their parents, those who live constantly in the presence of God increasingly reflect the beauty of God. You will see today's Annas, the children of Phanuel, in the people of mature age who live in awareness of God every day. On their faces of light, the beauty of serene old age is a joy to behold. They have aged gracefully. They are no longer torn apart by the untamed energies of youth, no longer play out the social pretences and games of mid-life. They let everything into God's hands. They are close to Heaven. And already they reflect the face of God... Phanuel.

PRAYERS

Inspired by the holy life of Simeon and Anna, we pray.

May our senior citizens age gracefully in prayerfulness and peace.
Lord, hear us.

Mary and Joseph did everything that the Law required. May they be an inspiration to all people in giving good example to their children.
Lord, hear us.

As Jesus grew to maturity in Nazareth, may our growing children mature physically, emotionally and spiritually.
Lord, hear us.

Let us pray for peace in families. Let there be no violence or abuse in any form. Let there be good communication between parents and children.
Lord, hear us.

(Pray for any personal, local or topical intention).

O God, let your face shed its light upon us, that we might reflect your beauty and love to all we meet this day. Through Christ, our Lord. Amen.

DECEMBER 31ˢᵀ

1 JOHN 2:18-21 | JOHN 1:1-18

1. On the last day of the year we look back in gratitude for all the blessings we have received in the past twelve months – blessings of life, of light and of love. A year is a substantial period of time from our perspective. But with God, a thousand years are like a single day. Our lifespan is only a tiny speck in relation to God's eternity. John's Gospel begins with a vast scenario. The story of Jesus did not begin on Christmas Day. His full story goes back even before Creation, before the stars, before any Big Bang. "He was with God in the beginning. Through him all things came to be. Not one thing had its being but through him."

2. John calls Jesus the Word of God. "The Word was made flesh and lived among us." He came to his own but many people did not accept him. But to all who did accept him, he gave the power to become the children of God. The power to become. Becoming demands constant growth. May the coming year be a time of further growth in our following of Christ who is the light of the world. Today let us look back for all we have received. And let us go forward with a fresh resolution to walk in the light of Christ, to become children of the light.

PRAYERS

At the close of this year we return to God in gratitude.

We thank you, Lord, for the Church, which has preserved the story of Jesus and handed it on to us. Continue to guide our Holy Father, Pope *(Name)* and all the successors of the Apostles.
Lord, hear us.

We thank you for the many blessings and graces we have received. In the coming year may we be faithful to you and grow ever closer to you.
Lord, hear us.

We thank you for family, friends and neighbours and for all who were kind to us. Bless and reward them.
Lord, hear us.

We pray for anybody we may have hurt in the past year. Lord, may they recover from any harm that we have caused.
Lord, hear us.

   (Pray for any personal, local or topical intention).

O God, the Beginning and the End, we thank you for the past year and entrust ourselves to your continuing care in the new year. Through Christ, our Lord. Amen

JANUARY 1ST

Solemnity of Mary, Mother of God

GAL 4:4-7 | LUKE 2:16-21

1. There is a tradition that the second half of the Hail Mary began in Ephesus in the year 431. At the Council of the Church held there, it was clarified that Jesus Christ was truly God and truly man. It followed that Mary should be called the Mother of God. Elizabeth had called her "the mother of my Lord". And Saint Paul wrote that "God sent his Son, born of a woman". Jesus was truly God and truly man. The people of Ephesus had a special devotion to Mary as she had gone there with the Beloved Disciple, Saint John. When they heard the decree of the Council, they danced for joy, chanting "Holy Mary, Mother of God, pray for us". Later, the prayer was slightly extended... "Pray for us sinners now and at the hour of our death". On the first day of the New Year, we invoke her intercession for a year of peace throughout the world.

2. New Year's Day is the eighth day of Christmas. On the eighth day, the child was circumcised and officially named. Mary's child was given the name Jesus, meaning the one who saves. It is a sacred name which should never be used with disrespect. "All beings in Heaven and on Earth should bend the knee at the name of Jesus." Mary was a person who treasured what she heard and pondered on it in her heart. Can we appreciate what the name of Jesus meant to his mother? In the years after her Son's return to Heaven, this sacred name was a total prayer for Mary. May it also be the centre of our prayer.

   Blessed be the name of Jesus, name of hope, name of divine forgiveness.

   Blessed be the name of Jesus, name of divine power, the name in which our prayers reach up to God the Father.

PRAYERS

Our New Year begins with the Solemnity of Mary, Mother of God. It is a day of prayer for peace throughout the world.

May this New Year be one of peace in every country. May there be an end to warfare and violence. May people in every land receive justice and enjoy peace.
Lord, hear us.

On the eighth day Jesus was circumcised and officially given his name. We pray that everybody will have a deep respect for his sacred name.
Lord, hear us.

May God bless our families, friends and neighbours this year and protect us from all harm.
Lord, hear us.

Through the intercession of Mary, Mother of God, we pray for people who are sick or who are going through a dark valley in life.
Lord, hear us.

(Pray for any personal, local or topical intention).

God our Father, we thank you for sending us your Son, Jesus, born of Mary. We make all our prayers in his sacred name. Amen.

JANUARY 2ND

1 JOHN 2:22-28 | JOHN 1:19-28

1. In John's Gospel, there are seven great statements of Jesus beginning with "I am..." the light of the world, the Bread of Life and so on. John the Baptist, the humble servant of the Lord, makes three statements beginning with "I am not". I am not the Christ, nor Elijah, nor the prophet promised in the time of Moses. It is good for us to know and accept our limitations. It relieves the pressure of pretence and role-playing. John was enthusiastic and courageous but he had the humility to know when it was time to step back from the limelight. He was a voice at the service of the Word.

2. John told the people that there was standing among them one unknown, the one who was to come after him. That same Jesus stands unknown in our world unless we witness to his presence. Is my life a voice preparing the way for Christ or do I obscure his presence? Am I a witness to God in family, workplace or social life? In my language, values, behaviour and attitudes? Does our parish community bring God's light to darkened lives, good news to the poor, hope to the downhearted, inner freedom to captives? Or is Christ standing unknown and unrecognised in our world?

PRAYERS

We pray that the Christian community of the Church will be a living voice making known the presence of God in our world today.
Lord, hear us.

We pray for those to whom God is unknown. May the light of God penetrate their darkness and light up their lives.
Lord, hear us.

In this New Year, may the good example of Christians be living proof of the healing power of the Holy Spirit.
Lord, hear us.

We pray for those who were glad to see the end of last year. May this coming year bring them better times and peace of mind.
Lord, hear us.

(Pray for any personal, local or topical intention).

O God, made known to us in the life of Jesus Christ, hear the prayers we offer in his name. Amen.

JANUARY 3RD

1 JOHN 2:29 – 3:6 | JOHN 1:29-34

1. John the Baptist identified Jesus as the Lamb of God who takes away the sins of the world. Lambs are gentle creatures. These gentle creatures were innocent victims which were sacrificed in atonement for the sins of people. Jesus died on the very day when thousands of lambs were being sacrificed in the nearby temple. Jesus not only made atonement for sins but in mercy, he took them away. At Mass we recall the words of John the Baptist. "Lamb of God, you take away the sin of the world, have mercy on us." Ponder on these words. Reflect on the wonderful mercy of God whose love is always greater than our sins. "Jesus, Lamb of God, have mercy on us."

2. In today's First Reading, John opens up a wonderful understanding of the Christian vocation. "Think of the love that the Father has lavished on us by letting us be called God's children." This is where the New Testament goes far beyond the Old Testament in revealing God's relationship with us. Each one of us is called to a life of personal intimacy with God. That is why Jesus told us to pray to God as our loving Father. Saint Paul wrote that if we are children of God, then we are heirs to the Kingdom of Heaven. He also said that the Holy Spirit within us helps us to recognise this personal calling from God and to cry out "Abba, Father". One of the joys of visiting the Holy Land is hearing little children calling "Abba". What we are to be in the future is greater still. All we know is that we shall be like God, because we shall see Him as He really is. That is what we call the beatific vision... all that God has prepared for those who love Him... a vision beyond anything we can even imagine.

PRAYERS

Lifted up in mind and heart by the beautiful words of Scripture, we pray.

May the Church be an oasis of mercy, where sinners can come to meet Jesus, the Lamb of God who takes away the sins of the world.
Lord, hear us.

John the Baptist was witness to Jesus and directed people to him. May the good example of Christians draw people to God.
Lord, hear us.

May we appreciate the love that God has for us by letting us be called the children of God and heirs to the Kingdom of Heaven.
Lord, hear us.

As Jesus was gentle as a lamb, may we be gentle in thought, word and action in our dealings with others.
Lord hear us.

(Pray for any personal, local or topical intention).

Merciful Father, your heart lavishes forgiveness on the sinner who repents. Hear our prayers offered in the name of Jesus Christ, our Lord. Amen.

JANUARY 4TH

1 JOHN 3:7-10 | JOHN 1:35-42

1. The meeting of Jesus with his first disciples is an event about searching, invitation and finding. John the Baptist looked at Jesus with a deep, searching gaze before he identified him as the Lamb of God. Later, Jesus gazed hard at Simon with searching eyes that saw his past, his present state and his future potential. He saw in him the Rock on whom he would build his future Church, so he gave him the new name, Peter (the Greek form) or Cephas (Aramaic).

2. Religions which do not have the revealed Word of God are described as people's search for God. But the Jewish-Christian tradition is drawn from God's invitation to people. Jesus is the Good Shepherd who searches for the lost sheep to take it home. He asked the two disciples of John the Baptist, "What do you want". They answered, "Master, where do you live?" He invited them to come and see. They spent the rest of the day with him. The Gospel notes that it was about the tenth hour, two hours before sunset. People liked to get home before darkness. It was journey's end for the searching soul had found home where Jesus lived. And where Jesus lived was in his union with the Father. Jesus constantly invites us to come and see... to spend time in prayer... and to be at home with him.

PRAYERS

Jesus asked, "What are you looking for?" Confident that he will hear us, we pray.

Lord, you called Simon Peter to be the rock on which you would build your Church. May your grace direct and guide Pope (*Name*) who is the successor of Peter in our time.
Lord, hear us.

You called the first disciples to come and follow you. May people today receive your call to dedicate their lives to your service and may those who receive your call accept it.
Lord, hear us.

Lord, we humbly ask you for the gift of prayer: that we might experience prayer as the invitation to be at home with you.
Lord, hear us.

For those who do not know you: break through the clouds which darken their lives and let the light of your face smile upon them.
Lord, hear us.

(Pray for any personal, local or topical intention).

O God, you look upon us with love and invitation. Hear our prayers in the name of Jesus Christ, your Beloved Son. Amen.

JANUARY 5TH

1 JOHN 3:11-21 | JOHN 1:43-51

1. Today we continue with Jesus calling the first disciples. Philip invited his friend Nathanael to come to Jesus. But Nathanael had a problem. "Can anything good come from Nazareth?" Nazareth was a village never even mentioned in the Old Testament. "Come and see," replied Philip. Jesus surprised Nathanael when he said he had seen him under the fig tree. It probably means that he had seen him in a discussion group or teaching situation as such groups regularly gathered outdoors under the shade of the large leaves of the fig tree. Jesus was impressed with the man's integrity. And this man who was incapable of deceit was granted the grace of believing in Jesus as the Son of God and the King of Israel. Philip had invited him to come and see. Now he had come and saw. He saw and believed.

2. Nathanael called Jesus the King of Israel. The Israelites were descendants of Israel whose previous name was Jacob. Jacob was the man who had the famous dream of the ladder linking Heaven and Earth. Jesus recalled that vision and told Nathanael to expect something similar. The next story in the Gospel is the wedding feast at Cana where Jesus worked his first miracle as a sign of the wedding of Heaven and Earth. The real ladder between Heaven and Earth is Jesus in whom divinity and humanity are united. The revelation of the divine glory of Jesus is part of the full feast of the Epiphany which will be celebrated tomorrow.

PRAYERS

As Nathanael came to Jesus, we now come with our petitions.

May we learn from the story of Nathanael not to judge people on the basis of where they have come from or any other source of prejudice.
Lord, hear us.

Philip brought his friend to Jesus. May it be our joy to bring somebody to Jesus, perhaps in a prayer group or retreat or charitable organization.
Lord, hear us.

Nathanael was called a man with no guile. May he be an inspiration to us to be totally truthful and honest.
Lord, hear us.

Like Nathanael, may we always worship Jesus as the Son of God.
Lord, hear us.

(Pray for any personal, local or topical intention).

Heavenly Father, hear the prayers we offer in the name of Jesus Christ, your Son, our Lord. Amen.

JANUARY 6ᵀᴴ

Feast of the Epiphany

ISAIAH 60:1-6 | MATT 2:1-12

1. Who is this child born at Bethlehem? Epiphany means the revelation of his glory to all nations. Gold for a king represents the coming of the reign of God. Frankincense is for the true priest who is the mediator between Heaven and Earth. Myrrh is an oil extracted from the bark of a tree and is used in the embalming of a dead body. It suggests that Jesus is the suffering servant who took the sins of the people on himself.

2. What gifts can we bring to Jesus? What can you give to somebody who has everything? Give him yourself, for he loves you and he wants you to be his friend. Give him your time, some quality time in prayer each day. Come to him with your problems for he has invited you to come with your burdens. Bring him your sinfulness and weakness, for he alone is our Saviour. Bring him your darkness, for he is the light of the world. Bring him your waywardness, for he is the true shepherd who guides us along the right path. Bring him your emptiness and hunger, for he is the Bread of Life.

PRAYERS

On this Feast of the Epiphany we come with our prayers and petitions.

The Response is: *O Lord, hear us we pray. O Lord, give us your love.*

May we bring gold to Jesus in committing our lives to his Kingdom, a kingdom of justice, peace and joy in the Holy Spirit.
O Lord, hear us we pray. O Lord, give us your love.

May we bring incense by recognising Jesus as the true priest or mediator, for nobody can go to the Father except through him.
O Lord, hear us we pray. O Lord, give us your love.

May we bring myrrh to Jesus in recognising his saving death and resurrection.
O Lord, hear us we pray. O Lord, give us your love.

(Pray for any personal, local or topical intention).

O God graciously hear our prayers in the name of your Beloved, Jesus Christ the Lord. Amen

JANUARY 7TH

1 JOHN 3:22 – 4:6 | *MATT 4:12-17. 23-25*

1. Imagine God the Father up in Heaven, one day looking down on the world. God is sad to see all the ways things went wrong... wars, injustice, inequality and so on. He asks God the Son: "Would you do a job for me. Would you go down to Earth to bring my people back from the reign of Satan. Bring them back to the reign of goodness, love, justice and peace". At Christmas we celebrated the coming down of God the Son to us. He grew to manhood and the time came to begin his mission. According to Matthew's Gospel, Jesus began by announcing to the people, "Repent, for the Kingdom of Heaven is close at hand".

2. The central theme of Matthew's Gospel is the Kingdom of Heaven. It is not a political kingdom, not a geographical territory. It means the reign of God in our minds, hearts and behaviour. It means resisting the misleading temptations of Satan. It calls for a change of life. So the first word of Jesus is "Repent". To repent means to change your mind and behaviour. The mission of Jesus is to establish the reign of God in our world. Jesus set out with two tactics: word and action. His words came in his preaching. His actions were works of healing. Many of these miracles of healing were described as casting out devils. Later in the Gospel, we will see the development of the Church as the task force to continue the work of the Kingdom.

PRAYERS

The people that walked in darkness has seen a great light. On those who dwell in the land and shadow of death a light has dawned. Let us pray with the Response: *Thy Kingdom come.*

In this new year may there be peace and justice in every country. *Thy Kingdom come.*

That a massive effort will be undertaken to feed the starving and house the homeless. *Thy Kingdom come.*

That a concerted effort will be made to protect the planet from the destructive results of global warming. *Thy Kingdom come.*

For the triumph of God's light over the powers of darkness. *Thy Kingdom come.*

(Pray for any personal, local or topical intention).

God, our Father, you so loved the world that you sent your Son to guide us in the way of your Kingdom. Graciously hear the prayers we offer in his name, Jesus Christ, our Lord. Amen.

JANUARY 8TH

1 JOHN 4: 7-10 | MARK 6: 34-44

1. Three lines stand out in today's Gospel.
   First, Jesus had pity on the people because they were like sheep without a shepherd.
   Second, the disciples said to Jesus, "This is a lonely place ... so send them away."
   Third, Jesus replied, "Give them something to eat yourselves."
   When the disciples gave up all they had, Jesus multiplied their generosity a thousand fold.

2. When the Sisters of Saint Teresa of Calcutta went to the slums of New York, they visited the old folk and those who lived on their own. They did simple jobs like sweeping the floor, preparing some food, washing clothes. Mother Teresa wrote that the worst disease today is not leprosy but the loneliness of not being wanted, being left out, being forgotten. The greatest scourge is to forget the next person, to be so suffocated by things that we have no time for the lonely Jesus... even a person in our own family who needs us. Mother Teresa's apostolate began with one person, a dying lady she picked up on a street. God who multiplied the five loaves and two fish multiplied her act of charity a thousandfold. Do not send them away. Begin with one. Give them something of yourself for their loneliness and hunger.

PRAYERS

Inspired by the compassion of Jesus, we pray.

That the Church may not be shut up in structures and laws. Rather, let it reach out to those who are on the margins of society.
Lord, hear us.

Although we might think that we have little to give, let us give it anyway, and may God do the multiplying.
Lord, hear us.

We pray for those who have no one to visit them. May the God of surprises inspire somebody to visit them.
Lord, hear us.

May the people who are forced to leave their homelands travel safely and receive a Christian welcome.
Lord, hear us.

   (Pray for any personal, local or topical intention).

O God, you are the Father of all. Fill us with your love and compassion to reach out to all who are hungry in body or in spirit. Through Christ, our Lord. Amen

JANUARY 9TH

1 JOHN 4:11-18 | MARK 6: 45-52

1. To be in a boat tossed about in a storm is terrifying. Worse again if it is in the darkness of night. Jesus had gone up the mountain to pray. This detail in the story connects it with the time after his Ascension, which is our time. Jesus may have gone away but he still was watching and aware of the plight of the boat and passengers. Jesus came to them and made himself known. "Courage! It is I! Do not be afraid." They were utterly and completely dumbfounded because they had not seen the meaning of the miracle of the loaves. One meaning of the multiplication of the loaves sees the miracle as an anticipation of the miracle of the Eucharist. We are in the boat of the Church. It is a time of storms and darkness. We might wonder "has God deserted us?" But no! Jesus may have ascended but he keeps a watchful eye on his Church at all times. He consecrates the bread and wine and invites us to receive. "Courage! It is I! Do not be afraid."

2. In today's First Reading, John writes beautifully about the transmission of love. Since God loved us we should love one another. As long as we love one another, God will live in us and his love will be complete in us. The transmission of God's love is not complete until we pass it on. Failing to do so is like a short circuit with electricity. If the wire is broken or disconnected, the power does not get through. We are to be the bearers of God's love. God is love and anyone who lives in love lives in God and God lives in that person. The message of yesterday's Gospel is to give what you have, no matter how small, and let God do the multiplying.

PRAYERS

Jesus told the apostles to have courage and to cast all fear away. So it is with great confidence that we pray.

The Church at times is like the apostles' boat battered by a storm. May we never despair, may we never lose confidence in Christ's presence with us.
Lord, hear us.

As we reflect on God's love for us, may we be inspired to complete God's love by passing it on to others.
Lord, hear us.

We pray for all whose lives are in storm and turmoil. May God come to them to give them courage and peace.
Lord, hear us.

We pray for those whose minds and hearts are closed to faith. May the gentle light of Christ break through their darkness and doubts.
Lord, hear us.

(Pray for any personal, local or topical intention).

O God, watch over us at all times and come to our aid in times of storm. Through Christ, our Lord. Amen.

JANUARY 10ᵀᴴ

1 JOHN 4:19 – 5:4 | *LUKE 4:14-22*

1. Our First Reading is from the First Letter of John. He gives us a theological understanding of love and follows with its practical application. John's understanding of love is based on the Blessed Trinity. Love begins in God the Father. The Father's love is shown to us in a human way in the life of Jesus Christ. And this love is poured into us by the Holy Spirit. With the grace of God, people become capable of supernatural love. John knows that love is not just a passing feeling or infatuation. He spells out two practical proofs of love. First, how can we say that we love God whom we have never seen if we do not love the people whom we do see. Anyone who says he loves God while he hates his brother is a liar. The second proof of loving God is keeping his commandments. Love begins in God the Father. It is manifested to us in the life of God the Son, Jesus Christ. The power of the Holy Spirit can enable us to overcome human limitations so as to love with a supernatural love.

2. In the Gospel, Jesus returns to Nazareth with the power of the Spirit in him. His words are gracious, full of grace. He has Good News... God-news for the people. He opens their eyes to see life in a new way. He liberates people from addictions, compulsions and obsessions. His work goes on today in all who are guided by the Holy Spirit to live with a positive, helpful, loving attitude to other people. This text is being fulfilled today even as you listen.

PRAYERS

In the early days of the Church, people were impressed by the way these Christians loved one another. So we pray.

May the Church, as a community of Christians, inspire all people to live together in peace and justice, in caring and sharing.
Lord, hear us.

May we cooperate with the Holy Spirit to overcome our natural limitations so as to see people through God's eyes and care for them with Christ's love.
Lord, hear us.

May our words be gracious rather than bitter, our judgements kind more than resentful, and our actions more helpful than hurting.
Lord, hear us.

Lord, deliver us from any bitterness we feel towards others.
Lord, hear us.

(Pray for any personal, local or topical intention).

O God, our Father, all life and love begin in you. Raise us up in the grace of the Holy Spirit as we pray in the name of Jesus Christ, your Son, our Lord. Amen.

JANUARY 11TH

1 JOHN 5:5-13 | LUKE 5:12-16

1. Today's First Reading from Saint John begins with a question: "Who can overcome the world?" When John writes about the world, he contrasts the world and the spirit. The world represents the unredeemed areas of life while the spirit means life redeemed by the grace of the Holy Spirit. The world then means our human limitations, sinful inclinations and negative reactions. Who can overcome this unredeemed world? Only the person who believes that Jesus Christ is the Son of God. To believe is much more than the mental acceptance of various doctrines. To believe really means to belong. To belong to Jesus Christ in mind, in decisions of the will and in behaviour. The doctrines we believe are called the creed. The word *creed*, comes from two Latin words, *cor-do*, which literally mean I give my heart. To believe is to make a commitment to Christ on every level of life. This trusting commitment of life is the way to overcome our worldly limitations and sinful inclinations.

2. We see an example of trust in Jesus in the Gospel story of the leper who came to Jesus. He didn't just come, but he fell on his face and implored Jesus. His actions show the depth of his desperation as well as his confidence in Jesus. Yet, he humbly accepts the will of God. "If you want to, you can cure me." Such a combination of desperation, trust, reverence, humility and acceptance make up a very mature faith. Faith opens up the healing hands of God. "Of course I want to," said Jesus, "be cured". Who can overcome our personal world of human limitations, negative reactions and bitter memories? Who can cure the leprosy of sinful compulsions and addictions? Jesus can, if we humbly hand over our problems to him every day in prayer.

PRAYERS

Encouraged by the humility and trust of the leper who came to Jesus, we pray.

We pray for the world in which we live. May this new year bring in the liberation of the world from warfare, violence and famine.
Lord, hear us.

May we humbly admit the problem areas of life where we have lost control. May we humbly throw ourselves at the feet of Jesus and implore his help.
Lord, hear us.

May the grace of God liberate our memories from bitterness and vengeance.
Lord, hear us.

Even Jesus felt the need to find a place where he could be alone to pray. May we follow his example.
Lord, hear us.

   (Pray for any personal, local or topical intention).

O God, we trust in your love and power to help us in all our problems as we pray in the name of Jesus Christ, your Son, our Lord. Amen.

JANUARY 12TH

1 JOHN 5:14-21 | JOHN 3:22-30

1. "He must grow greater, I must grow smaller." Tomorrow we will celebrate the greatest day in the life of John the Baptist when he was privileged to baptise Jesus in the River Jordan. But John was never one to boast about what he did. He always said that somebody greater was coming. He understood that his role was to prepare the way. He was a voice at the service of the Word. He was the friend at the service of the bridegroom. Jesus was the bridegroom in the marriage of God and humanity, the wedding of Heaven and Earth. Far be it from John to hog the limelight. He was happy to take the lesser role in the service of God.

2. When it was reported to John that people were going to Jesus, he wasn't one bit jealous. On the contrary, he was full of joy. "He must grow greater, I must grow smaller." Jesus must hold centre-stage while I slip into the wings. It takes great humility to step aside from the limelight for the sake of another. John is an inspiration to us to reflect on where we need to decrease so that Jesus might increase in our lives. Should I find more time for prayer? Should I be more willing to say "Yes" when somebody requests my time? Should I be more willing to lose an argument so as to maintain peace? "He must grow greater, I must grow smaller."

PRAYERS

Following the example of John the Baptist, servant of God, we pray.

Saint Paul described the Church as the Bride of Christ. May the beauty of the Church be cleansed of all sins and scandals.
Lord, hear us.

May we follow the humility of John the Baptist, always willing to push aside our selfish pride for the sake of the greater good.
Lord, hear us.

Like John the Baptist, may it be our great joy to be servants of God through service of people.
Lord, hear us.

May God bless and reward all the people who serve us every day, especially the people whose service we take for granted.
Lord, hear us.

(Pray for any personal, local or topical intention).

O God, may we recognise the talents you have given us and put them at your service in helping others. Through Christ, our Lord. Amen.

LENT

ASH WEDNESDAY

2 COR 5:20 – 6:2 | MATT 6:1-6. 16-18

1. Taking the ashes today is a public sign that one is going to do something for Lent. We can give up something or take on something. Better again, give up and take on. Giving up something we like is self-denial. It is the best way for training our willpower. Sports people know that skills are perfected by constant repetition. Virtues are perfected by habitual practice. Our willpower is perfected by the constant habit of self-denial.

2. Lent is a great incentive to take on some special action for a few weeks. Maybe avail of a retreat; more prayer at home; go to Mass more often. Replace compulsive television or internet by some spiritual reading. People who are addicted to computers or smartphone might consider one day each week free from gadgets, apart from what is necessary for work. Almsgiving is also mentioned in the Gospel. Having a box at home for a Third World charity is a great reminder. One other idea from today's Gospel is – don't be going around with a gloomy look, a sourpuss. Our works of penance are of little use if they do not bring us closer to God. And closer to God ought to be a source of great joy. Pass the message up to your face. Lent is a season of grace.

PRAYERS

Jesus prepared for his mission by forty days of penance. Let us accompany him for the forty days of Lent.

May Lent be a season of grace and spiritual growth in our lives. May we come closer to God.
Lord, hear us.

Grant us the spirit of self-denial, training our willpower to resist temptation.
Lord, hear us.

Make us more generous during Lent, especially in collecting for the Third World.
Lord, hear us.

May our Lenten observance develop the positive potential of our characters so that we become more pleasant, kind and helpful to others.
Lord, hear us.

   (Pray for any personal, local or topical intention)

O God, strengthen us during this season of Lent to grow closer to you and more helpful to people. Through Jesus Christ, our Lord. Amen.

THURSDAY AFTER ASH WEDNESDAY

DEUTERONOMY 30:15-20 | *LUKE 9:22-25*

1. Taking the ashes of Lent can be a very sobering experience if we ponder on the words: "Remember that you are but dust and unto dust thou shalt return". Keeping a compost bin is an eye-opener. When all the different forms of matter have broken down, what is left is pure, soft earth, perfect for potting plants at this time of year. Every material thing returns to earth. Today's Gospel repeats the sobering message. "What profit is it to have won the whole world but to have ruined your very self." What good is it to have climbed to the top of the ladder only to discover that you had scaled the wrong wall?

2. One of the great graces of Lent is the challenge to ask ourselves which road of life we are taking, the road to God or the road to perdition. In today's First Reading we heard: "I set before you life or death, blessing or curse. Choose life then that you and your descendants may live in the love of the Lord, your God". Lent is a challenge to stop drifting along aimlessly: a challenge to make a serious decision about where we want to go in life and after life. Every journey begins with one step. Every act of self-denial can be a step forward in following Jesus Christ. "If anyone wants to be a follower of mine, then renounce self, take up the cross every day and follow me." May your Lent bring you closer to God every day.

PRAYERS

Having listened to the Word of God about the challenge of Lent, we pray.

That Lent may be a season of renewal for the entire Church, drawing us closer to God.
Lord, hear us.

May the challenge of Lent help us to clarify the way we are called to live and strengthen our commitment to follow the way of Christ.
Lord, hear us.

We pray for all who are burdened with a heavy cross of suffering. May they recognise how close they are to Christ carrying his cross.
Lord, hear us.

We pray for family members and acquaintances who are drifting aimlessly in life. May they choose the fullness of life made known to us by Jesus Christ.
Lord, hear us.

(Pray for any personal, local or topical intention)

O God, may this season of Lent help us to know you more clearly and follow you more dearly. Through Christ, our Lord. Amen.

FRIDAY AFTER ASH WEDNESDAY

Isaiah 58:1-9 | *Matt 9:14-15*

1. Fasting is one of the practices recommended for Lent. Both readings at Mass today are about fasting. Fasting is beneficial for many reasons... maybe to lose weight or to get fit. The Pharisees fasted in preparation for the coming of the Messiah. Sadly, when the Messiah came, they did not recognise him. Jesus fasted in preparation for his ministry but he did not put the same emphasis on it as the Pharisees or the disciples of John the Baptist. We might consider two important ways of fasting during Lent. Fast from any behaviour that hurts another person, especially gossip or sarcastic remarks. And secondly, fast from saying "No" when asked to do something. Obviously there are times when you have to say "No," but if at all possible, say "Yes" when you are asked. Fasting with a scowl does no good for anybody. But fasting with a smile might transform the world, or at least a small part of it.

2. In the First Reading, Isaiah reminds us that doing penance or fasting is only hypocritical if our lives are a contradiction of charity and justice. "You oppress your workmen, you quarrel and squabble when you fast and strike the poor man with your fist, hanging your head like a reed, lying down on sackcloth and ashes. Is that what you call fasting?" It means far more to feed the hungry, shelter the homeless, clothe the naked and be reconciled with your own kin. "Then will your light shine like the dawn and your wound be quickly healed over." What I want is love, not sacrifice.

PRAYERS

Taking the lessons of Scripture to heart, we pray.

May all nations listen to the teaching of the Church about ending war, creating peace, and fostering justice for all people.
Lord, hear us.

This Lent, may we become aware of any fault of character that keeps us away from you. And give us the grace to overcome that fault.
Lord, hear us.

Give us the grace to overcome any behaviour which is hurting other people.
Lord, hear us.

May the challenge of Lent inspire us to do something to feed the hungry and shelter the homeless poor.
Lord, hear us.

(Pray for any personal, local or topical intention)

Father of all, guide us this Lent to work for a more just and caring society. Through Christ, our Lord. Amen.

SATURDAY AFTER ASH WEDNESDAY

ISAIAH: 58:9-14 | LUKE 5:27-32

1. The Pharisees basically were very good people, very zealous for the perfect observance of the Law. But maybe they were too good, too zealous, allowing no room for the limitations of people. They did not see eye-to-eye with Jesus who sat with sinners and shared meals with them. If a Pharisee organised a list of invitations to a meal, he started with who should be excluded. A tax collector like Levi would certainly be excluded. Top of the list of people that Jesus would have included were the very people the Pharisees excluded. We ask ourselves if we have a list of people we exclude. We avoid them. We refuse to greet them. We want nothing to do with them. What would Jesus do in our situation?

2. The Church, sadly, has often come across as very stern, very harsh in judging people. Little or no hope was offered to people who could not honestly promise never to sin again. The Catechism of the Catholic Church recognises that there are many psychological and social factors which make the hundred per cent resolution virtually impossible. Pope Francis recalled those words of the Catechism and he added that a small step in the midst of great human limitations can be more pleasing to God than the virtuous person who has never had such problems. Jesus saw himself as the doctor whose job is for the service of the sick more than for healthy people. "I have not come to call the virtuous, but sinners to repentance."

PRAYERS

Let us take the teaching of Jesus to heart as we pray.

May the Church show forth the compassionate face of Jesus in offering understanding and hope to all who are struggling with their weakness and broken resolutions.
Lord, hear us.

May this holy season of Lent bring back many people to the Sacraments.
Lord, hear us.

Lord, help us to see confession as a celebration of your victory over sin.
Lord, hear us.

Lord, help us to overcome the problems which cause us to exclude certain people from our lives.
Lord, hear us.

   (Pray for any personal, local or topical intention)

Merciful Father, help us in our weakness and reach out to us in your loving care. Through Christ, our Lord. Amen.

MONDAY

LEVITICUS 19:1-2. 11-18 | *MATT 25:31-46*

1. "When the Son of Man comes in his glory, escorted by all his angels, then he will take his seat on the throne of glory. The setting for the great judgement is awesome and frightening. But the judgement itself is a very simple process. "Whatsoever you did to the least of my brothers and sisters, that you did unto me." How can we say that we love God whom we have never seen, if we do not treat with love God's children whom we do see. Saint Teresa of Calcutta used to show people her five-finger exercise. Five words. YOU DID IT TO ME.

2. Lord, when did we see you hungry, thirsty, a stranger, in need of food or clothing, needing a visitor? Those who responded to the needs of ordinary people are amazed when told that it was the Lord they were serving. Equally, those who did not help people in need are shocked to hear that it was the Lord they were refusing. What God wants us to do may be here before our eyes. Some people waste their time and talents waiting for the heroic task to be undertaken. And all the while the service that God wants from us is the little deed done with a lot of love.

PRAYERS

Challenged by the teaching of Jesus, we pray.

May the Church be a community of believers who care for people and share with them.
Lord, hear us

Lord, open our eyes to see the needs of people, and open our hearts to come to their aid.
Lord, hear us.

Lord, bless and reward the people who give of their time and talents to help in voluntary organisations.
Lord, hear us.

Help us to be more aware of what we spend on selfish luxuries instead of sharing with people in need.
Lord, hear us.

(Pray for any personal, local or topical intention)

O God, the Father of all, may this season of Lent help us to grow in Christian charity. Through Christ, our Lord. Amen.

TUESDAY

ISAIAH 55:10-11 | *MATT 6:7-15*

1. In the Our Father, there are three God-petitions and four us-petitions. The God-petitions refer to God's name, God's Kingdom and God's will. We cannot add to God's glory but we ask that God's name will fill us with a deeper sense of both the heavenly majesty of God as well as the nearness of God as our Father. We desire the coming down of God's Kingdom to transform our world into justice, peace, compassion and sharing. Then we turn inwards by inviting God's will to be the energy of our hearts. The four us-petitions cover the dimensions of time - present, past and future. For today's needs, give us our daily bread, knowing that God already knows what we need. For our past sins we ask forgiveness as well as the grace to be able to forgive those who have offended us. For our future, lead us, not into any temptation or testing too great for us. Finally, deliver us from the clutches of the Evil One.

2. All that needs to be said in prayer is contained in the Our Father. Notice that the first person singular is never mentioned. All our prayer belongs to the community of the Body of Christ. Keep it simple. Our Father already knows what we need ever before a word is uttered. The Lord's Prayer can be committed to memory in a few minutes but it takes a lifetime to commit it to action. Words are hollow if they are not backed up in action. Praying for forgiveness must be backed up by a willingness to forgive others. Asking for our daily bread must be backed up by a willingness to share. Rather than babbling with many words, it is advisable to sit quietly with a short prayer lovingly repeated. Each line of the Our Father is a perfect prayer.

PRAYERS

As we take the teaching of Jesus Christ to heart, we pray.

Heavenly Father, may we have a deep reverence towards your holy name and a great trust in your fatherly providence.
Lord, hear us.

We earnestly desire God's Kingdom of justice, peace, compassion and caring.
Lord, hear us.

May God's will be what we always seek.
Lord, hear us.

Father, give us today our daily bread, answering all our needs which you already know.
Lord, hear us.

For the healing of the past: Father, forgive us our sins and enable us to forgive those who have offended us.
Lord, hear us.

For our future, lead us away from temptation and deliver us from the clutches of the Evil One.
Lord, hear us.

Heavenly Father, we unite all our prayers with those of Jesus Christ, your Son, our Lord. Amen.

WEDNESDAY

JONAH 3:1-10 | LUKE 11:29-32

1. A week into Lent, the Readings today encourage us to keep up our efforts at prayer, fasting and almsgiving. Our Lenten efforts are not only for ourselves. We are all members of the one body of Christ. The sins of one person drag down the spiritual health of the whole body. But the good works of one person lift up the entire body. The story of Jonah preaching in Nineveh should inspire us. Nineveh was an evil city. Jonah was a very reluctant preacher. But the people heard his warning and they repented. The city was saved. Nineveh can be seen in many places today where moral standards have fallen. No respect for the sacredness of life; serious abuse of drugs and alcohol; violence and robberies; sexual morality gone out of control. The story of Nineveh offers hope that the cycle of Evil can be halted. People can repent and change their ways. Your efforts during Lent have implications for the good of society. One greater than Solomon or Jonah is here. Christ is here and we are members of his Body. Keep up your good works.

2. Jonah must have been the most reluctant, half-hearted preacher who ever lived! Yet when he warned the people of Nineveh that they were on the road to perdition, they repented. Maybe it was sympathy for the poor fellow that touched their hearts. A stronger preacher might have been rejected. If Nineveh listened to such a half-hearted preacher as Jonah, there is no excuse for us. We have the words of Jesus. We are strengthened by Jesus in the Sacraments. We have the inspiring example of the saints and the wonderful letters of the popes. We have no excuse for not knowing the wisdom of Jesus.

PRAYERS

The story of Jonah and the conversion of Nineveh encourage us to pray for the conversion of the world today.

As the people of Nineveh listened to the preaching of Jonah and repented, may people today listen to the teaching of the Church and turn away from Evil.
Lord, hear us.

May our towns and neighbourhoods be free from crime so that people can live in peace.
Lord, hear us.

We pray especially for any family members or acquaintances whose way of life causes us great worry.
Lord, hear us.

   (Pray for any personal, local or topical intention)

O God, you desire that all people turn away from evil ways. May your goodness be known to people and attract them to conversion. Through Christ, our Lord. Amen.

THURSDAY

ESTHER 4-7 | MATT 7:7-12

1. Today's readings encourage us to pray with great confidence. When Queen Esther's life was in great danger, she turned earnestly to God. "Come to my help, for I am alone and have no helper but You." Jesus tells us to ask, to seek and to knock on God's door. We might say that we have often asked and we did not receive. Yet Jesus assures us that every prayer is heard. But it may not be answered exactly as we requested. God can see a bigger picture of life. A loving parent might answer a child's request in a different and safer way. Another possibility is that God answers our prayer but in a different place. For instance, we pray here for vocations to the priesthood but we see no result. However, other parts of the world have huge numbers of seminarians. Maybe it is an answer to our prayer but in a different country.

2. Sometimes God wants us to back up the words of prayer with good acts. Actions speak louder than words. A mother might tell a child, "Yes, I'll give you what you ask but first you must tidy up your room". "If you are bringing your gift to the altar, and there remember that your brother has something against you, go first to be reconciled with your brother and then come back to offer your gift." One great act of charity is to treat others as you would wish them to treat you. Prayer backed up with Christian action is extra powerful.

Prayer asks: fasting knocks on the door: almsgiving opens the door.

PRAYERS

After listening to the words of Jesus in the Gospel we pray. May we trust that every prayer is heard even if it is not answered in the way we expected.
Lord, hear us.

May we have the same attitude that Jesus had in the Garden of Gethsemane, "Not my will but thine be done".
Lord, hear us.

May we understand that sometimes God delays his answer until we treat other people as we would wish them to treat us.
Lord, hear us.

For those who have given up on prayer: may they experience the deep joy and confidence that come to a person who has a daily relationship with God.
Lord, hear us.

(Pray for any personal, local or topical need.)

Lord, increase our faith, deepen our trust and inflame our charity as we pray in the name of Jesus Christ, your Son, our Lord. Amen.

FRIDAY

EZEKIEL 18:21-28 | MATT 5:20-26

1. "If your virtue goes no deeper than that of the Scribes and Pharisees, you will not enter the Kingdom of Heaven." Entering into the Kingdom of Heaven means entering into the ideals of Jesus Christ – becoming Christian not only in name but also in reality. Don't stay on the surface of life but examine your inner attitudes. For instance, Jesus takes the commandment, "Thou shalt not kill". We might never actually murder anybody but Jesus asks us to go deeper in examining our conscience. There are many ways of being killers. We might never actually strike somebody but angry or sarcastic words can reduce a person to nothing. Putting a label on people, giving them offensive names will kill their right to be respected. Stony silence... deliberately avoiding a person... refusing to talk... these are examples of how relationships are murdered.

2. In yesterday's Gospel, Jesus said that one purpose of religious laws is to get us to treat others as we would wish them to treat us. Sometimes God delays in answering our petitions so as to gives us time to back up our words of prayer with action. "Be reconciled with another before you bring your gifts to the altar." God asks us walk the walk before we talk the talk. The challenge is to go deeper than the letter of the law: to go deeper into total self-honesty to see if we are Christian, not only in name, but also in reality. To enter into the Kingdom of Heaven means entering into the mind and ideals of Jesus Christ.

PRAYERS

As we take the teaching of Jesus to heart, we pray.

May we enter into the Kingdom of Heaven by living according to the ideals of Jesus Christ.
Lord, hear us.

As the psalmist wrote, "O God, you search me and you know me. You discern my purpose from afar". Grant us the grace to delve more deeply in self-honesty about how we live.
Lord, hear us.

Help us to control what we say about others so that we might not be killing a person's good name.
Lord, hear us.

We pray for people whom we may have hurt by action, attitude or word. May they recover from any injury we have inflicted on them.
Lord, hear us.

   (Pray for any personal, local or topical need.)

O God, our Father, to you every person is precious. Help us to treat others as we would wish them to treat us. Through Christ, our Lord. Amen

SATURDAY

DEUTERONOMY 26:16-19 | MATT 5:43-48

1. Our readings in Lent continue to challenge us. Today we are challenged about the limits we put on the scope of our love. Do we have one list of the people whom we respect and another list of the people we feel we have the right to hate? We regard them as enemies. There are enemies of God but God does not regard them as enemies. There are no limitations on God's love, no conditions attached. God's love is not limited to the observance of certain conditions like going to Mass or performing some penance. The amazing thing about God's love is that there is nobody outside its scope. The greatest sinner is as much God's creature as the greatest saint. We are called to be God's children and to be like God. It is a very lofty ideal to be perfect as our heavenly Father is perfect. The ideal is obviously beyond us but, at least, we can make a start. Ideals are like stars: we will never reach them but we chart our course by them.

2. How can we deal with our problem with the people who have wronged us or hurt us in any way? Here are three steps. First, wish them no harm. Move on from wishing them bad luck or that they will get their comeuppance. Second step, when you are ready, begin to pray for your enemy. The third step is to pray for yourself. Constantly ask the Holy Spirit to remove all bitterness from your heart. Ask for the grace to be more like God who sets no limitations on his love. In this way you will be more like your Father in Heaven for he causes his sun to shine on bad people as well as God, and his rain to fall on honest and dishonest people alike.

PRAYERS

In the light of the ideal of Christ we are moved to pray.

God loves all people and wishes that all would accept his love and be saved. By the grace of God, may we see people as Jesus Christ sees them.
Lord, hear us.

We pray for anybody who has abused us or hurt us in any way. May they be converted to a better way of living.
Lord, hear us.

Remove from our hearts all bitterness or thoughts of revenge.
Lord, hear us.

May the Holy Spirit help us to have a more positive attitude towards everybody.
Lord, hear us.

(Pray for any personal, local or topical need.)

Heavenly Father, we thank you for your unconditional love. May we who receive your love pass it on to others. Through Christ, our Lord. Amen.

SECOND WEEK OF LENT:

MONDAY

DANIEL 9:4-10 | LUKE 6:36-38

1. "Be compassionate as your Father is compassionate." Compassion means to feel with a person or to suffer with somebody. If we are condemning somebody, it is as if we are standing over the person like a judge. When we are looking down on somebody it is because we regard ourselves as belonging to a higher level. But if we are compassionate, if we are feeling with the person, then we are on the same level. The beauty of forgiveness is that we get back more than we have given. "Grant pardon, and you will be pardoned. Give, and there will be gifts for you: a full measure, pressed down, shaken together, and running over, will be poured into your lap; because the amount you measure out is the amount you will be given back."

2. There is a famous novel called *To Kill a Mocking Bird*. It is about a lawyer, Atticus Finch, who has to defend a young black man who has been accused of attacking a young white woman. The story is set in a very bigoted, racist town. Mister Finch has a conversation with his little daughter, Scout, who has been in trouble at school because of her fiery temper. Her dad tells her, "You never really understand a person until you consider things from his point of view – until you climb into his skin and walk around in it". Jesus wants us to develop the virtue of compassion. That is why he sat with sinners. He did not look down on them. He ate and drank with them. He felt for them. Who am I to judge others? Who am I who never climbed into that person's background or personal experience? There is a saying that to understand all is to forgive.

PRAYERS

Taking the teaching of Jesus to heart, we pray.

May the Church be faithful to the ideals of Jesus, full of understanding and compassion, celebrating God's mercy and giving hope to the sinner.
Lord, hear us.

Cleanse us of any self-righteousness which makes us feel superior to others.
Lord, hear us.

Help us to have a greater understanding of others so that we will be more compassionate towards them.
Lord, hear us.

In all our conversations may we be less judgemental and more compassionate.
Lord, hear us.

(Pray for any personal, local or topical need.)

O God, the Father of Mercy, help us to be more compassionate, like your Son, Jesus Christ, our Lord. Amen

SECOND WEEK OF LENT:

TUESDAY

ISAIAH 1:10. 16-20 | *MATT 23:1-12*

1. The Scripture readings for Lent were chosen to challenge our complacency and to shake up any smug satisfaction that "I am okay while other people are sinners". We are challenged to ask ourselves: do I practice what I preach? Do I expect higher standards from others than I would apply to myself? In other words, do I find excuses for my own failings but allow no excuses for others? In God's eyes, earthly honours or titles are of no value. What God values is humble service. "The greatest among you must be your servant."

2. The prophet Isaiah in the First Reading reminds us that religion is not just a private hotline between me and God. True religion must have a social awareness of needs of others. "Cease to do evil, learn to do good. Search for justice, help the oppressed, be just to the orphan, plead for the widow." The Word of God is like the surgeon's knife which reaches into any diseased part of life. But the Good News also tells us of God's forgiveness. "Though your sins are like scarlet, they shall be as white as snow; though they are red as crimson, they shall be as wool." When we examine our lives we should not become obsessed with our faults. We must also remember God's mercy .

PRAYERS

Having listened to the Word of God, we pray that we will put it into practice.

Let us pray for all who are called to leadership in the Church. May they never forget that their calling is to humble service rather than earthly honours and power.
Lord, hear us.

"You have only one Teacher, the Christ". Let us pray that Christ will always be the one who sets our ideals.
Lord, hear us.

May our Lenten resolutions remind us of the cries of the poor.
Lord, hear us.

We pray for the victims of war who have to flee from home and country. May they travel in safety and receive a Christian welcome.
Lord, hear us.

   (Pray for any personal, local or topical need.)

O God, we thank you for sending us Jesus Christ as our teacher and leader. May we build our lives on the foundation of his teaching, who lives and reigns with you for ever and ever. Amen.

WEDNESDAY

JEREMIAH 18:18-20 | *MATT 20:17-28*

1. The Apostles still had not absorbed one of the fundamental messages of Jesus. He was not going to be a political messiah. At the beginning of his ministry, he rejected Satan's temptation to seek earthly power and glory. The mother of the Apostles James and John came looking for top jobs for her boys in the Kingdom that Jesus often mentioned. The other ten Apostles were no better. They were indignant because they thought James and John were getting one up on them. Jesus must have sighed in disappointment that they had not got his message. His Kingdom would be one of humble service rather than self-advancement. "The greatest among you must be your servant. The Son of Man came not to be served but to serve, and to give his life for the ransom of many."

2. In the world of sport, some coaches have the motto, hammer the hammer. It means go for the leaders of the other team and hammer them. Minimize the leaders and you are on the way. Satan uses the same tactic. Go after the leaders of the Church. Pick up their human frailties. Let authority go to their heads. Clothe them like princes, call them by titles of eminence, kiss their rings, set them on an upward career. Pope Francis referred to Spiritual Alzheimer's which makes one forget his original spiritual vocation. Satan targeted the apostles with a certain amount of success. He continues to do so today. That is why we must always pray for those who are called to leadership in the Church. "The greatest among you must be your servant."

PRAYERS

We take to heart the teaching of Jesus to inspire our prayer.

We pray for the leaders of the Church. May they resist the temptation to use their position for their own advancement.
Lord, hear us.

For political leaders. May they understand that their power is a means of serving the nation in justice and honesty.
Lord, hear us.

Jesus gave his life for the ransom of many. May we be generous in giving time and attention to others.
Lord, hear us.

  (Pray for any personal, local or topical need.)

Heavenly Father, hear the prayers of your people gathered in the name of Jesus Christ, your Son, our Lord. Amen

THURSDAY

Jeremiah 17:5-10 | *Luke 16:19-31*

1. Jesus told many parables but only once did he give a name to a character. Lazarus, the poor, hungry, ulcerated man is the only character honoured with a name. Lazarus is a name meaning the compassion of God. What a blessed name for somebody whose life was one of pain and poverty! The only medical care he received was from the dogs who licked his sores. Dogs are known to be extraordinarily sensitive to pain and sores. The dogs that came to Lazarus were far more sensitive than the rich man with his grand house and surplus food inside the gate. There is nothing in the story to suggest that he acquired his wealth by unjust means. His sin was in what he failed to do: the sin of omission. Sins of omission are easily overlooked. There is an unhealthy sort of religion which is totally individualistic with no concern about social responsibilities.

2. There was a great gulf between the rich man and Lazarus at his gate. There is an even greater gulf in the judgement after death. There is an old tradition that it is not Saint Peter who is the porter at Heaven's gate but the people who were unjustly deprived in this life. They are the ones who say, "Yes, come in, welcome. I recognise you. You helped me". But to others they say, "Sorry, I do not recognise you. I never saw you helping anybody". Jesus once said, "Of him to whom much is given a great deal will be demanded". Who wants to be a millionaire? Could I handle the responsibilities and temptations that money would bring?

PRAYERS

As we are challenged by the Gospel, we pray.

Jesus clearly was on the side of the poor. May the Church continue its long history of caring for the poor in a vast variety of ways.
Lord, hear us.

May those who exercise great political or financial power work towards a fair distribution of the world's resources and the alleviation of famine.
Lord, hear us.

As the name Lazarus means the compassion of God, may poor people draw great consolation from their religious beliefs.
Lord, hear us.

Open our eyes, Lord, to our sins of omission.
Lord, hear us.

(Pray for any personal, local or topical need.)

O God, you hear the cries of the poor. May all of us hear their cry and do what we can to alleviate their suffering. Through Christ, our Lord. Amen.

FRIDAY

Genesis 37:3-4. 12-13. 17-28 | *Matt 21:33-43. 45-46*

1. The parable of the rebellious tenants is clearly directed against the Jewish religious leaders. They were plotting the death of Jesus. The First Reading today is a parallel story. Joseph was the most loved of the children of Israel, the son of his old age. His brothers were madly jealous. They sold him off as a slave for twenty silver pieces. Jesus was sold for thirty silver pieces. Both stories had happy endings. Joseph rose in rank and became the most powerful man in Egypt. He forgave his brothers and provided food for them when harvests failed. He became their saviour. Jesus was rejected and sold, but the resurrection changed everything. Joseph and Jesus turned out to be the rejected stone which later became the keystone to hold the structure together. The Jewish religious leaders were being told how they had lost their chance but now their privileges as God's chosen people would be extended to the Gentile nations.

2. In our time many people have rejected the Church. Some have rejected all religion. This can be seen as a challenge to the Church to renew enthusiasm for the ideals of God's Kingdom. We might have to let go of certain regulations and procedures which were useful in the past but give out the wrong message today. When the Church is seen to produce the fruits of the Spirit, then people will be attracted to Christ. A stone arch will collapse unless there is a proper keystone to hold everything together. When life falls apart one needs to find a source of meaning and unity. The challenge of the New Evangelisation is to witness that Jesus is the keystone to fullness of life. In the words of Pope Francis, "Jesus wants evangelisers who proclaim the Good News not only with words, but above all by a life transfigured by God's presence." (*The Joy of the Gospel*, 259).

PRAYERS

Trusting in Jesus as the keystone of life, we pray.

Let us pray for the Church: may criticism of the Church bring about a more humble Church, closer to the lifestyle and ideals of Jesus Christ.
Lord, hear us

We pray for the people who are being persecuted for their faith. May the Lord, who was himself rejected, support and strengthen them in their time of trial.
Lord, hear us.

For people who have rejected all religion: may they see their need for Jesus who is the Saviour holding all parts of life together.
Lord, hear us.

We pray for all who have been rejected in life. May they see Jesus as one who was rejected and come to know him as their forever friend.
Lord, hear us.

   (Pray for any personal, local or topical need.)

O God, loving Father of all, help us to live by the ideals taught us by your Beloved Son, Jesus Christ the Lord. Amen.

SATURDAY

MICAH 7:14-15. 18-20 | *LUKE 15:1-3. 11-32*

1. "This man welcomes sinners and eats with them". Jesus was a scandal in the eyes of the Jewish leaders because of the way he mixed with public sinners. So he told them the parable of the merciful father. When the son who was a waster and public disgrace came back, his father was moved with pity. He ran to the boy, clasped him in his arms and kissed him tenderly. He wasn't moved by anger, by reproach or blame. He was moved with pity. This is what mercy, *Misericordia*, means: a heart that feels, a heart full of pity. Such a contrast with the elder son who does not want to recognise "this son of yours" as his brother. He will not eat with his brother. He represents the religious leaders who would not mix with sinners. The father is equally full of pity for the elder son: "My son, you are with me always and all I have is yours". The Jewish elders may have rejected Jesus but he has not rejected them.

2. Our Lent will not be complete unless we avail of the Sacrament of God's mercy. Think of God's mercy waiting for you, like the Prodigal Son's father waiting for his child's return. Come in humble honesty to own up to your faults. There is no need to torture yourself because God already knows your sins. By having to put words on them, you are accepting responsibility for where you have fallen down. Humbly acknowledge the areas of life where you feel you should improve. Let the merciful Father embrace you. Relax in God's gentleness. Confession is not meant to be a torture chamber. It is the banquet of God's mercy. At the end of the banquet there is music and dancing. There is music in the wonderful words of absolution. And the dancing will be in the joy of your heart.

PRAYERS

As we are encouraged by the parable of the Merciful Father, we pray.

May our reflection on this parable help us to grow in our appreciation of God's wonderful mercy.
Lord, hear us.

May the Church be faithful to Christ in being a place where sinners are welcomed and helped in their struggles.
Lord, hear us.

Help us, Lord, to set aside all our fears and anxieties about confession. May we come to know the Sacrament as sitting down in the company of our merciful Saviour.
Lord, hear us.

May those who have strayed down the wrong paths of life come to their senses and return to the Lord who is waiting for them.
Lord, hear us.

   (Pray for any personal, local or topical need.)

Merciful Father, we thank you for showing us the face of mercy in the life of Jesus Christ, your Son, our Lord. Amen.

MONDAY

2 Kings 5:1-15 | Luke 4:24-30

1. No prophet is ever accepted in his own country. When Jesus went back to his own village he was rejected. Joseph's son! Follow him? Maybe I'd go to him to make a door or a table. He was too human for their admiration. There has always been the temptation to want a purely spiritual Christ without the messy aspects of human nature. Such an approach leads to a very self-serving spirituality devoid of any social responsibility. It produces people who are so heavenly minded that they are no earthly good. In the early Church, this led to a heresy called Gnosticism. Spiritual knowledge was all that mattered and there was no place for practical charity. In much the same way, many people find the Church too human for their liking. Their vision of a purely spiritual Church without human failures is nothing more than the figment of a romantic imagination. Jesus, though he was Son of God, was fully human. The Apostles were totally human. We should be glad that the Church is human and frail, because that means there is room for us in it. If it were a Church for perfect people we would have to leave.

2. Namaan, a successful commander of the Syrian army, an important man who enjoyed the ruler's favour, caught leprosy. A little slave girl from Israel, spoke of a man in Samaria with healing powers. So Namaan set out with big money and expensive gifts. He was taken aback when Elisha, the healer, did not come out to meet him personally. And the message he gave did not improve Namaan's humour. To bathe seven times in the Jordan, a river which was in no way the equal of the mighty rivers of his own land. He was about to leave in a state of high indignation until his servants pleaded with him: "If you had been asked to do something difficult you would have done it". His military reputation and impressive connections were no help. His money and expensive gifts counted for nothing. His journey towards healing involved a little slave girl, a prophet who did not come out to greet a VIP, and a featureless little river. But it was through all these ordinary little things that the healing power of God came to him. Patrick Kavanagh wrote of "the placeless Heaven that's beneath our noses." God is in the ordinary things of life. Imagine, God choosing a little piece of bread to be his embodiment as our food of life!

PRAYERS

After listening to the wisdom of God's Word, we pray.

Let us pray for our Holy Father Pope *(Name)* and for all who are called to lead the Church. May their faith withstand all opposition and rejection.
Lord, hear us.

We pray that people who are being persecuted because they are prophets of God, will be strengthened by God's grace.
Lord, hear us.

May our eyes be opened to recognise the presence of God in ordinary people and ordinary things.
Lord, hear us.

Namaan the leper was a general in the Syrian army. We pray for peace in Syria and in every war-torn land.
Lord, hear us.

   (Pray for any personal, local or topical need.)

God, our Father, hear our prayers offered in the name of Jesus Christ, your Son, our Lord. Amen

TUESDAY

Daniel 3:25. 34-43 | *Matt 18:21-35*

1. In the early pages of the Bible there is a wild character called Lamech. If anybody wronged him, he would seek vengeance seventy-seven times. It was a great advance when Moses limited vengeance to an equal amount: an eye for an eye and a tooth for a tooth. So it remained until Jesus set a new standard in the Sermon on the Mount. Do not seek any vengeance. Do not return evil for evil. Turn the other cheek. Go the extra mile. Peter, who had a fiery temper, sought a clarification. "How often must I forgive, will seven times be enough?" Jesus replied, "Not seven but seventy-seven times". The wheel has gone full circle from Lamech to Jesus. The kingdom established by Jesus was described by Pope Francis as a revolution of tenderness and compassion. The Catholic Catechism states that forgiveness shows how love is stronger than sin.

2. A heroic person during the Second World War was Etty Hillesum, a young Jewish woman in Holland, who died in a Nazi concentration camp. Speaking one day with her friend who was a communist she said: "Each of us must turn inward and destroy in himself all he thinks he must destroy in others. And remember that every atom of hate that we add to this world makes it still more inhospitable." Her communist friend interrupted, "But this is nothing only Christianity!"
Etty replied, "Yes, Christianity, and why ever not!" This young Jewish woman understood in mind and heart the teaching of Jesus in the Sermon on the Mount.

PRAYERS

After listening to the words of Jesus about forgiveness, we pray.

May we appreciate the forgiveness of God so deeply that it will be our joy to forgive others.
Lord, hear us.

May the world turn away from violence and vengeance, recognising that two wrongs do not make a right.
Lord, hear us.

May we play our part in the revolution of Jesus, working for a world of tenderness and compassion, bearing witness that love is stronger than sin.
Lord, hear us.

May we recognise that every atom of hate that we add to the world only makes it a more inhospitable place to live.
Lord, hear us.

(Pray for any personal, local or topical need.)

O God of mercy, transform our lives through the power of the Holy Spirit, so that the divine love within us will be greater than any wrongs we suffer. Through Christ, our Lord. Amen.

WEDNESDAY

DEUTERONOMY 4:1. 5-9 | MATT 5:17-19

1. "Do not think that I have come to abolish the Law or the Prophets. I have come, not to abolish them, but to fulfil them." When the Bible speaks about the Law – in the singular and with a capital letter – it refers to God's revelation about the meaning and direction of life. The Law is our side of the sacred covenant that promised God's protection. We call it Divine Law as opposed to the man-made regulations and directives that accumulate over the years. Moses, in today's First Reading, tells the people how fortunate they are to have a God so near them and whose Law is so clearly before them. The Jews regarded the Law as a safety-fence around them. Outside the fence lay danger: staying within the Law, one was safe. In the psalms there are some beautiful reflections on the gift of God's Law.
The Law of the Lord is perfect: it revives the soul.
Your Word is founded on truth: your decrees are eternal. (Ps. 118)

2. Moral decisions are far too serious to be left to the whims and fashions of the popular vote or opinion poll. A referendum is sometimes called in the immediate aftermath of a tragedy which has whipped up a massive surge of emotion. Recent referenda and elections in various countries have been directed by the social media. Slogans and emotive words have replaced reasoned debate. The Gospel tells of one opinion poll. By this popular vote, Jesus was condemned to death while Barabbas, a criminal, was released. We live in a world of rapid change. Too much change leaves people without any solid foundation. Sadly, in a culture that lacks solid beliefs and accepted guidelines, suicide has become an epidemic.
The lovers of your law have great peace: they never stumble. (Ps. 118)

PRAYERS

In the light of the Word of God we pray.

May the Holy Spirit guide the Church in giving clear moral guidelines to the world.
Lord, hear us.

May all those who make our laws and apply them respect the Law of God in their decisions.
Lord, hear us.

We pray for young people that they will find a meaning to life and follow the guidelines to a good moral life.
Lord, hear us.

O God, your Word is a lamp for our steps and a light for our paths. May we always walk in your light.
Lord, hear us.

   (Pray for any personal, local or topical need.)

O God, graciously hear these prayers which we offer to you in the name of Jesus Christ, your Son, our Lord. Amen.

THURSDAY

JEREMIAH 7:23-28 | LUKE 11:14-23

1. Today we hear the prophet Jeremiah say, "Here is the nation that will not listen to the voice of the Lord its God, nor take correction. Sincerity is no more, it has vanished from their mouths." Sadly, these words are as true today as they were when first written. When people let their hearts be hardened, they will not listen, much less take correction. People become so prejudiced that they will not accept what is perfectly obvious. Jesus had just worked a miracle in giving speech to a dumb man. But the people with closed minds came up with the most ridiculous argument. They claimed that Jesus was in league with evil spirits. The Devil may be evil but the Devil is not so stupid as to let his kingdom be divided against itself. The miracles of Jesus were signs that he was winning total victory over evil spirits. So powerful is God that with one finger he can win the battle with Evil.

2. The prophet Ezechiel foretold the time of Jesus. "I shall give you a new heart and put a new spirit in you. I shall remove your heart of stone and give you a heart of flesh." We hear these words in the liturgy of Easter as we celebrate the greatest miracle, the Resurrection of Jesus. The Resurrection is the total victory over Evil. As if it were a boxing match, Jesus took all the blows the Devil could throw against him through the connivance of Judas, Pilate, the Jewish leaders and others. He took the hatred and transformed it into love. He took the abuse and transformed it into forgiveness. He even took death and transformed it into eternal life. The Risen Lord is with us. His Spirit is within us. Be not afraid because Jesus has won the victory over Evil.

PRAYERS

We trust in the power of Jesus as we pray.

May the Church, guided by the finger of God, bring us God's Word and God's healing.
Lord, hear us.

May our eyes and ears be open to see and hear the signs of God's goodness all around us.
Lord, hear us.

May the Holy Spirit remove any hardness of heart which might prevent us from responding to God's love.
Lord, hear us.

We pray for those who refuse to believe. May the light of the Holy Spirit break through their darkness.
Lord, hear us.

(Pray for any personal, local or topical need.)

Father, as we prepare for the celebration of the death and resurrection of Jesus, open up our lives to listen to your Word so as to be guided by it. Through Christ, our Lord. Amen.

FRIDAY

HOSEA 14:2-10 | MARK 12:28-34

1. We have reached the second half of Lent. How are you getting on? How have you fared up to now? How can we judge what Lent has done for us? There is one sure test. It is the law of love, mentioned in today's Gospel. By their fruits you shall know them. Has Lent brought you closer to God... more prayerful... more regular participation at Mass... more reverential in language, especially regarding God's name? The second law of love questions your attitude towards people. Are you more respectful... more aware of people... more sensitive... more generous? Ponder on the four dimensions of love that Jesus mentioned.

    "With all your heart"... developing a personal relationship with God who calls you "Friend".

    "All your soul"... as the Psalmist said, "thirsting for God".

    "All your mind"... developing your knowledge of God through good reading and reflection.

    "All your strength"... expressing your love in practical acts of kindness, helpfulness and generosity.

2. *Love* is a word much used but often misused. The practical implications of love reach far beyond romantic infatuation or nice feelings about somebody. Saint Paul listed many of the practical proofs of love. Love is always patient... kind... never jealous or boastful. It is not arrogant or rude. It does not insist on its own way. It is not irritable or resentful. It does not rejoice at what is wrong but rejoices in the right. Love tolerates all things, hopes all things, endures all things. Acts of self-denial, such as fasting, are good for a variety of reasons. The best reason for any penance is to make us more reverential towards God and more respectful towards people. "This is far more important than any holocaust or sacrifice". This is what the Kingdom of God is all about. "By their fruits you shall know them."

PRAYERS

Our Gospel today recalls that the purpose of all the commandments is to develop our love of God and neighbour.

We pray that the Church will inspire the world to live according to the Kingdom of God, in love and justice, in peace and charity.
Lord, hear us.

May the grace of Lent bring us to a deeper reverence towards the one, true God.
Lord, hear us.

May this holy season produce the fruits of practical charity in our lives.
Lord, hear us.

May our eyes be opened to the needs of others and may we respond in kindness.
Lord, hear us.

(Pray for any personal, local or topical need.)

O God, in this holy season of Lent, fill our hearts with your love and keep us faithful in our religious practices. Through Christ, our Lord. Amen.

SATURDAY

HOSEA 5:15 – 6:6 | LUKE 18:9-14

1. In today's First Reading God tells us, "I want love, not sacrifice". In the Gospel we meet the Pharisee who was so zealous about fasting that he did twice what the law required. He also exceeded the legal requirements regarding the temple tax. Unfortunately, he was proud of all that he was doing. And pride made him think that he had the right to look down on others as despicable sinners. He thought that he was praying to God, but the god he worshipped was his own proud self. So we are told that he said this prayer to himself.

2. The tax collector said a humble prayer that pierced the clouds. "God, be merciful to me, a sinner." This prayer came straight from a humble heart. His prayer is simple and uncomplicated. Perhaps some good advice about prayer is less mouth and more heart! The sacred name of God or the name of Jesus is a prayer in itself. The essence of prayer is an awareness of God's presence. Prayer develops in response to the glimpses we get of God's relationship with us. There are five basic responses to God. They spell out the word ALTAR. Adoration responds to the glory of God. Love responds to the person of God. Thanksgiving is a return for the gifts of God. Asking expresses trust in God. Repentance is a humble apology to God. The tax collector makes the perfect prayer of repentance, "God, be merciful to me, a sinner."

PRAYERS

We take the parable of Jesus to heart as we pray.

May the observance of Lent produce the fruits of greater love for God and more respect for people.
Lord, hear us.

Cleanse us of all pride and our tendency to look down on others.
Lord, hear us.

We pray for people who are so burdened with guilt that they feel God would not want them. May they understand that the God of mercy is longing and waiting for their return.
Lord, hear us.

May the Church be known as the field hospital for those who are battered and bruised in the battlefield of life.
Lord, hear us.

   (Pray for any personal, local or topical need.)

O God of mercy, teach us to pray with the humble simplicity of the tax collector. Through Christ, our Lord. Amen.

MONDAY

ISAIAH 65:17-21 | JOHN 4:43-54

1. The court official who approached Jesus to heal his sick son showed great faith. Jesus did not travel with him but told him, "Go home, your son will live." He took Jesus at his word and started the journey home. His journey recalls the faith of Abraham, the first model of faith. Abraham was asked by God to leave his home and his father's country for a land that God would show him. He was promised a rich future but for many years, there was no sign of the fulfilment of God's promise. Ten times his faith was tested and seven times he was blessed with new hope. All he had to go on was his faith in God's promise. It was the same for the court official. The journey from Cana to Capernaum was thirty-five kilometres in hilly country. He had to travel through the dark of night and it was late the following day before he reached home and got the good news of his son's recovery. Our journey of faith is a combination of light and darkness, a flame by night and a cloud by day. Enough light to sustain us through the dark times. But also clouds of unknowingness when there are questions we cannot answer, mysteries we cannot comprehend. Saint John Paul II wrote that to believe is to abandon oneself to the Word of the living God, knowing and humbly recognising how unsearchable are his judgements and how inscrutable are his ways.

2. The man whose son was seriously ill got the good news that his son was cured. In today's First Reading Isaiah rejoices that the exile is over. The good news is that the people can move on from their painful past. No more will the sound of weeping be heard on their streets. Jerusalem will be a city of joy. One of the names we give to Jesus is Saviour. He saves us from the punishment due to sin. He stretched out his hand to save Peter from drowning. God will save us from any injustice or spiritual exile. He wants us to share his joy. With God on our side we can move on from a painful past.

PRAYERS

We take the lesson of the Gospel to heart as we pray.

Lord, may we listen to your Word with the same confidence that the father of the sick child showed when he trusted in the promise of Jesus.
Lord, hear us.

Let us pray for people who are going through a period of darkness. May their faith be sufficient support to keep them going.
Lord, hear us.

Let us join in prayer with parents whose child is sick.
Lord, hear us.

   (Pray for any personal, local or topical need.)

Your Word, O Lord, is a lamp for our steps and a light for our darkness. Support us on our journey of life. Through Christ, our Lord. Amen.

TUESDAY

EZEKIEL 47:1-9. 12 | JOHN 5:1-3. 5-16

1. When Jesus met the man who was thirty-eight years waiting at the pool, he asked him a surprising question: "Do you want to be well again?" Notice that the man did not answer the question directly. Instead, he began to blame others. "I have no one to put me in. Others get in before me." This is classical negative thinking. Poor little old me! Call it PLOM for short. As an antidote to his negativity, Jesus prescribed three actions. Stand up. Take up your mat. And walk. In John's Gospel, believing always involves trusting. There was so much authority in the voice of Jesus that the man trusted his legs. And they worked. The story challenges me to examine my own self-pity rating. To what extent do I hold on to negative memories? Do I blame others... nobody understands me... nobody helps me... others get there before me? Self-pity allows people to wallow in compensatory behaviour: compulsive drinking, eating, or immoral behaviour on the grounds that they are entitled to some compensation in a world where nobody understands. The words of Jesus are challenging. "Stand up. Take up your comfy blanket and walk." Challenging words, but life-giving words.

2. In John's Gospel, numbers are very significant. The crippled man was thirty-eight years waiting to enter the water which would liberate him and bestow fullness of life. This links up with the Exodus of the Israelite people who waited thirty-eight years before they could cross the water of the Jordan to enter the Promised Land. When John wrote his Gospel, he applied this story to the Jewish people who had not believed in Jesus. He lamented that they had not entered the water of Baptism to pass over into the fullness of life which Jesus brought. They were still wandering in the desert of unbelief.

PRAYERS

Encouraged by the healing power of Jesus, we pray.

Lord, may we draw strength from hearing your command to stand up, to let go of selfish comforts, and to walk with you this day.
Lord, hear us.

Help us to accept responsibility for our mistakes and to stop blaming others all the time.
Lord, hear us.

We pray for people with long-term ailments. Grant them patience and trust.
Lord, hear us.

May God bless and reward all who care for long-term patients.
Lord, hear us.

(Pray for any personal, local or topical need.)

O God, help us at all times to walk the road of life in the confidence that you are with us. Through Christ, our Lord. Amen

FOURTH WEEK OF LENT:

WEDNESDAY

ISAIAH 49:8-15 | JOHN 5:17-30

We are coming close to the Passion of the Lord. One of the many lessons we can draw from contemplating the death of Jesus is that there is still hope, even when it seems that the Lord has abandoned us. There was darkness over the Earth when Jesus died but the darkness did not last.

1. Nearly six hundred years before the time of Jesus, the Jewish people were forced into exile in Babylon. Many of them lost faith in God, thinking that God had abandoned them. However, great preachers sustained hope. In today's First Reading, Isaiah celebrates their return from exile. The people had complained, "The Lord has abandoned me, the Lord has forgotten me." Isaiah replied, "Does a woman forget the child at the breast or fail to cherish the son of her womb? Yet, even if these forget, I will never forget you." These are words of great encouragement for people who are in a dark space.

2. More barbaric than the Babylonian exile was the Nazi attempt to exterminate the entire Jewish race. Had God totally abandoned them? How could anybody believe that God had promised a covenant of protection for their race? But there were some heroic leaders who kept faith alive with the promise that the voice of the prophets speak more loudly than Hitler. Where was God in Auschwitz? Where was God on Calvary? The greatest Jew of all time was Jesus Christ. He entered into solidarity with all kinds of suffering: physical suffering, emotional suffering in seeing his mother at the foot of the cross, victim of false accusations and an unjust trial, abandoned and even betrayed by close associates. He even experienced the darkness of feeling abandoned by the Father. The cross of Jesus Christ is the greatest statement that God is with us even in the dreadful darkness of feeling abandoned. The darkness of Friday gave way to the light of Sunday. "Whoever listens to my words has eternal life."

PRAYERS

"I will never forget you, my people." Let us draw confidence from the words of Sacred Scripture as we pray.

As the preaching of great prophets like Isaiah sustained the faith of people in the past, so may the voice of the Church be a source of great strength to people who are being persecuted for their faith in our own day.
Lord, hear us.

May nobody, especially Christians, ever again inflict persecution by word or deed on the Jewish people.
Lord, hear us.

"Does a woman fail to cherish the child in her womb?" We pray for all expectant mothers: may they cherish the life of the child in the womb.
Lord, hear us.

We pray for those who have abandoned God. May they discover that God has not abandoned them.
Lord, hear us.

(Pray for any personal, local or topical need.)

O God, make your love known to us so that we might always know that you have not abandoned us. We offer this prayer in the name of Jesus Christ, your Son, our Lord. Amen.

FOURTH WEEK OF LENT:

THURSDAY

EXODUS 32: 7-14 | JOHN 5:31-47

1. Human beings were made in the image and likeness of God. We were given the gifts of intelligence and free will: the ability to think and the freedom to choose. We could not love without having the freedom to choose. Love is more than an attraction based on instinct or biological drives. Love involves a decision of the will. God honoured us with free will so that we might have the dignity of loving. God took a chance on us because there is also the possibility of refusing. In today's Gospel, Jesus is faced with Jewish leaders who refused to believe in him. He cites the evidence before their eyes... how John the Baptist spoke in his favour, the evidence of the works he did, the evidence of the scriptures they claimed to follow. But they refused to believe. As we go through life we make moral decisions every day, even without realising it. When we choose what is right, we are choosing God. When we do something that is wrong, we are in some way refusing God. Little decisions mount up and form our character either in the likeness of Christ or in a refusal of Christ. When we have to make a serious moral decision we should ask ourselves, what would God want us to do, how would Jesus act?

2. Two strong words are heard in today's readings. Refused and headstrong. God tells Moses that the people are headstrong... self-opinionated. Their minds were closed. They forgot the God who was their saviour and worshipped a calf fashioned from molten metal. When people are no longer guided by the law of God, what happens? "You look to one another for approval and are not concerned with the approval that comes from the one God." People become slaves to the latest fashion. Moral decisions, such as cohabiting before marriage, are justified on the grounds that everybody is doing it. "Jesus Christ is entitled to his opinion but this is my opinion." The psalmist wrote, "O God, you search me and you know me, you know my resting and rising, you discern my purpose from afar." The approval that comes from others is important, but in no way as important as the approval that comes from God.

PRAYERS

Taking the teaching of Jesus to heart, we pray.

May the Church be the light of the nations by proclaiming the ideals of Jesus Christ and the law of God by word and action.
Lord, hear us.

May the Holy Spirit help us to discern what God wants of us and may we have the strength of will to do what God wants.
Lord, hear us.

May those who want to remove any religious influence on society open their eyes to see how much religion has contributed to making the world a better place.
Lord, hear us

Give us patience, Lord, to tolerate people who are headstrong, self-opinionated and stubborn.
Lord, hear us.

   (Pray for any personal, local or topical need.)

O God, you have given your people many talents. Help us to use them in the service of your Kingdom, through Christ, our Lord. Amen.

FOURTH WEEK OF LENT:

FRIDAY

WISDOM 2:1. 12-22 | *JOHN 7:1-2. 10. 25-30*

1. We are two weeks away from Good Friday. The religious leaders had decided to get rid of Jesus. This was the only way they could silence him. The question arises, why did they kill that good man? He was healing people. He was a man of peace and compassion. Today's First Reading gives us an insight into the evil mind. "Let us lie in wait for the virtuous man, since he annoys us and opposes our way of life. Before us he stands, a reproof to our way of thinking." Our eyes are made for light but if our eyes are sore we want to shut out the light. The stomach is made for food, but if the stomach is sick, even the smell of food will upset it more. Similarly, our souls are made for God, but if the soul is sick, the person feels threatened in the presence of goodness. It was the goodness of Jesus that loomed as a threat to evil men.

2. Jesus once said, "Everybody who does wrong hates the light and avoids it, to prevent his actions from being shown up". So, when they could no longer avoid the light of Jesus, they decided to get rid of him by fair means or foul. The story is repeated throughout History. People found fault with the charitable work of Mother Teresa of Calcutta. People who defend the protection of life in the womb meet with bitter opposition. People who stand up for human rights put their lives in danger. There is a Chinese proverb that people throw sticks only at fruitful trees. "Blessed are you when people abuse you and persecute you and speak all kinds of calumny on my account. Rejoice and be glad, for your reward will be great in Heaven. This is how they persecuted the prophets before you."

PRAYERS

In the light of the Scriptures we pray.

May the Church always uphold the ideals of Jesus Christ in spite of dungeon, fire and sword.
Lord, hear us..

We pray for those who are suffering persecution today. May the Holy Spirit give them the strength of Christ. And may the day soon come when they can live in peace.
Lord, hear us

May we have the courage to stand up for our Christian beliefs and values in the face of opposition and cynicism.
Lord, hear us.

We pray for the conversion of those who are rejecting the light of Christ.
Lord, hear us.

(Pray for any personal, local or topical need.)

O God, in the spirit of the beatitudes, bless and reward all who suffer persecution for the sake of the Gospel. Through Christ, our Lord. Amen.

SATURDAY

JEREMIAH 11:18-20 | JOHN 7:40-52

1. Opinions were divided about Jesus, but the Jewish leaders had their minds made up to get rid of him. Long before the time of Jesus, the prophet Jeremiah was warned that there were people who were plotting to kill him. He compared himself to the trustful lamb being led to the slaughterhouse. John the Baptist identified Jesus as the Lamb of God. At the very time when the lambs were being sacrificed in the nearby temple, Jesus was dying on the cross. He became the innocent victim on behalf of sinful humanity. He entered into solidarity with all who are the victims of hatred, violence, injustice and bullying. He is the compassionate Saviour who accompanies us in our trials. He is the Lamb in whose blood we are redeemed. By his wounds, we are healed.

2. One of the Pharisees, Nicodemus, who was a secret follower of Jesus, called for a fair trial for Jesus. But he was shouted down. "Are you a Galilean too?" This is the old trick of name-calling or putting a label on somebody. Name-calling and slogans have become powerful weapons in gathering votes in recent elections and referenda. Many of today's voters do not read newspapers or follow television debates, but they are constantly active on Twitter or Facebook. Here, the short slogan has replaced rational debate. Slogans make no attempt to formulate a policy. Truth no longer matters. It is the age of post-truth. The social media offer a powerful voice to name-calling. "Sticks and stones may break your bones, but names will never hurt you." The old proverb is not true. Names are very hurtful. Name-calling is a vicious form of bullying. A text can travel the whole world in seconds.

PRAYERS

In the light of the sacred readings, we pray.

It was said of Jesus that nobody ever spoke like him. May we always look to his teaching to guide us.
Lord, hear us.

Jeremiah described himself as a trustful lamb being led to the slaughterhouse. We pray for the people of our own day who are being persecuted because of their religion.
Lord, hear us.

Jesus was an innocent victim denied a fair trial. We pray for people who have been the victims of false allegations.
Lord, hear us.

We pray for young people who have been bullied or mocked on the social media.
Lord, hear us.

   (Pray for any personal, local or topical need.)

O God, hear our prayers as we come to you in the name of Jesus Christ, your Son, our Lord. Amen.

MONDAY

DANIEL 13:41-62 | JOHN 8:1-11

1. The story of the woman condemned for adultery is paired with the story
    of Susanna. Susanna was freed when Daniel exposed the truth that it
    was her accusers who were the sinners. Similarly, Jesus challenged the
    woman's accusers to face the truth of their own sins. The Pharisees were
    exploiting the woman's case in order the catch out Jesus. Would he fail
    to carry out the letter of the Law or fail in mercy? It is reminiscent of the
    question about the lawfulness of paying tribute to Caesar. In that case,
    Jesus requested, "Show me a coin". It was a Roman coin. The answer was
    in their own pockets. If they accepted Roman money, then they accepted
    Roman taxation. In the case of the accused woman, Jesus again showed
    that the answer was in their own pockets… the pockets of their own past
    behaviour. "Let whoever is without sin cast the first stone."

2. "Woman, has no one condemned you?" Trembling, she answered, "No
    one, Sir". "Neither do I condemn you. Go and sin no more." Jesus is more
    eager to forgive than to condemn, to restore life rather than to destroy.
    A very important part of preparing for Easter is coming to meet the
    same Jesus in the Sacrament of Reconciliation. It is important to take an
    honest look at one's life. By putting words on our sins, we are admitting
    them and taking responsibility for them. This can be unpleasant. But
    confessing is a way of opening the door to let the badness out and let the
    goodness in. The goodness is God's merciful love. Go and sin no more.

PRAYERS

Encouraged by the story of God's mercy, we pray.

The power of celebrating God's mercy was conferred on the Church by the Risen Lord. May the Church be true to its calling as a hospital of recovery for all who have been wounded or contaminated by sin.
Lord, hear us.

Help us to overcome any fears or anxiety about confession. Help us to be humble and honest about ourselves since it is the truth that sets us free.
Lord, hear us.

Jesus was more interested in the woman's future than in her past. May the grace of the Sacrament help us to move on to a better life.
Lord, hear us.

Let us pray for people who have been falsely accused. May the truth come to light and their good name be restored.
Lord, hear us.

(Pray for any personal, local or topical need.)

God of mercy and forgiveness, help us to move forward from the sins of the past to the new life of grace. Prepare our hearts for Easter. Through Christ, our merciful Saviour. Amen.

TUESDAY

NUMBERS 21:4-9 | *JOHN 8: 21-30*

1. The First Reading and the Gospel are paired together as both mention being lifted up. Moses was instructed by God to fashion a bronze serpent and lift it up as a cure for people who had been bitten by a serpent. A serpent was regarded with fear because a snakebite could be fatal. But serpents were also held in awe because they regularly cast off their old skin and emerged with a new one. So, a serpent was a symbol of new life, which probably explains why a serpent coiled around a drinking vessel is the sign outside a pharmacy.

2. The hidden meaning of lifting up the serpent was revealed when Jesus was lifted up on the cross, and then in his Resurrection. The cross was an instrument for the execution of a criminal. The cross was regarded as a curse and whoever hung from a cross was regarded as cursed. But Jesus took the curse on himself and made the cross the tree of life. It was like the modern practice of immunisation. Health authorities try to anticipate the coming winter's flu strain. People are injected with a tiny amount which a healthy body can absorb and develop into a defence system against a stronger attack. Jesus the sinless one, when lifted up on the cross took sin on himself. The healthy body of the sinless Christ took the injection so as to immunise all the other members of his body. Saint Paul went so far as to say that God made the sinless one into sin, so that, in him, we might become the uprightness of God (2 Cor. 5:21). Jesus made this promise. "When I am lifted up from the Earth, I shall draw all people to myself." (John 12:32). Next week we will celebrate his death and resurrection.

PRAYERS

As we approach the celebration of the death and resurrection of the Lord, we pray.

On the cross Jesus revealed the total extent of his love for us. May we grow in our appreciation of his love.
Lord, hear us.

On the cross Jesus endured every kind of suffering to show his solidarity with us. May all who are suffering in any way recognise that Jesus is a companion who has shared their journey.
Lord, hear us.

The cross which was once a cursed thing was transformed by Jesus into a tree of blessings. We pray that anybody who feels under a curse may hold the crucifix and draw peace from the victory of Jesus.
Lord, hear us.

May the celebration of the passion and resurrection of Jesus be a source of great blessings in our parish.
Lord, hear us.

(Pray for any personal, local or topical need.)

O God, in your pity you loved the world so much that you sent down your Son to save us. Listen to our prayers as we are lifted up in the name of Jesus Christ, your Son, our Lord. Amen.

WEDNESDAY

1. "The truth will make you free." This is one of the wise sayings of Jesus. And where is this truth to be found? It is Jesus himself who is the way, the truth and the life. "If you make my Word your home, you will indeed be my disciples, you will learn the truth and the truth will make you free." The opposite of freedom is slavery. What Jesus meant by slavery was spiritual slavery. He said, "Whoever commits sin is a slave". Whoever has a habit of sin is not free. A person can be a slave to violent temper; to uncharitable gossip; to the practice of dishonesty. Any addiction is a slavery. A shameful addiction today is slavery to pornography. An alcoholic knows that one drink is too much, while twenty drinks will not be enough once he starts. Whoever is an addict to pornography loses the power to switch off. Like the alcoholic, what one must avoid is the first switching on.

2. Nowadays there is a great deal of confusion between freedom and permissiveness. Permissiveness wants to be free of any restrictions. The right to choose has become a slogan on posters and placards. But do we have the right to choose what is morally wrong? In the days of horse and carriage, a wealthy man bought a pair of magnificent, muscular horses. He tried to train them himself but no way could he control these frisky animals. So, he sent them off to a well-known trainer. A few weeks later, the horses were returned, now perfectly disciplined. What made the difference? The trainer explained: "You were training them to do what they wanted to do. I trained them to do what they ought to do". Freedom is not the permission to do whatever we want to do. True freedom is internal. It is the strength to do what we ought to do. God honoured us with the dignity of freedom so that we might have the ability to love, to choose what is right, and to have the strength to do it. "If you make my Word your home, you will indeed be my disciples, you will learn the truth and the truth will make you free."

PRAYERS

In the light of God's Word, let us pray.
May the voice of the Church guide us in the light of Christ's Word,
and direct our consciences so as to choose what is right in the eyes
of God.
Lord, hear us.

We pray for people who are being persecuted for their religious
beliefs and deprived of the freedom to practice their religion. May
this persecution cease.
Lord, hear us.

For people who are trapped in any form of addiction; may they find
freedom in admitting the truth of their problem with the help of
God, their Higher Power.
Lord, hear us.

For people who are slaves to sinful habits; may the grace of Easter
bring them liberation and new life.
Lord, hear us.

(Pray for any personal, local or topical need.)

God, our Creator, we thank you for the dignity of freedom and
the ability to love. Grant us the grace to make our home in the
wisdom of Jesus Christ, your Son, our Lord. Amen.

FIFTH WEEK OF LENT:

THURSDAY

GENESIS 17:3-9 | JOHN 8:51-59

1. Our First Reading and Gospel are linked together around Abraham. Four times we hear of the covenant God offered to Abraham. This covenant was a solemn promise that God would make the descendants of Abraham a great people under divine protection. The people, on their part, were to follow God's law as given in the Ten Commandments. The official signing of a covenant was not done in a solicitor's office but in some form of blood sacrifice. As years went by, the people drifted away from their side of the covenant. They were not living by the guidance of the Ten Commandments. It came to the point that some of the prophets told them that they had broken their covenant with God. However, they were promised that God would offer a new covenant. This covenant was brought by Jesus. This day week, Holy Thursday, we will recall the Last Supper. Jesus took the cup of wine and said, "This cup is the new covenant in my blood poured out for you".

2. Under the First Covenant, Abraham was promised that he would be the father of a multitude of nations, with land and prosperity. Jesus said, "Before Abraham ever was, I am". He is the Beginning and the End. All time belongs to him and all the ages. Jesus Christ, the Son of God, belongs to eternal, unending life. The covenant introduced by Jesus is not about life here on Earth but now God's promise is eternal life. We enter his covenant through the grace of Baptism, when we are given the power to become the children of God. If we develop this grace, we are part of the body of Christ and heirs of the Kingdom of Heaven. The highest point of the Christian year is at Easter when we renew the promises of our Baptism. We renounce the ways of Evil and renew our commitment to the light of Christ. "Dying you destroyed our death. Rising you restored our life. Lord Jesus, come in glory."

PRAYERS

As Holy Week draws nearer, we pray that we will be prepared in mind and heart.

At Easter we will renew the promise of Baptism to renounce Evil and to be faithful to Jesus Christ. Help us to live up to these promises.
Lord, hear us.

Jews, Muslims and Christians all trace their religion back to Abraham. May we recognise how we are united by faith in the one, true God. May there be an end to all religious hatred and war. May believers be united in confronting modern secularism.
Lord, hear us.

People threw stones at Jesus. We pray for people who are being persecuted for their faith today.
Lord, hear us.

(Pray for any personal, local or topical need.)

O God, may our celebration of Easter free us from our sins. Help us to remain faithful to a holy way of life and guide us to the inheritance you have promised, in the name of Jesus Christ, your Son, our Lord. Amen.

FRIDAY

JEREMIAH 20:10-13 | JOHN 10:31-42

1. They fetched stones to throw at Jesus. The stones can be taken as representing the different accusations made against Jesus. When we look at the design of a cross, we see four lines coming in from North, South, East and West, clashing at the centre. These lines represent the various plots to get rid of Jesus. Each plot needs the support of the others to achieve the death sentence. The prime movers are the religious leaders whose way of life is threatened by the ideals of Jesus. They need the support of the Roman power. Pilate can see that Jesus is innocent but there are hints that the Jews could ruin his reputation in Rome. He lacks the moral courage to face down these threats. His gesture of washing hands has become a symbol of the abdication of responsibility. Judas, one of the apostles, has become disillusioned since Jesus is not a military messiah. Slogans and accusations whip up the frenzy of the mob, the "rude and scoffing multitude". The alien forces clash at the centre where Jesus is the innocent victim. He is nailed to the cross by a variety of sins.

2. Easter Sunday will show the cross in a different light. The body of Jesus is not there. In the dawning light of the true New Age, the lines of the cross are coming out from the centre in an explosion of new life. The power of God has triumphed over Evil and Death. North, South, East and West, the healing power of God reaches towards the ends of the Earth. The Celtic monks drew a circle around the cross. A circle is a line with neither beginning nor end, a symbol of eternal life. The tree of death has become the tree of unending life.

PRAYERS

As we contemplate the cross of Jesus Christ, we pray.

May the cross of Jesus be a sign of great hope, representing the triumph of Goodness over Evil, of light over darkness.
Lord, hear us.

May the cross give us courage in knowing that Jesus is with us when we have some cross to carry.
Lord, hear us.

Jesus prayed for those who were putting him through terrible suffering. May we learn from him the lesson of not letting the wrongdoing of others poison our determination to love.
Lord, hear us.

We pray for the people who face the stones of persecution today for their Christian beliefs. May God grant them great courage and may the persecution cease.
Lord, hear us.

(Pray for any personal, local or topical need.)

O God of mercy, may our remembrance of the cross of Jesus lead us to the joys of Easter. We offer our prayer in the name of Jesus Christ, your Son, our Lord. Amen

SATURDAY

EZEKIEL 37:21-28 | JOHN 11:45-56

1. We read today that Jesus came to rescue people, to cleanse them, and to gather together in unity the scattered people of God. Let us think of scattered people. We are scattered when we have lost the way... when our brains have lost focus. We might say, "I'm all over the place. I don't know if I'm coming or going". The Greek word that we translate as devil is *diabolos*. This means the one who leads us astray... the one who divides... the one who scatters. Today's Gospel is set in the days when people from the country were coming to Jerusalem to purify themselves in preparation for the Passover. It reminds us to avail of the Sacrament of Purification we have in confession. Come to Jesus to be purified, to be cleansed, and to have your scattered life put back on track.

2. We know from the gospels that Jesus was very unhappy about what was going on in the Temple. Even at the age of twelve, he decided he would have to do something about it. He was particularly upset at the exploitation of the pilgrims who came to Jerusalem for the various festivals. The priestly classes were very wealthy. Archaeological excavations in recent years have yielded evidence of their luxurious houses. Jesus was a serious threat to their financial future. So, their leader, Caiaphas, put it bluntly: "You don't seem to have grasped the situation at all; you fail to see that it is better for one man to die for the people, than for the whole nation to be destroyed". What he was really saying is to get rid of this Jesus and our financial future is secure. But there is a delicious irony in what he said. Little did Caiaphas realise that Jesus was in fact dying for all people. At the very hour that the lambs of sacrifice were being killed in the Temple, Jesus was the Lamb of God dying on the cross for the salvation of all people.

PRAYERS

Having reflected on the Word of God, we pray.

May the Church's celebration of Holy Week be a time of grace and renewal.
Lord, hear us.

At the time of Jesus, the religious leaders were willing to kill him to protect their own interests. May our religious leaders today be people of honesty and integrity.
Lord, hear us.

The Devil is the father of lies who seeks to mislead us. Grant us the discernment and strength to resist his scattering.
Lord, hear us.

We pray that people will avail of the Sacrament of Reconciliation in preparation for Easter.
Lord, hear us.

   (Pray for any personal, local or topical need.)

God our Father, graciously hear the prayers we offer in the name of Jesus Christ, your Son, our Lord. Amen.

MONDAY

ISAIAH 42:1-7 | JOHN 12:1-11

1. The First Reading is taken from the second part of the Book of Isaiah. A change of leadership in Babylon brought the totally unexpected news that the Jews in exile were allowed to return to Jerusalem. Isaiah sees this liberation as the promise of a more wonderful liberation sometime in the future. He composed four uplifting poems about a future leader who will be a Servant of God bringing true justice to the nations. God's way of justice is not through vengeance or punishment. Rather, God's justice seeks the conversion of the sinner. "He does not break the crushed reed, nor quench the wavering flame." The identity of this Servant of God was not known until Jesus came. He came as a light to the nations. He opened the eyes of those who were spiritually blind. He offered people liberation from the slavery of sinful behaviour. He even raised the dead to life in anticipation of this own resurrection.

2. Lazarus had been brought back to life. His sisters, Martha and Mary, organised a celebratory meal in thanksgiving. Mary bought a very expensive ointment to honour Jesus. But dark clouds were looming. Judas complained that this extravagance was a waste of money which should be given to the poor. His concern was not for the poor but for the amount he could put into his own pocket. One wonders, was it Jesus who invited Judas to accompany him to the party? Was this a plea to Judas to change his mind? Jesus was the one who would not break the bruised reed. He tried to fan into flame any tiny spark of faith that remained in Judas. Sadly, Judas did not change. Jesus accepted Mary's extravagant gesture as an anticipation of his death. The raising of Lazarus caused many to believe in Jesus. But those who rejected him became even more determined to kill Lazarus in addition to Jesus. Violent murders rarely stop at one.

PRAYERS

This week we reflect on Jesus as the Servant of God who lay down his life for our sakes.

May the Church be true to its calling to serve the world with the light of Christ and with the message of hope for the sinner.
Lord, hear us.

May people who exercise political power do so as servants of justice, compassion and peace.
Lord, hear us.

May people who are trusted with public money resist the temptation of Judas to steal from the funds for his own use.
Lord, hear us.

May our cry for justice seek the rehabilitation of the sinner rather than vengeance and punishment.
Lord, hear us.

(Pray for any personal, local or topical need.)

Merciful Father, may the suffering and death of your Son, Jesus Christ, protect and strengthen us in our weakness. Through Christ, our Lord. Amen.

TUESDAY

ISAIAH 49:1-6 | JOHN 13:21-33. 36-38

1. Jesus was troubled in spirit. It shows the depth of his sorrow for Judas. The story of Judas is the classical path of temptation and fall. The first mention of Judas is when Jesus spoke about giving us his flesh to eat and his blood to drink, the doctrine of the Eucharist. Many people walked away from Jesus. Jesus let it be known that he knew that one of the apostles did not believe. It is likely that Judas was attracted to Jesus in the hope of a military messiah who would lead a revolution. Serious doubts began to grow in his mind. The Devil cannot enter into a person's free will unaided, so the evil spirit probes to find some personal weakness which will offer an opening. He found traits of dishonesty and greed in Judas. He was in charge of the common fund of the apostles and used to help himself from the contributions. Now the Devil put it into his mind that there was more money to be obtained by handing Jesus over to his enemies, thirty pieces of silver. But Judas had not yet made the final decision until the moment that Jesus handed him the piece of bread. Bread is known as the staff of life. Jesus was offering him life. Externally he accepted it but internally, his will made the final decision. He opened the door to Satan. Satan entered. Judas left the light and life offered by Jesus. Night had fallen.

2. Jesus was sorry to see Judas depart. But he also saw that this marked the beginning of his return to glory. "Now the Son of Man has been glorified." The story of Jesus did not end on Calvary. It has no ending because the story of Jesus is one of eternal glory. And he invites us to share it with him.

PRAYERS

As we have reflected on the temptation and fall of Judas, we are moved to pray.

For people who are being tempted to do something seriously wrong, may they see through the misleading of temptation and come to accept the help of God.
Lord, hear us.

For people who are plagued by doubts, may they humbly accept the wisdom of the Holy Spirit in Sacred Scripture and the teaching of the Church.
Lord, hear us.

We pray for people who have walked away from God. May they find that God has not walked away from them and that even one short prayer will bring them back.
Lord, hear us.

In our own small way, may we be agents of God's mercy to people who have strayed away like lost sheep.
Lord, hear us.

(Pray for any personal, local or topical need.)

Merciful Father, lead us not into temptation. Deliver us from the Evil One. Through Christ, our Lord. Amen

WEDNESDAY

ISAIAH 50: 4-9 | *MATT 26:14-25*

1. This day has traditionally been called Spy Wednesday. We have heard Saint Matthew's account of Judas. Matthew wrote especially to strengthen the faith of Jewish Christians. He takes every opportunity to show how Jesus fulfilled the Old Testament words or events. The money promised to Judas was thirty pieces of silver, the same sum offered in the Old Testament for the prophet Zechariah. It was the sort of price one would pay to purchase an injured slave, a paltry price. Judas was not just a spy. He did not merely betray Jesus, he handed him over. He could have betrayed him by handing over information about where to find Jesus. More than that, he personally led the soldiers and, worse again, it was with a kiss that he identified Jesus.

2. The passion of Jesus shows us how much he loved us by joining in solidarity with all who suffer. "Having loved those who were his in the world, he loved them to the utmost." He is with people who suffer physical pain and injuries. He stands with those who are victims of false allegations and unjust trials. He was disappointed at the absence of the apostles. He suffered deep family pain in seeing his mother at the foot of the cross, experiencing the sword of sorrow that Simeon had predicted many years previously. The deepest suffering was the darkness of feeling forsaken by the Father. "My God, my God, why have you forsaken me." That cold kiss of Judas shows Jesus experiencing the pain of people who have been betrayed in love. No matter what dark valley you travel, you are never alone. Somebody has been in there waiting to accompany you. That somebody is Jesus.

PRAYERS

After reflecting on the story of Judas betraying Jesus, we are moved to pray.

Scripture tells us that in Jesus, we have a compassionate High Priest who can understand suffering because he experienced it. May all who suffer find new strength when they recognise that Jesus is close to them.
Lord, hear us.

As Judas betrayed Jesus with a kiss, we pray for people who have been betrayed in love.
Lord, hear us.

Lord, grant us the protection of Mary, your Mother, who stood faithfully beside you on the cross.
Lord, hear us.

In our own small way, may we be a source of support and comfort to people who are suffering in any way.
Lord, hear us.

   (Pray for any personal, local or topical need.)

O God of mercy, may our celebration of your Son's Passion and Resurrection draw us closer to you. Through Christ, our Lord. Amen

THURSDAY

EXODUS 12: 1-8. 11-14 | 1 COR. 11:23-26 | JOHN 13:1-15

1. "It was before the festival of the Passover, and Jesus knew that the hour had come for him to pass from this world to the Father." The Jewish Passover celebrated their journey from slavery in Egypt to freedom in the Promised Land. Jesus gave new meaning to it in his passing from this world to the Father, from earthly life to heavenly life. The only way out of earthly life is through the door of death. The journey of Jesus was through his death into his resurrection. At the Last Supper, he set up a ritual for us to celebrate his Passover of death and resurrection. Not only to celebrate the events but to participate in them. "Do this as a memorial of me." We recognise this as the Mass.

2. There must be a Passover journey in our lives too. On several occasions in the Gospel, Jesus spoke of the necessity of dying to self-centredness, to take up the cross and follow him. Jesus performed the humble service of a slave when he washed the feet of his disciples. "I have given you an example so that you may copy what I have done to you". At the end of Mass, we are sent out on a mission to love and serve the Lord in humble service of other people. We receive the light of God's wisdom in the Liturgy of the Word. We receive the energy of Christian life in the Sacred Eucharist. At the end of Mass, we are honoured with the mission to carry Christ's light and energy to others.

PRAYERS

As we celebrate the institution of the Blessed Eucharist, we pray.

Holy Thursday is a day when priests renew their sacred promises. May all priests be renewed by the graces of the Eucharist. May they be faithful to their vocation.
Lord, hear us.

The harvest is great and the labourers are getting older. We ask you, Lord, to call many to dedicate their lives in priestly service.
Lord, hear us.

May we grow in appreciation of the wonder of the Lord's presence in the Bread of Life, come down from Heaven.
Lord, hear us.

As we reflect on Jesus performing the humble service of washing feet, may we be inspired to use our time and talents in helping others.
Lord, hear us.

We pray for family members and others who no longer believe in the Lord's presence in the Eucharist. Open their eyes to your presence, Lord, as once you opened the eyes of the disciples on the road to Emmaus.
Lord, hear us.

God, our Father, deepen our faith and strengthen our resolve to follow the humble service of Jesus Christ, your Son, our Lord.

Amen.

EASTER

MONDAY

ACTS 2:14. 22-23 | MATT 28: 8-15

1. "God raised this man Jesus to life, and all of us are witnesses to that." From the very beginning, efforts were made to deny the resurrection of Jesus and to deceive the people. However, the power of the Holy Spirit transformed the apostles and other disciples into living witnesses to the ongoing presence of the Risen Lord. Since the Second Vatican Council, there has been immense development in relations between Jewish and Christian scholars. One Jewish scholar, Pinchas Lapide, described the apostles as solid hillbillies from Galilee who were saddened by the death of Jesus but were changed within a short period of time into a jubilant community of believers. He concluded that only a resurrection could have accomplished that. The greatest proof of the resurrection is the existence of Christianity. It was said of the early Church, see how these Christians love one another. In coming weeks, each day at Mass we will hear how these early Christians lived. They were united in prayer, courage, caring and sharing. They were witnesses to the resurrection.

2. In proclaiming the mystery of faith, we do not say in the past tense that Christ rose. No, our proclamation is in the present tense, Christ is risen. His living presence is revealed in many ways but especially in the witness of Christian living. It is beautifully expressed in a reflection by Saint Teresa of Avila. "Christ has no body now but yours. No hands, no feet on Earth but yours. Yours are the eyes through which he looks with compassion on this world. Yours are the feet with which he walks to do good. Yours are the hands through which he blesses all the world. Yours are the hands, yours are the feet, yours are the eyes, you are his body. Christ has no body now but yours."

"God raised this man Jesus to life, and all of us are witnesses to that."

PRAYERS

As we gather to celebrate the Risen Lord among us, we pray.

Peter and the apostles were transformed by the Holy Spirit. May Pope *(Name)* and all our bishops be granted great wisdom and courage in leading the Church today.
Lord, hear us.

The early Christians, by their way of living, made a huge impression on people. By the grace of the Holy Spirit, may the Christian Church be a light to the world.
Lord, hear us.

Those who rejected Jesus misled the people by spreading lies about his resurrection. May those who mislead people today see the error of their ways and be converted to the truth.
Lord, hear us.

We thank you, Lord, for the improved relationship between Jews and Christians: may this mutual enrichment continue to grow.
Lord, hear us.

(Add prayers for personal, local or topical intentions)

Heavenly Father, graciously hear the prayers we offer in the name of our Risen Lord, Jesus Christ. Amen.

TUESDAY

ACTS: 2:36-41 | JOHN 20:11-18

1. The gospels give us several stories of encounters between the Risen Lord and various disciples. These stories reveal different ways of how we can encounter the Lord. The key to each story is the manner in which the Lord is recognised. At the start of today's story, Mary of Magdala was lost. She is pictured as standing outside the empty tomb, weeping. She was so depressed that even the sight of two angels did not excite her. Then Jesus appeared to her. He was different now. She did not recognise him by sight, nor by the sound of his voice. The key moment is when Jesus made himself known. He called her by name, "Mary". She knew him then. For many people, the beginning of faith is in sensing a personal call from God. The Risen Lord led her forward in faith. Her new relationship with him would not involve sight, hearing or touch. Her personal relationship would be in faith.

2. Mary of Magdala was called by name. The heartbeat of believing is a personal relationship with God. The Old Testament writer, Isaiah, had some beautiful expressions. "I have called you by your name, you are mine." "I have carved you on the palm of my hand." Pope Francis appealed to all Christians to work on this personal relationship. "I invite all Christians to a renewed personal encounter with Jesus Christ, or at least an openness to letting him encounter them. I ask all of you to do this unfailingly every day." Nothing should distract us from the joy of this Easter week. Jesus Christ is risen. Jesus invites you to share a personal relationship with him. In silent reflection try to hear him call you by your name. He wants you to know that he is your Saviour, your Lord and your friend.

PRAYERS

Gathered together in the presence of the Risen Lord, we pray.

Mary of Magdala recognised the Risen Lord when she was called by name. May we too receive the great grace of experiencing the Lord's invitation to a personal relationship.
Lord, hear us.

We pray for all who, like Mary, are deeply saddened by the death of a loved one: may their faith in the Risen Lord bring them great consolation.
Lord, hear us.

Mary was sent to the apostles to tell them that the Lord was risen. She became the apostle of the apostles. May the Church deeply respect the voice of women apostles.
Lord, hear us.

Today's psalm says, "The Lord fills the Earth with his love". Open our eyes to the presence of God all around us in the beauty of creation and in the goodness of people.
Lord, hear us.

(Add prayers for personal, local or topical intentions)

God, Creator and lover of all people, we humbly ask you to grant us the grace of a deep, personal relationship with your Son, Jesus Christ, the Risen Lord. Amen.

WEDNESDAY

ACTS 3:1-10 | LUKE 24: 13-35

1. The Risen Lord is with us as he was with the two disciples on the road to Emmaus. They had turned their backs on Jerusalem, the city of pilgrimage. Now they were heading towards Emmaus, a village famous for its mineral springs. They had lost hope when they saw Jesus crucified two days previously. The Risen Jesus at their side began to explain what the Scriptures had said about the Suffering Servant of God. Something started stirring in their hearts. The Scripture did not change what had happened on Friday, but what did change was their understanding of it. The Scripture does not change life but it gives us a new way of understanding what is happening. Next came the meal where Jesus repeated his actions at the Last Supper. He took the bread, said the blessing, broke it and gave it to them. At that moment their eyes were opened and they recognised him. Where can we meet the Risen Lord Jesus? Here at Mass we listen to his Word and then we repeat the actions of Jesus at the Supper: he took, he blessed, he broke and he gave. "Do this in memory of me." The two disciples were transformed. They recovered their direction, headed back towards Jerusalem and witnessed to the resurrection. At the end of Mass we are sent out to love and serve the Lord.

2. If you think you are a million miles away from God, guess who moved. It is consoling to see that while the two former disciples were leaving Jerusalem in favour of the comforting springs of Emmaus, Jesus was still with them. We might have deserted God but God never deserts us. But something prevented them from recognising him. What prevents us from recognising God's presence with us? Maybe it is some tragedy or disappointment, as happened to the two disciples who lost hope on Calvary. Are we too preoccupied with other interests? Too distracted by television, sport, scandals or personal anxiety? On the other side, what supports our awareness of God? Do we seek the light of God's wisdom in the Scriptures? Does the Eucharist open our eyes to recognise God's presence? Is our faith strengthened by personal prayer? Belonging to a prayer group? The good example of others? Involvement in a voluntary organisation? The beauty of Nature? There are many ways of becoming more aware of the presence of the Risen Lord.

PRAYERS

The Risen Lord was walking beside the two disciples but something prevented them from recognising him. Lord, grant us the grace of a living faith, and awareness of your presence.
Lord, hear us.

The words of Scripture enabled the two disciples to understand the tragedy of Good Friday in a new light. May all who have lost hope receive new light and direction from the Word of the Lord.
Lord, hear us.

The eyes of the disciples were opened at the breaking of bread. We pray for people who have drifted away from the Eucharist. May their eyes be opened to the awesome privilege of receiving Jesus as the Bread of Life.
Lord, hear us.

In the power of the name of Jesus, Peter brought healing to a crippled man. May all people recognise the sacredness and power of the name of the Saviour.
Lord, hear us.

(Add prayers for personal, local or topical intentions)

God our Father, graciously hear the prayers of all who gather here in the name of Jesus Christ, your Son, our Lord. Amen.

OCTAVE OF EASTER:

THURSDAY

ACTS 3:11-26 | LUKE 24: 35-48

1. This Easter week we hear the encounters of the Risen Lord with various disciples. In the light of these encounters, we recognise the presence of the Lord in various ways in our lives. In today's Gospel, the Risen Jesus identified himself by drawing attention to his wounded hands and feet. It is a reminder to us that Jesus entered into the wounds, pains and injustices of life. He explained to them that it had been written that the Servant of God would suffer on behalf of the people. Isaiah wrote about the Suffering Servant of God: "Ours were the sufferings he bore, ours the sorrows he carried. He was pierced through for our faults, crushed for our sins. On him lies a punishment that brings us peace and through his wounds, we are healed." So, as the Risen Jesus showed them his wounded hands and feet, he told them that in his name, repentance for the forgiveness of sins would be preached to all nations.

2. The Acts of the Apostles relates how the apostles urged people to turn away from sin and to receive forgiveness in the name of Jesus. Peter had healed a crippled man, not by his own power, but in the power of the name of Jesus. Jesus entered into the wounds of sin and injustice. He took on himself the burden of punishment. But in rising from the dead, he showed his victory over sin. We encounter him in the Sacrament of Reconciliation. It is worth pondering on the words of absolution. "God, the Father of Mercy, has reconciled the world with himself through the death and resurrection of his Son. He has sent the Holy Spirit for the forgiveness of sin. Through the ministry of the Church may he grant you pardon and peace. I absolve you in the name of the Father, the Son and the Holy Spirit."

PRAYERS

The Risen Lord told the apostles to witness to his power for the forgiveness of sins. May the Church continue the mission of the apostles in preaching the necessity of repentance and the joy of forgiveness.
Lord, hear us.

May all of us appreciate the joy of meeting with the merciful Saviour in the Sacrament of Reconciliation.
Lord, hear us.

May the memory of the sufferings of Jesus be a source of strength and comfort for all who are suffering in any way.
Lord, hear us.

The sacred name of Jesus calls down his presence and power in our lives. May we have a deep reverence for this divine name.
Lord, hear us.

(Add prayers for personal, local or topical intentions)

O God our Father, we thank you for sending your Beloved Son who took our sins upon himself. In his name we pray, through Jesus Christ, our Lord. Amen.

FRIDAY

ACTS 4: 1-12 | JOHN 21: 1-4

1. The miraculous catch of fish throws light on the presence of the Risen Lord in the mission of the Church. The key to each encounter story is the way in which Jesus makes himself known. In this story, the moment of recognition is when they see the huge haul of fish. The beloved disciple said "It's the Lord". It touched their memory of a similar catch at the beginning of the public ministry of Jesus. On that morning, Jesus told them, "From now on, it is people whom you will catch". As long as they laboured through the night, they caught nothing. But once they took direction from the Word of the Lord, their catch was enormous. Today's First Reading tells of the enormous number, five thousand, joining the small community of believers. The mission of the Church is a combination of direction from the Word of God, matched with human effort.

2. The nets were not torn, just as the cloak of Jesus, woven in one piece, was not torn on Calvary. It is the Greek word for torn that gives us the word *schism*, meaning the tearing of the unity of the Church. The prominence of Peter indicates his special role in the Church. In the Acts of the Apostles, he is filled by the Holy Spirit as he preaches fearlessly and with divine wisdom. The number of fish, one hundred and fifty-three, has been interpreted in many ways. The most common interpretation is that it represents the number of species of fish known at that time. Thus it expresses a mission to all nations. Where do we encounter the Risen Lord? Like Mary Magdalene, in a personal call by name. With the Emmaus disciples, in the Eucharistic breaking of bread. In the healing power of the wounds of Jesus. And, in today's Gospel, we meet the Lord in the community of believers known as the Church.

PRAYERS

Inspired by the miracle of the many fish, we pray.

As the Holy Spirit gave extraordinary wisdom and courage to Saint Peter, we pray for the same gifts for Pope *(Name)*, the successor of Peter.
Lord, hear us.

When it is dark all around us and our labours bring in empty nets, may we hear your Word giving us new direction.
Lord, hear us.

The untorn nets were a symbol of the unity of the Church. May the various Christian families come together, enriching one another from their own traditions.
Lord, hear us.

The apostles left all to commit themselves to the mission of Jesus. May the call of Jesus Christ touch the lives of many to give their lives in the service of the Church.
Lord, hear us.

   (Add prayers for personal, local or topical intentions)

O God, graciously hear our prayers in the name of Jesus Christ, your Son, our Lord. Amen.

SATURDAY

ACTS 4: 13-21 | MARK 16: 9-15

1. During the week, we have reflected on encounters of the Risen Lord with various disciples. Today we have Mark's very brief summary of the appearance to Mary Magdalene and to the disciples on the road to Emmaus. One detail that Mark adds is that there were seven devils driven out of Mary Magdalene. She must have been a notorious sinner. It just shows us that even the worst sinner could yet become a saint. As for the apostles, the Risen Lord reproached them for their incredulity and obstinacy. Yet in the next breath, he told them to go out to the whole world and proclaim the Good News to all creation. How on Earth were they going to do it? The answer will come in tomorrow's Gospel. "As the Father sent me, so am I sending you. He breathed on them and said, 'Receive the Holy Spirit'." The apostles were men transformed. The mission of Jesus is not finished. It is carried on by the Church, the community of believers.

2. In the Acts of the Apostles, we read that the Jewish religious leaders were astonished at the wisdom and assurance of these men whom they regarded as uneducated laymen. Even the threat of imprisonment did not deter them. Regarding proof of the Resurrection, the fact that the tomb was empty proves nothing, as the body might have been removed and hidden elsewhere. The greatest proof of the Resurrection was the transformation of the apostles in the power of the Holy Spirit. It remains the same today. The greatest proof of the truth of Christianity is the witness of life shown by Christians. The transforming power of the Holy Spirit is to be seen in the fruits of the Holy Spirit. Love, joy and peace are proofs of a relationship with God. Patience, kindness and goodness show Christian relationships with people. Trustfulness, gentleness and self-control manifest an inner serenity of soul.

PRAYERS

"Go out to the whole world: proclaim the Good News to all creation."

We pray that the Church today, under the guidance of Pope *(Name)*, may continue to bring the message of Jesus Christ to all people.
Lord, hear us.

Jesus had cast out seven devils from Mary Magdalene. Even the worst of sinners is not beyond the grace of conversion. We pray for the conversion of sinners.
Lord, hear us.

May those who are being arrested for their Christian beliefs receive the power of the Holy Spirit which sustained the apostles when they were arrested.
Lord, hear us.

May the transforming power of the Holy Spirit be seen in the way that we live; may we be charitable and helpful; may our faces be bright with joy and peace.
Lord, hear us.

(Add prayers for personal, local or topical intentions)

May God our Father graciously hear the prayers we offer in the name of Jesus Christ, our Risen Lord. Amen.

MONDAY

ACTS 4:23-31 | JOHN 3:1-8

1. "Unless a person is born from above, he cannot see the Kingdom of God". What is this Kingdom of God? The Kingdom is the ideal that Jesus set up, a world where people would live according to God's plan, a world of peace, justice, truth, charity, compassion and sharing with others. A world where God reigns, not Evil. We will never see that ideal world unless we start off afresh with the ideals of the Sermon on the Mount where Jesus describes how to live as children of God. This conversion of life is like a new birth. It cannot happen without the grace of the Holy Spirit. "What is born of the flesh is flesh: what is born of the Spirit is spirit." In John's writings, we often see that contrast between the flesh and the Spirit. The flesh stands for knowledge without the aid of grace: the spirit is the source of seeing with the eyes of faith. This applies especially to believing in the miracle of the Eucharistic presence. The flesh sees only bread: the spirit, believing in the words of Jesus, sees with the eyes of faith that "the bread that I shall give is my flesh for the life of the world".

2. Being born again means experiencing the presence of God in a new way. For some this experience comes in a sudden radical conversion. For people who have always lived good lives, cradle Christians, a reawakening can come through an inspiration or a sudden jolt that shakes one out of complacency. As a man said at the end of a Cursillo weekend, "I am very tired now but I am awake for the first time". Saint Francis of Assisi saw Christ in a new way the day he embraced a leper. He wrote in his Last Testament: "What before seemed bitter was changed into sweetness of soul and body." Saint Teresa of Calcutta experienced a new calling the day she picked up a dying woman on the street. All of us need to be shaken from our slumbering complacency from time to time. We need to be born again... and again... and again so that we might be servants of the reign of God on Earth.

PRAYERS

As we celebrate the presence of the Risen Lord among us, we pray.

The early Christians, filled with the Holy Spirit, proclaimed the Christian message boldly. May the voice of the Church continue to proclaim Christian faith and Christian ideals to the world.
Lord, hear us.

May we see the Kingdom of God in a world where there will be no wars and no wrongdoing in a kingdom of justice, peace and joy in the Holy Spirit.
Lord, hear us.

May all of us be born again in a spiritual reawakening from time to time.
Lord, hear us.

May our world be blessed with prophetic people whose example inspires others to work for God's Kingdom.
Lord, hear us.

(Add prayers for personal, local or topical intentions)

God, our Father, look upon your people with kindness. May the Holy Spirit reawaken us to the fullness of our Christian calling, through Christ, our Lord. Amen.

TUESDAY

ACTS 4:32-37 | JOHN 3:7-15

1. "The wind blows wherever it pleases. You hear its sound but you cannot tell where it comes from or where it is blowing. That's how it is with all who are born of the Spirit." We cannot see the wind, but we can see its effects – in the slanting of the smoke, the racing of the clouds, or the scattering of the leaves. It's the same with the Holy Spirit. We do not see the Holy Spirit but we see the fruits of the Holy Spirit in the lives of people. The early Christians were fully committed to the ideals of the Sermon on the Mount, which is the charter of the Kingdom of God on Earth. They were united in heart and soul, praying together, faithful to the teaching of the apostles and sharing their material possessions with one another. Their way of life was a witness to the Holy Spirit.

2. A lady who had cataracts removed from both eyes described the change in her life. "I had forgotten what colour was like." We can drift along in life or drift along in prayer, but we are only half-awake. In T.S. Eliot's play on Thomas Becket, the women of Canterbury were living, but only partly living. Every now and then we need to get the colour restored, to have our faith refreshed. The evidence of being born again is not a matter of feeling, but in a way of living. The wind is seen in its effects. The evidence of being born of the Holy Spirit is a life bearing the fruits of the Spirit. The early Christians were a great model.

PRAYERS

The early Church was a model of Christian caring and sharing. May the Church in our times by example and by word inspire the world to a fair sharing of the wealth of the world's resources.
Lord, hear us.

May we be alive to the breath of the Holy Spirit and produce the fruits of love, joy and peace.
Lord, hear us.

May our relationships with people be marked by patience, kindness and goodness.
Lord, hear us.

May we have great inner strength sustaining us in trustfulness, gentleness and self-control.
Lord, hear us.

(Add prayers for personal, local or topical intentions)

All-powerful God, help us to witness to the power of the Holy Spirit in the way that we live. Through Christ, our Lord. Amen

WEDNESDAY

Acts 5:17-26 | John 3:16-21

1. Today's Gospel is one of the most uplifting readings we will ever hear. "God loves the world so much that he gave his only Son, so that everyone who believes in him may not be lost but may have eternal life." Jesus was not sent to condemn people but to save us. God did not wait for us to be perfect before he loved us. God's love is not something that has to be deserved or merited. God is love and his love is never less than one hundred percent. Even the worst sinner is still loved by God. Store up today's Gospel in your minds. God loves us. God's love for us is shown especially in the life and example of Jesus Christ. God desires the all people would be saved and share in the joy of eternal life. The fullness of eternal life is in the future, but we can have a foretaste of eternal life if we commit ourselves fully to union with God in all we think and do.

2. If God desires that everybody should be saved, how can there be a hell? God does not want anybody to be condemned, but we can condemn ourselves if we reject the light of Christ. "On these grounds is sentence pronounced: that though the light came into the world, people have shown that they prefer darkness to the light because their deeds were evil". Hell is self-inflicted by our own choices of sinful behaviour. The punishment of sin is inbuilt, leading to the sadness of exile from God, disruption of harmony in relationships and in alienation from our true selves. Everyone who does wrong hates the light and avoids it for fear his actions should be exposed. The Good Shepherd constantly seeks the one who is lost. And God so loves the sinner that there is rejoicing in Heaven when the sinner returns.

PRAYERS

Encouraged by the beautiful words of Jesus, we pray.

God loves the world and all his creatures. May we appreciate this love and may we do all we can to make the world a more loving place for all.
Lord, hear us.

We pray for all who are walking in darkness at the moment: may they experience God's love leading them out of darkness into the light.
Lord, hear us.

For the conversion of those who have been drawn into the ways of sin: may they find the grace of repentance and return to the light and life of Christ.
Lord, hear us.

Lord, you sent an angel to release the apostles from jail. May your grace assist all who are struggling to be free from any form of addiction.
Lord, hear us.

(Add prayers for personal, local or topical intentions)

God of love and mercy, graciously hear the prayers we offer in the name of Jesus Christ, your Son, our Lord. Amen.

THURSDAY

ACTS 5:27-33 | JOHN 3:31-36

1. "Anyone who believes in the Son has eternal life, but anyone who refuses to believe in the Son will never see life." The fullness of eternal life will be experienced only in the future, after death. But even in this life there can be a foretaste of what is to come. That is why today's Gospel speaks in the present tense... "anyone who believes in the Son has eternal life". Believing is more than accepting various doctrines. Believing involves belonging, belonging to Jesus Christ in a personal relationship. Our doctrines are listed in what we call a *creed*. This word, creed, comes from the Latin word for *the heart*. To be a believer means to belong to Jesus in mind, heart and behaviour. It is a foretaste of eternal life.

2. Let us reflect on some of the privileges of believing. Pope Francis, in *The Joy of the Gospel*, wrote that those who accept the offer of salvation are set free from sin, sorrow, inner emptiness and loneliness. Jesus in his immense compassion takes away the sins of the world. What an extraordinary privilege to celebrate divine forgiveness! Friendship with Jesus frees us from inner emptiness and loneliness. He is a constant friend. We can talk to him any time. He gives new meaning to life. He raises us up to the privilege of being children of God and heirs of the Kingdom of Heaven. He gives us the privilege of calling God "Our Father." We are never alone when we have Jesus as our friend. "Anyone who believes in the Son has eternal life". An intimate, daily, personal relationship with Jesus is a foretaste to the fullness of eternal life.

PRAYERS

Reflecting on the privileges of believing, we pray.

The risen Lord sent the apostles to proclaim the Good News to all nations. May the Holy Spirit inspire the Church in our time in proclaiming the message of Jesus to the world.
Lord, hear us.

May the Holy Spirit help us to appreciate the fullness of life that grows through a personal relationship with Jesus.
Lord, hear us.

For those who refuse to believe; may the light of the Holy Spirit shine through their darkness.
Lord, hear us.

In today's First Reading, Peter said that obedience to God comes before obedience to men. May our politicians and lawmakers take heed of these words.
Lord, hear us.

(Add prayers for personal, local or topical intentions)

God our Father, you sent your Beloved Son to be for us the way, the truth and the life. Hear the prayers we offer in his name, Jesus Christ, the Lord. Amen.

SECOND WEEK OF EASTER:

FRIDAY

ACTS 5:34-42 | JOHN 6:1-15

1. Today we commence eight days with Chapter 6 of John's Gospel, which is all about different hungers and different forms of bread. Bread is such a common food that it is called "the staff of life". In the Our Father, when we ask for all we need today, the word *bread* is sufficient to cover everything. In this chapter, the first bread is to feed bodily hunger. Holy talk is not much use to people who have no food. Jesus responded to that need of the people who had nothing to eat. The second hunger is the need for direction and meaning in life. Jesus answered that hunger through the wisdom of his teaching. As the Chapter develops, the third hunger is for life beyond the grave. Jesus spoke in the future tense: "The bread that I shall give you is my flesh for the life of the world. Whoever eats my flesh and drinks my blood has eternal life and I shall raise him up on the last day." But it all began with ordinary bread for the body.

2. The one who had the five loaves and two fish was a small boy. The loaves were of barley, a very rough kind of bread. It didn't look too promising. But when it is given in generous love, God will do the multiplying. We might feel that we are nobodies. We have no great talents. We have nothing to give. There are charitable organisations who are always looking for helping hands. If we give the little we have, we can trust God to do the multiplying. One of the mottoes of Saint Teresa of Calcutta was: do the little thing with a lot of love.

PRAYERS

We turn to God who fed the multitude in the miracle of the loaves and fish.

It is a huge scandal that despite all our scientific advances and modern technology, there are millions of people without enough food. May the wealthy nations apply the necessary resources to feed the hungry.
Lord, hear us.

May God bless and multiply the great work being done by charitable organisations.
Lord, hear us.

Lord, help us to be generous in offering the little talents we have to help other people. May we do the little act with a lot of love.
Lord, hear us.

The apostles were glad to have the honour of suffering humiliation for the sake of Jesus. May those who are burdened with any cross carry it in union with Jesus.
Lord, hear us.

(Add prayers for personal, local or topical intentions)

O God, we thank you for all you have given us. Hear our prayers in the name of Jesus Christ, our Lord. Amen.

SATURDAY

ACTS 6:1-7 | JOHN 6:16-21

1. In John's Gospel, the important events of Jesus' ministry are set in the context of Jewish feasts. Jesus brought new meaning to those feasts. Chapter Six, all about the Bread of Life, is set in the time of the Passover. This great feast recalled how the destroying angel passed over the tents and houses marked with the blood of a lamb. The chosen people passed safely through the Red Sea. They passed from slavery into freedom. Passing through the sea is recalled as Jesus came walking over the stormy sea and the disciples' boat quickly reached shore safely. All this was a sign of the new Passover when Jesus passed from this world to the Father.

2. Passing through water was part of the original celebration of Baptism. The candidate descended a few steps into a large bath of water. Water was poured over the head or else the person was briefly immersed in the water. Then the newly baptised came out of the water and was clad in a white garment which was worn for a week. Entering the bath signified entering the tomb with Jesus. Emerging in the white garment was a symbol of sharing in the resurrection. Saint Paul explained this better than anybody. "By our Baptism into his death we were buried with him, so that as Christ was raised from the dead by the Father's glorious power, we too should begin living a new life." At Easter we renewed our baptismal promises. We renounced sin and committed our lives to following Christ. The Christian Passover is a lifelong journey of turning away from sin and walking in the light of Christ.

PRAYERS

After reflecting on the meaning of Baptism, we pray.

The water of Baptism expressed our entry into the death and resurrection of Jesus. May we constantly die to sin and walk in the light of Christ.
Lord, hear us.

Lord, when all is dark and we are tossed about in the storms of life, grant us the faith to know that you are near and you will direct us to safety and peace.
Lord, hear us.

As the Christian community grew, the apostles realised that they would need many helping hands. May our parish community make full use of the local talents to create a neighbourhood of caring Christians.
Lord, hear us.

Lord, bless and reward all people who generously give time to local organisations.
Lord, hear us.

(Add prayers for personal, local or topical intentions)

O God, graciously hear the prayers we offer in the name of Jesus Christ, your Son, our Lord. Amen.

MONDAY

ACTS 6: 8-15 | JOHN 6:22-29

1. News of the multiplication of bread and fish spread rapidly. Crowds gathered, maybe to get free bread or see some other stupendous miracle. In John's Gospel, miracles are usually called signs. A sign is a pointer beyond itself, directing us where to go. Jesus asked them to go beyond the idea of bread for the body. "Work for the food that endures to eternal life, the kind of food the Son of Man is offering you." They asked him, "What must we do if we are to do the works that the Father wants?" "You must believe in the one he has sent." In John's Gospel belief is never a noun, it is always a verb. Belief is more than the mental acceptance of various doctrines. To believe is to belong... to belong to Jesus in mind, in heart and in behaviour. A person who accepts all the doctrines but who does not behave in a Christian way is not a true believer. The people had accepted bread from Jesus. Now he asked them to go beyond bread and to accept the giver of the bread. Faith is the personal acceptance of a relationship with Jesus.

2. At the close of the Jubilee Year 2000, Pope John Paul II wrote a document about the beginning of the new millennium. There have been many changes in society, new problems have arisen and new questions are being asked. People wonder if we need a new formula. Pope John Paul II replied that we are not saved by a formula but by a Person and the assurance that he gives us, "I am with you". Accept Jesus, the giver of bread. There are many types of hunger besides the empty stomach. Hunger for meaning, for hope, for love, for appreciation, for being wanted, for serenity and stability. Work for the food which endures to eternal life. Believe in Jesus, trust in him and walk the road of life with him.

PRAYERS

Encouraged by the words of the Gospel, we pray.

As we reflect on bread, we pray for the people who are starving.
May the wealthy nations and millionaires contribute generously
to the alleviation of world hunger.
Lord, hear us.

For people who are spiritually or emotionally hungry: may they
find their answers in Jesus Christ.
Lord, hear us.

May we never become so preoccupied with earthly matters that
we forget about the food that endures to eternal life.
Lord, hear us.

Like Stephen in the First Reading, may people who present
Christian ideals on radio or television be filled with courage and
wisdom by the Holy Spirit.
Lord, hear us.

(Add prayers for personal, local or topical intentions)

God our Father, guide us at all times in the way of Jesus Christ, our
Lord. Amen.

TUESDAY

ACTS 7:51 – 8:1 | JOHN 6:30-35

1. The people asked Jesus, "What sign will you give us to show that we should believe in you?" The multiplication of loaves and fish was not enough for them. They wanted another sign. People who ask for signs, even when one is given, usually ask for another one to be sure. There comes a stage when one must go beyond questions and make a commitment. The questioning person wants to see in order to believe. The believer replies, "I see because I believe." Jesus promised, "He who comes to me will never be hungry; he who believes in me will never thirst."

2. The people reminded Jesus of the manna from Heaven. There were some outstanding features in the manna. First of all, it was a gift from God. God rained down bread from Heaven for them to eat. When they saw it for the first time, they were amazed. The word *manna* means "what is that?" Amazement. There was an element of testing and trust attached to this amazing food. They were to gather only enough for one day... to trust that God who fed them today would do so tomorrow. There is a lovely reflection on the manna in the Book of Wisdom: "You gave them the food of angels... containing every delight... satisfying every thirst... conforming to the taste of whoever ate it... transformed into what each eater wished." The manna was a sign of all that Jesus would bring... bread from Heaven... satisfying every need... containing every delight... conformed to what each person needs. The amazing gift of God. If we really appreciated the presence of Jesus in the Blessed Eucharist, we would never need any other signs.

PRAYERS

Lord, deepen our faith in your presence in the Eucharist. May we never receive casually, but always with a sense of amazement and reverence.
Lord, hear us.

Grant us a deep trust in the Eucharist as the greatest source of spiritual strength, satisfying every hunger, conformed to every need.
Lord, hear us.

For those who no longer come to the Eucharist: open their eyes so that they might see what they are missing.
Lord, hear us.

For priests who celebrate the Eucharist: each day strengthen them in their vocation. Call many more to minister at the altar.
Lord, hear us.

(Add prayers for personal, local or topical intentions)

O God, as you answered the needs of the people in the desert, graciously hear our prayers in the name of Jesus Christ, your Son, our Lord. Amen.

WEDNESDAY

ACTS 8:1-8 | JOHN 6:35-40

1. Sometimes we say that God can write straight on crooked lines. Today's First Reading from the Acts tells how tragedy turned into a blessing. Bitter persecution of Christians in Jerusalem forced them to flee. It turned out to be a blessing for people in other places because the fleeing disciples brought the Good News of Jesus with them. Many were converted and there was great rejoicing in many places.

2. Listen to the Good News of today's Second Reading, from John's Gospel. "I am the Bread of Life. Whoever comes to me will never be hungry. Whoever believes in me will never thirst." By believing in Jesus, people were receiving a very noble moral code and the message of God's mercy to the sinner. They got the answers to the hungers of the spirit. And above all they got the news of resurrection from the dead, news which satisfied the thirst for immortal life. "It is my Father's will that whoever sees the Son and believes in him shall have eternal life, and that I shall raise him up on the last day." So, there are two important messages for us today.

   God can turn a tragedy into a source of blessings.

   The greatest news of all is Easter: the resurrection of Jesus from the dead and our invitation to be raised up with him in the next life.

PRAYERS

"I am the Bread of Life. Whoever comes to me will never hunger. Whoever believes in me will never thirst." May our faith develop a deep personal relationship with Jesus to satisfy our deepest questions and hungers.
Lord, hear us.

Persecution of Christians in Jerusalem resulted in spreading the Good News to other places. We pray for Christians who are being persecuted today. May God strengthen and console them with many blessings.
Lord, hear us.

"It is the will of Him who sent me that I should lose nothing of all that he has given me." We pray for family members and others who have strayed away from God. May the gift of faith come alive in them.
Lord, hear us.

May our departed relations and friends enjoy the eternal life promised by Jesus.
Lord, hear us.

(Add prayers for personal, local or topical intentions)

Merciful Father, the giver of every good gift, graciously hear the prayers we make in the name of Jesus Christ, your Son, our Lord. Amen.

THURSDAY

ACTS 8:26-40 | JOHN 6:44-51

1. "No one can come to me unless he is drawn by the Father who sent me." Faith is a gift from God. It should never be taken for granted. In the majority of cases, God's gift comes through people. The greatest cradle of faith is a Christian family. It is said that faith is not so much taught as caught. It is fascinating to see how a little child picks up ideas and words. A child seems to know instinctively when he/she has picked up a naughty word. Maybe the child senses the reaction of adults to the word. In a Christian home, a child catches a sense of God. Christmas has a meaning, the crib and the cross are explained, bedtime prayers open up the mind to a greater world. Belief in God is caught in the atmosphere of the home. The Christian child is drawn to God. Faith is a gift from God and the best way to keep this gift is by sharing it with others. Parents will find their own faith coming to life when they share it with their children.

2. In olden days, Roman emperors sought to distract the minds of people from social injustices by placating them with bread and circus. The circus meant entertainment. Nowadays, people are distracted from the serious questions of life by hollow entertainment and the artificial demands of consumerism... all the things I must have. Today's shallow living has borne poisoned fruit in restlessness, loneliness, impermanent relationships, dependence on drugs, and worst of all, suicides. As Chesterton remarked, when people do not believe in something, then they will believe in anything. So, there are substitute gods in horoscopes, the spirit of trees or the power of stones. Belief in Jesus is the way to eternal life. The divine wisdom which Jesus brought to the world is the Bread of Life. "I am the Bread of Life".

PRAYERS

"Nobody comes to me unless he is drawn by the Father who sent me." We thank you, Lord, for the gift of faith. May we treasure our faith and nourish it by prayer and good reading.
Lord, hear us.

May all parents pass on faith and prayer to their children and may their own faith grow as they do so.
Lord, hear us.

May all teachers and preachers of the Word be guided by the Holy Spirit.
Lord, hear us.

In the First Reading, Philip was travelling on the road to Gaza. This territory is frequently associated with conflict. May a just settlement bring peace to Gaza and to every area of conflict.
Lord, hear us.

(Add prayers for personal, local or topical intentions)

Heavenly Father, we thank you for the light of faith. May we always walk in your light, through Christ, our Lord. Amen.

FRIDAY

ACTS 9:1-20 | JOHN 6:52-59

1. "The bread that I shall give is my flesh, for the life of the world."
Up to this point Jesus had given people two kinds of bread. First, he multiplied the loaves of bread to feed their bodily hunger. The second bread he gave was in the wisdom of his teaching to answer the hungers and questions of the mind. Next he began to speak of a future bread... "the bread that I shall give". It was not yet given. What was this future bread? "The bread that I shall give is my flesh for the life of the world." It is understandable that the people could not initially understand this promise. Jesus repeated the promise by rephrasing it six more times. Seven statements. In John's Gospel, seven is the divine number. Jesus repeatedly linked this future bread with life. Believers see this future bread as the promise of the Blessed Eucharist. At the Last Supper, the time had come. Jesus took the bread and said: "This is my body... this is my blood". For thirty years or so, the Son of God lived on Earth in a body of human flesh and blood. Before leaving this world, he instituted a new way of living among us. Now he is embodied in the consecrated bread and wine. "My flesh is real food, my blood is real drink." "The bread that I shall give"... that is the promise of the Eucharist.

2. "Whoever eats my flesh and drinks my blood lives in me and I live in him." This is a lesson Saint Paul learned on the day of his conversion. The Risen Lord said to him: "I am Jesus and you are persecuting me". The lesson was that to touch these Christian followers was to touch Jesus himself. How can this be? Go back to the words of the Gospel. "He who eats my flesh and drinks my blood lives in me and I live in him. As I who am sent by the living Father, myself draw life from the Father, so whoever eats me will draw life from me." Our belief in the presence of the Risen Jesus in the Eucharist is based entirely in the words of the Gospel and Saint Paul.

PRAYERS

Having listened to the words of Jesus about giving us his flesh to eat and his blood to drink, we pray.

May God strengthen our belief in the presence of Jesus Christ in the Blessed Eucharist.
Lord, hear us.

"Whoever eats me will draw life from me." May Holy Communion be a constant source of spiritual energy in us. May we grow in the likeness of Christ and become what we receive.
Lord, hear us.

For family members and friends who have drifted away from the Eucharist: may they humbly accept the teaching of Jesus and return to the table of the Lord.
Lord, hear us.

We pray for priests and for vocations to the priesthood so that people may not be deprived of the Eucharist because of the lack of priests.
Lord, hear us.

(Add prayers for personal, local or topical intentions)

Heavenly Father, hear the prayers of your people gathered here in the name of Jesus Christ, your Son, our Lord. Amen.

SATURDAY

ACTS 9:31-42 | JOHN 6:60-69

1. After hearing the promise of Jesus to give us his flesh to eat and his blood to drink, many of his followers turned away from him. Jesus did not call them back to say that he had meant it only in a symbolic way. No, he meant it to be taken literally, that he would be the Bread of Life in the consecrated bread and wine. He appealed to the people to postpone their decision: "What if you should see the Son of Man ascend to where he was before". The presence of the Lord in the Eucharist can be understood only in the light of the Resurrection. It is the Risen Lord who comes to us. Since his death, he is no longer present on Earth in a body of flesh and blood. His new embodiment is in the consecrated bread and wine. Saint Paul expressed this Christian belief in writing to the Corinthians: "The blessing-cup which we bless, is it not a sharing in the blood of Christ? And the loaf of bread which we break, is it not a sharing in the body of Christ?" (1 Cor. 10:16). "Do this in memory of me."

2. "It is the spirit that gives life, the flesh has nothing to offer." In John's writing, worldly knowledge is sometimes called the flesh, and it is contrasted with the knowledge which faith brings, which is called the spirit. Worldly or scientific knowledge is based on human investigation. A scientific analysis of the consecrated bread would not reveal the divine presence, just as a scientific examination of the body of Jesus while on Earth would not have revealed his divine identity. That is what Jesus meant in saying that the flesh has nothing to offer. "It is the spirit that gives life". The spirit refers to the knowledge given by the Holy Spirit, and this is the knowledge we call faith. Belief in the presence of the Lord in the consecrated bread and wine is based entirely on the words of Scripture. Peter spoke up on behalf of believers: "Lord, to whom shall we go? You have the message of eternal life, and we believe; we know that you are the Holy One of God."

PRAYERS

In the light of the teaching of Jesus, we pray.

Saint Peter, as spokesperson for the apostles, proclaimed that Jesus had the message of eternal life. May his successor today, Pope (*Name*), be guided and strengthened by the Holy Spirit, in the proclamation of the Gospel to all nations.
Lord, hear us.

Sometimes we might find doctrines hard to understand or explain: may we have the humility to accept the teaching of Jesus as handed down to us in the Church.
Lord, hear us.

For family members and others who no longer come to the Eucharist: may they be open to the light of the Holy Spirit leading them to faith.
Lord, hear us.

We pray for vocations to the priesthood, so that people might not be deprived of the Eucharist because of the lack of priests.
Lord, hear us.

(*Add prayers for personal, local or topical intentions*)

Heavenly Father, we thank you all your gifts and especially for the privilege of receiving your Beloved Son as the Bread of Life. Through Jesus Christ, your Son, our Lord. Amen.

FOURTH WEEK OF EASTER:

MONDAY

ACTS 11:1-18 | JOHN 10:1-10

1. In the Holy Land, one still sees the shepherd leading the flock from the front. They know his call. Jesus is our true shepherd. He does not drive us from behind. He does not beat us with a stick. He leads us by his teaching, his ideals and his example. When we have moral decisions to make, the question we should ask ourselves is – what would Jesus do? What did he say? How did he act? We come to recognise his voice by becoming familiar with the gospels. The Good Shepherd guides us along the right path. He is true to his name. Near restful waters he leads me to revive my drooping spirit. Sheep find it hard to drink from swiftly flowing water, so the shepherd finds a pool of restful water. We cannot drink of God's presence if life is too hectic and noisy. We need the pool of quiet time to sit with the Lord and revive our drooping spirits.

2. "The thief comes only to kill and steal and destroy." There are many false shepherds today. There are many strange voices that mislead people... into foggy thinking that all religions are of equal value... or into a moral vagueness which no longer recognises what is sin... or towards materialistic progress as the goal of life... or to pop culture which makes an idol of some current celebrity. The thief comes only to kill and steal and destroy faith. Jesus came so that we might have life and have it to the full.

PRAYERS

The shepherd leads the flock and guides them along the right path. May we always follow the voice of Jesus and never be misled by false shepherds.
Lord, hear us.

The shepherd feeds the flock. He has prepared a banquet for me in the sight of my foes. May the banquet of the Eucharist be our strength against all temptation.
Lord, hear us.

The shepherd protects the flock. May the Lord accompany all who are in the valley of darkness because of depression, sadness or addiction.
Lord, hear us.

Lord, bless and guide all our Church shepherds. Keep them faithful to their calling and ministry.
Lord, hear us.

(Add prayers for personal, local or topical intentions)

God, our Father, lead to the fullness of life all who follow the voice of Jesus Christ, your Son, our Lord. Amen.

TUESDAY

ACTS 11: 19-26 | JOHN 10:22-30

1. In John's Gospel some of the most important events in the ministry of Jesus take place in the context of Jewish feasts. Jesus brings the meaning of each particular feast to a new level. Today's Gospel is set at the time of the feast of the Dedication of the Temple. This celebrated the rededication or reconsecration of the Temple after it had been defiled by pagan worship. Jesus had already foretold the destruction of this Temple. "Destroy this Temple and in three days I will raise it up." The three days refer to his resurrection. After rising from the dead and returning to the Father, Jesus would be the new centre of worship. True worship would not be confined to any particular mountain or stone building. Jesus was asked if he was the Christ, meaning the consecrated one, the anointed one of God. Jesus answered, "I and the Father are one." True worship from then on would not involve sacrificing animals in the Temple. True worship would be through Jesus as our Mediator with the Father: with Jesus as our brother in humanity; in Jesus as members of his body.

2. Christ could say, "I and the Father are one." A follower of Christ can say, "I and Christ are one." Today's Reading from Acts recalls how the followers of Christ were called Christians. Another name for Baptism is christening. Say it slowly... Christ-ening. Immediately after the Baptism by water, the newly baptised is anointed with the sacred oil of chrism. This prayer is said. "As Christ was anointed Priest, Prophet and King, so may you live always as a member of his body, sharing everlasting life." We share in his priesthood when we join with Christ in the Eucharist. We follow Christ the Prophet when we listen to his voice and live by his teaching. We belong to Christ the King when we live by his rules of life. What a privilege it is to be one with Christ, to be a Christian, to be Christ-ened.

PRAYERS

As Christians, belonging to Christ, we pray with confidence.

That the Church will always be true to Christ in proclaiming his teaching to the world.
Lord, hear us.

Grant us the grace of a deep appreciation of the wonderful privilege of participating in the priesthood of Jesus Christ at Mass.
Lord, hear us.

Since our christening, we are Christian in name: may we be Christian in fact by living according to the ideals of Christ.
Lord, hear us.

We remember those who are being persecuted because they are Christian. Lord, protect them and may their persecution cease.
Lord, hear us.

   (Add prayers for personal, local or topical intentions)

Heavenly Father, hear the prayers we offer in the name of our High Priest, Jesus Christ, the Lord. Amen.

WEDNESDAY

ACTS 12:24 – 13:5 | JOHN 12:44-50

1. In today's Gospel, John concludes his account of the public ministry of Jesus by recalling some of his key ideas. In the opening chapter John tells us that no one has ever seen the Father. Human eyes could not take the resplendent light of God's glory. God's light came to us filtered through the humanity of Jesus, the Word made flesh. "Whoever sees me sees the One who sent me." After the Last Supper, Jesus said to Philip, "To have seen me is to have seen the Father". The evangelist John has been depicted in art as an eagle. The eagle is reputed to be the only creature that can look directly into the light of the sun without damaging its eyes. John's writings direct our eyes into the inner life of the Blessed Trinity as made known to us in the life of Jesus, the Word made flesh. God has spoken to us in a language that we can understand, the story of a human life. If you want to know what God is like, the surest way is to keep looking at what Jesus was like.

2. Today's Gospel concludes the public preaching of Jesus, but the First Reading shows how his mission was carried on in the Church in the power of the Holy Spirit. For two thousand years, the mission of the Church has continued down the centuries to our own time. On the day of our Christening, our baptismal candle received light from the paschal candle which represents the light of the Risen Lord. Jesus told his disciples, "You are the light of the world, you are the salt of the earth." Pope Francis said that our attitude ought to be not just: "I have a mission" but "I am a mission on this Earth; that is the reason why I am here in this world". Bring the light of Christ to somebody today... an act of kindness, a smile, a cheerful word or a remembrance in prayer.

PRAYERS

May the Church, in the power of the Holy Spirit, continue to proclaim the Word of God to all nations.
Lord, hear us.

Open our eyes, Lord, to the small needs of people so that we might bring the light and smile of Jesus to their lives.
Lord, hear us.

For people who have rejected the light of Christ: may they hear his invitation to repent and to come back to his light.
Lord, hear us.

For those who are walking in the dark valley of depression, sadness or sorrow: may they remember that the Good Shepherd is walking with them.
Lord, hear us.

(Add prayers for personal, local or topical intentions)

Heavenly Father, graciously hear the prayers of your people gathered here in the name of Jesus Christ, our Lord. Amen.

THURSDAY

ACTS 13:13-25 | JOHN 13:16-20

1. One of the most important sermons of Jesus was given in action before it was explained in words. He took on the humble service of washing the feet of his disciples. Jesus always avoided the pomp of being treated like royalty. And that is what he wants of his Church too: no pomp, but a Church of humble service, especially to the poor. "If I, the Lord and Master, have washed your feet, you must wash each other's feet. I have given you an example so that you may copy what I have done to you." No servant is greater than his master. Then Jesus promised that "happiness will be yours" if you follow his example of humble service. Mother Teresa of Calcutta had what she called her Business Card, five short steps. The fruit of silence is prayer; the fruit of prayer is faith; the fruit of faith is love; the fruit of love is service; the fruit of service is peace. As Jesus promised: "Happiness will be yours if you behave accordingly". It is in giving that we receive.

2. The first major document of any Pope is regarded as an outline of his vision of the Church. Pope Francis' first document was called *The Joy of the Gospel*, that same happiness which Jesus attached to humble service. He said it is a temptation to want a purely spiritual relationship with Christ without flesh, without the cross. That sort of religion avoids the messy business of being involved in the needs and pains of people. Being so heavenly minded that one is no earthly good! In contrast to the happiness of serving others was the fate of Judas who was serving himself by betraying Jesus for thirty silver pieces. His life ended in suicide. Pope Francis referred to slow suicide. "We do not live better when we flee, hide, refuse to share, stop giving and lock ourselves up in our own comfort zone. Such a life is nothing less than slow suicide." Remember the humble example of Jesus. "I have given you an example so that you may copy what I have done for you."

PRAYERS

Inspired by the humble service of Jesus, we pray.

May the Church let go of the trappings of pomp and inspire the world in the example of humble service.
Lord, hear us.

Jesus promised happiness to those who would follow his example: may we learn that it is in giving that we receive.
Lord, hear us.

Help us, Lord, to be less self-centred and locked up in ourselves: open our eyes and hearts to be at the service of others.
Lord, hear us.

Bless and reward all those who give their time and talents in works of voluntary service.
Lord, hear us.

(Add prayers for personal, local or topical intentions)

God, our Father, graciously hear the prayers we offer in the name of Jesus Christ, our Lord. Amen.

FRIDAY

ACTS 13:26-33 | JOHN 14:1-6

1. For the next three weeks, our Gospel readings will be taken from what Jesus said to the apostles at the end of the Last Supper. They were very troubled as he told them that he was going away. So he consoled them that his going away would be for their benefit in many ways. "Do not let your hearts be troubled. Trust in God still and trust in me." Where he is going to is Heaven. "I am going to prepare a place for you." What a wonderfully consoling message! "There are many rooms in my Father's house. I shall return to take you to myself". The Christian understanding of death is that the Risen Lord will come to take his faithful to Heaven.

2. Thomas was one of those people who always has a question. "Lord, we do not know where you are going, so how can we know the way?" The question allows Jesus to make his great answer: "I am the Way, the Truth and the Life. No one can come to the Father except through me." He is the Way, whose teaching guides our behaviour and shows us how to live. He is the Truth in whom the searching mind will find ultimate meaning and satisfaction. He is the Life who has conquered death. He offers eternal life to all who live by his way and believe in his truth.

PRAYERS

"No one can come to the Father except through me". So, we pray in the name of Jesus.

"Do not let your hearts be troubled. Trust in God still and trust in me." May all who are deeply disturbed mentally or emotionally draw great confidence from the words of Jesus.
Lord, hear us.

"I am going now to prepare a place for you." May the promise of Jesus be a source of consolation and peace to people who are terminally ill.
Lord, hear us.

May all who are sad at the loss of a loved one be consoled by the words of Jesus today.
Lord, hear us.

For all who are mixed up and without direction in life: may they turn to Jesus and find in him the Way, the Truth and the Life.
Lord, hear us.

(Add prayers for personal, local or topical intentions)

All our prayers we offer to the Father in the name of Jesus Christ, our Lord. Amen.

SATURDAY

ACTS 13:44-52 | JOHN 14:7-14

1. The apostles were disturbed because Jesus was going away from them so he offered them motives for consolation. There are greater days ahead. The time when Jesus was with the apostles was great. God was present in the person of Jesus. "To have seen me is to have seen the Father." People saw him, heard him, even touched him. They saw his miracles. How could the time after his presence be greater? All would be revealed at the coming of the Holy Spirit. The times ahead would be greater in the expansion of the mission of Jesus. He confined himself to a small geographical region. With the power of the Spirit in them, the apostles brought the message of Jesus far and wide. Today's First Reading describes the happiness of many pagans when Saint Paul brought them the Good News.

2. A second way that the time after the resurrection would be greater is in Christian prayer. Prayer would have a new power because it is in the name of the Risen Jesus. Peter healed a crippled man in the name of Jesus. Worship of God would no longer be in the sacrifice of animals. Prayer in the name of Jesus means being united with him in his return to the Father. That is why the celebration of the Eucharist is the greatest prayer. In the living memory of the death and resurrection of Jesus, we offer all honour and glory to the Father, through Jesus, with him and in him. Through him as our mediator, since no one can go to the Father except through him. With him who became one with us in human flesh and blood. In him, as members of his body. The mission of Jesus was once the mission of one. Now it is the mission of millions. And that includes you.

PRAYERS

Consoled and encouraged by the words of Jesus, we pray.

May the Church continue the mission of Jesus in bringing the Good News to all nations.
Lord, hear us.

The preaching of Paul brought great happiness to people. May our faith be a source of great joy in our lives.
Lord, hear us.

"Whatever you ask for in my name, I will do". May we have a profound belief in the power of the sacred name of Jesus.
Lord, hear us.

For those who have no faith or religion, may they come to know Jesus Christ and through him receive the joy of the Gospel.
Lord, hear us.

   (Add prayers for personal, local or topical intentions)

Heavenly Father, graciously hear the prayers we offer in the name of Jesus Christ, your Son, our Lord. Amen.

MONDAY

ACTS 14:5-18 | JOHN 14:21-26

1. The conversation of Jesus with the apostles after the Last Supper is full of consolation, hope, strength and peace. If we obey the Commandments and love God, then we are preparing our souls to be a home for God's presence. "If anyone loves me, he will keep my word and my Father will love him, and we shall love him and make our home with him." This is the divine indwelling. Some say it is religion's best-kept secret. God is at the centre of my being. Perhaps we have too much babbling in words, and too much chasing off to distant places. Constant prayer develops the habit of attentiveness to God. What we need in this bustling, noisy world of today is inner silence to nurture attentiveness to God who is at home within us.

2. "The Advocate, the Holy Spirit, whom the Father will send in my name, will teach you everything, and remind you of everything that I have said to you." For many centuries, the role of the Holy Spirit was seriously neglected. In the only Eucharistic Prayer at that time, Eucharistic Prayer No. 1 today, there was no mention of the Holy Spirit. The Spirit was the forgotten Paraclete. Some people describe their experience of the indwelling Spirit as the fourteen inch drop... from the brain to the heart... from a remote God up there to God within... from a brain-centred prayer battling with distractions to an awareness of God in everyday life. God is UP, but God is also IN.

PRAYERS

Inspired by the beautiful doctrine of the divine indwelling, we pray.

The apostles were transformed at the coming of the Holy Spirit at Pentecost. May the Church in our day be powerfully guided by the wisdom of the Holy Spirit.
Lord, hear us.

"Blessed are the pure in heart for they shall see God." May the light of the Holy Spirit enable us to recognise the presence of God within us and all around us.
Lord, hear us.

May the Holy Spirit inspire our minds with the wisdom of Christ's teaching.
Lord, hear us.

May the Holy Spirit, also known as the Consoler, bring peace of mind and heart to all who are deeply troubled.
Lord, hear us.

(Add prayers for personal, local or topical intentions)

Glory be to the Father, and to the Son and to the Holy Spirit, as it was in the beginning, is now and every shall be. Amen.

TUESDAY

ACTS 14:19-28 | JOHN 14:27-31

1. "Peace I bequeath to you, my own peace I give you, a peace the world cannot give, this is my gift to you." Jesus spoke these comforting words just before his Passion began. Judas had left the table and gone into the darkness. Jesus knew the suffering he was about to face. "The prince of this world, that is, the Devil, is on his way. But he has no power over me." Jesus then tells us the secret of his inner peace. "I love the Father and I am doing exactly what the Father told me." His unconditional trust in God the Father is the source of his deep, inner peace... a peace deeper than suffering... deeper than any mischief the Devil could conjure up. In God's will is our peace.

2. In today's First Reading we meet with that great disciple of Christ, Saint Paul. In his missionary journeys, he endured multiple forms of hardship. He was so badly beaten up in one town that he was left for dead. But he recovered consciousness and off he went with his companions to preach the message of Christ in other towns. We read that his preaching put fresh heart into the disciples and he urged them to persevere in the faith. He opened up the door of faith to the pagans. This phrase, the door of faith, was used as a motto for the Year of Faith. Paul's inner strength came from his relationship with Jesus. "All I want is to know Jesus Christ and the power of his Resurrection, and to share in his suffering by reproducing the pattern of his death." Paul, like Jesus, had a deep reservoir of peace that carried him through all suffering. "Peace I leave you, my peace I give you."

PRAYERS

Trusting in the Lord's gift of peace, we pray.

May the voice of the Church be like that of Saint Paul who put fresh heart into peoples' lives and encouraged them to persevere in the faith.
Lord, hear us.

May there be an end to all warfare so that all people will enjoy the peace that the Lord wants us to have.
Lord, hear us.

For those who are suffering persecution on account of their religion. May the persecution cease as justice and peace are restored. May they know that God is with them at all times.
Lord, hear us.

For people who suffer from fears and anxiety: may the Holy Spirit enable them to hand over their problems so that they can live in Christ's peace.
Lord, hear us.

(Add prayers for personal, local or topical intentions)

God our Father, you sent your beloved Son to show us the way to peace: hear the prayers we offer in his name, Jesus Christ the Lord. Amen.

WEDNESDAY

ACTS 15:1-6 | JOHN 15:1-8

1. Remain in me... make your home in me... abide in me. These are variations in translating the beautiful invitation of the Lord. The idea is so important that it is repeated ten times in this chapter. Home is where you belong, where you are welcome when you return. A Christian is as much at home with Christ as the branch is with the tree. The life of a Christian is rooted in Christ and always returns to him for meaning, sustenance and energy. "Apart from me you can do nothing." Take a burning coal out from the fire and it loses its glow. Cut off the branch and it withers. It is impossible to live a vibrant Christian life without a steady prayer-life.

2. This is blossom time in the Northern hemisphere and fruit-picking time in the South. Blossoms and fruit do not grow on the main trunk or sturdy branches but on the fragile twigs and tendrils. When we hear our vocation to bear fruit for Christ, our first reaction might be a sense of our inadequacy. But many of the people who bore fruit in God's service were conscious of past failures. Moses had killed a man. King David's moment of lust instigated a train of evil deeds. Paul had persecuted the followers of Jesus. Bearing fruit for Christ can be in teaching, parenting, works of compassion, uplifting words and in many other ways. The great secret of bearing fruit is keeping contact with home. And home means a daily relationship with Jesus. Cut off from him we can do nothing.

PRAYERS

"I am the vine, you are the branches." We pray that we will remain in contact with God every day, and will never allow ourselves to be cut off from him.
Lord, hear us.

Lord, may your words always remain in our minds and hearts, inspiring us to lives of love and service.
Lord, hear us.

May we never bury our talents because of shyness or fear: may we be generous with our time towards making our neighbourhood a better place.
Lord, hear us.

For people who have allowed themselves to be cut off from God: may the invitation of divine mercy call them back home.
Lord, hear us.

(Add prayers for personal, local or topical intentions)

Heavenly Father, hear our prayers as we are united with Jesus like the branches are one with the vine. Through Jesus Christ, our Lord. Amen.

THURSDAY

ACTS 15:7-21 | JOHN 15:9-11

1. One of the great tragedies of our time is the plight of those who are homeless. Thousands are homeless because they were driven out by war or persecution. Others are homeless because of personal problems or financial reasons. There is also the condition of spiritual homelessness. Home is where we live, where we are loved, where we return. Jesus offers us a spiritual home. A house is not a home unless there is love in it. Jesus tells us, "Make your home in my love. If you keep my commandments you will remain in my love. I have told you all this so that my own joy may be in you, and your joy complete".

2. Henri Nouwen was a wonderful writer and counsellor, but he suffered from periods of darkness and low self-esteem. During one of his low periods, he met Mother Teresa of Calcutta. He told her of his problem. She gave him a double piece of advice. Never do anything you know to be wrong... just as Jesus said to keep his commandments. And her second advice was to spend one hour each day adoring the Lord. She assured him he would be alright. He took her advice and later wrote about it. "She punctured my big balloon of complex self-complaints. She pointed me beyond myself and brought me to a place of real healing." Keep away from any form of badness and find time every day to be at home with God. Jesus promises us a spiritual home filled with joy. "I have told you all this so that my own joy may be in you and your joy complete."

PRAYERS

Inspired by the words of Jesus, we pray.

May the Church be a community united in God's love and compassion, reaching out in practical works of mercy and showing the face of joy.
Lord, hear us.

With the psalmist we pray: Lord, make me know your love and show me the way I should walk.
Lord, hear us.

For people who are homeless: may persecution of people cease; may homeless people be treated with great dignity.
Lord, hear us.

For those who are spiritually homeless: may they come to know that Jesus is sitting by the well, waiting to satisfy their inner thirst.
Lord, hear us.

(Add prayers for personal, local or topical intentions)

Loving Father, hear our prayers in the name of Jesus Christ, your Son, our Lord. Amen.

FRIDAY

ACTS 15:22-31 | JOHN 15:12-17

1. Our mission in life is to know God's love and to pass it on. "Love one another as I have loved you." In today's Gospel there are several I – You statements revealing the intimacy of Christ's relationship with us. I have loved you as the Father loves me. I lay down my life for you. I share the fullness of joy with you. I call you friends. I have made known to you everything I have learnt from my Father. I chose you. I commissioned you to go out and to bear fruit. We come to know our identity through the quality of our inter-personal relationships... the I – You relationships. My identity as a Christian grows in appreciating that I am loved by God... that Jesus laid down his life for me... that he calls me friend... that he has called me and commissioned me to go out and to bear fruit. "Love one another as I have loved you". That is our Christian mission.

2. If we are overwhelmed by our unworthiness or uselessness, remember that the part of the fruit tree which bears fruit is the most fragile tip of the branch. In the wonderful ways of providence, God has chosen humble people to bear fruit. They know their own weakness but also know their dependence on God. Store up in your memory these inspiring words of Jesus as addressed to you personally. I have loved you. I call you friend. I have called you to bear fruit. Listen to Jesus saying these words to you time and time again.

PRAYERS

Inspired by the loving invitation of Jesus to be united with him, we pray.

May the Church be a community of people united in friendship with God, inspiring the world to live in justice, harmony and peace.
Lord, hear us.

May we grow in our appreciation of the friendship Jesus wishes to share with us.
Lord, hear us.

By the grace of God, may our lives enrich other people with the fruits of kindness and compassion.
Lord, hear us.

For people who suffer from low self-esteem: may the friendship of Jesus help them to realise how much they are loved by God.
Lord, hear us.

(Add prayers for personal, local or topical intentions)

God our Father, may we live each day in the knowledge that you love us and call us to bear fruit. Through Jesus Christ, our Lord. Amen.

SATURDAY

ACTS 16:1-10 | JOHN 15:18-21

1. Jesus is the vine and we are the branches. The vine is such a vigorous plant that it needs to be pruned twice in the year if it is to bear a good crop. The first pruning is in springtime. Many sprouting branches are cut off. Jesus told the apostles, "You are pruned already by means of the Word I have spoken to you." This first pruning took place when Jesus spoke of giving us his flesh to eat and his blood to drink. Many followers cut themselves off that day and left Jesus. The apostles were among those who stayed with him. The second pruning of the vine is in August, a month before harvesting. Branches that carry little or no fruit are cut off to allow the sap to swell out the stronger fruit. This later pruning refers to the time after Jesus when his followers would be tested under persecution, just as he was persecuted. The first pruning was about faith. The second pruning would be about faithfulness in spite of dungeon, fire and sword.

2. "If they persecuted me they will persecute you". Persecution of Christians is rampant today in many countries. Even in our own country, followers of Christ face hostility, cynicism, bitterness and hatred. The early Christians considered it a privilege to suffer in the name of Christ. Opposition is a challenge to prove our faithfulness. "If they have persecuted me they will persecute you too."
   "Blessed are you when people abuse you and persecute you and speak all kinds of calumny against you falsely. Rejoice and be glad, for your reward will be great in Heaven."

PRAYERS

Encouraged by the Word of God, we pray.

For those who are persecuted or mocked because of their Christian faith: may they find the strength to be faithful as they remember that Jesus is with them.
Lord, hear us.

As Jesus prayed for those who persecuted him, may we overcome all bitterness and pray for the conversion of those who mock us.
Lord, hear us.

For any family members or acquaintances who have become bitter critics of religion: may the light and love of the Holy Spirit break through their bitterness.
Lord, hear us.

Saint Paul's crossing over into Macedonia represents the coming of Christianity to Europe. Europe is now the most pagan and secularised continent. May the people of Europe return to the teaching and ideals of Jesus Christ.
Lord, hear us.

(Add prayers for personal, local or topical intentions)

Lord God of mercy, watch over those you have called. Strengthen them in time of opposition. This we ask in the name of Jesus Christ, our Lord. Amen.

MONDAY

ACTS 16:11-15 | JOHN 15:26 – 16:4

1. Sometimes we hear the Holy Spirit called the Paraclete, at other times, the Advocate. These names are identical in meaning. Paraclete is a Greek word and Advocate is the Latin equivalent. Either name means the One-called-alongside. During the life of Jesus, the presence and power of God could be seen physically in the life and actions of Jesus Christ. Saint John's First Letter refers to Jesus as the first Advocate and to the Holy Spirit as another Advocate. The Holy Spirit is like the wind. We do not see the wind but we can see its effects in the direction of the clouds or the slanting of the smoke. The presence and power of the Holy Spirit are to be seen in the people whose lives are a witness to God's grace for all to see. The Holy Spirit's presence is shown in gifts such as wisdom, prayerfulness, extraordinary courage, forgiveness, generosity and love.

2. Another name of the Holy Spirit is Comforter. Comfort comes from two Latin words. *Cum* meaning with, and *fortis* meaning strong. Comforter means that one is strong with the help of the Holy Spirit. Jesus told the apostles to be prepared for times of persecution and hardship. But they would be strong with the Holy Spirit at their side. The power of the Holy Spirit could be seen in the transformation of the apostles. They found it hard at times to grasp what Jesus was saying. After his death, they were locked away in fear. After Pentecost, they were transformed into men with God's wisdom and extraordinary courage. The story of the early Church comes to us in what is called *The Acts of the Apostles*. It should really be called *The Acts of the Holy Spirit*.

PRAYERS

Opening up our hearts to the Holy Spirit, we pray.

That Pope *(Name)* and all our bishops may be powerfully guided by the Holy Spirit.
Lord, hear us.

For those who are being persecuted , like the early Christians: may the Holy Spirit strengthen them so that their faith is not shaken.
Lord, hear us.

May our prayer-life grow in greater awareness of the Holy Spirit in our lives.
Lord, hear us.

May the Holy Spirit bring light to those who are in darkness and consolation to those who are depressed.
Lord, hear us.

(Add prayers for personal, local or topical intentions)

God our Father, hear our prayers, through your Son, Jesus Christ, in the unity of the Holy Spirit. Amen

TUESDAY

ACTS 16:22-34 | JOHN 16:5-11

1. Saint Irenaeus lived about a hundred years after the time of Jesus. He wrote a beautiful meditation on the return of the Prodigal Son and how his father hugged him back home in welcome. In his imagination, Irenaeus pictured the two hands of the father. One hand is visibly taking the hand of the son in warm welcome. The other hand is not visible as it is behind the son, drawing him closer in a loving hug. The visible hand represents Jesus who sat with sinners and ate with them. The unseen hand represents the Holy Spirit. The Holy Spirit is not seen directly but the warm embrace of the Holy Spirit transforms life. The Holy Spirit is the Advocate, the Friend at our side and within us.

2. Jesus explained to the apostles that it was good that he was departing. "Unless I go, the Advocate will not come to you; but if I go I will send him to you." The mission of Jesus was in a physical body, confined by the limitations of physical life. His mission was confined to a small territory, to a small section of the world's population and in one language. The Holy Spirit is as free as the wind, not confined in human limitations. The Holy Spirit, descending in the form of tongues of fire, inspired the Church to speak in every language, to every race and nation, to the ends of Earth. When Jesus died on the cross it seemed that Satan, the prince of this world, had triumphed. But the Resurrection changed everything. And the wisdom of the Holy Spirit proved how right Jesus was in everything he said or did... even in his death.

PRAYERS

The promise of the Holy Spirit encourages us to pray with the Response: *Come, O Holy Spirit.*

May the Holy Spirit constantly renew the heart of the Church as a community united in faith and love.
Come O Holy Spirit.

May the Holy Spirit renew the face of the Earth, inspiring nations to put away the weapons of war and to develop the Earth so that every country has adequate food supplies.
Come, O Holy Spirit.

May we grow each day in awareness of the presence of the Holy Spirit beside us and within us.
Come, O Holy Spirit.

May the Holy Spirit, the Comforter, come to the assistance of all who are burdened with grief or sadness.
Come ,O Holy Spirit.

(Add prayers for personal, local or topical intentions)

God, our Father, embrace us with the invisible hand of the Holy Spirit and the visible hand of Jesus, in whose name we pray.

WEDNESDAY

ACTS 17:15.22 – 18:1 | JOHN 16:12-15

1. "I still have many things to say to you but they would be too much for you now. But when the Spirit of Truth comes, he will lead you to the complete truth." Somebody who listened to a politician speaking said that while he understood each word, he hadn't a clue what the man was talking about. There are different levels of knowledge. There is head-knowledge and there is heart-knowledge. A pupil acquires head-knowledge, while it is a disciple who gets heart-knowledge. A pupil might get a degree in head-knowledge Theology without being a believer. A disciple is a believer who makes a personal commitment to follow the ideals of the teacher. Credo means that I give my heart.

2. A man who left the priesthood later admitted that he was so caught up in sitting-theology that he neglected kneeling-theology. It is the Holy Spirit who enables a person to make the fourteen-inch drop, from the brain to the heart. The story of Jesus is not just about what happened in the past. For the committed believer, the story of Jesus touches on what is still happening. As Saint Paul said in Athens, "In him we live and move and have our being". The prayerful reading of Scripture tells what God did in the past so that we might see what God is saying today... regarding the Church, regarding the world, and regarding ourselves. "When the Spirit of Truth comes, he will lead you to the complete truth... since all he tells you will be taken from what is mine."

PRAYERS

Under the guidance of the Holy Spirit, we pray with the Response: *Come, O Holy Spirit.*

That Pope (*Name*) and all teachers in the Church will be powerfully guided by the Holy Spirit.
Come, O Holy Spirit.

That political leaders and lawmakers might be open to the light of the Holy Spirit.
Come, O Holy Spirit.

That we might be true disciples, committed to Jesus and to his ideals.
Come, O Holy Spirit.

For those to whom God is unknown: may the light of the Holy Spirit penetrate their darkness and draw them to God.
Come, O Holy Spirit.

(Add prayers for personal, local or topical intentions)

Send forth your Spirit, O Lord, to renew the heart of the Church and the face of the Earth. Through Christ, our Lord. Amen.

THURSDAY

ACTS 18:1-8 | *JOHN 16:16-20*

1. Today is the fortieth day of the Easter season. It should be the Feast of the Ascension but for pastoral reasons this celebration is postponed until Sunday. Forty is a number associated with a time of preparation. The Hebrew people took forty years to reach the Promised Land. Later, the prophet Elijah was fed by bread from an angel, which energised him to walk for forty days and nights until he met with God on the holy mountain. And Jesus prepared for his public ministry with forty days of prayer and fasting. In the Acts of the Apostles we read that after his resurrection, the Risen Lord continued to appear to the disciples for forty days and told them about the Kingdom of God. "In a short time you will no longer see me. You will be sorrowful but your sorrow will turn to joy." Jesus allowed the apostles the traditional time, forty days, to be prepared for his final departure.

2. The forty days between Easter and the Ascension was a time of transition. This transition gave them time to move gradually from knowing Jesus by physical sight towards knowing him through faith; a transition from sorrow to joy; from his physical presence to his sacramental presence. Today is the fortieth day. Pentecost will be the fiftieth day. The nine days between today and Pentecost form the original novena. The apostles returned to the upper room in Jerusalem where they were united in prayer together with Mary, the mother of Jesus and other disciples. It is important that for the next nine days we should be united in prayer inviting the Holy Spirit to renew the heart of the Church and the face of the Earth.

PRAYERS

Let us join with Mary and the disciples in the upper room in preparing for Pentecost. The Response to the prayers is, *Come, O Holy Spirit.*

On the Mount of the Ascension, the Lord told the disciples to prepare for the coming of the Holy Spirit. May we keep our minds open to the inspiration of the Holy Spirit.
Come, O Holy Spirit.

Jesus promised the apostles that their sorrow would be turned into joy. May the Holy Spirit bring the consolations of faith to all who are under a cloud of sorrow.
Come, O Holy Spirit.

May the Holy Spirit, the teacher of faith, continually enlighten all bishops, priests and ministers of the Gospel.
Come, O Holy Spirit.

May all of us be strengthened in faith by the coming of the Holy Spirit.
Come, O Holy Spirit.

(Add prayers for personal, local or topical intentions)

God our Father, graciously hear our prayers offered in the name of Jesus Christ, our Risen Lord. Amen.

FRIDAY

ACTS 18: 9-18 | *JOHN 16:20-23*

1. When Jesus was telling the apostles that he was soon going away, they felt sad, helpless and lost. But he consoled them that later they would see it as part of a greater plan. He compared their sadness to the suffering of a mother at childbirth before the joy of holding her newborn baby in her arms. "I shall see you again, and your hearts will be full of joy, and that joy no one shall take from you."

2. Cecil Day Lewis wrote a very poignant poem called *Walking Away*. He recalled the day when his seven-year-old son played his first football match. After the game the boy drifted away to follow his pals. The sensitive eye of the poet saw this as the first indication that his son would develop his selfhood and the parent would have to let him walk away. The last three lines of the poem describe how this first parting was...

> *Saying what God alone could perfectly show*
> *How selfhood begins with a walking away*
> *And love is proved in the letting go.*

The pattern is repeated in every parent-child relationship: when to hold on, when to let go; when to permit and when to forbid; when to insist and when to back down; when to refuse and when to consent. Even the apostles had to learn when to let go of the physical presence of Jesus. But it was then that their new selfhood as the Church came to birth in their transformation by the Spirit of Pentecost.

PRAYERS

United with Mary and the disciples in the upper room, we prepare for Pentecost.
The Response is *Come, O Holy Spirit.*

May the Holy Spirit every day renew the heart of the Church in the service of the Kingdom of God.
Come, O Holy Spirit.

Through the power of the Holy Spirit, may the Church inspire the political leaders of the nations towards justice and peace in every country.
Come, O Holy Spirit.

May the Holy Spirit guide all parents and children in the difficult decisions they have to make.
Come, O Holy Spirit.

May the Holy Spirit show us when and how to let go in order to move forward.
Come, O Holy Spirit.

(Add prayers for personal, local or topical intentions)

Send forth your Spirit, O Lord, to renew the heart of the Church and the face of the Earth. Through Christ our Lord. Amen.

SATURDAY

Acts 18: 23-28 | John 16:23-28

1. "I have come from the Father and I have come into the world. Now I am leaving the world to go to the Father." The story of Jesus is like a triangle: a line down, a line along the base and a line going back up to the starting point. Jesus came down to us, for God so loved the world that he gave his only Son. The baseline of the triangle expresses how the Word was made flesh and lived among us. Jesus lived a human life. He was a helpless baby, he grew, he worked as the son of a carpenter, he felt tired, hungry and thirsty. He entered into full solidarity with human nature. At the end of the baseline is the cross on which he died. But the triangle is not complete at the cross. He rose from the dead and in his Ascension he returned to his Father. His journey from human life through his death and return to the Father is called the Paschal mystery, from the Hebrew word for *a journey*. We are invited to join him in his return to the Father every time we participate in the celebration of the Eucharist.

2. Three times in today's Gospel Jesus speaks of praying in his name. His name calls up his presence and his power. The Catechism of the Catholic Church teaches us: "Christian liturgy not only recalls the events that saved us but actualises them, makes them present. The Paschal mystery of Christ is celebrated, not repeated. It is the celebrations that are repeated, and in each celebration there is an outpouring of the Holy Spirit that makes the unique mystery present" (Par. 1104). Jesus invites us to share in his return to the Father. All honour and glory is given to the Father through Jesus, with him and in him. Through him as the only mediator or way to the Father; with him as our brother in human life; and in him as members of the body of which he is the head.

PRAYERS

As we are in the novena preparing for the coming of the Holy Spirit, we pray with the Response: *Come, O Holy Spirit.*

May the Holy Spirit deepen our understanding of the unsurpassable value of the Mass.
Come, O Holy Spirit.

May we never disrespect the sacred name of Jesus. May we remember that his presence and power are invoked when we pray in his name.
Come, O Holy Spirit.

For people who are terminally ill: may the Holy Spirit take away all fear from their hearts; help them to look to the future in the hope of joining with Jesus in the glory of Heaven.
Come, O Holy Spirit.

May our family members and acquaintances, who no longer come to Mass, be enlightened by the Holy Spirit, the Spirit of Truth.
Come, O Holy Spirit.

(Add prayers for personal, local or topical intentions)

Heavenly Father, hear the prayers we offer in the sacred name of Jesus Christ, your Son, our Lord. Amen.

MONDAY

ACTS 19:1-8 | JOHN 16:29-33

1. "Be brave: I have conquered the world." In John's Gospel, these are the last words that Jesus said to the disciples. Jesus is soon to leave them and there will be times of persecution ahead. So he encourages them to be brave. The time will come when they will be scattered. In fact, the scattering began when Judas left the group. But Jesus reassures them that they will never be alone. He will be only the distance of a prayer away from them. They are to remember that he told them: "I call you friends." We do not need a mobile phone or any modern technology. He is our friend for life and his contact number is his sacred name, Jesus.

2. "Be brave: I have conquered the world." As we prepare for next Sunday's celebration of Pentecost, we remember how the coming of the Holy Spirit transformed the disciples and took away all fear from them. The Holy Spirit is the Advocate, the friend called to our side. Saint Paul has a wonderful message about the Holy Spirit helping us when our prayer dries up. "The Spirit comes to help us in our weakness, for when we do not know how to pray properly, then the Spirit personally makes our petitions for us in groans that cannot be put into words" (Rom. 8: 24). Be assured that God is always with us. Prayer is our link with God. "In the world you will have trouble. But be brave: I have overcome the world."

PRAYERS

This week we join with the apostles in preparing for the Feast of Pentecost. The Response is *Come, O Holy Spirit.*

That the power of the Holy Spirit will always be seen in the life of the Church.
Come, O Holy Spirit.

That the inspiration of the Holy Spirit will lead nations to put away the weapons of war so that all people can live in peace.
Come, O Holy Spirit.

That all who suffer from anxiety and fear may they find courage in remembering that Jesus has overcome the world.
Come, O Holy Spirit.

When our prayer has dried up, may we persevere in the belief that as long as we have the will to pray, the Holy Spirit is praying within us.
Come, O Holy Spirit.

(Add prayers for personal, local or topical intentions)

Heavenly Father, united in the Holy Spirit, we pray with confidence in the name of Jesus Christ, your Son, our Lord. Amen

TUESDAY

ACTS 20:17-27 | JOHN 17:1-17

1. The Gospel for the next three days is taken from the farewell prayer of Jesus before he left the disciples. He raised his eyes to Heaven. The traditional definition of prayer is the raising of the mind and heart to God. "Father, glorify your Son, so that your Son may glorify you; and through the power over all mankind that you have given him, let him give eternal life to all those that you have entrusted to him." Jesus is praying that his disciples will share in divine glory. "And eternal life is this: to know you, the only true God, and Jesus Christ whom you have sent." To know you... this is not head-knowledge but heart-knowledge. Not the knowledge of facts, but the intimate knowledge of a personal relationship. Knowing God as our Father, our Creator and provider ... the One who hugs the returning sinner, the One who so loves the world that he sent Jesus Christ as our Redeemer. It is the Holy Spirit who gives the grace to know God in this intimate, personal way.

2. Saint Paul wrote beautifully about our relationship with God. "The Spirit enables us to cry out 'Abba, Father!' The Spirit himself joins with our spirit to bear witness that we are children of God. And if we are children, then we are heirs, heirs of God and joint heirs with Christ, provided that we share his suffering so as to share his glory" (Rom. 8: 15-17). This is the week of preparing for Pentecost. Let our prayer be an invitation to the Holy Spirit to grant us an intimate knowledge of God our Father, and of Jesus Christ whom the Father has sent us.

PRAYERS

In the light of the prayer of Jesus, we pray.
The Response is: *Come, O Holy Spirit.*

That the Holy Spirit of Pentecost will always be renewing the Church as the community of disciples of Jesus.
Come, O Holy Spirit.

That the Holy Spirit will inspire us with a deep personal relationship with God the Father and with Jesus Christ, our Saviour.
Come, O Holy Spirit.

That the Holy Spirit will renew the face of the Earth by inspiring all people to turn away from violence and to live in peace.
Come, O Holy Spirit.

We pray for all who are suffering: may the Holy Spirit, the Comforter, bring them healing and inner strength.
Come, O Holy Spirit.

(Add prayers for personal, local or topical intentions)

Come, Holy Spirit, fill the hearts of the faithful and renew the face of the Earth.

WEDNESDAY

ACTS 20:28-38 | JOHN 17:11-19

1. We are reading these days from the farewell prayer of Jesus after the Last Supper. Jesus is praying for the disciples who would take on his mission. Joining Jesus in this prayer is an ideal way of preparing for Pentecost. Jesus asked for special blessings for the future leaders of the Church. "Keep them true to your Name," united with God and with one another. Then he prayed, "Share my joy with them to the full." Joy is much deeper than pleasure. Pleasure depends on external factors which are pleasing to the senses. Joy is internal. It grows out of security and the experience of love. The disciples would have to face opposition and persecution. Jesus prayed that they would have inner joy which would be deeper than any suffering. Then Jesus asked the Father to protect them from the Evil One. He was not taking them into some sheltered sanctuary. Their mission would be in the world of harsh reality. "I am not in the world any longer, but they are in the world." Pope Francis called for a Church which is bruised, hurting and dirty because it has been out on the streets, rather than a Church which is unhealthy from being confined and from clinging to its own security. Protect this Church... that is the prayer of Jesus.

2. "Consecrate them in the truth; your Word is truth." Consecration with holy oil originally meant more than a tiny dab of oil. It meant being soaked with the oil, seeping into the body. Soak them in the truth as they absorb the wisdom and guidance of the Word of God. Next Sunday, Pentecost, we will celebrate the answer to the prayer of Jesus as the apostles are consecrated for their mission in the outpouring of the Holy Spirit.

PRAYERS

As we prepare for Pentecost we join with Jesus in his prayer for the Church.
The Response is, *Come, O Holy Spirit, come.*

May all members of the Church be so secure in their relationship with God that their lives will be a living witness to the joy of the Gospel.
Come, O Holy Spirit

May the Holy Spirit protect the Church from all evil.
Come, O Holy Spirit

May the Church be consecrated in the truth by constantly absorbing the Word of God.
Come, O Holy Spirit.

Saint Paul reminded the people that there is more happiness in giving than in receiving. May it be our delight to help others and may we appreciate the kindness of others.
Come, O Holy Spirit.

(Add prayers for personal, local or topical intentions)

Come, Holy Spirit. Renew the heart of the Church; renew the face of the Earth.

THURSDAY

ACTS 22:30; 23:6-11 | JOHN 17:20-26

1. We are coming very close to Pentecost, next Sunday. Our Gospel reading takes us into the mind and heart of Jesus in his farewell prayer for the future Church. He prays not only for the disciples but also for the disciples of later times. The great desire in his heart is that they might all be one. Sadly, there have been many splits and divisions. Today's First Reading tells of the divisions between Sadducees and Pharisees in the Jewish world. Christians, followers of Jesus Christ, are in no position to point the finger at others. Our history is marked with differences, disputes, divisions, hatred and prejudice. Religious wars are a horrible contradiction but they are still happening. Ecumenism is encouraging us to move on from past prejudices: to see the grace of God in other traditions: to learn from one another. "Father, may they all be one... as you are in me and I am in you."

2. Jesus prayed: "May the love with which you loved me may be in them, and so may I be in them." Next Sunday, Pentecost, we will celebrate the coming of the Spirit of Divine Love. Tongues of fire came to rest on the heads of the apostles. The tongues were separate but all were parts of the one fire, the fire of God's love. Preparing for Pentecost, we unite in the prayer of Jesus that all may be one.

PRAYERS

As we prepare for the Feast of Pentecost, we pray with the Response: *Come, O Holy Spirit.*

May the Holy Spirit help us all to heal the misunderstandings of the past so that all Christians will be united in the love of Christ.
Come, O Holy Spirit

For all divided families: may they move on from the wrongs and hurts of the past to the joy of being reunited.
Come, O Holy Spirit

For an end to all racial prejudice and tribal hatred. For justice and peace in every land.
Come, O Holy Spirit

That God's love might be in us so that we become bringers of love to others.
Come, O Holy Spirit

   (Add prayers for personal, local or topical intentions)

Come, Holy Spirit: renew the unity of the Church; renew the face of the Earth.

FRIDAY

ACTS 25:13-21 | JOHN 21:15-19

1. Today's Gospel recalls the day when the Risen Lord appointed Peter
    as the leader of the community of his followers. Jesus once identified
    himself as the Good Shepherd who was willing to lay down his life for
    the flock. When his earthly life was over, he appointed Peter to be the
    principal shepherd: "Feed my lambs, feed my sheep." And he predicted
    that Peter also would lay down his life for his beliefs. What we might call
    the interview for the role of leader is unusual. Three times Jesus asked
    him, "Do you love me?" One obvious interpretation of the three times
    links the occasion with the night when Peter had three times denied
    that he had any association with Jesus. The third time Jesus asked him,
    "Do you love me?," Peter was really upset. The probing question moved
    Peter to cast away any mask and to reveal his inner heart. "Lord, you
    know everything; you know that I love you." It was an upsetting process,
    but the Lord used it to help Peter recognise all the loyalty that was deep
    in his heart, though for a time it was hidden under feelings of guilt.

2. The unusual interview used by the Risen Jesus focused on two qualities
    required for Christian leadership. The first quality is a humble awareness
    of one's own frailty. The second quality is love for Jesus, greater than any
    other love. Coupled with this love is absolute trust in the power of the
    Holy Spirit. As we prepare for the Feast of the Coming of the Holy Spirit,
    let us pray for the constant renewal of a Church in humble service and
    trusting love.

PRAYERS

As we come close to the Feast of Pentecost, let us pray with the Response: *Come, O Holy Spirit.*

For Pope *(Name)*, the successor of Saint Peter as the chief shepherd of the flock: may the Holy Spirit fill him with divine wisdom, warm compassion and courage in facing problems.
Come, O Holy Spirit.

That all people in positions of authority might use their power in humble service.
Come, O Holy Spirit.

For all who are burdened with guilt from sins of the past: like Peter, may they experience the loving mercy of the Risen Lord.
Come, O Holy Spirit.

May the Holy Spirit renew the face of the Earth by inspiring all people to put aside the weapons of war and to enable all nations to live in peace.
Come, O Holy Spirit.

(Add prayers for personal, local or topical intentions)

Father of mercy, send your Holy Spirit to cleanse our hearts of sin and to strengthen our love and loyalty. This we ask in the name of Jesus Christ, your Son, our Lord. Amen.

SATURDAY

ACTS 28:16-20. 30-31 | JOHN 21:20-25

1. Tomorrow will be the Feast of Pentecost, the birthday of the Church in the power of the Holy Spirit. Throughout the seven weeks of the Easter season, our daily Gospel has been from Saint John. Today we hear the ending of John's Gospel. The writer vouches for the truth of what he had written. Then he humbly signs off saying that there were many other things that Jesus did, but the whole world would not hold all the books that would have to be written. The fact is that the story of Jesus did not finish at his return to Heaven. The story of Jesus continues in the life of the Church, which is the community of believers, inspired by the Holy Spirit.

2. A wise man once said that his favourite translation of the Gospel was his mother's translation. "She translates it into life." The Bible may be the story of what God did and said in the past, but it is a light on what God is saying and doing in our own time. When we become familiar with the Word of God, we are better able to discern how God is inspiring, questioning, challenging, or consoling us today. The Holy Spirit inspired the writing of the Bible. It is the same Holy Spirit who inspires our reading of the Sacred Text. The Holy Spirit enables us to translate the words into life. On the Eve of Pentecost, let us open up our minds and hearts to the inspiration of the Holy Spirit.

PRAYERS

On the Eve of Pentecost, we invite the Holy Spirit to renew the heart of the Church and the face of the Earth. The Response to the prayers is: *Come, O Holy Spirit.*

When the Holy Spirit came down to the disciples, the Church, as the community of believers, came to life. May the Holy Spirit continue to breathe fresh vitality into the Church.
Come, O Holy Spirit.

May the light of the Holy Spirit show us how to translate the Word of God into how we ought to live.
Come, O Holy Spirit.

May the inspiration of the Holy Spirit move the world's leaders to renew the face of the Earth by ending all wars and enabling all people to live in peace.
Come, O Holy Spirit.

May the Holy Spirit, the Comforter, grant inner strength to all who are suffering in any way.
Come, O Holy Spirit.

(Add prayers for personal, local or topical intentions)

Come, O Spirit of Pentecost. Renew the heart of the Church and renew the face of the Earth. We offer our prayer in the name of Jesus Christ, the Lord. Amen.

ORDINARY TIME

MONDAY

MARK 1:14:20

1. Today we commence reading from Mark's account of the public ministry of Jesus. He proclaimed the Good News from God. "The time has come and the Kingdom of God is at hand. Repent, and believe the Good News." The mission of Jesus will be to inaugurate the reign of God on Earth. For too long, people had been misled into a world of injustice, war, violence and inequality. Now the reign of Satan is about to be challenged by Jesus in word and action. "Repent, and believe the Good News." We are challenged to think again about our values and behaviour. The wrong ways must be replaced by the ideals of Jesus.

2. The ideals of the Kingdom will need a task force to implement them. So, Jesus called disciples who would be the foundation members of the Church in the service of the Kingdom. Casting nets and mending nets represent mission and maintenance, the twin arms of the apostolate. Mission to those not yet in Christ's net. Maintenance in the routine tasks of serving those who are already disciples. Catholic evangelisation has been compared to a fisherman waiting for the fish to jump into the boat. Today's world is becoming increasingly secular. Pope Francis said that Jesus wants evangelisers who proclaim the Good News not only with words, but above all by a life transfigured by God's presence. The charity of works is the unmistakable proof of the charity of words.

PRAYERS

Taking our inspiration from the Word of God, we pray.

Let us pray that the Church will always be faithful to its mission of serving the Kingdom of God.
Lord, hear us.

May the teaching of Christ inspire all people to turn away from injustice and violence so that all people can live in peace, according to God's plan.
Lord, hear us.

As the Apostles bravely followed the call of Christ, may our young people today be open to the call of Christ to dedicate their lives in the service of the Church.
Lord, hear us.

Let us pray for people whose lives are in danger because of their religious beliefs. May their persecution cease.
Lord, hear us.

(Add prayers for any local, personal or topical intention)

God our Father, graciously hear the prayers of your people gathered in the name of Jesus Christ, your Son, our Lord. Amen.

TUESDAY

MARK 1:21-28

1. Jesus began his mission saying that the Kingdom of God is close at hand. "Repent, and believe the Good News". This episode in the synagogue is the first inkling of the great power struggle which took place when Jesus set about repossessing the world from the occupying forces of Evil. He backed up his words with authority shown in works of healing. The exorcism stories are a dramatic way of presenting the divine power and authority of Jesus.

2. Notice how the work of the evil spirit brings about confusion of the mind, frenzied convulsion and loud cries. The Devil's name - *diabolos* - means one who confuses the mind and leads a person astray. In contrast to the noise of the Devil, the work of Jesus is with quiet strength. "Be quiet." In times of distress, return to quiet prayer. Godly power is gentle. True wisdom needs no shouting. "Be still, and know that I am God."

PRAYERS

Encouraged by the divine power shown by Jesus, we pray.

The quiet authority of Jesus brought healing and peace to people who were tormented by inner demons. We pray for all people who are deeply distressed in mind and spirit. May the Lord grant them inner peace.
Lord, hear us.

May the Church serve the Kingdom of God on Earth by proclaiming the Word of God with authority.
Lord, hear us.

In times of distress may we draw strength from the final petition of the Our Father, deliver us from Evil.
Lord, hear us.

May the Lord grant peace to all who suffer from inner demons, anxiety, addiction, uncontrolled temper, obsessions or compulsions.
Lord, hear us.

(Add prayers for any local, personal or topical intention)

Heavenly Father, graciously hear our prayers in the name of Jesus Christ, your Son, our Lord. Amen.

WEDNESDAY

MARK 1:29-39

1. Word spread rapidly that Jesus was healing people. We can understand why people flocked to him, crowding around the door. Jesus was becoming the victim of his own success. Healing people was part of his mission but not the whole story. He needed to get away. Even Jesus felt the need for quiet prayer. Each one of us needs to know where we can find a quiet place or time to sit with God.

2. We begin our day before the mirror, grooming cosmetically to face the world. Try to get some moments of morning prayer to groom yourself spiritually so that you will face the day with a Christian mind and heart. Then, at the end of the day, reflect on what has happened. Think of the graces, the gifts of God, the good experiences of the day now closing. Each night focus for a little while on one particular blessing of that day. One is enough. Then thank God. It sets you up for restful sleep.

PRAYERS

Inspired by the teaching and example of Jesus, we pray.

May the Church continue the mission of Jesus in proclaiming the Kingdom of God on Earth through teaching and healing.
Lord, hear us.

Jesus was a source of healing for people. We bring to him the needs of our family, neighbours and friends who are suffering in body, mind or spirit.
Lord, hear us.

Jesus felt the need to withdraw for quiet prayer. May we develop the habit of finding a quiet place where we can reconnect with God every day.
Lord, hear us.

May the open doors of our churches represent an invitation to come in and find peace in the presence of the Lord.
Lord, hear us.

(Add prayers for any local, personal or topical intention)

God of mercy and compassion, listen graciously to the prayers of your people gathered in the name of Jesus Christ, your Son, our Lord. Amen

THURSDAY

MARK 1:40-45

1. The leper pleaded on his knees, "If you want to, you can cure me." Jesus replied, "Of course I want to!" He stretched out his hand and touched the leper. In this touch, he was acting against all religious and medical protocol. Did Jesus catch leprosy? No, but the leper caught cleanliness. He was cured. Who are the outcasts today? Who are the victims of social prejudice? Who are cast out by the limitations of my charity? The leper I must face is within myself – my prejudices, hardness of heart, and areas of unforgiving.

2. A dishevelled man in a nursing home had a nervous habit of swivelling his head and spit, spit, spit... It was upsetting a burly man who hurled abusive names at him. But a sensitive lady took pity on him, sat beside him and asked his name. No answer except spit, spit, spit... Gently she asked again. This time he repeated the hurtful name the bully had given him. "But what is your real name?" Spit, spit, spit... "Patrick," he answered.
"Do they call you 'Pat'?"
No spit this time: "Yes".
She sat beside him at the next meal.
The following morning he appeared in a clean shirt, his hair groomed. The nervous twitch had gone and the spitting had ceased. "If you want to, you can cure me." Kindness can work miracles.

PRAYERS

As the leper brought his petition to Jesus, we are moved to bring our needs too.

Jesus felt compassion for the leper who was a social outcast. May his Church on Earth show a special concern for the outcasts of today.
Lord, hear us.

We pray for all who work in caring for the sick and elderly. May their hearts be full of compassion and their gentle hands bring God's healing to the sick and handicapped.
Lord, heal us.

May we overcome all fears and inhibitions which block us from reaching out in kindness to others.
Lord, hear us.

We ask you, Lord, to bless and reward all who have been kind to us.
Lord, hear us.

(Add prayers for any local, personal or topical intention)

God of mercy and compassion, look kindly upon your people gathered here in the name of Jesus Christ, your Son, our Lord. Amen.

FRIDAY

MARK 2:1-12

1. Four friends of the crippled man carried him to Jesus. It is an image of how we can carry people to God through prayer. We are not told anything about the faith of the man on the stretcher. What impressed Jesus was the faith of his friends. Very often, when people are sick, they don't have the energy to pray. It is consoling to remember that other people, through their faith, are carrying our petitions to God.

2. Mark is a superb storyteller who draws us into the heart of what is happening. He makes us follow the eyes of Jesus as he sees the different people in the room. Looking down, he saw the crippled man in need of healing in soul and body. Looking up, he saw the friends and their faith. Looking around, he saw the silent critics. Looking within, he saw the faith of some and the negative thoughts of others. Where do I stand in the story? What does Jesus see in me? Am I that weak and helpless person lying on the stretcher? Am I the negative critic and fault-finder? Or am I blessed to be one of the faith-friends who carry people to Jesus in prayer?

PRAYERS

Encouraged by the example of the four friends who brought the crippled man to Jesus, we now bring our needs and the needs of the Church to him.

We pray that people will recognise our churches as houses of divine mercy where people will come to receive God's forgiveness and peace.
Lord, hear us.

Four friends carried the crippled man to Jesus. We carry the needs of family, friends and neighbours to the Lord. (Let us pause for a moment to mention in silent prayer the names of those we carry).
Lord, hear us.

There were people who found reason to be critical of Jesus even when he was healing people. Lord, cleanse us of the negative thoughts that make us critical of others.
Lord, hear us.

Lord, bless and reward the good friends who prayed for us and helped us when we needed their support.
Lord, hear us.

(Add prayers for any local, personal or topical intention)

Heavenly Father, hear the prayers of your people united in the name of Jesus Christ, the Lord. Amen.

SATURDAY

MARK 2:13-17

1. Jesus scandalised the pious people of his day by mixing among sinners and eating with them. The name, Pharisees, means the Separated Ones. They kept themselves separated from any contamination with pagans or people who were regarded as sinners. Sinners were left without hope. Jesus came as the human face of God's mercy. He got close to the sinners and urged them to come close to him. He came, not for the sake of the virtuous, but as a doctor coming to those who are sick. Although we are unworthy, he invites us to his table in the Eucharist.

2. Table-fellowship was hugely significant in olden times. To share food with somebody was a sharing of life. A missionary from Papua New Guinea met a tribe where a hunter might travel for days without eating his catch until there were others to share the food. In today's busy world, some families hardly ever sit together to share food. It's a time of fast-food, the stand-up snack and avoidance of company. Worst of all is the table where people are more interested in Facebook or YouTube than in their companions at the table. The word *companion* comes from the Latin for sharing bread. Food is a gift from God to nourish the body and to nurture relationships.

PRAYERS

In the light of the Word of God, let us pray.

Jesus went out of his way to show sinners that he wanted them as his companions and friends. May all who feel burdened with guilt experience the invitation of Jesus to leave their past behind, and to develop a personal relationship with Jesus as their friend.
Lord, hear us.

The tax collector, Levi, heard the invitation of Jesus to follow him. We pray for vocations, that men and women will respond to God's call to dedicate their lives in his service.
Lord, hear us.

We thank you, Lord, for the food on our tables. We pray that table-fellowship will nurture the unity of families.
Lord, hear us.

We pray for those without food. May the resources of science and wealth be directed towards the provision of food for everybody on this planet.
Lord, hear us.

(Add prayers for any local, personal or topical intention)

God, our heavenly Father, graciously hear the prayers of your people gathered in the name of Jesus Christ, your Son, our Lord. Amen.

MONDAY

MARK 2:18-22

1. There is a time to fast and a time to celebrate. We know that Jesus fasted but he was not in favour of multiplying fasts. There is a temptation to think that salvation depends on the number of Brownie points we can accumulate, instead of depending totally on the mercy of the Saviour who embraces us as a loving spouse in the wedding of Heaven and Earth. As the Letter to the Hebrews states, Jesus can sympathise with us because he too lived in the limitations of human weakness. Many of us were taught how to confess but not how to celebrate God's mercy. The loving mercy of God is more powerful than our merits, our endeavours and our penances. If you believe in Jesus as your Saviour, pass the message up to your face!

2. The parables of the New Patch and the Old Wineskins challenge us. The Spirit of God brings a powerful energy. Am I stuck in a rut? Can I accept that times have changed and changed times need new initiatives? Do I believe in the power of the Holy Spirit to renew the Church in fresh ways? Am I open to new challenges? Do I support efforts at parish renewal? To live is to change and to change often is to grow.

PRAYERS

Enlightened by the Word of God, we pray.

Let us pray that the Church may be open to constant renewal in the power of the Holy Spirit.
Lord, hear us.

Jesus Christ is the bridegroom and the Church is his bride. As members of the Church we are children of God. Lord, fill us with joy as we remember how close you are to us.
Lord, hear us.

Let us pray for people who find change difficult: may they receive the grace to move forward in hope and trust.
Lord, hear us.

May those who are burdened with a huge sense of guilt find peace in the mercy of our loving Saviour.
Lord, hear us.

(*Add prayers for any local, personal or topical intention*)

God of mercy and compassion, graciously hear the prayers we offer in the name of Jesus Christ, your Son, our Lord. Amen.

TUESDAY

MARK 2:23-28

1. Jesus had great respect for laws but he recognised that there was a hierarchy of importance among laws. He saw that an act of kindness or healing was more important than some of the prohibitions set down regarding observance of the Sabbath. What is demanded by charity is more important than rules or precepts of the Church. For instance, it is more important to care for a sick patient than to neglect the patient so as to fulfil the obligation to go to Sunday Mass. "The Sabbath was made for man, not man for the Sabbath."

2. In his Exhortation on the *Joy of the Gospel*, Pope Francis wrote: "In her ongoing discernment, the Church can also come to see that certain customs not directly connected to the heart of the Gospel, even some which have deep historical roots, are no longer properly understood and appreciated. Some of these customs may be beautiful, but they no longer serve as a means of the community of the Gospel. We should not be afraid to re-examine them. The Church has rules or precepts which may have been quite effective in their time, but no longer have the same usefulness for directing and shaping people's lives. Saint Thomas Aquinas pointed out that the precepts which Christ and the apostles gave to the people of God 'are very few'" (*The Joy of the Gospel,* 43). For instance, the custom of "churching" for a mother after childbirth would not be acceptable today.

PRAYERS

In the light of the Scriptural Readings, we pray.

That the Church may not be so caught up in legalism as to neglect the more important demands of compassion and charity.
Lord, hear us.

The Lord's Day is a very important part of the week. Sunday is meant to offer soul-time, family time and time for God. We pray that people will rediscover the importance of the sacred day.
Lord, hear us.

That we might be willing to let go of customs and regulations which have lost their power to serve the Gospel.
Lord, hear us.

   (Add prayers for any local, personal or topical intention)

O God, graciously hear the prayers of your people gathered in the name of Jesus Christ, your Son, our Lord. Amen.

WEDNESDAY

MARK 3:1-6

1. The place was holy: the synagogue was the local house where the people gathered to study the Law and to pray. The day also was holy: the Sabbath was a day of holy restfulness. But the critical attitude of many to the healing work of Jesus was anything but holy. The critics were hoping to find something to use against Jesus. The man with the withered hand represents a withering religion: a severe notion of God; a cold, heartless judgement of others; a legalistic approach without any of the warmth and joy of charity.

2. Jesus was angry. He looked angrily at his silent, obstinate critics. If Jesus could be angry, then anger in itself cannot be always bad. Anger is the proper response to some wrong or injustice. What matters is what we do with anger. Anger is negative when it turns into hatred or violence. But anger is good when it provides the impetus and energy to work for justice or correction of what is wrong.

PRAYERS

We take the teaching and example of Jesus to heart as we pray.

Lord, may our religion be a source of love, joy and peace. Save us from the false religion that breeds withering looks, cold silence and severe judgement of others.
Lord, hear us.

The critics of Jesus began to plot against him. May those who suffer from the scheming of others know that Jesus is on their side as he too was a target for scheming minds.
Lord, hear us.

Lord, help us to control our anger. May anger be a constructive power for justice rather than a destructive power.
Lord, hear us.

Let us pray for the well-being of anybody whom we have hurt by angry words or actions.
Lord, hear us.

(Add prayers for any local, personal or topical intention)

O God of gentle love, hear our prayers offered in the name of Jesus Christ, your Son, our Lord. Amen

THURSDAY

MARK 3: 7-12

1. Great crowds had followed Jesus but he warned the people strongly not to make him known. This is called the messianic secret. There are several suggestions as to why he called for secrecy. One reason is that he did not want to raise false expectations among those who were looking for a military messiah who would lead a revolution against the occupying forces of Rome. Galilee was simmering as a result of multiple forms of taxation and a depressed economy. The area was ready for a call to arms. So, Jesus had to be very careful not to raise false expectations. He certainly did not want to start a war. His intention was to start what Pope Francis called "a revolution of tenderness."

2. The messianic secret is more prominent in Mark's Gospel than in the others. Mark wrote for Christians in Rome who were suffering persecution. Some were raising the question, if this is what Christianity brings us, where is God? The most popular form of literature at that time in Rome was drama. Mark wrote as a dramatist. Throughout his Gospel, Jesus is not recognised as the Son of God until the moment of his death. Then, a Roman centurion was so impressed at the events on Calvary that he said: "In truth this man was Son of God". The drama of Mark's writing is that God's presence was recognised only in the suffering and death of Jesus. Mark's message for a suffering people is that Jesus is here now, with the persecuted people.

PRAYERS

As we take the message of the Gospel to heart, we pray,

Jesus avoided titles of honour and earthly power. May our Church leaders follow his example of humble service.
Lord, hear us.

Great crowds came to Jesus as news of his ministry spread near and far. May the witness of Christian lives draw people to God.
Lord, hear us.

People reached out to touch Jesus in the hope of healing. We reach out to Jesus now in the name of our family, friends and acquaintances who are unwell.
Lord, hear us.

We pray for people suffering persecution because of their religion. May they know that the Lord is with them. May there be a speedy ending to their persecution.
Lord, hear us

(Add prayers for any local, personal or topical intention)

God, our Father, graciously hear our prayers, in the name of Jesus Christ, our Lord. Amen

FRIDAY

MARK 3:13-19

1. The twelve apostles chosen by Jesus were very ordinary folk. From what we know about them, they did not look likely to belong to any prominent religious organisation, much less to be the leaders. Simon Peter, a fisherman, drew his sword on a man and cut off his ear. The brothers, James and John, were named Boanerges, the Sons of Thunder. We get a hint of their fiery characters from the day they asked Jesus would they call down fire from Heaven on an inhospitable Samaritan town. Thomas was stubborn and sceptical. Simon the Zealot belonged to an armed organisation intent on driving out the Romans. Side by side with him was Matthew who had collected taxes for these Romans. In the company of Jesus, political differences melted away: fiery tempers were calmed. Jesus had the eye of the artist, able to see the extraordinary potential of ordinary people.

2. To be an apostle means to be sent out on a mission. The first disciples of Jesus were called as the task force to carry on the mission of Jesus to establish the Kingdom of God on Earth. At our Baptism, we received the candle of light lit from the Paschal Candle which represents the Risen Christ. He said to his followers, "You are the salt of the earth, you are the light of the world". Each one of us must ask... What sort of light am I? Would the world be a darker place without my light? The motto of the Christophers is: if everybody lit just one little candle, what a bright world it would be.

PRAYERS

In the light of our readings of Sacred Scripture, we pray.

For Pope (*name*) and all our bishops who are the successors of the apostles: grant them the wisdom to guide the Church in the service of the Kingdom of God on Earth.
Lord, hear us.

May all of us recognise that we are to be apostles of Jesus Christ. May we be a source of light for those who walk in darkness. May we be the salt preserving what is good and healing what is wrong in our society.
Lord, hear us.

May each one of us be a light of kindness to somebody today.
Lord hear us.

We thank you, Lord, for the people who brought light to us when we needed it. Bless and reward them for their kindness.
Lord, hear us.

(Add prayers for any local, personal or topical intention)

O God, you honour us by calling us to serve in your Kingdom. Hear our prayers offered in the name of your Son, Jesus Christ, the Lord. Amen.

SATURDAY

MARK 3:20-21

1. The crowds around Jesus were so demanding that his relatives began to worry about his well-being. They came to the conclusion that he had taken leave of his senses... bonkers mad... maybe under the power of some evil spirit. Why didn't he stick to his carpentry? His mother must be so embarrassed! To make matters worse, he was being investigated by important people from Jerusalem. It can be difficult for dreamers and idealists who strive to make things happen. No prophet is accepted in his own town.

2. What about Mary among these anxious relatives? Did she think that her son was out of his mind? Not for a moment. Having lived with her son for so many years, she would have known that there were depths of thought in his mind. She never forgot what he had said when he was only twelve years of age about being busy with his Father's affairs. Puzzling words which she and Joseph did not fully understand. She stored it in her heart and pondered on it. She was prepared for the extraordinary events now happening. We do not know if she said anything to the relatives. We see her standing there in silence. It is the sacred silence of faith when faced with mystery.

PRAYERS

With Mary, we ponder on the Word of God and pray.

Mary is mother and model of the Church, the community of believers. May the Church, like Mary, grow in wisdom through pondering on the Word of God.
Lord, hear us.

There were so many demands on Jesus that he had no time to eat. There are many people who are very generous with the time they give to others. Lord, bless them, protect them and reward them.
Lord, hear us.

When people make demands on our time, may we be patient and compassionate.
Lord, hear us.

Sometimes people who have high ideals are victims of mockery and cruel humour. We pray that idealists will have the courage to persevere.
Lord, hear us.

(Add prayers for any local, personal or topical intention)

Loving Father, graciously hear the prayers of the community of believers, offered in the name of Jesus Christ, your Son, our Lord. Amen.

MONDAY

Mark 3:22-30

1. The critics of Jesus were faced with the fact that Jesus was healing people and bringing them peace of mind. They were so hardened in prejudice that they could not accept that the power of Jesus came from God. If not from God, then where did his power come from? They said that his power came from the prince of devils. Jesus pointed out the stupidity of this. The Devil may be evil but is not so stupid as to have his army of spirits warring against one another. Prejudice causes the mind to be so blind that even obvious facts are not accepted. Prejudice hardens the will to the extent that a person is immoveable.

2. What is blasphemy against the Holy Spirit? Why is it the only sin that cannot be forgiven? There is no sin that God is unwilling to forgive. But the grace of forgiveness has to be accepted. Blasphemy against the Holy Spirit is the absolute refusal to accept God's offer of forgiveness. Two statements in John's Gospel offer an explanation. "He came to his own domain and his own people did not accept him" (John 1:11). We have to accept what God offers. The second statement is about rejecting the light. "On these grounds is sentence pronounced: that though the light came into the world, people have shown that they prefer darkness to light because their deeds were evil" (John 3:19). People can become so enslaved in evil ways that they reject God's offer of forgiveness. And that is blasphemy against the Holy Spirit.

PRAYERS

Having reflected on the Gospel, we pray.

May the Church always guide people in the light and truth of Jesus Christ.
Lord, hear us.

Let us pray that people who are slaves to evil ways may turn away from sin and accept the grace of God's forgiveness.
Lord, hear us.

Let us pray for people who are being persecuted on account of their religious beliefs. Grant them inner strength. May those who persecute them turn away from evil and violence.
Lord, hear us.

For any of our family or acquaintances who have turned away from God. May the light of Christ shine through their darkness.
Lord, hear us.

   (Add prayers for any local, personal or topical intention)

Merciful Father, graciously hear the prayers we offer in the name of Jesus Christ, your Son, our Lord. Amen

TUESDAY

MARK 3:31-35

1. Wouldn't it be grand if we could enter a Time Machine and go back to Galilee in the days of Jesus! See him face to face, hear his voice and witness a miracle! Yet, the evidence of the Gospel is that many who did see him and hear him did not believe in him. Some of his relatives thought that he was mad, possibly under the influence of an evil spirit. Gathered around Jesus we see a circle of people listening to him. Outside the immediate circle stand his mother and cousins. Having a relationship with Jesus through faith is more important than actually seeing him in the flesh. "Blessed are those who have not seen but yet believe" (John 20:29). Mary, the Mother of the Lord, is the greatest model of faith.

2. The new family of Jesus is composed of people who hear the Word of God and put it into practice. Saint Teresa of Calcutta developed her apostolate on a simple plan. Meet Jesus in the Blessed Eucharist and then go out to serve Jesus in the poor and dying. At the end of Mass, we are sent out of the church with a mission. Go now to love and serve the Lord.

PRAYERS

Inspired by the light of the Gospel, we pray.

May our local parish be a community of people who listen to the Word of God and are inspired to put the message into action.
Lord, hear us.

We pray for all who feel like spiritual outsiders. They find it hard to pray and have more questions than answers. May the light of the Holy Spirit penetrate their darkness and enable them to believe and to belong.
Lord, hear us.

As we leave the church after Mass, may we be strengthened to bring the presence of Christ to all we meet today.
Lord, hear us.

For any of our family or acquaintances who no longer come to Mass: may the witness of a joyous relationship with God show them what they are missing.
Lord, hear us.

(Add prayers for any local, personal or topical intention)

Merciful Father, graciously hear the prayers of your family gathered here in the name of Jesus Christ, your Son, our Lord. Amen

WEDNESDAY

MARK 4: 1-20

1. The parable of the sower and the seed questions us about how deeply we listen to God and to one another. The lines of a song by Simon and Garfunkel come to mind: "People talking without speaking, people listening without hearing". Jesus described four levels of hearing.

    The seed on the edge of the path is a message that comes in one ear and out the other. Nothing has registered.

    After Mass can I remember anything that was read? The seed on rocky ground represents shallow listening. Something registers for a little while but is soon forgotten.

    The seed choked by thorns represents our good intentions which are choked by material concerns and preoccupations.

    Finally, the seed lands in good soil and it grows and bears fruit. The instruction of Jesus is, "Listen, anyone who has ears to hear!"

2. The seed is the Word of God. When one looks at a small, shrivelled, dead-looking seed, it is hard to imagine that this little thing is a source of life. It has the potential to become a flower or a vegetable, or a stalk of wheat, maybe a tree. But the seed is no use if it is left in the paper packet. It is dynamic only when it is buried in the soil. The Word of Scripture is not dynamic if it is left on the paper page. It has to be planted in the earth of life. Because our scriptures were written long ago and in a very different culture, at first sight they may appear dead and irrelevant. But taken in faith, Scripture is a dynamic seed that questions, shapes and directs life. Approach the Bible with the expectation that this Word of God is just what I need today. Have patience and allow it time to take root.

PRAYERS

As we are challenged by the parable of the seeds, we pray.

O God, we thank you for your life-giving Word. May the teaching of the Church always guide us according to your Word.
Lord, hear us.

May the Holy Spirit who inspired the writers of Sacred Scripture continue to inspire us as we listen to the sacred Word.
Lord, hear us.

We pray that the sacred words we hear may take root in our lives to bring forth the fruits of Christian life.
Lord, hear us.

May our minds and hearts be attentive to people so that we might really hear what they are saying or trying to say.
Lord, hear us.

(Add prayers for any local, personal or topical intention)

God, our Father, hear the prayers we offer in the name of Jesus Christ, the Word made flesh. Amen

THURSDAY

MARK 4: 21-25

1. Today's Gospel can be summarised in a few words: pass on the light. The light of God came into the world in Jesus Christ. Then he told his followers, "You are the light of the world, you are the salt of the earth". He didn't say "You shall become". No, he said "you are the light already". Don't be afraid to let it shine. A movement called the Christophers use the motto, "Better to light one candle than to curse the darkness". There may be somebody in a dark place at the moment who can be reached by nobody else but you. It's amazing really, but God is counting on you to bring light to that person. If everyone lit just one little candle, what a bright world it would be.

2. One of the many gems of wisdom used in the A.A. Fellowship is the message: "You keep your sobriety by giving it away". Helping another person increases our own resolve. It is the same with faith. When we openly share our spiritual life with another person, especially if we help that person, we find that our own faith is strengthened. It is in giving that we receive. Pass on the light.

PRAYERS

Taking our light from the Word of God, we pray.

May the Church be true to its mission to be the light of the nations.
Lord, hear us.

Through the witness of our life, may we be bringers of light to people who are in a dark space at the moment.
Lord, hear us.

Thank you Lord, for those who have been a light to us in any way. Bless and reward them.
Lord, hear us.

Lord, take away our fears so that we will always have the courage to stand up for our Christian ideals.
Lord, hear us.

(Add prayers for any local, personal or topical intention)

Merciful Father, graciously hear the prayers we offer in the name of Jesus Christ, the Lord. Amen

FRIDAY

MARK 4: 26-34

1. Technology has changed our lives in many ways. We have light, heat and music at the flick of a switch; instant communication with any part of the world; a tablet for virtually any pain. And yet, there are times when there is no instant answer. We need patience. Jesus looked to the fields for a parable on the subject. A lot happens between planting and harvesting so the farmer has to let nature take its course. The growth of God's Kingdom goes through times of great progress and periods of spiritual recession, day and night. We are in a spiritual winter now in Western Europe, but there are other regions where religion is flourishing. In the garden, winter enriches the earth as frost hastens the decay of compost. We must trust in God's providence that our spiritual winter will bring about a healthier Church.

2. Small seeds can grow into mighty trees, but it takes time. Many people are distressed at the changes for worse in society. Yet there are many signs of improvement... in care for the planet, concern for justice, involvement of people in parish ministry, prayer groups and love of the Bible. It's not all bad news. Church history shows that the worst of times produced the greatest saints and reformers. Trust in God who will not be short of an answer.

PRAYERS

Taking the Word of God to heart, we pray.

May the Church be like a fertile field receiving the seeds of God's Word and, in time, producing a rich harvest.
Lord, hear us.

We pray for people who feel overwhelmed by scandals and bad news. May their eyes be opened to the goodness and kindness of people all around us.
Lord, hear us.

May our television, radio and newspapers give more publicity to the Good News and highlight the inspirational stories of those who plant the seeds of goodness.
Lord, hear us.

We may never perform heroic deeds, but let the tiny seed we can sow improve the quality of life for people.
Lord, hear us.

(Add prayers for any local, personal or topical intention)

O God, master of the harvest, hear the prayers we offer in the name of Jesus Christ, the Lord. Amen.

SATURDAY

MARK 4: 35-41

1. Some years ago, we had the Year of Faith. On all posters and documents, the logo for the year was the boat in a storm, today's Gospel. It was a very appropriate image of the Church in our times. In the storm-tossed boat, Jesus was asleep. To many, it seems that God is asleep and not hearing our prayers. The apostles were frightened. When they woke Jesus, he asked, "Why were you frightened? How is it that you have no faith?" Our faith is tested in times of scandals and storms. One writer said that in his reading of History, there were five times when the Church had gone to the dogs... but it was the dogs who died! "Be still and know that I am God."

2. Julian of Norwich lived in the 14th Century. She suffered serious illness for years. The population of Europe was decimated after a succession of plagues. There were revolts and wars everywhere. The Church was in a frightful mess. Talk about the boat in a storm! Dame Julian received a simple revelation from God. God showed her a little thing, the size of a hazelnut, in the palm of his hand. "What can this be," she wondered. God answered: "It is all that is made". She reflected: "It lasts and always will because God loves it. And in the same way, everything has its being through the love of God." He's got the whole world in his hand and he won't let us down.

PRAYERS

Mindful of God's eternal love, we pray.

The Church is a boat on stormy seas at the moment. May we never lose faith in the presence of the Lord, even when he seems to be asleep.
Lord, hear us.

For people who are suffering persecution because of their religion: may they draw courage from remembering that God is with them.
Lord, hear us.

When our lives are tossed about in turmoil, may we draw hope and courage as we remember that God, our loving Creator, is always holding us on his loving hand.
Lord, hear us.

Let us pray for people who have lost hope. May the light of God's love shine into their darkness.
Lord, hear us.

(Add prayers for any local, personal or topical intention)

O God, our loving Creator, hold us in the palm of your hand as we pray in the name of Jesus Christ, your Beloved Son, our Lord. Amen.

MONDAY

MARK 5:1-20

1. When Mark wrote his Gospel, his immediate audience was the Christian community in Rome which was suffering persecution. The most popular form of literature in Rome was drama. Mark described the pacifying of the demented man as a dramatic conflict with evil spirits. Their name was Legion, the same as a battalion of the Roman army. Mark was clearly linking the story with the violent persecution of Christians in Rome. By the power of Jesus, this evil legion was so utterly defeated that they had no place to hide. Even the pigs refused to shelter them! It is a story of great drama, with the message to put total trust in Jesus, whose power is so much greater than that of any army of evil spirits.

2. In biblical times, any mental disturbance was regarded as possession by an evil spirit. Nowadays, medical science would diagnose it as an illness. Yet, people frequently refer to their problems as their inner demons: uncontrolled rage, addiction, slavery to pornography, inner darkness, constant pessimism, greed, uncharitable judging and suchlike behaviour. The good news is that the power of prayer brings us the grace of Jesus, who brought peace and self-control to demented people. Three steps towards healing are Name, Tame and Re-Aim. Name the problem with the humble admission that it is out of control. Tame it by handing it over to God, maybe hundreds of times every day. Then, with God's support, re-aim life to walk with Jesus every day. In the Gospel story, the man who was seriously demented became a missionary proclaiming all that Jesus had done.

PRAYERS

Drawing confidence from the healing power of Jesus, we pray.

Christ has the power to overcome all evil forces. Let us pray for the Christians who are being persecuted by evil legions today.
Lord, hear us.

For all who are struggling with any addiction or inner demon which they cannot control: may they hand it over to God every day and walk in his strength.
Lord, hear us.

We pray for the families who live with unhappy people who cause great upsets at home. Grant them the serenity to accept the things they cannot change.
Lord, hear us.

Everyone was amazed at the power of Jesus. May we reflect in amazement at all that he has done for us.
Lord, hear us.

(Add prayers for any local, personal or topical intention)

Heavenly Father, lead us not into temptation and deliver us from Evil, through Christ, our Lord. Amen.

TUESDAY

MARK 5:21-43

1. These two miracles reveal the divine power of Jesus. He is the Saviour or Saver who can save the life that is wasting away. And he can restore life to the dead. We can apply the power of Jesus to our moral life. Our spiritual life bleeds away as a haemorrhage when guilt drags us down, fears paralyse us, negative thinking darkens the mind, past failures puncture hope. Conversion begins when we reach out and touch the Lord as he goes by. Jesus can also restore life to those who are spiritually dead. He has the power but we must make the first step by reaching out to touch him in faith and confidence. "Your faith has restored you to health; go in peace and be free from your complaint."

2. In this account of the two miracles, there are eight references to hands or touching. Saint John Paul II in his youth wrote a poem about hands. It began, "Hands are the heart's landscape". He was looking at his own tired hands after a day of heavy work in a stone quarry. If I were to meditate on my hands, what would I see? Are they like a fist, hard, hurtful and violent? Knotted in tension and self-protection? Grasping, greedy, pampered? Or do I rejoice to see hands that are open, welcoming, soothing, caring? Artistic, creative, playful? Hands that join together in prayer as the energies of life are united and point upwards towards Heaven? The hands of Jesus welcomed, touched, lifted up and restored life. He has no hands now but ours.

PRAYERS

The healing power of Jesus gives us the confidence to pray.

Lord, we ask you to come to our family members and neighbours who are sick. Lay your hands gently upon them and restore them to health.
Lord, hear us.

Too often our prayers are half-hearted and distracted. Grant us the sort of faith that make us really reach out to touch the Lord and release his power.
Lord, hear us.

We pray for all who work in medical care. May they be aware that they are the hands of God for their patients. May they treat every patient with Christian dignity.
Lord, hear us.

(Add prayers for any local, personal or topical intention)

O God of life and love, hear the prayers we offer in the name of Jesus Christ, our Lord and Saviour. Amen.

WEDNESDAY

MARK 6:1-6

1. *The Valley of Squinting Windows* was the catchy title of a novel by Brinsley MacNamara. Its dominant theme was local begrudgery. A prophet is only despised in his own town, among his neighbours. The problem is as old as humanity. Even Jesus was the object of local negativity. Most of the locals were astonished when they heard him. They were amazed at his miracles. Yet their small minds and bitter hearts found reasons to reject him. If you feel that you are not properly understood or appreciated, then you are in good company because it happened to Jesus. We have to ask ourselves how much we appreciate our neighbours. There are people who are emotionally drained because of lack of affirmation. Do we take the goodness of others for granted? Show them your appreciation, thank them, affirm them. It can mean so much to people.

2. Nazareth took people by surprise. Never mentioned in the Old Testament. A migrant workers' town, for tradesmen and labourers building the new city of Sepphoris for Herod. Could anything good come from Nazareth? How could the Messiah come from such an unimportant place? Who could have imagined the long-awaited Messiah working at a carpenter's bench? God's ways are not always our ways. God's presence is here for us in the ordinary matters of daily life... at the work desk, the kitchen sink, in the people I meet. May God open our eyes to recognise his presence in the ordinary events of life.

PRAYERS

Mindful of God's presence everywhere, we pray.

Let us pray for our local parish: that the talents of people may be recognised and used for the service of the local community.
Lord, hear us.

May the grace of God free us from envy and begrudgery which poison our acceptance of others.
Lord, hear us.

Let us pray for people who are bullied and who are never thanked or appreciated for what they do.
Lord, hear us.

Open our eyes to the goodness of people we meet every day. Let us not take them for granted. May we offer them appreciation and gratitude.
Lord, hear us.

(Add prayers for any local, personal or topical intention)

O God, the giver of every good gift, graciously hear our prayers in the name of Jesus Christ, your Son, our Lord. Amen.

THURSDAY

MARK 6:7-13

1. When Jesus sent out the apostles to extend his mission, he said more about their lifestyle than about what they should preach. As Saint Francis put it, preach at all times, sometimes using words. What you are thunders so loudly that I cannot hear what you are saying. We are so bombarded today with advertising pressure, slogans and biased media that people are rightly suspicious of words. Pope Paul VI pointed out that if people today listen to evangelisers, it is because first they are witnesses. What sort of witness did Jesus emphasise for the apostles? Don't be burdened with unnecessary accumulation of goods. Cooperate with others. Trust in God's providence and trust in the goodness of others. Bring peace and joy to all you meet. Avoid confrontation. Let the joy of your personal relationship with God pass the message up to your face. What Pope Francis called "sourpuss religion" would put anybody off. The charity of works is the unmistakable proof of the charity of words.

2. What can you do to bring a family member back to religion? Angry confrontation usually does more harm than good. Does anybody ever win an argument? Getting in the last word is never a sign of convincing the other person. The louder the voices, the more each side is hardened in their opinion. Nobody is ever convinced without first being open to a change of opinion. Loud exchanges close the door to any change of heart. That is why Jesus instructed the apostles: "If people refuse to listen to you, walk away and shake off the dust from under your feet as a sign to them". What can you do? Be gentle. Respect the other person, even if you do not agree. Give witness by how you live, trust in God and pray. Change of heart has to take place before there is change of mind. And change of heart takes time.

PRAYERS

Taking to heart the instructions of Jesus to the apostles, we pray.

May the witness of the leaders of the Church avoid the pitfalls of triumphalism and legalism. May the holiness of the Church be seen in lives of humility and simplicity, in reverence towards God and deep respect for one another.
Lord, hear us.

May we be bringers of peace to every house we enter.
Lord, hear us.

May the Holy Spirit guide us in the delicate matter of instructing others.
Lord, hear us.

The apostles were sent out with the healing power of Jesus. We bring to God the names of our family and acquaintances who are ill. (Silent pause).
Lord, hear us.

(Add prayers for any local, personal or topical intention)

God of tender compassion, hear our prayers, in the name of Jesus Christ, your Son, our Lord. Amen.

FRIDAY

MARK 6:14-29

1. Herod's family background was partly pagan and partly Jewish. It probably suited his political career to have a foot in both camps. But the result was that he was neither one nor the other. As Jesus remarked, you cannot serve two masters. Herod arrested John because he had condemned Herod's marriage to his own brother's wife. Yet, the Jewish side of his personality made him fear John because he recognised him as a good and holy man. And he liked to listen to John. He was seriously mixed up. Herod clearly had an interest in spiritual matters but he sat on the fence without making a commitment. There's a growing number of people who settle for religiosity rather than religion. Religiosity has an interest in spiritual matters with making a commitment. "I am very spiritual but I am not religious." Saint John Paul II wrote that it is a contradiction of Christianity to settle for a life of mediocrity, marked by a minimalistic ethic and a shallow religiosity. The Book of Revelation has a warning for the people of Laodicea. "Since you are neither hot nor cold, but only lukewarm, I will spit you out of my mouth." Credo, I believe, means "I give my heart to God," not just passing a passing interest.

2. There is a time to confront and a time to avoid confrontation. Reflecting on yesterday's Gospel we suggested that there are times when confrontation does more harm than good. But there are other times when it is necessary to confront openly. For Evil to triumph, all that is needed is for good people to stay silent. There is great wisdom in the Serenity Prayer. "God grant me the serenity to accept the things I cannot change; the courage to change the things I can; and the wisdom to know the difference."

PRAYERS

Reflecting on today's Gospel, we pray.

As members of the Catholic Church, may we be committed believers, giving ourselves 100% to Christian beliefs and morals.
Lord, hear us.

May all Christian politicians have the courage to stand up for the Christian ideals which protect life and family stability.
Lord, hear us.

John the Baptist and thousands of martyrs suffered death for their religion. We pray for those who are being persecuted today. Lord, grant them great inner strength. And may the injustice of persecution soon cease.
Lord, hear us.

May people who have become half-hearted in their religion wake up to the seriousness of having God in their lives.
Lord, hear us.

(Add prayers for any local, personal or topical intention)

O God, the beginning and end of life, graciously hear our prayers in the name of Jesus Christ, your Son, our Lord. Amen

SATURDAY

MARK 6:30-34

1. "Come apart to a quiet place all by yourselves and rest for a while."
    The apostles had been very busy so Jesus recommended a rest from
    activity. Come away... to a quiet place... rest a little. Unless we come
    apart, we run the risk of being torn apart. We all need moments to
    reconnect... to rejoin Jesus. Obviously coming to Mass is a good way...
    visiting a church... sitting in silence for a while. Find out what works
    for you. Where can you find the quiet space where you can be alone
    with God? God won't mind if you are sipping a cup of coffee! Come and
    find rest for your soul.

2. The busy apostles had no time even to eat. In spite of all the labour-saving
    devices we have today, people were never so busy. The hectic world of
    business is dominated by four P-words: profit, productivity, pace and
    pressure. The four F-words (good F-words!) are under pressure: family,
    friends, festival and fun. When work dominates, even recreation is called
    a workout. Little things matter a lot, like eating with others instead of a
    hurried snack alone, sitting at a table instead of standing, using a teapot
    rather than a bag-in-cup, placing a saucer under a cup. Ban phones from
    the table! People were like sheep without a shepherd so Jesus set out to
    teach them at some length. What the world needs are people of vision,
    contemplatives who can lead the aimless sheep: people of true holiness
    and wisdom to restore the big picture of life's meaning.

PRAYERS

Let us take up the invitation of Jesus to come apart to pray.

The people were like sheep without a shepherd so Jesus set out to teach them. May the Church continue his work by guiding people to the One who is the Way, the Truth and the Life.
Lord, hear us.

May we accept the invitation of Jesus to treasure the quiet moments when we sit with him and find peace.
Lord, hear us.

For people who are torn apart by pressure, fear or anxiety. May they learn how to come apart to rest awhile in that peace which only God can give.
Lord, hear us.

May our homes be tabernacles of God's presence and centres of peace.
Lord, hear us.

(Add prayers for any local, personal or topical intention)

God, our Father, graciously hear the prayers of your people gathered in the name of Jesus Christ, your Son, our Lord. Amen.

MONDAY

MARK 6:53-56

1. In Mark's Gospel, it is amazing how often Jesus touches others and allows himself to be touched. Somebody who begs is known as a toucher. And Jesus is somebody who would be regarded as a soft touch because of his compassion with the poor and suffering. Pope Francis wrote about the closeness of Jesus to people. He looked into their eyes with deep understanding. He looked at the rich young man and loved him. He drew near to the blind man. He touched the leper. He ate and drank with people who were regarded as sinners. He allowed a woman who had been given a bad name to wash his feet with her tears. He was sensitive to Nicodemus' position in the Jewish Council so he received him at night. To be a true follower of Christ one must share the lives of others, listening to their concerns, helping them materially and spiritually in their needs, rejoicing with those who rejoice, weeping with those who weep. Arm in arm with others, we are committed to building a new world. (Pope Francis: *The Joy of the Gospel*, 269)

2. It is a temptation to be the sort of pious Christian who wants the comfort of a purely spiritual Christ, while keeping aloof from other people and their demands. As a character in the Peanuts cartoon said, "I love humanity: it's people I can't stick". Quoting Pope Francis: "Sometimes we are tempted to be that kind of Christian who keeps the Lord's wounds at length. Yet Jesus wants us to touch human misery, to touch the suffering of others". While giving a few coins to a poor person on the street, it means so much more if we make eye contact with the person, say a few words, and hand the money rather than throw it into a cap or a box. The personal contact might mean more than the coins. (Pope Francis: *The Joy of the Gospel*, 88 & 270)

PRAYERS

Like the people in the Gospel, we reach out to touch the Lord in prayer for all our needs.

May the Church always be a hospital of compassion and peace for all who have been wounded in the battlefield of life.
Lord, hear us.

We join our prayers with those of the people who are reaching out to the Lord for healing.
Lord, hear us.

We ask God to work through the hands of those in the caring profession. May their touch be welcoming, warm and full of care for all their patients.
Lord, hear us.

For people who have been the victims of inappropriate touching: may they be released from their hurt and enabled to move forward in life.
Lord, hear us.

(Add prayers for any local, personal or topical intention)

God, our Father, you have shown us the face of mercy in the life of your Son, Jesus Christ. Graciously hear the prayers we offer in his name. Amen.

TUESDAY

Mark 7:1-13

1. Jesus was deeply disturbed by the travesty of religion enmeshed in legalism. "You put aside the Commandments of God to cling to human traditions." In the life of the Church, human regulations brought in eminent titles, episcopal palaces, expensive garments, cold protocol and other trappings of power which may have been meaningful in their time but are off-putting for people today. The Church is not meant to be a museum of dead fossils. Jesus set up a Church to be missionary, to be with the people, giving them meaning, hope, direction, compassion and God's love above all. We must not be afraid to let go of obsolete customs or rules in order to be more relevant to the needs of our time. The guiding challenge must always be, what would Jesus do? What would Jesus say? Would Jesus recognise the Church today as the Church that he set up?

2. "This people honours me with their lip service while their hearts are far from me." Sometimes we have too many words in prayer. It can happen that prayers get in the way of prayer! A spate of words allows no time for listening. Here is some good advice for prayer: less lip and more heart. Allow time for the fourteen-inch drop, from the brain to the heart.

PRAYERS

Guided by the teaching of Jesus in word and example, we pray.

That the Church might be free of any sort of legalism or bureaucracy that would get in the way of compassion and human understanding.
Lord, hear us.

We pray for people who resist any kind of change. Enable them to see the difference between the unchangeable law of God and the human traditions, which meant a lot in the past, but are no longer helpful.
Lord, hear us.

We ask God for the grace of deep prayer: that we might grow in a heart-to-heart relationship with God.
Lord, hear us.

(Add prayers for any local, personal or topical intention)

God, our Father, graciously hear the prayers we offer in the name of Jesus Christ, your Son, our Lord. Amen.

WEDNESDAY

MARK 7:14-23

1. Jesus called the people to him and asked them to do two things: listen and understand. We listen to the Word of God when we read the Bible or when we hear it read, just as we are doing here at Mass. Listen with a desire to hear God's Word. Listen, and then understand. The best way to understand is to reverse the word... *stand-under*. Stand under God's Word as a light on life. The Word of God questions us, challenges us, corrects us, directs us and puts shape on our lives. In today's Gospel Jesus has a gem of wisdom. "Nothing that goes into a person from outside can make him unclean. It is things that come out of a person which show whether somebody is clean and beautiful within".

2. Cleanliness is next to godliness. The proverb is not referring to the absence of a bit of dirt under the fingernails. The cleanliness that makes a person like God is in the heart. A clean heart inspires a life of kindness and compassion, and works of justice and helpfulness. But what comes out of the unclean heart is a list of moral ugliness. Jesus gave us a list of twelve evil fruits of the heart. Fornication, theft, murder, adultery, avarice, malice, deceit, indecency, envy, slander, pride and folly which means denial of God's existence. This list sounds like the promotion of a television series. A wise writer in the Old Testament tells us that charm is deceitful and beauty is vain. Outer beauty is desirable but what matters far more is what we are in the sight of God.

PRAYERS

Mindful of the teaching of Jesus, we pray.

May the Church be always guided by the Holy Spirit in bringing the light of God's Word to all nations.
Lord, hear us.

May we stand under the light of God's Word when we seek direction in life.
Lord, hear us.

We pray for people who have gone astray. May the light of God shine through their darkness and draw them home to God.
Lord, hear us.

May we co-operate with the grace of God in the ongoing conversion of our hearts from being self-centred, judgmental and hurtful.
Lord, hear us.

(Add prayers for any local, personal or topical intention)

O God of light and love, hear our prayers offered in the name of Jesus Christ, your Son, our Lord. Amen.

THURSDAY

MARK 7:24-30

1. The story of healing is serious business but there is playfulness here too. The distraught mother who came to Jesus was a pagan. Jews regarded themselves as the specially chosen children of God. Other people were sometimes referred to as dogs, good friends maybe, but not family. Calling somebody a dog sounds racist and offensive to our ears but there is a hint of humour in the exchange between Jesus and the mother. We need to appreciate that serious religious teaching by means of humour was common among Jews. Maybe the tone of voice was playful and took all offence out of it. The tone said more than the words. The woman is smart enough to enter the game. "Ah yes, sir, but the house-dogs under the table can eat the children's scraps". Whereupon, Jesus gave her the happy news of the healing of her daughter. Serious, yet playful. It is important to take God seriously. But enjoy God's playfulness too. Think of Saint Teresa of Avila, falling into the river and saying to God, "If that is the way you treat your friends, no wonder you have so few of them!"

2. Scraps, crumbs from the table. The mother had such trust in Jesus that the smallest crumb from his hand would be enough. Somebody might not have a great brain or the ability to understand big words, yet a few little scraps from the Lord's teaching can be the basis of a great faith. It often happens that an uneducated person has more wisdom than somebody with lots of brains.

PRAYERS

Encouraged by the story in the Gospel, we pray.

May the Church be like Christ in appreciating the goodness of people regardless of their religion.
Lord, hear us.

Free us from prejudice which would make us reject people on the grounds of race, colour or religion.
Lord, hear us.

May our relationship with God be at once serious and playful.
Lord, hear us.

May the Lord who answered the pagan mother's plea for the healing of her daughter hear our prayers for our sick relatives, neighbours and friends.
Lord, hear us.

(Add prayers for any local, personal or topical intention)

O God, the giver of every good gift, graciously hear the prayers we offer in the name of Jesus Christ, your Son, our Lord. Amen.

FRIDAY

MARK 7:31-37

1. The actions of Jesus in touching the ears and mouth of the deaf-mute may be repeated in the ceremony of Baptism. This prayer accompanies the action: "The Lord Jesus made the deaf hear and the dumb speak. May he soon touch your ears to receive his word, and your mouth to proclaim his faith, to the praise and glory of God the Father." My ears have been sanctified but do I keep them open to God's Word, listening to it, reading it and pondering on it? Am I open to what other people are saying? Do I try to hear what they find hard to say? Do I hear the pleas of those in need? Or do I have ears that are itching for scandal?

2. In Baptism, my mouth was sanctified for the praise and glory of God. Are my words worthy of a baptised Christian? A poisoned tongue spits out cynicism, deceit, hurt, character assassination, anger and blasphemy. Does the tongue which receives Jesus in the Eucharist profane his holy name? My tongue has been sanctified to spread good news of love, peace, consolation, gratitude, prayer and laughter. We have the choice of using our tongues for blasphemy, obscenity and hurt or to be the instrument of thanks, praise and prayer.

PRAYERS

Our blessed ears have heard the Gospel of the Lord and now our blessed tongues express our petitions in prayer.

May the leaders of the Church deeply ponder the Word of God so that their teaching might be an inspiration to the whole world.
Lord, hear us.

We thank you, Lord, for sanctifying our ears and mouth in the Sacrament of Baptism. May our ears be open to what is good but closed to what is harmful.
Lord, hear us.

May our gift of speech never be abused in profanity and scandal. Rather, may our tongue be organs of faith, hope and love.
Lord, hear us.

Let us pray for people who have problems with hearing or impediments of speech. May God bless them with great inner strength.
Lord, hear us.

(Add prayers for any local, personal or topical intention)

O God, our Creator, you have endowed us with many great gifts. Hear our prayers in the name of Christ, our Lord. Amen.

SATURDAY

MARK 8:1-10

1. For three days people had stayed with Jesus but now they had run out of food. Were they impractical people, careless, or bad planners? Or was it that they were so caught up and passionate about Jesus that they overlooked the need to get provisions? Let us accept that it was their passion for the teaching of Jesus that caused them to forget. The American humorist, Dom Marquis, wrote a poem about his friend Archy the Cockroach and a moth. The moth is so attracted to light that he was trying to break into an electric light bulb to fry himself on the wires. Archy the Cockroach does not agree with the moth but he admits: "I don't agree with him... but at the same time I wish there was something I wanted as badly as he wanted to fry himself." Maybe that explains why the people overlooked their lack of provisions. The words of Jesus were feeding all sorts of hungers of the soul, so much so that, for some time, they forgot the hunger of the body.

2. The actions of Jesus as he took, he blessed, he broke and he gave, anticipated the institution of the Eucharist at the Last Supper. Jesus felt sorry for the hungry crowd who had stayed on to listen to him and he fed them by the miraculous multiplication of the seven loaves. This anticipated his compassion for us in all our spiritual needs on the pilgrimage of life. And so, he chose to remain among us in the Bread of Life, his flesh to eat and his blood to drink, the blood of the new covenant.

PRAYERS

Jesus felt sorry for the people so he fed them by the miraculous multiplication of the seven loaves. We are inspired to pray.

The Church has always been in the forefront of caring for the poor and hungry. May the rich world listen to the Church's teaching about a fair sharing of the world's resources.
Lord, hear us.

We thank the Lord for the gift of the Eucharist. May our faith in the Lord's presence grow ever deeper. May the Bread of Life be a constant source of strength.
Lord, hear us.

We pray for family members and acquaintances who no longer come to the Eucharist. May they come to realise what they are missing.
Lord, hear us.

Jesus told the apostles to gather up what was left over. May we be careful not to waste food as that is a form of robbing the poor and hungry.
Lord, hear us.

(Add prayers for any local, personal or topical intention)

Thank you, Father, for all your gifts and graciously hear the prayers we offer in the name of Jesus Christ, our Lord. Amen

MONDAY

Mark 8:11-13

1. The critics of Jesus were demanding a sign from Heaven to test him. Jesus knew that any sign would make no difference as they had closed their minds about him. They had even suggested that his miraculous powers came from an evil source. What can you do with people who are totally locked up in negative prejudice? You can always pray for them. Confrontational arguments rarely do any good. Change of mind will never occur unless there is some possibility of change of heart. There were some occasions when Jesus did enter into debate with his critics. But in this instance, he sensed that his critics were so prejudiced that there was no chance of moving them. He gave a sigh straight from the heart and said: "Why does this generation demand a sign? No sign will be given to them." Then he left them where they were. They were not prepared to listen.

2. The miracles of Jesus were called signs: signs to fill the mind with wonder and move the heart to believe. Jesus gave many signs full of wonder. The world is full of wonder for those who have eyes to see. The vast expanse of the universe; the intricate cycle of the seasons; the beauty of the Earth – these are signs of the artwork of God. The life of Jesus reveals the wonder of the face of mercy. The lives of the Saints manifest the wonder of the power of the Holy Spirit. As G.K. Chesterton said, the world is not lacking in wonders but in *wonderment*. In order to believe, one must have a mind open to wonder.

PRAYERS

In the light of the Word of God, we pray,

May the Church at all times be a living witness to the ideals and compassion of Christ.
Lord, hear us.

That we might be free of blind prejudice which would prevent us from seeing and hearing with open minds and hearts.
Lord, hear us.

That we might have the grace to stop criticising people, always looking for faults, putting a negative spin on anything they do.
Lord, hear us.

Let us pray for people who have been hurt by criticism. May they find the grace to forgive and to move on from their hurts.
Lord, hear us.

   (Add prayers for any local, personal or topical intention)

O God, the source of all wonder and beauty, graciously hear the prayers we offer in the name of Jesus Christ, our Lord. Amen.

TUESDAY

MARK 8:14-21

1. Today's Gospel is about forgetting and remembering. The apostles had forgotten to take any food and they had only one loaf with them in the boat. What they were forgetting was that in Jesus they had the greatest food of all, the Bread of Life in person. Jesus leads them on playfully. "What do you mean, no bread? Have you no perception, no understanding? Are your eyes closed and your ears clogged? Remember the times I fed the multitudes. Remember the baskets you filled with leftovers." The miracles of Jesus in multiplying bread and wine prepared the disciples to believe what he said at the Last Supper... "This is my body"... "This is my blood, the blood of the new covenant." Then he said, "Do this in memory of me." The celebration of Eucharist is rooted in memory. Ritual celebrations keep memory alive. The Lord has invited us here to share in the merits of his death and to rise with him in glorifying the Father.

2. When a nation loses its native language, it loses its memory, identity and legitimate pride. People familiar with Irish history can recognise the depressed condition of the Irish nation in the 19th Century after the rape of the native language and culture. Today we are witnessing the emergence of a post-Christian people who have lost their Christian language and identity. It is a form of spiritual Alzheimer's. The names of God or Jesus have lost sacred meaning. The President of a nation can give a Christmas message without mentioning Christ. Sunday is for sport or shopping. Easter is a spring holiday. Children are coming into school without knowing a single prayer. The Jews have a saying that God has no grandchildren. If religion is not passed on by the parents, the next generation is lost to the Church. "Do this in memory of me." Remember, lest we forget.

PRAYERS

Listening to the Readings at Mass keeps our memory alive. So, we pray.

May the voice of the Church keep the memory of Jesus Christ fresh in the minds of people.
Lord, hear us.

May the memory of the miracles of Jesus in multiplying the bread and wine strengthen our faith in the presence of the Lord in the Blessed Eucharist.
Lord, hear us.

We pray that all parents will instruct their children in religious faith and prayer.
Lord, hear us.

May people who have lost their religious memory remember the Lord and his teaching, and allow themselves to be found by the Good Shepherd.
Lord, hear us.

   (Add prayers for any local, personal or topical intention)

O God, the giver of every good gift, thank you for the gift of memory. Hear our prayers in the name of Jesus Christ, your Son, our Lord. Amen.

WEDNESDAY

MARK 8:22-26

1. CYCLE A

The healing of the blind man is different to the other miracles of Jesus. It is not done in an instant by the touch or word of Jesus. It is a gradual process. The word *gradual* comes from the Latin word for a step. Gradual means step by step. Even when the man began to see, it was in a very imperfect way. "I can see people: they look like trees to me, but they are walking about." Jesus laid his hands on the man's eyes again, and then he saw clearly. This step-by-step description represents stages of growing in faith. Pope Francis drew from his pastoral experience among people when he recognised the little step somebody took, although it was far short of total orthodoxy. Forms of popular piety might be frowned on by rigid theologians but they are very important to some people. A person may not be ready to make the full journey of faith but even one small step is very important.

2. CYCLE B

The Letter of Saint James points to a way we can grow in faith. "Accept and submit to the Word which has been planted in you." The seed of faith is in us from the day of Baptism. The seed has to be nurtured in our earthly, everyday lives. The Word of God is like a mirror revealing what we look like. It shows up where we have to improve. Saint James gives two important areas to work on: control of our tongues and practical assistance to those who need help.

PRAYERS

Enlightened by the Sacred Readings, we pray.

May the Church be a light to all nations, proclaiming the wisdom of God by word and action.
Lord, hear us.

Sacred Scripture is a mirror showing us what we look like and where we have to improve. May we put into action the lessons we have learned.
Lord, hear us.

May all our politicians and lawmakers be guided by the light of Christ.
Lord, hear us.

People brought the blind man to Jesus for healing. We now bring to Jesus all those who are struggling in darkness, that he may touch their eyes and banish their darkness.
Lord, hear us.

(Add prayers for any local, personal or topical intention)

O God of light, we thank you for the gift of sight. Graciously hear our prayers in the name of Jesus Christ, our Lord. Amen.

THURSDAY

MARK 8:27-33

1. CYCLE A

"Who do you say I am?" If you were approached by somebody doing a religious survey and were asked what Jesus means to you, how would you answer? There are many ways to answer but here are three very important beliefs. Jesus is more than human. He is divine, the Second Person of the Holy Trinity. Secondly, he is God come among us in human form. If you want to know what God is like, look at the human life of Jesus Christ, what he said, what he did, how he reacted in situations, his values and ideals. God has spoken to us in a human language that we can understand. Thirdly, Jesus is not just a figure of the past. He is risen and he is present in our lives if only we can become aware of it. He invites you into a personal, daily relationship. He wants to be your friend.

2. CYCLE B

Saint James writes in a down-to-earth, challenging way. He wants practical action to prove the validity of pious talk. Talk, even holy talk, is cheap. Faith without good works is dead. Hypocritical piety is usually a cop-out from practical charity, and charity begins at home. Catholics have rightly insisted that good deeds are necessary for salvation. That is what Jesus taught us. It is for feeding the hungry, clothing the naked, looking after the sick and so on that the reward of Heaven is given to people.

PRAYERS

Enlightened by the Word of God, we pray

It was Peter, the first Pope, who declared his belief that Jesus was the Christ, the Anointed One. We pray for the successor of Peter, Pope *(name)*, that his faith might be an inspiration to all the Church.
Lord, hear us.

Lord, we believe, help our unbelief. May our commitment to Jesus grow ever stronger.
Lord, hear us.

May our faith inspire us to act with Christian compassion and service.
Lord, hear us.

For the people we know who have drifted away from believing: may they experience the joy of accepting the invitation of Jesus to a personal friendship.
Lord, hear us.

(Add prayers for any local, personal or topical intention)

O God our Father, you so loved the world that you gave your Beloved Son to lead us in the truth. Hear the prayers we offer in his holy name. Amen.

FRIDAY

MARK 8:34 – 9:1

1. "If you want to follow me, you must renounce your self-centredness, take up your cross and follow me". A little story about Saint Teresa of Calcutta. After their morning hour of adoration of Christ in the Eucharist, the sisters were heading out to serve Christ among the poor. One young sister looked very sad, all locked up in herself. Mother Teresa called her aside and asked her, "Did Jesus say 'take up your cross and go ahead of me' or 'take up your cross and follow me'?" The sister rightly answered, "Follow me." She began to smile. Message received. The cross is the symbol of total self-giving. "Having loved his own who were in the world, he loved them to the end." Jesus gave a powerful lesson of humble service when he washed the feet of his disciples. To follow Christ is to undertake a life of self-giving in practical love for others. That is why Jesus spoke of the necessity of renouncing self-centredness.

2. Pope Francis called it a form of slow suicide when we cut ourselves off from others, refuse to share, stop giving, talk to nobody, and lock ourselves up in our own comforts. He also wrote that when we live out a spirituality of drawing nearer to others, and seeking their welfare, our hearts are opened to the Lord's greatest and most beautiful gifts. Peace and joy are among these beautiful gifts. "It is more blessed to give than to receive." (Pope Francis: *The Joy of the Gospel*, 272)

PRAYERS

In the light of the teaching and example of Jesus, we pray.

May the Church be faithful to the example of Jesus in being a community of believers who avoid self-centredness and who care for others.
Lord, hear us.

May the powerful leaders of wealthy corporations have a conscience about relieving world poverty.
Lord, hear us.

We pray for people who are burdened with a heavy cross. May the Lord give them great inner strength and peace.
Lord, hear us.

May the Lord bless and reward people who generously give time to helping people in need.
Lord, hear us.

(Add prayers for any local, personal or topical intention)

O God of infinite love, hear the prayers we offer in the name of Jesus Christ, the Lord. Amen.

SATURDAY

MARK 9:2-13

1. Jesus took three apostles, Peter, James and John, with him up a high mountain where they could be alone. From a mountain height, one gets a panoramic view of the winding of rivers, the meeting of roads, the outline of fields. It is an experience that opens up the mind. The poet William Blake described it like this.

> "Great things happen when men and mountain meet
> This is not done while jostling in the street."

On the high mountain Peter, James and John were granted a new understanding of Jesus. They got a little glimpse of his divine glory. They had to come down from the height but memory kept the experience alive. The three needed this memory as they were to be the witnesses of the agony of Jesus in Gethsemane. Later, as pillars of the early Church, they experienced many difficult times. The Second Letter of Peter lets us know how they tapped into this precious bank of memory. "We were with him on the holy mountain". We must treasure our moments of insight and tap into the bank of golden memories when the going is hard.

2. "This is my Son the Beloved. Listen to him". In our technological world today, it is hard to listen attentively. People flee from silence by inserting earphones. Saint Teresa of Calcutta had her own version of a business card... five short lines.

> "The fruit of silence is prayer;
> the fruit of prayer is faith;
> the fruit of faith is love;
> the fruit of love is service;
> the fruit of service is peace."

The path is prayer... faith... love... service... peace.

PRAYERS

"This is my Son, the Beloved. Listen to him." Let us pray.

Peter, James and John, pillars of the Early Church, were strengthened by the Lord for the days ahead. May the leaders of the Church in our time receive divine assistance for their difficult task.
Lord, hear us.

May we grow in our ability to listen to God.
Lord, hear us.

May we learn how to escape from the rush and bustle of life and to cultivate silence.
Lord, hear us.

(Add prayers for any local, personal or topical intention)

O God, our heavenly Father, graciously listen to our prayers, in the name of your Beloved Son, Jesus Christ, our Lord. Amen.

MONDAY

MARK 9:14-29

1. "I believe, Lord, help my unbelief." The prayer of the father of the epileptic boy is one of the great prayers to remember. There are two aspects to believing. One is the mental acceptance of certain doctrines or beliefs. The other aspect is more in the heart than in the head. It means a personal trust or confidence in God. In fact the word *creed,* or *credo* in Latin, means 'I give my heart'. Faith is often spoken of as a journey. It is a lifelong commitment, hopefully a continual growth in commitment. A prominent theologian, Gerald O'Collins, said that, at best, we should describe ourselves as becoming believers. The founder of Cursillo, Eduardo Bonnin, described himself as an apprentice Christian, still learning, always on the journey of faith. If God was small enough for our minds to understand fully, then God would be too small for the deep longings of the heart.

2. "Everything is possible for anyone who has faith." There are many things we cannot do on our own. But when we enter into a partnership with Jesus, we are a winning combination. "All wisdom is from the Lord" (Ecclesiasticus, Cycle I). This divine wisdom is part of the Twelve Steps of Rehabilitation. After admitting that one is powerless with a problem, one moves forward to handing it over to a higher power. As Jesus said, this demon can only be driven out by prayer.

PRAYERS

Let us pray with the Response: *I believe, Lord, help my unbelief.*

The boy brought to Jesus suffered from epilepsy. We pray in the name of all who suffer from epilepsy or any form of seizure.
I believe, Lord, help my unbelief.

That our faith may continue to grow.
I believe, Lord, help my unbelief.

Let us hand all our problems and fears over to God's care.
I believe, Lord, help my unbelief.

For all who feel spiritually cold or who feel miles away from God, we pray.
I believe, Lord, help my unbelief.

(Add prayers for any local, personal or topical intention)

O God, without you we are powerless, but with you all things are possible. Graciously hear our prayers in the name of Jesus Christ, our Lord. Amen.

TUESDAY

MARK 9:30-37

1. Jesus had a hard time trying to convince the apostles what he was really about. Several times he told them that he would be rejected, put to death and rise again. This was so totally against their expectations that they could not take it in. This is a classic case of denial when the truth is unpalatable. Among themselves, they were arguing about which one of them was the greatest. They were still thinking of prestige and power in the kingdom Jesus which was continually talking about. But Jesus had not come as a military messiah. His revolution was about a conversion of life, a revolution of compassion and tenderness.

2. To bring home his message, Jesus set a little child in front of the apostles. Many creatures in the wild are able to walk about from the moment of birth. The human brain is so large and complex that it takes a long time to develop. The human child is virtually helpless for months. The helpless child represented the help that people need. Greatness, according to Jesus, is in coming to the aid of those in any kind of need. "Anyone who welcomes one of these little children in my name welcomes me. And anyone who welcomes me, welcomes not me but the one who sent me." Greatness in the Kingdom of God is not in having power and wealth, but in humble service.

PRAYERS

We take to heart the teaching of Jesus as we pray.

May the Church be a living community of believers who are compassionate, generous, humble and helpful.
Lord, hear us.

Free us, Lord, from proud ambition and the desire to dominate others.
Lord, hear us.

May we recognise that the way we treat others is really the way we treat God.
Lord, hear us.

May God bless and reward people who volunteer their time and talents to help people in any need.
Lord, hear us.

(Add prayers for any local, personal or topical intention)

God, the giver of every good gift, hear the prayers we offer in the name of Jesus Christ, the Lord. Amen

WEDNESDAY

MARK 9:38-40

1. In Saint Mark's Gospel, the evil spirits call Jesus by some very holy names such as "Holy One of God." They use these holy titles, not in adoration, but in the belief that if they say the right name or title, they will get his power. They were not far off the mark. The fact is that when we pray in the name of Jesus Christ, we are united with his power. "Whatever you ask for in my name I will do, so that the Father may be glorified in the Son" (John 14:13). The sacred name, used with faith, calls up the presence of Jesus. And with his presence comes his power. The faithless use of the name of Jesus or God is appalling. One wonders what an outsider must think of our religion if that is the disrespect we show to our God and Saviour. Nothing shows up the shallowness of faith so much as the abuse of the name of God. The name of Jesus is a prayer, not a curse word.

2. The apostle John had a problem because "a man who is not one of us" was casting out devils in Jesus' name, so "we stopped him". But Jesus did not agree. "Anyone who is not against us is for us." Miracles of healing are not confined to the Catholic Church. Retreat Centres host ways of meditating, breathing exercises and gentle movement which are not specifically Christian, but neither are they anti-Christian. These exercises are bringing great inner peace and healing to people. Inner demons of violence, addiction, anxiety and fear are being cast out. "Anyone who is not against us is for us." The apostle John wanted to stop the man who was healing. The more mature John in the First Epistle of John wrote that "God is love, and whoever remains in love remains in God and God in him". God's presence and power are not confined to any one Church.

PRAYERS

Saint Paul wrote that every knee should bend at the name of Jesus. Let us pray with the Response: *Blessed be the name of Jesus.*

Let us pray for a deep reverence for the sacred name of Jesus, our Lord and Saviour.
Blessed be the name of Jesus.

For people who habitually abuse the sacred names; may they realise what they are saying and change their language.
Blessed be the name of Jesus.

Miracles of healing were worked in the name of Jesus. Now we bring to Jesus our friends and relations who are sick in body, mind or spirit.
Blessed be the name of Jesus.

May the name of Jesus be the most loved word in our vocabulary.
Blessed be the name of Jesus.

(Add prayers for any local, personal or topical intention)

God, the Father of all nations, graciously hear the prayers we offer in the name of Jesus Christ, our Lord and Saviour. Amen.

THURSDAY

MARK 9:41-50

1. "If anyone gives you a cup of water to drink because you belong to Christ, then I tell you solemnly, he will most certainly not lose his reward." You belong to Christ. In Baptism you were Christ-ened. It was revealed to Saint Paul on the road to Damascus that when he was persecuting Christians, he was persecuting Christ. It follows that the way you treat other people is the way you treat God. If you want to know how much you belong to Christ, not only in name, but in fact, check up on how you treat other people. As Saint John put it, how can you say that you love God whom you have never seen if you do not love the people whom you do see. Saint Teresa of Calcutta liked to remind people of the five-finger exercise. YOU DID IT TO ME.

2. "Anyone who is an obstacle to bring down one of these little ones who have faith would be better thrown into the sea with a great millstone round his neck." This must have been the strictest warning Jesus ever gave. Do not be an obstacle to the faith of anybody, but especially to the faith of an impressionable child. Perhaps Jesus could foresee the abuse of children by people who were trusted, especially by church personnel. It is only in recent times that the depth of hurt inflicted has been recognised. We must continue to pray for people who have been abused, as well as for true repentance on the part of anybody who has abused or hurt others.

PRAYERS

As we are challenged by the teaching of Jesus, we pray.

May the Church be a community of believers who are a help, not a hindrance, to one another in our relationship with God.
Lord, hear us.

If we have been an obstacle to anybody's faith may the Lord forgive us and enable the person we have harmed to recover.
Lord, hear us.

For people who have been seriously abused or bullied: may God's grace heal their deep wounds and enable them to move forward in peace.
Lord, hear us.

Let us pray for the conversion and repentance of people who have abused, bullied or misled other people.
Lord, hear us

(Add prayers for any local, personal or topical intention)

O generous God, you reward even the smallest act of kindness. Hear and answer the prayers we offer in the name of Jesus Christ, the Lord. Amen.

FRIDAY

MARK 10:1-12

1. The Gospel today is about marriage. There used to be a saying that a wedding was for a day while a marriage was for life. Nowadays, it is often a case that a wedding is for a weekend – or longer, if one were to include stag or hen parties – but the marriage is until further notice. Pope Francis gave very practical, simple advice about the importance of three words. PLEASE; THANKS; SORRY. "Let us not be stingy about using these words, but keep repeating them, day after day. There are certain silences that are oppressive, even at times within families, between husbands and wives, between parents and children, among siblings. The right words, spoken at the right time, daily protect and nurture love." (Pope Francis: *The Joy of Love*, 133) PLEASE – THANKS – SORRY.

2. The First Reading for each Cycle offers further practical advice for friendship in marriage.

CYCLE I

(Ecclesiasticus) Marriage is helped by a kindly turn of speech and a courteous way of speaking. Shouting and name-calling are OUT. Fair weather friends will use you when it suits them but desert you when you are down. A faithful friend is a sure shelter, a rare treasure, something beyond price.

CYCLE II

James lists important ingredients for the wedding cake: no complaining; great patience; no swearing or offensive language; total honesty with one another; let your "yes" be yes and your "no" be no. Married friendship grows where these qualities are taken seriously.

PRAYERS

Taking the advice of Sacred Scripture to heart, we pray.

For all married couples: with the help of the grace of God may their friendship grow stronger through all the ups and downs of life.
Lord, hear us.

For marriages that are under strain: may they be open to God's grace as they overcome their difficulties; may they rediscover the love that first brought them together.
Lord, hear us.

We pray for children who grow up in an unhappy home: let no lasting harm come to them.
Lord, hear us.

For people who work in Marriage agencies or counselling: may God's wisdom always guide them.
Lord, hear us.

(Add prayers for any local, personal or topical intention)

O God, our Creator, you draw people together to unite them in love and to bring new people into life. Graciously hear our prayers for all married couples. Through Christ, our Lord. Amen.

SATURDAY

MARK 10:13-16

1. People were bringing little children to Jesus for him to touch them. It is a beautiful picture, the way he took them in his arms, laid his hands on them and blessed them. Sadly, not all contact with children has been holy. Children have been subjected to physical, emotional and even sexual abuse. One very sad outcome of the abuse of children is the way that, in the interests of safety, children are being taught to distrust adults. And there are restrictions on what adults can do for children. One hopes these children will not grow up into adults who are incapable of trusting anybody.

2. The apostles thought that bringing the children to Jesus would be an intrusion on his precious time. But when Jesus saw what was happening, he wanted the children to come. He took the occasion to focus on the children as models of innocence and trust. Children are totally dependent on others and they know it. They respond to gestures of love. They have a great capacity for wonder. When they receive gifts their faces light up with joy. Jesus is not asking us to be childish but to rediscover the virtues of children.

PRAYERS

Jesus said that the Kingdom of God belongs to the childlike people who harm nobody and trust in God.

Let us pray that all children will have the good fortune to grow up in an atmosphere of love and trust.
Lord, hear us.

We remember the children whose childhood is destroyed by war or famine: may those who cause war wake up to the reality of the pain they are causing.
Lord, hear us.

For all who have suffered abuse or bullying in childhood: with God's help may they be enabled to let the hurts behind and now go forward with dignity and confidence.
Lord, hear us.

May all of us recognise our dependence on God and have a deep confidence in God's protection and care.
Lord, hear us.

(Add prayers for any local, personal or topical intention)

O God, loving Father of all, hear the prayers we offer with childlike trust, through Christ, our Lord. Amen.

MONDAY

MARK 10:17-27

1. "What must I do to inherit eternal life?" What must I do to be saved, to get into Heaven? The way to get into Heaven is to let Heaven get into me: that is, to let God's thoughts into my thoughts, to let God's values become my values. The first truth about being saved is that it is a gift offered in God's kindness. It is something far beyond anything we could earn, merit or deserve. The second truth about being saved is that God's wonderful gift must be accepted with our co-operation. In the understanding of those times, the rich young man regarded his wealth as a sign of God's blessing. He felt entitled to hold onto his wealth. He was delighted to receive but not willing to give. He wanted to get into Heaven but he would not let the Kingdom of Heaven and its ideals into his way of thinking. His face fell at the challenge and he went away sad, for he was a man of great wealth.

2. Mark's Gospel brings us very close to the actions and reactions of people. Look at the contrast between the face of Jesus and the face of the rich young man. "Jesus looked steadily at him and loved him." What a beautiful picture! A face of light and warmth. Eye contact that was personal. Words of invitation... "Follow me". Now look at the man who ran up to Jesus and knelt piously before him. "Good master, what must I do to inherit eternal life?" Jesus invited him to sell his property portfolio and give the money to the poor. Now look at the change in his appearance. "His face fell at these words." His face was like a plastic mask that came too close to the fire and it melted away into a sad mess. Pope Francis wrote that whenever our interior life becomes caught up in our own concerns, there is no longer any room for others, no place for the poor, no listening to God. A person becomes resentful, angry and listless. The rich young man went away sad.

PRAYERS

As we are challenged by the teaching of Jesus, we pray.

May the lifestyle of people who represent the Church be faithful to the example and teaching of Jesus in his concern for the poor.
Lord, hear us.

May people who are wealthy see their responsibility to share with God's beloved poor.
Lord, hear us

May the people who lack the necessities of life receive a fair share of the world's resources.
Lord, hear us.

We pray that many young people will experience the invitation of Jesus to follow him and may they dedicate their lives to his service.
Lord, hear us.

(Add prayers for any local, personal or topical intention)

O God, we thank you for all the good things we have received. May we be generous in sharing with others. Through Christ, our Lord. Amen.

TUESDAY

MARK 10:28-31

1. In yesterday's Gospel a rich young man was too fond of his possessions to accept the invitation of Jesus to follow him. But Peter, spokesman for the apostles, reminded Jesus that they had left fishing boats, profitable jobs, homes and families for his sake. He reassured them that they would be repaid a hundred times over, in this life and the next. A certain parish priest complimented a local farmer on his generous contribution to every noble cause. The man replied: "No problem, Father, you see God has a bigger shovel." That farmer knew his Gospel. God rewards with a bigger shovel.

2. "Many who were first will be last, and the last first." The Last Day will be full of surprises, some pleasant, others not too pleasant. Those who were persecuted, bullied and humiliated in this life will be called to the front seats. But the bullies, and those who deprived the poor of their just demands will be sent to the back of the queue. Many who climbed to the top of the ladder of power, or wealth or prestige will get the horrible surprise that they climbed the wrong wall. "Many who were first will be last, and the last first."

PRAYERS

In the light of God's Word, we are encouraged to pray.

For those who have dedicated their lives to God in religious commitment, may they be rewarded with spiritual richness in prayer, peace of mind and joy in their relationship with God.
Lord, hear us.

That many young people will hear the call of Christ to follow him and that they will respond with total trust.
Lord, hear us.

We pray for the people who are being persecuted every day for their religious beliefs. May God give them great inner strength and may their persecution come to a speedy end.
Lord, hear us.

For those who are being bullied and humiliated: may they be comforted by the words of Jesus that the last will be first and the first last.
Lord, hear us.

   (Add prayers for any local, personal or topical intention)

O God, the Father of all, graciously answer the prayers we offer in the name of Jesus Christ, your Son, our Lord. Amen.

WEDNESDAY

MARK 10:32-45

1. They were going towards Jerusalem. Jesus went on ahead like a man on a mission. The apostles followed. They were in a daze. They could not take in what he was saying about being arrested and crucified. It was unthinkable. They heard him talk about a kingdom. But it wasn't to be a kingdom of power and domination, which was the way of the world. The way of Jesus was in humble service. "The Son of Man did not come to be served but to serve, and to give his life for the ransom of many." Christian greatness means acting justly, loving tenderly and walking humbly with our God.

2. Ambition is good. It sets our ideals and a target to aim at. It is a source of energy and dedication. But ambition is harmful when it becomes selfish. The brothers James and John were ambitious in a selfish way. They wanted the top seats in the Kingdom. Obviously, they still did not know what Jesus meant by the Kingdom of God on Earth. Saint Paul directed the people of Corinth to be ambitious for the higher gifts, especially for love. Then in his famous hymn to love he listed the practical expressions of love which is generous, patient, kind, never resentful or jealous, always putting the other person first. "Anyone who wants to be great among you must be your servant, and anyone who wants to be the first among you must be the slave to all." It took some time, but eventually James and John understood what Jesus meant by the Kingdom, and they generously gave their lives to its service.

PRAYERS

In the light of the Gospel, let us pray.

For all who are called to positions of power in the Church: may no false ambition or careerism lead them away from the Gospel ideal of humble service.
Lord, hear us.

May all who exercise political power put aside personal gain as they work for a just and caring society.
Lord, hear us.

We pray for all who have to drink from the cup of suffering. May God strengthen them and ease their burdens.
Lord, hear us.

We pray for vocations to the priesthood and apostolic life.
Lord, hear us.

   (Add prayers for any local, personal or topical intention)

O God, hear our prayers offered in the name of Jesus Christ, your Son, our Lord. Amen.

THURSDAY

MARK 10:46-52

1. The prayer of the blind man, Bartimaeus, is a model of petition in its reverence, simplicity, perseverance and trust. There is reverence in the way Jesus is addressed with a messianic title, Son of David. His prayer is as simple as could be, with no unnecessary words or complicated explanations. He shows perseverance in the way he shouted all the louder when people tried to stop him. The inner voices that tend to stop our prayer are feelings of unworthiness, doubts and guilt. The blindness of Bartimaeus reminds us that faith is only dim light. Bartimaeus was a beggar and we are all beggars before God.

2. The prayer of Bartimaeus has inspired the Jesus Prayer. One holds onto a short aspiration centred on the sacred name of Jesus. An aspiration means a breathing... a breathing enriched with the sacred name. The rhythm of breathing sets the gentle pace of the prayer. Of course, distractions will enter the mind. Once you realise your mind has drifted away, gently come back to the little aspiration you have chosen. Jesus Mercy. Jesus Lord. Jesus Saviour. Jesus Friend.

PRAYERS

As we draw inspiration from the prayer of Bartimaeus, we pray.

The Church is called the Light of the Nations. Protect and guide Pope *(name)* and our Bishop *(name)* as they lead us through our spiritual blindness with the light of Christ.
Lord, hear us.

Let us pray for all who suffer from poor eyesight, that God will grant them great strength of spiritual sight.
Lord, hear us.

We thank you, Lord, for our parents, teachers, priests and others who have passed on the light of faith to us: bless and reward them.
Lord, hear us.

May we have the reverence, perseverance and confidence that Bartimaeus had as he prayed.
Lord, hear us.

May the prayerful repetition of the sacred name of Jesus fill us with his presence and power.
Lord, hear us.

(Add prayers for any local, personal or topical intention)

Heavenly Father, you sent your Beloved Son as the light of the world. Strengthen our faith as we pray in his name, Jesus Christ, our Lord. Amen.

FRIDAY

MARK 11:11-26

1. Sometimes the prophets in the Old Testament performed dramatic actions to bring home a lesson. It is in that line of dramatic gesture that we are to understand the strange action of Jesus in cursing the poor fig tree. The tree that no longer bore fruit was a metaphor for the temple religion which had lost its sanctity. It had become a robber's den where innocent pilgrims were exploited through a variety of taxes. It had become a centre of business rather than a house of prayer. Even as a boy of twelve, Jesus was appalled at what he saw in the temple. He resolved to be busy about his Father's house. The sight of the fig tree withered away was a prophecy of the destruction of the temple which had happened by the time the gospels were written.

2. What about the statement that faith can move mountains? The context is important. It has to do with forgiveness. "When you stand in prayer, forgive whatever you have against anybody so that your Father in Heaven may forgive your failings too." The mountains to be moved are in the memory: memories of being hurt, bullied, wronged, betrayed. Human nature on its own may find it impossible to overcome these hurtful memories. We need faith in the power of the Holy Spirit. God wants us to cast these mountains of negative feelings into the sea of his merciful love. There will be joy in Heaven and on Earth when you open your heart to God's healing mercy. Father, forgive us our sins as we forgive those who have offended us.

PRAYERS

Enlightened by the Word of God, we pray.

May the Church always be faithful to its mission and never lose its apostolic fruitfulness.
Lord, hear us.

May our church buildings be centres of prayer, places where we come closer to God and where we find peace.
Lord, hear us.

May religion never be used to exploit people.
Lord, hear us.

We pray that any bitterness or hatred in our memories may be cast like mountains into the sea of God's healing mercy.
Lord, hear us.

(Add prayers for any local, personal or topical intention)

Father of mercy, graciously hear the prayers we offer in the name of Jesus Christ, your Son, our Lord. Amen.

SATURDAY

MARK 11:27-33

1. "What authority do you have for acting like this?" Authority is almost like a dirty word in this age of permissiveness. Authority is seen as a power from above crushing my rights, or an invasion of my personal space. It's a time for my rights with no mention of my responsibilities. "Women's right to choose". To choose what? This is the age of ME... my rights, my choice, my space. There is little mention of my responsibilities, my duties, my faithfulness. Authority is linked to author. Christian authority is a responsibility to be faithful to the author of our faith, namely Jesus Christ. Christian authority is not about power, but about serving people with the true meaning of life.

2. "Who gave you the authority to act like this?" The enemies of Jesus were trying to trap him. On a radio chat-show one night, three priests were being interviewed about the supports and stresses of a priest's life. One mentioned the stress of preaching. The interviewer excitedly jumped in. "Preaching! Who gave you the right to tell anybody how to live?" Preaching or teaching the Christian message does not come from a right but from the responsibility or duty to pass on the teaching of Jesus Christ. And if we are to talk about rights, people have the right to hear the divine truth. It was Jesus, the author of our faith who said, "Go, teach all nations." We would have fewer murders, fewer suicides, more stable marriages, and a better world to live in if people listened to the teaching of Jesus.

PRAYERS

Enlightened by the teaching of the Gospel, we pray.

May the Church at all times be faithful to its responsibility to pass on the wisdom of Jesus Christ.
Lord, hear us.

May our political leaders recognise their responsibility to protect the rights of all people, from womb to tomb.
Lord, hear us.

May parents be faithful to their promise to pass on the truths of the faith to their children.
Lord, hear us.

May those who constantly criticise the Church open their eyes to the immense work the Church does for justice, peace, care of the sick and feeding the hungry.
Lord, hear us.

(Add prayers for any local, personal or topical intention)

O God, the author of all that is good, continue to inspire us to be faithful to the teaching of Jesus Christ, in whose name we pray. Amen.

MONDAY

MARK 12:1-12

1. God sent prophets and inspirational leaders, but people rejected them because their preaching was a threat to their way of living. Finally, God sent his Beloved Son, Jesus Christ. He was a man of noble ideals, compassionate to all who were suffering, a bringer of healing and peace. Yet he was rejected. Why? Our eyes are made for light, but if the eye is sore, we cannot stand the light. Our tummies are made for food, but when the tummy is sick, we cannot stand even the smell of food. The soul is made for God, but the soul that is sick is threatened by the goodness of God. When we hear criticism of our religion, remember that the criticism probably reveals more about the sick soul of the critic than the object of the criticism.

2. Jesus was rejected, but in the providence of God, the rejected stone became the keystone to hold all of life together. Before cement was invented, the stability of a stone structure depended on the interlocking of the stones. The cornerstone locked the walls together. If the cornerstone was the correct shape, any vibration or big wind actually clamped the stones more tightly together. Jesus, by rising from the dead, became the keystone that holds life together. When life threatens to fall apart, then more than ever we realise how much we need God to hold all together. "The stone rejected by the builders has become the cornerstone."

PRAYERS

In the light of God's Word, we pray.

May the Church as the community of believers, bring the light of Christ to all people.
Lord, hear us.

For all who feel rejected, cast aside or undervalued: may they be consoled in remembering that Jesus too was rejected but was later recognised as the cornerstone of life.
Lord, hear us.

For all who are searching for meaning and direction in life; may they turn to Jesus whose example is the way, whose teaching is the truth, and who leads us to eternal life.
Lord, hear us.

Lord, open our eyes and hearts to anybody whom we have rejected or undervalued, and help us to make it up with them.
Lord, hear us.

(Add prayers for any local, personal or topical intention)

O God, the bringer of new life, graciously hear the prayers we offer in the name of Jesus Christ, our Risen Lord. Amen.

TUESDAY

MARK 12:13-17

1. "Should we pay taxes to the Romans or not?" The question was put to Jesus as a trap. If he advocated not paying the taxes, he would be in trouble with the Romans, but if he was in favour of paying, he would be in trouble with the nationalists. Jesus turned the question back on those who asked it. He suggested that they had the answer in their own pockets. If you have Roman money, if you avail of their great engineering projects, their roads and bridges, their aqueducts and water cisterns, do you expect to get it all without taxation? Give back to Caesar what you get from belonging to the Empire. Then Jesus added the punchline. Give to God what belongs to God. Total separation of politics and religion is not feasible because we have dual citizenship, of Earth and of Heaven. Secularism denies our responsibilities towards God: selfish piety reneges on earthly and social responsibilities. Religion and politics live in holy harmony in the person who is fully responsive to God and to society.

2. Total honesty is in short supply today, but it has always been that way. The alliance of Pharisees and Herodians, traditional enemies, was a dishonest, hypocritical partnership. Pharisees were determined to keep separated from all foreign culture, while the Herodians owed their power through wheeling and dealing with the Romans. Normally Pharisees and Herodians would be at loggerheads with each other. Notice their hypocrisy in calling Jesus an honest man. Jesus, the light of the world, immediately saw through their hypocrisy. We can fool some of the people some of the time but we cannot fool God at any time. As a psalm says: "O God, you search me and you know me. You discern my purpose from afar. All my ways lie open to you."

PRAYERS

Jesus is the true light who can read our innermost intentions. So, we pray.

That the Church will be a shining model of honesty and truthfulness to inspire the world.
Lord, hear us.

May our politicians be totally truthful and honest in all their dealings.
Lord, hear us.

May all of us be truthful and honest, knowing that we can never deceive God.
Lord, hear us.

We pray for people who have suffered because of the dishonesty or lies of others.
Lord, hear us.

(Add prayers for any local, personal or topical intention)

O God of light, to your eyes, all of life is an open book. Hear the prayers we offer in the name of Jesus Christ, our Lord. Amen.

WEDNESDAY

MARK 12:18-27

1. Sadducees took their name from Zadok, high priest in the time of King David. Most of them belonged to the priestly party who worked in the temple. They had turned it into a lucrative business centre where innocent pilgrims were ripped off by multiple taxes. It did not suit them to believe in a judgement after death, so they set up a hypothetical case to trap Jesus. There was an ancient law that where brothers lived together, if one of them died and his widow was childless, then the next in line should marry the widow. In this case, a woman was married to all of seven brothers in succession without bearing a child. Which of them would be her husband if there is life after death? Jesus told them that they understood neither the scriptures nor the power of God. The laws of physical life such as the need for procreation would not apply in the next life. It still happens that people take one or more selected texts of the Bible, do not balance these quotations with other texts and they end up in error. They do not understand the scriptures nor the power of God. A little knowledge is a dangerous thing.

2. The Sadducees made their wealth by exploiting people. Saint Paul said that the love of money is the root of all evil. Maybe not all evil, but certainly the root of many evils. The social documents of all the recent popes are very critical of the exploitation of the poor nations, of economics without conscience, of the selfish destruction of Nature's balance. The gap between rich and poor is increasing all the time. One recent survey showed that the sixty-two richest people in the world together own more than the combined wealth of 50 % of the world's population. Half the population of the world are trying to survive on less than €2 a day. The rich nations are exploiting the natural resources of the poor nations. If there is to be any justice at all, there has to be a day of reckoning, a judgement to be faced at the end of life. The last shall be first and the first shall be last.

PRAYERS

Having listened to the Word of God, we are moved to pray.

May the teaching of the Church always remind people that we have here no lasting city but seek one that is to come.
Lord, hear us.

May our belief in the resurrection of Jesus Christ fill us with hope of one day sharing eternal life with God and with our loved ones who have passed away.
Lord, hear us.

Let us pray for an ending to the exploitation of the poor nations of the world and that they will get a fair share of the world's resources.
Lord, hear us.

May the people who have great wealth come to know the joy of sharing: may they contribute generously to the provision of food and basic health care for those in need.
Lord, hear us.

(Add prayers for any local, personal or topical intention)

O God, the Father of all, thank you for all you have given us. Graciously hear the prayers we offer in the name of Jesus Christ, our Lord. Amen.

THURSDAY

MARK 12:28-34

1. "Listen, Israel, the Lord our God is the one Lord." The First Commandment of love reaffirms the unique position of God. It involves being serious, not lukewarm, about God, about spiritual matters and the eternal dimension of life. Listen to God above the calls of materialism, consumerism, power, pleasure or being top of the class. Loving God with all your heart means a serious commitment to God. All your soul refers to your deepest longings and desires: "My soul is thirsting for you, my God" (Ps. 62). All your strength is a commitment to practical action since faith without good works is dead.

2. "Love your neighbour as yourself." Psychology recognises the need for self-esteem. The psalmist prayed, "I thank you, Lord, for the wonder of my being". To celebrate our self-worth is not pride, but a recognition of God as our Creator, Redeemer and Sanctifier. Mary's prayer is a model of attributing greatness to God. "The Almighty has done great things for me, holy is his name". Not to love ourselves is an insult to God's work of art. The greatest source of healthy self-esteem is to glimpse even a little of the immense love of God for us. People who have low self-value probably take themselves too seriously and God not seriously enough. That is why love of God is the First Commandment and then love of self and others.

PRAYERS

The laws of religion are there to help us to love God with all our heart, all our soul and strength, and to love our neighbour as ourselves. So we pray.

May the Church be true to its calling as a community of people recognisable by love of God and care for one another.
Lord, hear us.

May we grow each day in a personal, loving relationship with God.
Lord, hear us.

I thank you, Lord, for the wonder of my being. May we recognise how much you love us.
Lord, hear us.

We pray for people with low self-esteem or who feel unloved. May the light of God's love shine through their darkness.
Lord, hear us.

(Add prayers for any local, personal or topical intention)

O God, our Creator, Redeemer and sanctifier, we praise and thank you. May the love in our hearts grow each day. We offer our prayer through Christ, our Lord. Amen

FRIDAY

MARK 12:35-37

1. CYCLE A

   In the Gospel today, Jesus refers to himself as Lord. When we call him Lord, we are expressing our belief that he is more than human. We believe that he is divine, the Son of God, the Second Person of the Blessed Trinity. Saint Paul tells us that at his name, every knee should bend and every tongue confess that Jesus Christ is Lord. Our First Reading, from the Book of Tobit, gives us a suitable prayer for blessing the name of Jesus, the Lord.

   > Blessed be God!
   > Blessed be his holy name!
   > Blessed be all his holy angels!
   > Blessed be his great name for evermore!

2. CYCLE B

   We often refer to Jesus as Our Lord. We believe that he is more than human. He is divine, the Son of God, the Second Person of the Blessed Trinity. Not only is he Lord, but he is Our Lord. He is not just a figure of past history. He is present in our lives. He is our Saviour and Redeemer. In today's First Reading, Saint Paul recalls how the Lord rescued him in times of danger and persecution. Blessed be Jesus, our Lord and Saviour.

PRAYERS

Here at Mass, we gather as a community in the name of Jesus Christ, Our Lord.

We pray that there will be only one God in our lives, the true God revealed by Jesus Christ, Our Lord.
Lord, hear us.

Jesus is not merely My Lord, but Our Lord. May our faith never be self-centred, but may we recognise how we are brothers and sisters as members of the Body of Christ.
Lord, hear us.

At the name of Jesus, every knee should bend and every tongue confess that Jesus Christ is Lord. May we have a deep respect for the sacred name of Jesus.
Lord, hear us.

We call on the name of Jesus as we pray for friends who are sick or going through a dark time.
Lord, hear us.

(Add prayers for any local, personal or topical intention)

Heavenly Father, we thank you for sending us your Beloved Son as our Saviour and Lord. We offer all our prayers in his name. Amen

SATURDAY

MARK 12:38-44

1. In religious affairs there are takers and there are givers. Takers use religion for their own advancement. Jesus told the apostles to beware of the scribes with their long robes, eminent titles and places of honour. What was worse was the way they "swallowed the property of widows, while making a show of lengthy prayers". The scribes were part of the temple personnel. They were highly paid. The money came from donations and a variety of taxes ripping off innocent pilgrims. The behaviour of the scribes has always been a temptation for church leaders. Careerism replicates the outward show of the scribes in the expensive robes, titles of eminence and places of honour, far removed from the simplicity of Jesus and the apostles. A great teacher of the past said that to use God is to kill him. If I use God for my own purposes, then I am the god I worship. The scribes were takers. The poor widow was a giver who gave all she had. She was praised by the Lord.

2. The poor widow gave all she had. This was only a week or so before another widow, Mary, stood at the foot of the cross and gave up all she had to God. Saturday is Mary's day, going back to the Saturday between Good Friday and Easter Sunday. Saint John wrote that she stood beside the cross. This is a picture of strength, not swooning or crying aloud. Standing. In the confusion after the death of Jesus, on Holy Saturday, she stood in faith and trust because she clearly remembered what Jesus had said about rising from the dead. That's why Saturday is her day. May Mary, the faithful Mother on Holy Saturday, support all who are experiencing grief or darkness.

PRAYERS

In the light of the Gospel, we pray.

May our religious leaders resist all temptations to use their position for their own advancement and prestige.
Lord, hear us.

The poor widow, who gave all she had , trusted that God would not let her down. May we have great trust in God's loving care.
Lord, hear us.

May the example of the generous widow inspire us to be generous givers.
Lord, hear us.

May Mary, who stood beside the cross of her Son, support all who grieve at the loss of a loved one.
Lord, hear us.

(Add prayers for any local, personal or topical intention)

O God, the giver of every good gift, and support of all who trust in you, hear the prayers we offer in the name of Jesus Christ, your Son, our Lord. Amen.

MONDAY

MATTHEW 5:1-12

1. We get a better understanding of the Beatitudes if we translate them with the word *Blessed* rather than *Happy*. Happy is an emotional condition, whereas blessed refers to our standing in God's eyes. The popular understanding at that time was that God's blessings were seen in prosperity, power, prestige and popularity. Jesus saw these as temptations towards pride and self-importance. The people who were most open to God's real blessings were the poor and powerless, those who mourned for past misdeeds, those who strove for justice and mercy, the pure of heart who see things from God's point of view, and those who were persecuted on account of their Christian ideals. Blessed are they, for God's reward awaits them.

2. Thomas Monaghan, a devout Catholic, was the sole owner of *Domino*, the world's largest pizza delivery service. He sold it for a billion dollars to devote his life and money to charitable causes. What challenged him was reading C.S. Lewis on the sin of pride. "Pride leads to every other vice: it is the complete anti-God state of mind ... Each person's pride is in competition with everyone else's pride." In the Beatitudes, Jesus turned the values and attitudes of the world upside down. His mission was the Kingdom of God on Earth.

PRAYERS

As our lives are challenged and inspired by the Beatitudes of Jesus, we pray.

May the Church be true to the spirit of the Beatitudes, inspiring the world towards the sharing of wealth, and towards justice and peace.
Lord, hear us.

May all political leaders use their power and influence to make the world a better place for all.
Lord, hear us.

May those who work for justice and peace see their work bear fruit.
Lord, hear us.

We pray for people who are suffering persecution or mockery on account of their religious beliefs. May they know that God is on their side and may they see the end of their persecution.
Lord, hear us.

(Add prayers for any local, personal or topical intention)

O God, the source of every blessing, direct our lives away from earthly temptations, so that we might live in the light of Jesus Christ, your Son, our Lord. Amen.

TUESDAY

MATTHEW 5:13-16

1. "You are the salt of the earth, you are the light of the world." Salt and light express two different kinds of leadership. Salt grains are tiny, hardly seen but very effective. Salt works in many ways. Before modern refrigeration, salt was the only way to preserve food. It preserves what is good and it heals, though it might sting in doing so. In cooking, salt is intended to draw out the juicy flavours of food. We are called to preserve what is good, to heal where necessary and to draw out what is beautiful in people. Salt is a hidden power but light has to be apart from an object to shine on it. "No one lights a lamp to put it under a tub." Light represents a leadership that stands apart in order to show the way and to point out the faults. The most effective type of leadership is good example. "Your light must shine in the sight of people, so that, seeing your good works, they may give the praise to your Father in Heaven". The Cursillo movement encourages people to make a friend, be a friend and bring a friend to Jesus.

2. Before Pope Francis was elected Pope, he was in a group of Cardinals discussing the situation of the Church and what kind of Pope was required. He made an interesting point. Remember the place in the Bible where Jesus says, "I will come knocking on your door to let me in". Maybe we should think of Jesus knocking on the inside and saying, "Please let me out". Let me out, bring me to all the people who need me. "You are the salt of the earth. But if salt becomes tasteless, what can make it salty again." When the people were hungry, Jesus told the apostles, "Give them something to eat yourselves." Christ is counting on you.

PRAYERS

Enlightened and encouraged by the light of Jesus, we pray

That the Church will always be a light to the world leading it to justice, peace and care of the poor.
Lord, hear us.

That in the little corner of the world where we live, we might be salt preserving good morals, healing what is contaminated and drawing out the hidden beauty of people.
Lord, hear us.

We pray for people who live in darkness and depression. May the kindness of people bring light and joy to their lives.
Lord, hear us.

May our local parish be a vibrant Christian community where the different talents of people are utilised to the full.
Lord, hear us.

   (Add prayers for any local, personal or topical intention)

O God we thank you for the talents you gave us. May we develop them and use them to make the world a better place. Through Jesus Christ, our Lord. Amen.

WEDNESDAY

MATTHEW 5:17-19

1. "Do not imagine that I have come to abolish the Law or the Prophets. I have not to abolish them but to complete them." Sometimes we cannot see the forest for the trees. It happened to the Jewish religion, and it happens today also. Jews themselves have a joke that wherever there are two Jews, there are three opinions. The fundamental rules were few, but the scholars added hundreds of interpretations which evolved into rules. One original commandment was, "Keep holy the Sabbath day". Gradually this became a tangled web of prohibitions. They had paralysed the joy of the Sabbath. Jesus showed a holy disregard for these human regulations. When he was asked which was the most important commandment, he boiled it all down to love of God and love of people.

2. The legalism which Jesus opposed will always be a temptation for the Church. Some regulations and customs which were once very helpful now have the opposite effect. Cardinals and bishops were treated like princes, living in palaces, wearing expensive rings and ornate garments, and being addressed by titles of eminence. Such customs tend to turn people away nowadays. Some priests developed scrupulosity because of the many serious regulations during Mass. Pope Francis used the image of a museum of dead fossils to describe a Church that is so locked up in past customs that it loses missionary fervour and lacks enthusiasm for people who are living without the light of Christ. Jesus said, "I have not come to abolish the Law or the Prophets but to complete them".
(Pope Francis: *The Joy of the Gospel,* 95).

PRAYERS

We take the teaching of the Lord to heart as we pray.

That the Church will be guided by the Holy Spirit in adapting to the different questions and problems that we face in our times.
Lord, hear us.

May those who make the laws of the state never forget the pillars of God's law.
Lord, hear us.

May people who find change hard to make become more flexible for the sake of the greater good.
Lord, hear us.

May people who were hurt by stern authority or rigid legalism receive the grace to move on from these past hurts.
Lord, hear us.

   (Add prayers for any local, personal or topical intention)

O God, the source of wisdom, may your law be the guiding light of our lives, through Christ, our Lord. Amen.

THURSDAY

MATTHEW 5:20-26

1. Jesus set about bringing people back from human regulations to the original purpose of the commandments. He contrasts "What you have heard" with "But I say to you". He takes the commandment, "Thou shalt not kill". Interpretations of the law allowed multiple exceptions. It became a duty to stone people to death for blasphemy or for adultery. Armies were sent out to smite the enemy. One very odd line in a holy psalm says, "The first born of the Egyptians he smote, for his love endures forever". A strange sort of love! Jesus wanted people to get back to the original, positive values which the commandments were designed to protect. "Thou shalt not kill" is a commandment respecting the sacredness of life. "I have come that you may have life and have it to the full". It is the duty of a Christian to protect life, to work for the improvement of life through justice and peace, to make this world, this parish, a better place to live. In the words of Martin Luther King, "We must learn to live together as brothers and sisters or perish together as fools."

2. While we might never physically kill anybody, there are yet many ways we might squeeze the life out of people. Gossip kills a person's good name. Remember, gossip is toxic, and through the power of social media, a rumour can travel to any part of the world in seconds. Sarcasm kills. Cynicism kills. Lack of affirmation kills. Constant carping and criticism destroy a person's confidence. A killjoy poisons the atmosphere. "Thou shalt not kill." That commandment touches our lives in many ways.

PRAYERS

Inspired by the teaching of Jesus, we pray.

For an end to all warfare: that people will live together in harmony and peace; and may our streets be safe and free from senseless violence.
Lord, hear us.

Lord, help us to control our anger. May we never destroy anybody's life by sarcasm or uncharitable gossip.
Lord, hear us.

For the protection of the environment and a deep respect for all of God's creation.
Lord, hear us.

We pray that families who are divided might come together in a spirit of reconciliation.
Lord, hear us.

(Add prayers for any local, personal or topical intention)

Heavenly Father, Creator of all life. May your children on Earth live together in harmony, justice and peace. Through Christ, our Lord. Amen.

FRIDAY

MATTHEW 5:27-32

1. Jesus took up the Sixth Commandment, "Thou shalt not commit adultery". Various regulations allowed many exceptions to the commandment. Jesus went beneath the letter of the law to probe the interior honesty of our relationship with God. What he said about lust shows how this vice is the opposite of the Beatitude, "Blessed are the pure of heart for they shall see God". The person who is pure of heart sees God in people and will regard others with respect and dignity. But the heart that is full of lust does not see God's creation in people. They are there to be used. Exploitation of people in the sex-trade is a massive problem. It is even worse where children are exploited. Pornography is a serious addiction. As with any addiction, a person loses freedom, becomes a slave. Who wants to be trapped in slavery? An alcoholic needs to avoid only one drink, the first one. The sex-addict needs to avoid the first switching on. "If your eye causes you to sin, cut it out." Jesus did not mean self-mutilation, but he did mean cut out the wrong behaviour.

2. "You have heard it said... but I say to you." Jesus struck a blow for gender equality. The interpretation of the Law was done by the Scribes, all of whom were men. Women were treated like chattels, or disposable property. The male Scribes found a variety of reasons to allow men to divorce and remarry. But the wife was simply dismissed. A woman did not have the right to sue for divorce. If a woman who was divorced at her husband's request remarried, she was then regarded as an adulteress. But Jesus claimed that the same law should apply equally to men, so that the man who married a divorced woman also committed the sin of adultery. It was a case of gender equality.

PRAYERS

As we take the moral teaching of Jesus to heart, we are inspired to pray.

"Blessed are the pure in heart for they shall see God." Lord, enable us to look on other people as God's creation, who are to be treated with dignity and respect.
Lord, hear us.

Cleanse our hearts of any tendency to see others as instruments to be used for personal gratification.
Lord, hear us.

We pray for people who are addicted to pornography. May they be released from this slavery.
Lord, hear us.

We pray for people who, through violence or desperate circumstances, are forced into the sex-trade. May they be released and have their dignity restored.
Lord, hear us.

(Add prayers for any local, personal or topical intention)

O God, you created man and woman in your own image and likeness. May we see people as your creation. Through Christ, our Lord. Amen.

SATURDAY

MATTHEW 5:33-37

In today's Gospel, Jesus continues to bring people to the values protected by the commandments. We need never swear on oath if we are totally committed to truth at all times.

1. CYCLE A

   Saint Paul in the First Reading speaks of the new creation, the new standard of morality expected of Christians. We are to be people of the truth. The Devil is the father of lies. In fact, the word *devil* originates in a Greek word for one who misleads people. The most effective lie is the half-truth. That's the psychology of the story of the temptation of Adam and Eve. The forbidden fruit is attractive to look at, but the poisonous outcome is not mentioned. It takes courage to stand up for the truth. It may mean swimming against the current of public opinion. But we are called to be ambassadors for Christ, people of the truth.

2. CYCLE B

   When Elisha was called to follow the great prophet, Elijah, he made a total commitment to it. He burned his plough and slaughtered his ploughing oxen. There would be no turning back. In the spirit of Jesus, his "Yes" meant yes and his "No" meant no. Jesus said that anything more than this comes from the Evil One. The vows of marriage or religious profession are sacred and there must be no turning back. The father of lies, Satan, will plant attractive thoughts of the forbidden fruit in the mind. These are only half-truths. The sharp fishing hook is cleverly camouflaged under some attractive bait. In our courts, people swear under oath to tell the truth, the whole truth and nothing but the truth. Are they serious about the oath they take? People of truth do not need any oath.

PRAYERS

Inspired by the Word of God, we pray.

Saint Paul said that the Church is the pillar and the ground of truth. May the Holy Spirit always inspire the Church in proclaiming the truth as taught by Jesus Christ.
Lord, hear us.

May we always be people of the truth in what we do and what we say.
Lord, hear us.

May we be faithful to our religious promises so that our "Yes" means yes and our "No" means no.
Lord, hear us.

May we be honest in all our dealings.
Lord, hear us.

(Add prayers for any local, personal or topical intention)

O God of light, you know our inmost thoughts and desires. Help us to walk at all times in the ways of truth, honesty and fidelity. Through Christ, our Lord. Amen.

MONDAY

MATTHEW 5:38-42

1. Jesus wants us to replace thoughts of retaliation or vengeance with the power of Christian love. In primitive times, vengeance had no controlled limits. Moses set the limit of equal measure, an eye for an eye and a tooth for a tooth. But, as Martin Luther King said, this policy will result in blindness and hunger. So, Jesus went beyond equal retaliation. "You have heard it said... but I say to you, let there be no retaliation." Never let the badness of the other person bring out the badness hidden in your own heart. Never let the other person set the agenda of your life. Never let the rivers of Christian love be poisoned or polluted by the wrongdoing of others.

2. Some people say we have become too soft in our preaching. So much talk about love and mercy. Let's get back to the Last Judgement, back to fear and trembling. Has Hell been forgotten? They have a point. We cannot neglect the Final Judgement or the reality of Hell. However, the emphasis on love and mercy is far more demanding than a religion based on fear of damnation. Jesus calls for an interior conversion of mind and heart. Many people whose religion was based on God as a strict judge acted with unchristian severity towards others. The religion of interior conversion is a constant battle to overcome all negative instincts producing hatred and revenge. We cannot do it on our own, but we can reach this conversion with the grace of the Holy Spirit. Saint Paul says, "As God's fellow workers, do not neglect the grace of God that you have received".

PRAYERS

Jesus is the model of total love and forgiveness. Let us pray that we might become more like him.

May we be open to the grace of the Holy Spirit, leading us to an inner conversion of mind and heart so that we become more like Christ in our reactions.
Lord, hear us.

For people who are suffering persecution: by the grace of God, may they have an inner strength that enables them to remain calm and strong.
Lord, hear us.

By the grace of God, may we be strong enough to overcome all natural instincts to seek revenge when wrong has been done to us.
Lord, hear us.

We remember those who have been deeply hurt or abused. May they have the grace to move on in life without being weighed down by the hurts of the past.
Lord, hear us.

(Add prayers for any local, personal or topical intention)

God of mercy and compassion, graciously listen to the prayers we offer in the name of Jesus Christ, your Son, our Lord. Amen.

TUESDAY

MATTHEW 5:43-48

1. We are reading this week from the Sermon on the Mount, where Jesus sets before us the very lofty ideals of the Kingdom of Heaven on Earth. Today he tells us there are to be no limitations or conditions attached to true Christian love. Christian love is not the product of natural attraction which makes us like some people more than others. Nor is it the product of our feelings. It is a decision we make, an act of the will. The decision is to be an agent of God's love to everybody: a decision to push on with positive energy. It is a powerful river that resists being poisoned by the wrongs that other people do. We are children of God who causes sun to shine and rain to fall on bad people as much as on good people.

2. God's love is unconditional. There are no terms or conditions attached. God does not say "I love you on condition that you go to Mass or do certain penances". God loves the sinner as much as the saint because God is 100% love and is incapable of loving anybody 50%. That is very consoling, but it is also very demanding because we are called to be perfect just as our heavenly Father is perfect, which, of course, is an ideal beyond our ability. But fear not. God in his mercy bestows supernatural grace through the Holy Spirit. Super-natural... above and beyond what our natural powers can reach. However, even with supernatural grace, we do not attain divine perfection. Again, God's mercy provides for us. God provides the merciful process of purification known to us as purgatory. Do not think of purgatory as a place of punishment. No, it is a process of cleansing the smudges and stains of our earthly imperfections as we are drawn closer to the perfect vision and reflection of God. Thank you, God, for your unconditional love and your mercy to us in our imperfections.

PRAYERS

———

Heavenly Father, we thank you for your unconditional love and your understanding of our imperfections. With the gift of supernatural grace, help us to move beyond the limitations we set on our charity.
Lord, hear us.

May your Kingdom come as your ideals are established in our minds, hearts and behaviour.
Lord, hear us.

Forgive us our trespasses and enable us to forgive anybody who has wronged or hurt us.
Lord, hear us.

We pray for anybody who has been deeply hurt or betrayed. May God's healing Spirit bring them renewed peace and strength.
Lord, hear us.

(Add prayers for any local, personal or topical intention)

O God of infinite love, graciously listen to the prayers we offer in the name of Jesus Christ, the Lord. Amen.

WEDNESDAY

Matthew 6:1-6. 16-18

1. Jesus showed extraordinary mercy to sins of weakness. But there was one sin that really upset him, religious hypocrisy: performing religious acts for the sake of gaining the admiration of people. We all need approval and affirmation. We would dry up if we never received appreciation or gratitude. But it must never be the main motive for performing acts of generosity, prayer or penance. We have to keep going even if we never experience any human appreciation. It is enough to know that God sees what we are doing. God wants to see us being generous, prayerful and disciplined. The desire to do what God wants is what matters.

2. "When you pray, go to your private room and, when you have shut the door, pray to your Father who is in that secret place." When Jesus lived, houses were small and only the very wealthy had private rooms. So Jesus was speaking about finding a quiet place within oneself. Shut the door. Leave your distractions outside for a few minutes. Just God and you. Listen, think, remember, pray. Value this time when you are alone with God. Remember, you are God's creation, God's work of art. You are precious in his eyes. God is with you. God is in you. Discover who you are. Learn to love silence. Pray to your Father who is on that secret place.

PRAYERS

Let us take the teaching of Jesus to heart as we pray.

May our religious leaders today be models of generosity, prayerfulness and self-discipline.
Lord, hear us

Lord, deliver us from hypocrisy and wanting to show off how good we are.
Lord, hear us.

Grant us the grace of quiet prayer where we shut the door to have a quiet place to develop our awareness of God's presence with us.
Lord, hear us.

May we be sensitive to the needs of people who need words of appreciation and affirmation.
Lord, hear us.

(Add prayers for any local, personal or topical intention)

Heavenly Father, you see all that is done in secret and reward it. Hear our prayers in the name of your Beloved Son, Jesus Christ, our Lord. Amen.

THURSDAY

MATTHEW 6:7-15

1. The Our Father must surely be the greatest lesson ever on prayer. There are three God-petitions and four us-petitions. Thy name, thy kingdom, thy will. In the first line we raise up mind and heart in revering God's holy name. In one sense God is as distant as Heaven, yet God is as near as a personal relationship. So we address God as our Father in Heaven. Then we call on God to come down, thy Kingdom come. May our world be filled with the reign of God in justice, peace and joy, as God would have it. Up... down... and then within us. May God's will be at the centre of our lives.

   Next we have the four us-petitions. For today and its needs, give us. Bread expresses all we need. For our past, forgive us our sins and enable us to forgive others who have offended us. For our future, do not put us to a test that would be too great for us. Finally, save us from the Evil One. It takes a brief time to learn this prayer by rote but it takes a lifetime to know it by heart.

2. If God already knows our needs, why must we ask him? God does not need our words. It's we who need the words for a variety of reasons. Having to use words clarifies many things for us. Words of petition clarify our need of God. Words make us more humble, more aware of our powerless plight without God. Having to repeat our petition over a period of time is a means of deepening our faith. Having to ask for forgiveness makes us more aware of our duty to forgive others. Words enable us to carry the needs of others to God. And shared words are a means of praying with others.

PRAYERS

Taking the lesson of Jesus to heart, we pray.

O God, our Creator and Father, may we honour you through reverence for your holy name.
Lord, hear us.

May your Kingdom come in a world where war shall be no more, all people will have food, and the commandments are obeyed.
Lord, hear us.

May your will be what we desire at all times.
Lord, hear us.

Give us the bread of all we need this day for health and well-being.
Lord, hear us.

Father, forgive us our sins and enable us to forgive all who have hurt us.
Lord, hear us.

Father, take us by the hand and deliver us from all evil.
Lord, hear us.

All our prayers we offer in union with Jesus Christ, our Lord. Amen

FRIDAY

MATTHEW 6:19-23

1. Years ago, in the royal court, a very important figure was the court jester. Part of his job was to humour the king when he was in bad form. One day the jester rubbed up the king in the wrong way. The king was furious and he gave the jester a dunce's hat to wear every day until he met a person more foolish than himself. Years later the king was close to death and not resigned to his fate. The jester, the king's friend for many years, asked him: "Whenever you were travelling abroad, didn't you send your ambassador to arrange the protocol?" The king replied, "Yes, I did." "Didn't you carefully plan your schedule for every day?" "Yes, I did." "Well here you are on the most important journey of your life and you made no arrangements. Take back this cap you gave me, for I have found a man more foolish than myself."

   "Do not store up treasures for yourself here on Earth ... for where your treasure is there will be your heart also."

2. "If your eye is sound, your whole body will be filled with light. If your eye is diseased, your whole body will be all darkness." There is an old saying that the eye is the window of the soul. The poet, Francis Langbridge described two ways of looking at life.

   > "Two men look out through the same bars:
   > One sees the mud, and one the stars."

   The eye of the artist can see beauty where nobody else can. One of the Beatitudes of Jesus says that the pure of heart shall see God. The way we see and judge people reveal as much about our inner life as about the object of our judgement. The pure of heart will see other people with the compassion of God, whereas the sick soul looks for the faults of people. "Blessed are the pure of heart for they shall see God."

PRAYERS

In the light of the Gospel, we are moved to pray.

May the teaching of the Church always remind us that we have
here no lasting city but seek one that is to come.
Lord, hear us.

May we resist the temptations of consumerism which convince us
that we must have things we really do not need.
Lord, hear us.

Open our eyes to the wonder and beauty all around us so that we
might praise you every day.
Lord, hear us.

Heal our diseased minds so that we will see what is good in people
rather than what is bad.
Lord, hear us.

(Add prayers for any local, personal or topical intention)

Heavenly father, graciously hear the prayers we offer in the name
of Jesus Christ, your Son, our Lord. Amen.

SATURDAY

MATTHEW 6:24-34

1. A key to understanding the Sermon on the Mount is to notice how often God is called Father. In the entire Old Testament, God is called Father only fourteen times, and not in the sense of a personal relationship. But in the Sermon on the Mount, God is called Father fifteen times, and always referring to a personal relationship. Today's Gospel is about drawing confidence from the loving care of the Father rather than trusting in material things. Jesus pointed to the adornment of fields and the beauty of the birds. It is a pagan mistake to set our hearts on material things. Set your hearts on God's Kingdom and all these other things will be given you as well. So, do not worry about tomorrow: tomorrow will take care of itself. In the words of a song:

    "See the birds and flowers, how they neither sow nor spin,
    Trust in God our Father, you can put your trust in him."

2. "By their fruits you shall know them." Where life is built around material things, people are insecure, anxious and never satisfied. Today we have more money but less contentment, bigger houses and smaller families, more options open but less fidelity. We produce too much food for the market but not enough to feed the hungry. We can communicate with any country in an instant but may not know our next-door neighbour. We have more labour-saving devices but less time. We can reach outer space but are out of touch with the inner space of the soul. There are three things that last, faith, hope and love. Set your hearts on faith which enables us to know God; hope which draws confidence from God; and love which enables us to enjoy God.

PRAYERS

Trusting in the loving providence of God, we pray.

May those who hold financial and political power have a conscience about sharing the world's resources and putting a speedy end to world-hunger.
Lord, hear us.

Free us from the temptations of consumerism persuading us to want what we really do not need.
Lord, hear us.

May our eyes be open to the simple beauties of life and so increase our trust in God's providence.
Lord, hear us.

We pray for people who are trapped in anxiety and compulsions. May they learn from Jesus how to let go and let God.
Lord, hear us.

(Add prayers for any local, personal or topical intention)

God our Father, you provide for all your creatures. May we trust totally in your providence, through Christ, our Lord. Amen.

MONDAY

MATTHEW 7:1-5

1. Hypocrisy is something that crops up very often in Matthew's Gospel. Today, it is the hypocrisy of commenting on another person's faults without first sorting out our own which may be far worse. "Take the plank out of your own eye first and then you will see clearly to take the splinter out of your brother's eye". When we are honest about our own lives, we become more humble and compassionate. We are less judgemental. With eyes of compassion, we begin to see clearly. We begin to see the bigger picture of where the other person is coming from. Our tone of voice is gentler. Confronting a person in a stern way might do more harm than good. That's like the half-blind person damaging the eye that has the speck of sawdust in it. The best person to speak with an alcoholic is someone who has humbly admitted to having the problem. To judge another person properly we need self-honesty, humility, compassion and gentleness.

2. A speck of sawdust in somebody's eye but a full plank in your own! Surely there was a touch of humour in Jesus' voice. The audience would have enjoyed this exaggeration. A touch of humour is a good way to attract attention. The humorous image would remain in their memory and so would the moral. When you point a finger at another person there are three fingers pointing back to yourself. Very often, what irritates you in another person is something in your own personality that you have not faced. Why are you irritated? Why do you judge this person? "The judgements you give out are the judgements you will get." The conscience you are most responsible for is your own.

PRAYERS

As we take the teaching of Jesus to heart, we are inspired to pray.

Lord, when we come to you for mercy and forgiveness, we trust in your understanding of human nature. Help us to show the same understanding when we are tempted to judge others.
Lord, hear us.

Open our eyes in self-honesty so that we might see clearly what we should sort out in our own lives.
Lord, hear us.

Lord, help us to control our tongues and our tendency to gossip.
Lord, hear us.

We pray for people whose good name or self-confidence has been ruined by gossip and rumour.
Lord, hear us.

(Add prayers for any local, personal or topical intention)

God of mercy and compassion, hear the prayers we offer in the name of Jesus Christ, our Lord and Saviour. Amen.

TUESDAY

MATTHEW 7:6. 12-14

1. Always treat others as you would like them to treat you; that is the meaning of the Law and the Prophets. Every religion or philosophy of life has a similar Golden Rule: do not do to others what you would not wish to be done to you. But there is a significant difference in the way Jesus put it. He phrased it in a positive way. "Always treat others as you would like them to treat you." The plan of Jesus is that charity is to be pro-active. He goes beyond the negative language of "Do not do to others". Negative rules are very good but they can be understood as applicable only within certain conditions. With Jesus, charity takes the initiative. Christian love is a decision of the will to be determined to love, regardless of whether a person deserves it or not. "Treat others as you would like them to treat you."

2. "Enter by the narrow gate, since the road that leads to perdition is wide and spacious, and many take it." We are nearing the end of the Sermon on the Mount. Jesus asks us to make a commitment to follow his ideals. Modern permissiveness is weak on commitment. People want the space to change track to whatever suits ME at any given time. Yet we see how focused sports people are on strict diets, sleep patterns, exercises, and development of basic skills. The undisciplined athlete is a born loser. Jesus urges us to stop messing about in regard to what we believe, how we behave and how we worship God. We are to have the narrow focus of the dedicated athlete. "Enter by the narrow gate".

PRAYERS

The teaching of Jesus is a map for the road that leads to salvation. So we pray.

Jesus has given us the truth and shown us the way. May we make a clear commitment to follow his truth and his way.
Lord, hear us.

We pray for those who have strayed away from Jesus as they want to experiment with different theories and behaviour. May they come to the realisation that lack of clear commitment leads us nowhere.
Lord, hear us.

May we always be guided by the Golden Rule of treating others as we would wish them to treat us.
Lord, hear us.

Let us pray for anybody whom we have harmed because we did not treat them with Christian love.
Lord, hear us.

(Add prayers for any local, personal or topical intention)

God our Father, may your grace always guide us to follow Jesus on the road that leads to salvation. Through Christ, our Lord. Amen.

WEDNESDAY

MATTHEW 7:15-20

1. CYCLE A

"Beware of false prophets who come disguised as sheep but underneath are ravenous wolves. By their fruits you shall know them". Instead of identifying other people as false prophets, let us focus on ourselves and ask what kind of fruits or witness we produce. Is my religion a very private affair, me and God in a private box, with no concern or sharing with others? Am I so heavenly-minded that I am no earthly good? Am I so critical and pessimistic that I am what Pope Francis called a sourpuss? Am I open to change, or do I cling rigidly to customs and regulations which were helpful in the past but have lost their significance today? Is my life producing good fruit? Or bad fruit? Do I have a pious exterior hiding a bitter heart? By their fruits you shall know them.

2. CYCLE B

When the Israelites returned to Jerusalem after their captivity in Babylon, things were in a bad way. Many false prophets were misleading the people towards pagan rituals. Then one day, while repairing the temple, an ancient scroll was discovered. It was a portion of the Law of God which was part of Israel's covenant with God. King Josiah was inspired to start a religious reform. The false prophets were banished and the practice of child sacrifice was stopped. Many other documents were discovered. They were inspired to weave these writings into a single text. This collection was the beginning of the written Bible as we know it. The false prophets were replaced by the true prophets who prepared the way for Jesus Christ.

PRAYERS

In the light of our Scripture readings, we pray.

At a time when many false prophets are leading people astray, we pray that the Holy Spirit will guide Pope *(name)* and our bishops as true shepherds of the flock of Christ.
Lord, hear us.

May the proof of our faith be seen in the evidence of how we live as kind, compassionate and prayerful Christians.
Lord, hear us.

We thank God for the people who have handed on the faith to us, who taught us or inspired us. May our lives bear fruit as an inspiration to others.
Lord, hear us.

Let us pray for family members or acquaintances who have been led astray by false prophets. May they return to the light of Christ.
Lord, hear us.

(Add prayers for any local, personal or topical intention)

God our Father, continue to send holy leaders to inspire the Church. We offer these prayers in the name of Jesus Christ, our Lord and Saviour. Amen.

THURSDAY

MATTHEW 7:21-29

1. The Sermon on the Mount closes with the parable of the rock and the sand. It is very pertinent to our time, when there has been a flood of changes and the collapse of many traditions. The teaching of Jesus is a solid rock on which the house of life can be built, withstanding every crisis, opposition and change of fashion. There is today a fog of vagueness regarding doctrine and a mist of uncertainty about morality. Pick-and-choose religion selects what is comforting and rejects what is demanding. The umbrella of pluralism shelters a reprehensible tolerance of disobeying the commandments. Pious talk without practical action is not a solid foundation. The advice of Jesus is to listen and obey, to hear and to do the will of the Father.

2. People today lack stability. They change jobs, addresses and partners. They find it hard to make a life-commitment which closes the doors on other options. The feeling is that all choices are on the menu and we ought to have the option to try them. Full commitment of life, in marriage or religious profession, is a prospect too daunting for people who lack inner stability. Little wonder that there is deep insecurity. Many people struggle to find a lasting meaning to life. Jesus said that you cannot build a house on shifting stand. But the Lord God is an everlasting rock.

PRAYERS

Let us take the words of Jesus to heart as we pray.

The apostle Simon was given a new name, Peter, meaning a rock. Let us pray for his successor today, Pope *(name),* that his life and teaching may be a solid rock of fidelity to Christ and a source of stability in a changing world.
Lord, hear us.

May our religion be deeper than pious talk. May we listen deeply to the Word of God and translate it into practical action.
Lord, hear us.

For people who suffer from insecurity and constant anxiety: may the Lord grant them the grace to trust totally in God as an everlasting rock of stability.
Lord, hear us.

For married couples who are going through a shaky time: may the grace of the Sacrament of Matrimony restore their loving friendship.
Lord, hear us.

(Add prayers for any local, personal or topical intention)

O God, whose love endures forever, strengthen our inner backbone of trust as we pray in the name of Jesus Christ, your Son, our Lord. Amen.

FRIDAY

MATTHEW 8:1-4

1. At the end of the Sermon on the Mount, Matthew tells us that the teaching of Jesus made a deep impression on the people because he taught them with authority, unlike the scribes. The authority of Jesus was proved in the evidence of his divine power to heal people. The scribes accumulated many regulations about washing and cleansing, but they lacked the power to cleanse and heal. There were heartless laws about avoiding lepers and not touching them. So it was a great shock when Jesus touched the leper. But this touch conferred divine healing. Contrary to what people expected, Jesus did not catch the leper's disease: but the leper caught the cleanliness of Jesus. Sometimes we are tempted to hide behind human regulations and rubrics as an excuse for not reaching out to people with a touch of God's love which gives hope to the sinner.

2. The leper said to Jesus, "If you want to, you can heal me." "Of course I want to." Surely, a smile on the face of Jesus touched the leper's life ever before his hand touched him. Centuries before that day, against all the odds, Abraham and Sarah received the gift of a son and heir. This child was given a very beautiful name, Isaac, which means the smile of God. We are the recipients of many smiles of God, many blessings, each day, but we may not notice them. It is a very helpful practice at the end of each day to reflect on the unnoticed blessings or smiles of the day. Then pick just one of them and thank God for it.

PRAYERS

Encouraged by the story of Jesus healing the leper, we pray.

May the ministry and teaching of the Church bring the smile of God and the joy of the Gospel into our lives.
Lord, hear us.

May we never hide behind rigid rules as an excuse for not responding to the needs of people.
Lord, hear us.

We pray for people who are like spiritual lepers as their happiness is being eaten away by darkness, failure or anxiety. May they be touched by the hand of Jesus and get a smile back on their faces.
Lord, hear us.

May our presence be a source of hope and joy for the people we meet today.
Lord, hear us.

   (Add prayers for any local, personal or topical intention)

O God of love and compassion, graciously hear the prayers we offer in the name of Jesus, Christ, your Son, our Lord. Amen.

SATURDAY

MATTHEW 8:5-17

1. Jesus was astonished at the faith of this centurion, an officer in the Roman army. Normally it's the people who are astonished at the works of Jesus. We can see three aspects to this faith which Jesus found astonishing. First of all, the centurion's faith was shown in his care for his sick servant: not a family member but a servant. Then we see his profound humility and reverence: "I am not worthy to have you under my roof". Thirdly, we see his absolute confidence in Jesus. There is no need for Jesus to come. One word from Jesus would be sufficient. As a military man, the centurion lived in a world where the word of authority was obeyed without question. He believed that a word from the authority of Jesus would be carried out. The prophecy of Isaiah was fulfilled: "He took our sicknesses away and carried our diseases for us."

2. What a fantastic privilege it would be if Jesus were to come to your house today. But, by the grace of God, you have an even greater privilege. Jesus is coming to you personally in Holy Communion. We make the humble words of the centurion our own. "Lord, I am not worthy that you should enter under my roof, but only say the word and my soul shall be healed."

PRAYERS

As the Roman officer brought his petition to Jesus, we are inspired to come with confidence.

We pray for a lively faith which will inspire our lives, especially faith in the presence of Jesus Christ in the Blessed Eucharist.
Lord, hear us.

For family members and others who no longer come to Mass: may they receive the grace of believing in the Lord's presence as the living Bread come down from Heaven.
Lord, hear us.

As the centurion pleaded on behalf of his sick servant, we carry to the Lord the needs of those who are sick in any way.
Lord, hear us.

May the divine energy we receive in the Bread of Life inspire us to bring the love and compassion of the Lord to the people we meet this day.
Lord, hear us.

(Add prayers for any local, personal or topical intention)

Almighty Father, you sent down your Beloved Son to carry our diseases for us. Hear the prayers we offer with confidence in the name of Jesus Christ, our Lord. Amen.

MONDAY

MATTHEW 8:18-22

1. Today we meet with two people who declared an interest in following Jesus, but he warned them about the cost of discipleship. One was a scribe, a man who had a well-paid job. Jesus challenged him about leaving his financial security to take up an itinerant life without the security of knowing where the next meal or bed would come from. Many of the great saints showed extraordinary trust in God's providence. Mother Teresa of Calcutta often received great donations from a certain wealthy business man. When he was selling out his business, he wanted to set up a trust fund which would offer financial security for the future of Mother Teresa's work. But the great little woman would not accept it because it would go against her understanding of the Gospel. Her trust was not in a bank account but in the providence of God.

2. The second applicant who was keen to follow Jesus said, "But first let me go and bury my father". Jesus challenged him in a way that is difficult to interpret. "Leave the dead to bury their dead: your duty is to go and spread the news of the Kingdom of God". Family duties can be discharged by others who have not received the powerful energy of a missionary vocation. Missionaries, from Abraham down to our own day, have made heroic sacrifices in leaving family and homeland to serve the call of God. All of us are called to leave our comfort zone, and to be generous with our time, in order to deepen our commitment to God, particularly through helping people in need.

PRAYERS

In the light of God's Word, we pray.

That the people who feel the call of God to serve the Gospel might overcome their fears by trusting absolutely in God's support.
Lord, hear us.

We thank you, Lord, for all who have made personal sacrifices to serve us in the Church. Continue to support them, especially when they are feeling low.
Lord, hear us.

May all of us be prepared to leave our comfort zone in order to help others in various ways.
Lord, hear us.

The harvest is huge but the labourers are getting older. We pray for vocations to the priesthood and religious life.
Lord, hear us.

(Add prayers for any local, personal or topical intention)

O God, the giver of every good gift, support us at all times. We offer our prayers in the name of Jesus Christ, your Son, our Lord. Amen.

TUESDAY

MATTHEW 8:23-27

1. On the voyage of life, storms blow up. We pray but get no answer. It seems that God is out of reach, his phone is switched off, he is asleep. No, God is there all the time, watching us from a distance. Some of the great saints experienced long periods of darkness. Saint Thérèse of Lisieux wrote that in her early days in the convent, she felt as if she was the favourite toy of the Child Jesus. Later she experienced deep desolation and darkness. Now she was the toy that was thrown away. God allows these times of darkness to stretch and deepen our little faith. Thomas Merton wrote that in daylight we can see the objects that are near us, but it is only in the darkness of night that we can see the distant stars. Trust God in times of darkness. God is using the night of faith to make our faith deeper than a matter of how we feel.

2. Saint Teresa of Calcutta lived the last forty years of her life with no consolations or light in prayer. She was wise enough to know that feelings are a poor guide regarding prayer. She had a vision once when Jesus repeated his words from the cross: "I thirst". From this, she understood that her spiritual dryness was a way of sharing in the thirst of Jesus. For anyone who is in a desert of prayer, it is helpful to recall the words of Saint Paul: "The Spirit comes to help us in our weakness, for, when we do not know how to pray properly, then the Spirit personally makes our petitions for us in groans that cannot be put into words; and he who can see into all hearts knows what the Spirit means, because prayers that the Spirit makes for all God's holy people are always in accordance with the mind of God." If all you can muster in prayer is a groan or a sigh, that's OK with God. Leave it to the Spirit to make sense of it.

PRAYERS

We draw confidence from the Gospel as we pray.

The Church today is a boat on very stormy seas. Reach out your saving hand, Lord, to lead us safely through these difficult times.
Lord, hear us.

When our faith is being tested in darkness, may we always trust that God is with us and has not forsaken us.
Lord, hear us.

We pray for people who are fleeing from persecution or warfare, crossing the sea in untrustworthy boats. May their voyage be safe and may they find a better life.
Lord, hear us

For those who are tossed about in mental storms or emotional distress: may they find peace.
Lord, hear us.

(Add prayers for any local, personal or topical intention)

O God, you never forsake us. You watch over us at all times. Hear the prayers we offer in the name of Jesus Christ, our Lord. Amen.

WEDNESDAY

MATTHEW 8:28-34

1. It is extraordinary how the evil spirits call out to Jesus with the most holy titles. In today's Gospel, they call him Son of God. Far from adoring Jesus, what they are doing is trying to get hold of his power through the use of his name. Names were very significant in those times. A name called up the presence of the person, and in the presence was the power of the person. Maybe if they hit the right title, they might get hold of his power. Of course it did not work out as they wanted. Jesus told us to pray in his name. All our prayers at Mass are directed to the Father in the name of Jesus, that is, through him as our Mediator, with him as one who took our human nature to himself and in him as parts of the body of which he is the head. In the Acts of the Apostles, there is a wonderful story of how Peter said to a crippled man, "I have neither silver nor gold, but I will give you what I have: in the name of Jesus Christ the Nazarene, walk!" People who have a deep reverence for the name of Jesus walk tall because they live with the presence and power of Jesus.

2. What about the herd of pigs? The evil spirits cry out, "Have you come to torture us?" They know they are defeated. But where can they go? As a last resort they ask for the lowest of the low, into the pigs. But even the pigs did not accept them so they charged down the hill into the lake. This story confirms the complete victory of Jesus over the evil spirits. The evil spirits continue their efforts to lead us astray. Fear not, we have the greater power of Jesus on our side. He is with us. He came as a doctor to bring healing and peace. And the last line of his prayer is "Deliver us from Evil".

PRAYERS

Jesus once said, "Have courage for I have overcome the world." So, with confidence, we pray.

May we grow in our reverence towards the name of Jesus, knowing that in him, we receive the power to overcome every temptation to Evil.
Lord, hear us.

May people who are deeply disturbed in mind or spirit receive the peace promised by Jesus.
Lord, hear us.

That the evil people who are the cause of war and violence be converted to the ways of peace and justice.
Lord, hear us.

May people who are struggling with inner demons and addictions receive the grace of peace and strength.
Lord, hear us.

   (Add prayers for any local, personal or topical intention)

O God, your power over Evil was shown in the life of Jesus Christ. Grant serenity to all who pray in the name of Jesus Christ, the Lord. Amen.

THURSDAY

MATTHEW 9:1-8

1. "Courage, my child, your sins are forgiven." Why did Jesus offer forgiveness of sins before healing the paralysis of the body? Inner healing of the spirit is often connected with healing of the body. Physical healing is hindered as long as a person is trapped in a web of negative thoughts and feelings. Even before Jesus mentioned forgiveness, he called for courage. "Your sins are forgiven." The inner relief of receiving forgiveness opened up new possibilities for the patient. He was now ready to receive physical healing.

2. Are you ready to accept God's forgiveness, or do you continue to confess sins for which you have already received forgiveness? Has your self-esteem gone too low? Are you paralysed by the weight of guilt? We confess our sins in the context of a sacrament. Sacraments are celebrations of God's grace and blessing. The point of confessing is not to tell God what he already knows. It is we who need to hear ourselves admitting what wrongs we have done and where we need God's help. When we receive absolution, it is God telling us, "Your sins are forgiven. Rise up, take up your mat and walk". We can now walk out renewed and refreshed. A feeling of awe came over the people when they saw what healing Jesus brought. And they praised God.

PRAYERS

Jesus is the Lamb of God who takes away the sins of the world. So we pray with confidence.

May the Church be a hospital of healing for all who have been wounded in the battlefield of life.
Lord, hear us.

May we grow in a mature use of the Sacrament of Forgiveness.
Lord, hear us.

In our prayer we carry to God all who are spiritually paralysed in guilt and negativity.
Lord, hear us.

For all who are physically handicapped: may they have great friends to support them.
Lord, hear us.

   (Add prayers for any local, personal or topical intention)

O God of mercy and forgiveness, hear our prayers in the name of Jesus Christ, our Lord. Amen.

FRIDAY

MATTHEW 9:9-13

1. Matthew had a beautiful name. It means the gift of God. Hardly the name we would give to a tax collector. At that time, tax collectors had ample scope for overcharging people. So they were regarded as sinners and banned from Jewish worship. But in a moment of grace, Jesus passed by. He looked at Matthew and called him to follow. Leaving all behind him, Matthew became a disciple. Then he was chosen as one of the twelve apostles. Later he was author of one of the Four Gospels. We can say of Matthew that he was someone who became his name... a gift of God. We ask ourselves, who would I nominate as someone who has been a gift of God to me? And then we ask, am I a gift of God to other people?

2. The name Pharisees means the Separated Ones. They came to prominence two hundred years before the time of Jesus, when it was necessary to warn people to keep away from the pagan customs of their Greek rulers. But they went too far with this avoidance of any contact with people regarded as sinners. Eating and drinking with people meant sharing life with them. Jesus was a scandal to them when he ate with a sinner like Matthew. But he had come to give hope to the sinners and outcasts. "It is not the healthy who need the doctor but the sick. What I want is mercy, not sacrifice. And indeed I did not come to call the virtuous, but sinners."

PRAYERS

We thank God for all the people who have been God's gift to us some time or other.

May the Church be a community of believers whose way of life makes each one of us a gift of God to others.
Lord, hear us.

May God bless and reward all who have been a great gift to our lives.
Lord, hear us.

As we reflect on Matthew the tax collector, we pray that people who handle public money may always be upright and honest in their dealings.
Lord, hear us.

Lord, save us from the temptation of the Pharisees to judge and condemn others.
Lord, hear us.

(Add prayers for any local, personal or topical intention)

O God, the giver of every good gift, graciously hear the prayers we offer in the name of Jesus Christ, our Lord. Amen.

SATURDAY

MATTHEW 9:14-17

1. "Do not put new wine into old wineskins: the skins will burst and the wine will be lost." Before glass bottles were available, people used leather skins to carry liquids. Leather gradually dried out and hardened. New wine created gas as it fermented. This would burst the old skins which had no flexibility. Fresh new skins were required. Remaining rigidly with customs and regulations which have lost their significance may be good for history, but not for evangelisation. You cannot put the new evangelisation, which recent popes have promoted, into old birettas!

2. Jesus found that the religious structures of his time were stagnant and self-serving. There was no hope for the sinners who were treated as cursed. Jesus saw that a patch-up reform would solve nothing. In the Sermon on the Mount, he went beyond the traditions and regulations which were handed down, to the original vision and values of the commandments. The problem with many traditionalists is that what they want to preserve are selected parts of history and selected customs and rubrics. In the spirit of the Sermon on the Mount, true traditionalists go back to the original message and its implementation. They ask what did Jesus do? What did he say? How did he respond to situations? What would he do today? The inflexible upholders of human traditions were so threatened by the reform of Jesus that they plotted his death.

PRAYERS

Jesus, the Bridegroom of the Church is always with us, so we pray with confidence.

May the Church, the Bride of Christ, proclaim the joy of the Gospel to all people.
Lord, hear us.

May the Holy Spirit open up our closed minds and soften our inflexible ways which resist any reform. Help us to treasure the past without being imprisoned in it.
Lord, hear us.

May the Holy Spirit give us fresh courage to express the original message of Jesus in ways that appeal to the people of our time.
Lord, hear us.

We pray for people who find any change difficult. May they have greater trust that the Holy Spirit is active in the Church.
Lord, hear us.

(Add prayers for any local, personal or topical intention)

God, our Father, graciously listen to the prayers we offer in the name of Jesus Christ, your Son, our Lord. Amen.

MONDAY

MATTHEW 9:18-26

1. Today we have two miracles of Jesus and each one involves hands and touching. A twelve-year old girl had died and her father bowed low before Jesus, pleading: "Come and lay your hands on her and her life will be restored". In the second story, a woman with an embarrassing bleeding for twelve years reached out in faith to touch the fringe of Jesus' cloak. Jesus saw her faith. "Courage, my daughter, your faith has restored you to health." Pope Francis, in his letter on the *Joy of the Gospel*, wrote that we may be tempted to be the kind of Christian who keeps the Lord's wounds at arm's length. Yet Jesus wants us to touch human misery, to touch the suffering flesh of others. In one of his homilies, he suggested that when we give something to a poor beggar, look at the person and hand the money rather than throw it into a cap. The personal touch might mean more than the coins.

2. Many Catholics express their faith with their hands: rubbing statues, caressing a little crucifix, lighting candles, being blessed with relics. These expressions are sometimes criticised as being superstitious. Jesus thought otherwise. He understood how the woman expressed her faith by touching the fringe of his garment. If it was good enough for Jesus, it should be good enough for us. The faith of this woman is celebrated in a popular hymn.

> Reach out and touch the Lord as he goes by:
> You'll find he's not too busy to hear your heart's cry.
> He is passing by this moment, your needs to supply.
> Reach out to touch the Lord, as he goes by.

PRAYERS

Today's two miracles of Jesus remind us of the sacredness of touch and the healing energy of God in our hands.

Lord, bless the hands of those who bring us the Eucharist, who lay hands upon the sick, and who raise a hand over a penitent as a sign of the Holy Spirit.
Lord, hear us.

Bless the hands of those who feel a deep need to touch some holy object as a support to their faith.
Lord, hear us.

Bless our hands so that they will never be used in violence: may our hands be helpful, uplifting and caring.
Lord, hear us.

We pray for those who are spiritually dead. May they feel the hand of Jesus inviting them to wake up and start living again.
Lord, hear us.

(Add prayers for any local, personal or topical intention)

God, our Father, graciously hear our prayers as we reach out to you in the name of Jesus Christ, our Lord. Amen.

TUESDAY

MATTHEW 9:32-38

1. The people were harassed and dejected, like sheep without a shepherd. They were leaderless. Jesus felt sorry for them. Feeling sorry with people is compassion, suffering with. This is the meaning of mercy. The English word *mercy*, does not capture the real meaning of the Latin word, *misericordia*. The first part *miseri* refers to feeling sorry; *cordia* refers to the heart. Misericordia literally means the heart that feels. The Irish word, *trócaire*, is an accurate translation of Misericordia. One of the ways offered by philosophers to prove the existence of God is the theory that there must have been some being before anything was created or moved. God was called the Unmoved Mover. A great Jewish theologian, Abraham Heschel, rejected that title and called God the Most Moved Mover. God is moved in mercy, compassion and tenderness towards us. Jesus felt sorry for the people.

2. Jesus was moved because the people were leaderless, so he set out to proclaim the Good News to them. What is this good news? First of all, there is a God. You are God's creation. God loves you, cares for you, and wants your friendship. The second part of the Good News is the reality of sin. People strayed from God's ways and messed up the world. But God did not leave us unaided in that mess. God loved us so much that he sent us his Beloved Son, so that we might not be lost and leaderless. The third step of the Good News is the invitation of God to a close, personal relationship. But the harvest is huge. There are millions of people today who need to hear the message of Jesus. Ask the Lord of the harvest to send labourers to his harvest field. Pray every day for vocations to the priesthood, to religious life, to any commitment of life serving the Kingdom of God on Earth.

PRAYERS

Jesus felt sorry for the people who were leaderless and dejected so he sent out his disciples to be shepherds to lead the flock.

We pray for Pope *(name)* and our bishops who are ordained as shepherds of Christ's flock. Guide them with divine wisdom and courage.
Lord, hear us.

The harvest is great, the labourers are few and getting older. May the call of God touch many people to dedicate their lives to the service of the Gospel.
Lord, hear us.

It is a stressful time for overworked priests. May God's grace sustain them when they feel overwhelmed and exhausted.
Lord, hear us.

We received the light of Christ at our Baptism. May we bring that light to everyone we meet today and every day.
Lord, hear us.

   (Add prayers for any local, personal or topical intention)

O God, our Creator and Saviour, graciously listen to the prayers we offer in the name of Jesus Christ, our Lord. Amen.

WEDNESDAY

MATTHEW 10:1-7

1. The apostles chosen by Jesus were unlikely leaders if one were to be guided by human estimation. By God's grace, fiery Simon became Peter, the Rock. The brothers, James and John, were known as Boanerges, the Sons of Thunder. They channelled their excesses to heroic martyrdom and deep contemplation. Simon was a Zealot, a revolutionary prepared to take up arms against the Romans. Matthew collected taxes for the Romans. Political differences melted away in the company of Jesus. Jesus had an extraordinary ability, the eye of the artist, to see potential in unlikely people. Perhaps we should think again about somebody we have mentally dismissed.

2. Although the harvest was vast, the missionary strategy of Jesus was to begin work with a small group in a limited area. Jesus would have agreed with the marketing policy of a certain multinational company: think globally but act locally. It is a temptation to talk big and do nothing. The Christian mission begins at home. Make it recognisable as a Christian house with religious emblems such as holy water, a crucifix, a statue. Let there be prayer, grace before meals, respect for God's name. The best means of evangelisation is not talk but the witness of life. Support the activities in your parish. When volunteers are required, don't be leaving it to others. You are an apostle, a bringer of light.

PRAYERS

Encouraged by the example and teaching of Jesus, we pray.

For Pope *(name)* and our bishops, the successors of the apostles. May they be inspired in wisdom and courage by the Holy Spirit who transformed the first apostles.
Lord, hear us.

May our local parish be alive with the Spirit of Christ.
Lord, hear us.

The greatest strength in evangelisation is the witness of Christian living. May our lives be a light to inspire others.
Lord, hear us.

May we have the eyes of Jesus to see the potential of people more than their faults.
Lord, hear us.

(Add prayers for any local, personal or topical intention)

O God of love, graciously answer the prayers we offer in the name of Jesus Christ, our Lord. Amen.

THURSDAY

Matthew 10:5-15

1. When Jesus sent out the first apostles, he instructed them to be bringers of peace to every house they entered. Let us reflect on the Peace Prayer associated with Saint Francis of Assisi. This prayer asks for the grace to be instruments or channels of God's peace. "Where there is hatred let me bring your love"... not just my love but God's love. Responding to hatred by a return of hatred only increases the problems of the world. Somebody must take the initiative to put an end to the cycle of hatred adding to hatred. "Where there is injury, let me offer pardon." Jesus, in the Sermon on the Mount, asked his followers to show that patient love is more powerful than bullying or violence. Where there is doubt, may I be a witness to the light of faith. Where there is despair, let me be a bringer of hope. Where there is darkness, let me bring the light of Christ. With God's help, may I turn sadness into joy.

2. One of the keys to serving peace is to stop feeling sorry for ourselves... victims of PLOM, poor, little, old me! So we pray that we might think of others before our own comfort.

   "Grant, that I may not so much seek to be consoled as to console, to be understood as to understand, to be loved as to love." We learn that it is in giving that we receive; in pardoning that we are pardoned; and in dying that we are born to eternal life.

   "Whatever house you enter, let your peace descend upon it." That is our apostolate, to be instruments of God's peace to others.

PRAYERS

We are called by Jesus to be apostles of peace to all. So we pray.

For an end to all war and violence: may there be justice and peace in every land.
Lord, hear us.

For all who are the victims of war and persecution: may people who are forced to leave their homeland travel safely, and may they be welcomed with Christian dignity.
Lord, hear us.

May there be peace in our minds and hearts so that we can be bringers of peace to others.
Lord, hear us.

May there be peace in families. May divided families be reconciled again.
Lord, hear us.

(Add prayers for any local, personal or topical intention)

O God, the Father of all, hear our prayers for peace, in the name of Jesus Christ, your Son, our Lord. Amen.

FRIDAY

MATTHEW 10:16-23

1. "Remember that I am sending you out like sheep among wolves." When Matthew wrote his Gospel, Jews who had become Christians were regarded as heretics. They were banned from entering the local synagogue, and refused service in local shops. What was very painful was division within families, brother betraying brother to death, and the father his child. In some places, there was violent persecution and these Christians had to flee from their home place. These were people whom Matthew had in mind when he wrote his Gospel. He reminded them that Jesus was arrested, tried and executed. What they were going through brought them very close to Jesus. The Holy Spirit would be the source of their wisdom and perseverance.

2. Sadly, persecution of Christians is as bad today as in any time of the past, although it gets very little mention in the media. We may not have to face martyrdom or physical persecution, but we may have to live with very anti-Christian media and unbalanced reporting. We may be the target of cynical workmates. Even at home, in the family, we might be victims of mockery. Jesus has promised to be with us. "You will be hated by all people on account of my name: but those who stand firm to the end will be saved".

PRAYERS

We take to heart what Jesus said about being persecuted, and so we pray.

For an end to all persecution, warfare and violence: that all people may be able to live in peace.
Lord, hear us.

For the victims of religious persecution who are forced to flee from their homes: may they find a place to live with peace and dignity.
Lord, hear us.

For people who are mocked because of their Christian beliefs: may the Holy Spirit give them great inner peace and strength.
Lord, hear us.

Where families are divided on religious issues, may they have the grace of reconciliation.
Lord, hear us.

(Add prayers for any local, personal or topical intention)

O God, the Father of all, may the differences between people be overcome through peaceful means. This we ask in the name of Jesus Christ, our mediator and Lord. Amen.

SATURDAY

MATTHEW 10:24-33

1. Once upon a time... not too long ago... it took courage of a sort not to go to church in holy Ireland. People who did not go to church were regarded as odd, or maybe worse. They swam against the social tide which equated church attendance with respectability. How things have changed! Now it takes courage to witness to Christian beliefs and ideals. One has to swim against the current of popular opinion stirred up by social media brain-washing and cynical agnosticism. Three times in today's Gospel Jesus repeats "Do not be afraid". This is the phrase most often repeated in the Bible. God knows that we are cowards so he continually exhorts us to have courage, to have confidence . If people opposed Jesus and called him diabolical names, why should we be surprised if we have to put up with a little of the same? We are in good company, we are with Jesus.

2. Pope Francis compared priests to aeroplanes: they make news only when they crash! The wonderful contribution of the Church to education, culture, medical care, feeding the hungry, working for justice and peace, is being airbrushed out of history. But Jesus tells us not to be afraid because the time will come when the full truth will be recognised. "Everything now covered will be uncovered and everything now hidden will be made clear". Be not afraid: God sees the full picture. "So, if anyone declares for me in the presence of others, I will declare myself for them in the presence of my Father in Heaven. But the one who disowns me in the presence of others, I will disown in the presence of my Father in Heaven." Be not afraid: God is with us. "Blessed are those who are persecuted in the cause of right, theirs is the Kingdom of Heaven."

PRAYERS

Encouraged by the exhortation of Jesus not to be afraid, we pray.

May the Church always be faithful to the ideals of Christ in the face of opposition and cynicism.
Lord, hear us.

When we are faced with criticism, may the Holy Spirit strengthen us to remain calm and charitable.
Lord, hear us.

May we always take heart from the words of Jesus urging us not to be afraid.
Lord, hear us.

Let us pray for those who oppose Christian ideals and constantly criticise the Church. May their eyes be opened to see all that the Church has done and continues to do for the betterment of life.
Lord, hear us.

(Add prayers for any local, personal or topical intention)

O God, your all-seeing eye watches over us always. Continue to guard us from all evil as we pray in the name of Jesus Christ, your Son, our Lord. Amen.

MONDAY

MATTHEW 10:34 – 11:1

1. In the early days of the Church, Jews who became followers of Christ continued to go to the temple and to the local synagogue. Soon there were more Christians from a Gentile background but the Jewish Christians maintained their Jewish prayers. About forty years later, the Council of Jews made the decision to ban the followers of Jesus from the local synagogues and shops. It resulted in very painful divisions in families, setting a man against his father, a daughter against her mother, and so on. It was in this context that Matthew wrote his Gospel. He appealed to Jews to see in Jesus the fulfilment of their own scriptures. And he encouraged Christians to see this painful family division as taking up the cross to follow Christ faithfully. Francis of Assisi suffered a similar painful break with his father in order to follow his calling. Family opposition or criticism may have to be overcome to follow Christ's call, perhaps in going to Mass or adoration, or in giving time to a Parish Council or voluntary charitable organisation. But, God will reward you.

2. Reward is promised three times in today's Gospel. Saint John Bosco did marvellous work for young people in Turin, providing them with education and a future. His inspiration spread to other countries. On one occasion his work took him to Paris. He sought lodging from a local priest. His clothes were poor and dusty from his travels, so all he was offered was a mattress among boxes up in the garret. Years later, when John Bosco's canonisation seemed likely, the priest admitted that if had known that his visitor was a future saint, he would have treated him with greater respect. But a Christian welcome is not to be confined to future saints. "If anyone gives so much as a cup of water to one of these little ones because he is a disciple, he will most certainly not lose his reward." Three times, Jesus promises the reward.

PRAYERS

Encouraged by the teaching of the Gospel, we pray.

May the Church be a family of the followers of Jesus Christ, supporting one another in prayer and in charitable action.
Lord, hear us.

May we be serious, not half-hearted, in following Christ, willing to sacrifice anything that gets in the way of our commitment.
Lord, hear us.

For people who meet with opposition to their religion, especially in the family circle: may God grant them the courage to persevere and may their witness bring about the conversion of their critics.
Lord, hear us.

May the promise of God's reward keep us going when situations are hard and the cross is heavy.
Lord, hear us.

(Add prayers for any local, personal or topical intention)

O God, the Father who sees all that we do, reward our little acts of kindness. Through Christ, our Lord. Amen

---

TUESDAY

MATTHEW 11:20-24

1. Jesus began to reproach the towns where most of his miracles were worked because they refused to repent. To repent means to change, to change our way of thinking and our way of living. Jesus began his preaching with the message to repent and believe. Notice that he said repent before believe. It may be necessary to make a change before one can make an act of faith. Believing is more than mentally accepting various matters of doctrine. There are people who are 100% orthodox in matters of doctrine while they are bitter and cruel. Believing begins in a willingness to change attitudes and behaviour. Many of the people who saw the miracles of Jesus made no effort to repent, to change their attitudes and behaviour. Believing means giving our hearts to God in the way we think, in our attitudes, our values and behaviour.

2. We read all sorts of health warnings or advice on diets and exercise... but are we willing to change? There was never so much sex education but this knowledge has not stopped the alarming increase in sexually transmitted disease and unwanted pregnancies. Knowledge without willpower is useless. Take the scandalous problem of world hunger. With modern science, medical advancements and rapid communication, we have the knowledge to solve the problem, but do we have the willpower? We need a change of heart, we need to repent. Jesus reproached the people who saw his miracles but refused to change their ways. Are we any better? Are we willing to change ways that harm our health... harm our family... harm our world?

PRAYERS

Jesus reproached the people who saw his miracles but refused to change their ways.

May the Church always challenge us to change our attitudes and values so that we can follow Christ more closely.
Lord, hear us.

May those who have great financial and political power have the will to address the scandal of world hunger.
Lord, hear us.

May we be Christian not only in name but in our values, our attitudes and our behaviour.
Lord, hear us.

We pray for family members or friends who have drifted away from religion. May they discover their need of God and be willing to make any necessary changes to their way of living.
Lord, hear us.

(Add prayers for any local, personal or topical intention)

Heavenly Father, you gave your Beloved Son, Jesus Christ, to lead us to salvation. Hear the prayers we offer in his name, Jesus Christ, the Lord. Amen.

WEDNESDAY

MATTHEW 11:25-27

1. "I bless you, Father, Lord of Heaven and Earth, for hiding these things from the learned and clever and revealing them to mere children." When we become aware of some favour or blessing, we can turn back to God in praise and thanks. It is easy to return thanks when things are going well and we are aware of God's favours. But it takes great faith to return thanks when matters are not going smoothly. The context of today's Gospel is when Jesus reproached the people who saw his miracles but refused to change their ways. Yet, in this disappointing moment, Jesus found a reason for giving thanks. There were other people who took his teaching to heart with childlike trust. "I bless you, Father for these trusting, unsophisticated people."

2. It is a great spiritual exercise to train ourselves to thank God for the blessings of each day. At the end of the day, reflect on what has happened. Pick out one particular moment or experience of blessing. The day's special blessing does not have to be something pleasant. It may have come in a painful encounter. It is only when we reflect on it that in hindsight we recognise that God was saying something to us in that painful moment. Blessings sometimes come in strange disguise. Some brave soul scratched these lines on the wall of an internment camp. "I believe in the sun when it is not shining. I believe in love even when I see it not. I believe in God even when he is silent."

PRAYERS

Gathered together, we join with Jesus in giving thanks for all God's blessings. We pray with the Response: *We bless you, God.*

For all the blessings of life and light and love that we have received.
We bless you, God.

For sustaining and supporting us when times were hard.
We bless you, God.

For all the people who revealed your face to us... a trusting child, a word of encouragement when we needed it, somebody's heroic courage, for joy at a time of adversity... for all who have been a blessing for us.
We bless you, God.

May each one of us be a source of blessing to somebody today.
We bless you, God.

(Add prayers for any local, personal or topical intention)

O God, the source of every blessing, look with kindness on all who gather here today in the name of Jesus Christ, your Son, our Lord. Amen.

THURSDAY

MATTHEW 11:28-30

1. Today's short Gospel is surely one of the most comforting passages of the Bible. It is an invitation from Jesus: "Come to me all you who labour and are burdened, and I will give you rest." His plan is simple. Let us shoulder this together and share the burden. He takes the example of two farm animals harnessed together to pull a heavy load. In those days the harness, or yoke, was made of wood. It was very carefully shaped to the measurements of the animals' necks and shoulders. If the two pulling the load are out of step the yoke cuts into the shoulders. But pull together in harmony and the burden is light. "Learn from me," said Jesus. Come at my pace. I am gentle and humble of heart. Gentleness will not force the pace. Humility will not seek to dominate. Come at my pace. We will share the burden and you will find rest for your soul.

2. The plan of rehabilitation in the Twelve Steps of Alcoholics Anonymous might well have been developed from the invitation of Jesus. It begins with the acceptance that there is a problem gone out of control. There is a burden which can no longer be shouldered alone. The problem is then handed over to the Higher Power. "Come to me. I am gentle and humble of heart." You too will have to be gentle with yourself and in dealing with your past. You too will have to be humble and totally honest about yourself. It is the truth that will set you free. You will find peace. There is no burden that cannot be carried when we combine with Jesus.

PRAYERS

Today Jesus invites us to come to him with our burdens and problems.

Lord Jesus, we take up your invitation to come to you. We lay our burdens and anxieties at your feet, confident that you will help us.
Lord, hear us.

May we learn from your gentleness not to become angry. May we learn from your humility not to be rebellious.
Lord, hear us.

We remember family and friends who are heavily burdened with health problems: we bring them to you in prayer.
Lord, hear us.

For people who are struggling with any addiction: may they find in you the higher power they need.
Lord, hear us.

(Add prayers for any local, personal or topical intention)

O God of understanding and compassion, hear the prayers of all who come to you in the name of Jesus Christ, your Son, our Lord. Amen.

FRIDAY

MATTHEW 12:1-8

1. The Pharisees put too much focus on what was forbidden on the Sabbath. Jesus wanted to get back to its original meaning. Sabbath means a day of rest. At a time when most manual workers were slaves, granting them one day's rest in the week was wonderful. On the first page of the Bible, God worked for six days before resting on the seventh day. God blessed the seventh day and called it holy. So the first thing to be called holy was not a place, nor a book, but the day of rest. A modern Jewish writer, Jonathan Sacks, in his book *Faith in the Future*, wrote beautifully about the Sabbath: "The Sabbath is our moment of eternity in the midst of time. Within the cycle of the week, it creates a delicate rhythm of action and reflection, making and enjoying, running and standing still. Without the pause to experience family, community and God, we risk making the journey while missing the view." Remember... and keep holy the day of rest.

2. In the Christian calendar, Sunday is the day of holy rest. It is the day of the Resurrection and the day of Pentecost. It is time to slow down in holy restfulness: time for our souls, time for family and time for God. Show me what you do on Sunday and I will know how important your God is to you. Saint Augustine wrote beautifully about Sunday, our Christian Sabbath. "We shall rest and we shall see; we shall see and we shall love; we shall love and we shall praise." Sunday is God's gift of soul-time, family-time and God-time.

PRAYERS

The Third Commandment reads: Remember and keep holy the Sabbath Day.

We thank God for the holy day of rest every week. May we remember to keep God at the centre of that day.
Lord, hear us.

May our Sunday be a time for greater family togetherness.
Lord, hear us.

May our Sunday be a time for prayer and spiritual growth.
Lord, hear us.

Let us thank God for the Jewish people and the rich faith they have passed on to us. May they never again suffer from anti-Semitism.
Lord, hear us.

   (Add prayers for any local, personal or topical intention)

O God, who declared the Sabbath a holy day, hear the prayers we offer in the name of Jesus Christ, our Lord. Amen.

SATURDAY

MATTHEW 12:14-21

1. "He will not break the crushed reed nor put out the smouldering wick." These words of Isaiah paint a beautiful picture of the pastoral plan of Jesus. The Pharisees treated sinners as outcasts, cut off from God. Jesus was a scandal in their eyes because he sat down with these outcasts and chatted with them. He introduced these sinners to the God of mercy. He gave them hope. Hope gives direction. It may be a long journey to perfection but it begins with one step. Pope Francis wrote that a small step, in the midst of great limitations, can be more pleasing to God, than a life which appears outwardly in order but it never has to confront great limitations.

2. Saint Pope John XXIII had a similar gentle, merciful approach. When he was Bishop of Venice, one of his priests was the subject of scandalous rumours. The future Pope, Cardinal Roncalli, called in to visit the priest. The poor fellow probably expected a stern warning. However, Cardinal Roncalli sat down and they had a friendly chat. Then the Cardinal knelt down in front of the priest and asked him to hear his confession. In his gentle, positive way he reminded the priest of who he was and what he could be. The tiny spark among the ashes was fanned into a flame. A priest who was at breaking point was given hope, direction and dignity. That was how Jesus treated sinners who struggled with human weakness. "He will not break the crushed reed, nor put out the smouldering wick."

PRAYERS

Inspired by the memory of the mercy of Jesus, we pray.

May the Church, inspired by the example of Jesus, be an oasis of mercy where the sinner will find compassion, hope and direction.
Lord, hear us.

When we have to correct somebody, may our words never be so stern as to quench that person's spirit. Guide us towards restoring their dignity and hope in genuine repentance.
Lord, hear us.

We pray for people who have been tortured in the confessional. Help them to leave the hurt behind and to come to know the Sacrament as a meeting with God's mercy.
Lord, hear us.

For those who are heavily burdened with guilt: may they come to the Lord and allow his merciful love to take away their burden.
Lord, hear us.

(Add prayers for any local, personal or topical intention)

God of mercy and compassion, thank you for showing us the face of mercy in the life of Jesus Christ. Graciously hear the prayers we offer in his name. Amen.

MONDAY

MATTHEW 12:38-42

1. Some of the scribes and Pharisees asked Jesus for a sign. They were not looking for evidence to believe in him. They were trying to trying to get him into a spot of bother. As Jesus pointed out to them, he had already given more than enough signs. Even when his miracles could not be denied they refused to accept these as signs from God. They accused him of being in league with the Devil. The greatest sign would be his rising from the dead. They bribed the guards at the tomb to say that while they were asleep, the disciples came and stole the body. Their problem was prejudice. The prejudiced mind has already decided and will not be moved. All the arguments in the world will not change the prejudiced mind. It is really frightening to see how immoveable the prejudiced mind is. There are none so blind as those who will not see.

2. Prejudice continues to thrive. One sees it in racial hatred, religious rivalry, followers of different teams, local begrudging and so on. Prejudice has been at the root of war, racial discrimination, persecution of minorities, bullying and dreadful injustices. What can we do if we have a tendency towards prejudice? Open your eyes and try to see people as Jesus would see them. Try to focus on something good in the person. Maybe the person has come from a very hurtful background. Remember the admonition of Jesus, let whoever is without sin cast the first stone. Who am I to judge? Saint Paul, in his famous hymn to love, says that love is always ready to make allowances, to trust, to hope and to endure whatever comes. Recall the words of Jesus: Judge not and you will not be judged.

PRAYERS

We take the teaching of Jesus to heart as we pray.

For those who are so prejudiced against the Church that they cannot see any good in it: open their eyes and hearts to recognise the amount of work for justice and care for the poor that the Church has inspired.
Lord, hear us.

Free us from the prejudice that hardens our hearts against certain people.
Lord, hear us.

Open our eyes to enable us to see what is good in people.
Lord, hear us.

We pray for the victims of prejudice in discrimination, persecution, bullying, name-calling, or character defamation. May they be consoled in remembering that Christ too was the victim of prejudice in many ways.
Lord, hear us.

(Add prayers for any local, personal or topical intention)

O God, the Father of all, help us to love all people as your creation. Through Jesus Christ, your Son, our Lord. Amen.

TUESDAY

MATTHEW 12:46-50

1. It might seem at first sight that Jesus was neglecting his mother and relations. He wasn't neglecting his family but extending it. "Who is my mother?," he asked. She was the greatest disciple he ever had. She is the one who said, "Let it be done to me according to thy Word." Jesus was extending his family by welcoming in all those who strive to do the will of the Father in Heaven. Mary is the perfect model of the obedience of faith.

2. All of us who gather at Mass belong to the extended family of Jesus. Our relationship with God is never just a private affair – me in my box with God, you in your box. There is a false piety which never shows any concern for others. So heavenly minded but no earthly good. The motto for the Eucharistic Congress in Dublin read, Communion with Christ, Communion with one another. Think of the model of prayer that Jesus taught us. The first personal singular is missing from the Our Father. It says Our Father, not My Father. Give us, forgive us, lead us, deliver us. It is always in the plural, members of the one family of Christ. God is addressed as Our Father. If we take those two words seriously, there is no basis for exploitation of others, discrimination, racism or prejudice. If we are members of the extended family of Jesus, then others are our brothers and sisters, and should be treated as such. Furthermore, Mary, the mother of Jesus is our mother too. Brothers, Sisters, we are one!

PRAYERS

We gather together at Mass as the extended family of Jesus.

May the Church be a community of disciples who will be recognised as people who care for each other as brothers and sisters.
Lord, hear us.

We ask God's blessing on our families, for our health, unity and support for one another.
Lord, hear us.

We pray for families who are going through a difficult time. May they see the solution to their problems with the help of God.
Lord, hear us.

As we remember the departed members of our families, we pray that we will all be reunited in the family of God in Heaven.
Lord, hear us.

(Add prayers for any local, personal or topical intention)

God, our Father, hear the prayers of your family united in the name of Jesus Christ, your Son, our Lord. Amen.

WEDNESDAY

MATTHEW 13:1-9

1. Jesus did not tell any parable about the qualities of preaching, but this parable of the sower and the seed is about how people listen to the Word. The point of the parable is not about the quality of the soil, or about the seed, but about how people receive the seed of the Word. Every preacher or teacher has to remember that what is communicated is not necessarily what is said, but what is heard. Everything that is heard has been filtered through the mind of the listener. One listener is delighted while another gets nothing out of the sermon. There were very different reactions to the preaching of Jesus. Some people were filled with awe at his gracious words, while others were filled with anger and hardened in their prejudice. The sermon is the same: it is the listening that makes the difference. The parable of the sower and the seed challenges us about how we listen.

2. Some seed fell on the edge of a path, on hard soil. Birds gobbled it up before it got into the soil. Our minds are miles away and we do not hear anything. The shallow soil is okay on the surface but rocky underneath. This is the shallow person who is caught up in superficial matters. This person is more likely to remember who sat in which seat, or how somebody was dressed, than to remember anything that the readings said. Some seed started to grow but the shoot was choked by thorn bushes. Sometimes good intentions do not last long because the mind is too preoccupied by other concerns and worries. Finally, there is the good soil which produces a crop in various amounts. If one prepares the soil beforehand, there is every chance that the seed will flourish. Before reading the Scriptures or listening to a talk, pray to the Holy Spirit for the preacher and for yourself. Ask God for a living Word. Have a positive attitude that this reading or talk is just what I need today. Even if the preacher is poor, his incompetence might touch the compassionate quality of your heart.

PRAYERS

As we listen to the parable of the sower and the seed, we are challenged about the depth of our listening.

May those who are ordained to preach the Word of God, love Sacred Scripture, give time to it, grow with it and bring it to the people.
Lord, hear us.

May all of us make the deliberate effort to be more attentive to God's Word and less distracted.
Lord, hear us.

May we learn how to apply the Word of God to our lives.
Lord, hear us.

May we be less preoccupied with things of little importance and give more time to God's Word.
Lord, hear us.

(Add prayers for any local, personal or topical intention)

O God, your Word is a lamp for our steps and a light for our paths. Direct our footsteps in following the way of Jesus Christ, your Son, our Lord. Amen.

THURSDAY

MATTHEW 13:10-17

1. "The reason that I talk to them in parables is that they look without seeing and listen without hearing or understanding." Jesus knew that people would listen to stories and remember them. And a humorous story has a better chance of being remembered. Recent studies show that Jewish rabbis often used humour to convey serious lessons. As the story is planted in the memory, so too is the important moral which, in time, will bear fruit. As a young priest, Pope Francis took the advice of an experienced preacher that every sermon should have an idea (substance), a sentiment (feeling) and an image (picture): the sentiment touches the heart, the image fires the imagination and the idea carries the teaching.

2. The stories of Jesus are called parables. Parable sounds like parallel. A parable is a story that runs parallel to life. It is like a mirror that travels beside you in which you can see yourself. Your memory recalls the story. The penny drops when you begin to see yourself in the story. You are inspired or challenged, consoled or corrected. As Jesus said in Nazareth, "This text is being fulfilled today even as you listen". The Word of God is something alive and active, reaching into our secret emotions and thoughts. The best sermon is the one that makes you do your own thinking.

PRAYERS

Taking the lessons of Jesus to heart, we pray.

Thank you, Lord, for understanding the limitations of our distracted minds. You gave us simple, homely stories that we can remember and ponder. May all who preach the Word have the grace to touch the minds and hearts of people.
Lord, hear us.

Open our ears so that we might listen more attentively and take your teaching to heart.
Lord, hear us.

Open up our imaginations so that your teaching will be a dynamic seed bearing fruit in our lives.
Lord, hear us.

May people who are searching for meaning and direction in life find what they need in the words of Sacred Scripture.
Lord, hear us.

   (Add prayers for any local, personal or topical intention)

Your Word, O Lord, is a lamp for our steps and a light for our lives. Listen graciously to the prayers we offer in the name of Jesus Christ, your Son, our Lord. Amen.

FRIDAY

MATTHEW 13:18-23

1. A seed is not much use if it is left in the paper packet. It has to be planted in the earth. Neither is the seed of God's Word effective if it is left on the paper page. It has to be planted in the earth of life. Three students of theology were discussing the merits of various translations of the Bible. The college gardener working nearby overheard the learned discussion. "Excuse me," he said, "but I think my mother has the best translation. She translates it into life". Pope John Paul II recommended that we should listen to the Word of God in a living encounter which questions, shapes and directs our lives. The Word of God is not a relic of the past. It is a living seed that bears fruit when it is planted in the earth of our lives.

2. The one who received the Word in rich soil is a person who hears it and understands it. What does understand mean? Perhaps we should reverse the word. Instead of saying under-stand, say stand-under. Stand under the light. The psalmist said that the Word of God is a lamp for my steps and a light for my path. A great blessing in recent years has been the popularisation of *Lectio Divina*, a very old way of praying with Sacred Scripture. It is a prayerful reading of a text, searching for what God said or did in the past. What is God saying or doing in this passage? Then connect the passage with life today: plant the seed in the earth of our experiences today. In the light of what God did or said in the past, we are enabled to see what God is saying or doing today. In this way, we stand under the light of God's Word. The one who received the seed in rich soil is the person who hears it and puts it into action.

PRAYERS

We thank God for the light of his Word as we pray.

May the Church be inspired and directed in its teaching by the light of the Word of God.
Lord, hear us.

May we continually grow in our love for the Scriptures so that the seed of God's Word will find fertile soil in our lives.
Lord, hear us.

May we be Christian in name and in fact, through the transformation of our thoughts, our values and our behaviour under the light of God's Word.
Lord, hear us.

May people who are searching for meaning and direction in life find inspiration in the Word of God.
Lord, hear us.

(Add prayers for any local, personal or topical intention)

O God, your Word is a lamp for our steps and a light for our paths. May our lives bear fruit as we follow the light of Jesus Christ, your Son, our Lord. Amen.

SATURDAY

MATTHEW 13:24-30

1. The mission of Jesus was to establish the rule of God, the Kingdom of God on Earth. The Church would be the task force to continue his mission. The parable of the darnel intertwined with the wheat is consoling. The Lord knows our imperfections. The Church is a mixture of divine power and human frailty. If the Church were only for perfect people, most of us, probably all of us, would not be allowed membership. Thank God for this mixture of saintly people who might yet become sinners and sinners who might yet be saints. By the way, if you find the perfect Church, you are bound in conscience to join it, but remember, once you have joined, it will no longer be perfect!

2. The parable of the wheat and darnel may also be applied to us as individuals. In a sense, there is no such thing as a weed. See the same plant in the wild and we call it a wild flower. Weeds are wild flowers in the wrong place. Seven particular plants are known as the seven deadly sins: pride, covetousness, lust, envy, anger, gluttony and sloth. Some of these wild energies give us a lot of trouble. Lord, take this lust out of my life! Take this anger out of my life! God is the wise gardener who knows that anger is an energy intertwined with the determination to act for justice or to correct what is wrong. Lust is an offshoot of interest in people, curiosity and the ability to love. These untamed energies are wild flowers in the wrong place. Take anger and lust totally out of life and one is no better than a passionless stone. Treat your wild energies with respect. Channel them in the right direction.

*"We are not wholly bad or good / who live our lives under Milkwood,
And thou I know will be the first / to see our best side not the worst."*

– Dylan Thomas

PRAYERS

Blessed be God who has made us such a complex mixture of matter and spirit, laughter and tears, growing and dying.

Let us pray for the Church, a mixture of divine power and human limitations. May God's inspiration guide us with wisdom and protect us from serious mistakes.
Lord, hear us.

For the sins of the Church we ask forgiveness, and pray that they will never happen again.
Lord, hear us.

Lord, help us to control our wild energies and enable us to use them for a good purpose.
Lord, hear us.

May we look beyond the darnel of faults in other people to see the good wheat in their lives.
Lord, hear us.

(Add prayers for any local, personal or topical intention)

O God, you are the wise gardener of life. Help us to grow despite our faults. Through Christ, our Lord. Amen.

MONDAY

MATTHEW 13:31-35

1. The parables of the Mustard Seed and Spoon of Yeast are very inspiring. From small beginnings great movements can emerge. The tiny, yellow mustard seeds are so light that they are easily blown on the wind so that the plant spreads far and wide. What about the yeast, also known as leaven? A housewife is baking bread, mixing the dough. Some of yesterday's dough has been kept. By this time it is going sour, fermenting, beginning to bubble. A little of this bubbling stuff is mixed with today's baking. Without this bubbly stuff, the new bread will be flat and stodgy. But the bubbles of yeast allow pockets of air which make the new bread soft and light. Like the tiny mustard seed, God can use some unknown person to start something great. And, like the fermenting dough, God can inspire somebody of dubious background to do great work. Oskar Schindler, a Catholic, was a man with a very shady background. Yet he became somebody who saved thousands of Jews from extermination.

2. Many of us see disturbing images of the dreadful results of war, famine, homelessness and poverty. We are disturbed but do nothing about it. The dreadful images turn sour within us and often they can make us cynical about politicians and negative about life. But the energy generated in fermentation can be used for a good cause. Mary's Meals is a charitable organisation which feeds over a million schoolchildren every day. It was started by two brothers in Scotland after seeing the suffering of children in Bosnia shown on the television news. They decided to take a week off work in a fish farm to organise a collection. The response was overwhelming. It grew and grew at a fantastic rate. Now over a million children, who previously were deprived of education because they had to work at home, every day get both food and education. The Kingdom of God is like pinch of sour leaven which can bubble up into the best of bread. Never despair of what God can do from the most unlikely beginning.

PRAYERS

Inspired by the parables of the tiny seed and the yeast, we pray.

May the Church never forget its small and humble beginnings. May we resist the temptation to become proud and triumphalist.
Lord, hear us.

O God, you can make the small seed grow. You can turn the sour yeast into something useful. Take our little efforts and use them as you will.
Lord, hear us.

May God bless the charitable organisations who work to alleviate poverty, homelessness and hunger.
Lord, hear us.

May each of us enrich this day by some act of kindness or care for somebody.
Lord, hear us.

(Add prayers for any local, personal or topical intention)

God, our Father, graciously hear the prayers we offer in the name of Jesus Christ, your Son, our Lord. Amen

TUESDAY

MATTHEW 13:36-43

1. Jesus explained the parable of the darnel in the wheat-field. The sower of the good seed is the Son of Man, that is, Jesus himself. The field is the world; the good seed represents people who follow Christ's ideals; the darnel is planted by the Evil One. The Devil hates the Church. In a sense, the day the Devil stops attacking the Church will be a bad day because it will only happen if the Church is up to no good. We get upset when somebody says hurtful things about the Church. While some critics go over the top, we should be grateful when their criticism shows up issues that should be corrected. Many of our critics do us a great favour.

2. The Church is a mixture of divine grace planted in the earth of human lives. The wheat crop is far from perfect. The Church is far from perfect. And thank God for that because it is there for the likes of you and me. As one writer expressed it: "I don't like the sins and scandals of the Church, but I do love the Church which finds room for sins and sinners." Another writer said that if you do not love the Church with all its faults and failings, then your idea of the Church is nothing more than the figment of a romantic imagination.

PRAYERS

Having reflected on the parable of the darnel in the field of wheat, we pray.

For the Church: may the uncovering of scandals in the Church be the source of purification and reform.
Lord, hear us.

May those who hold high office in the Church be free of worldly ambition.
Lord, hear us.

May they see their ministry as humble service of the Kingdom of God on Earth.
Lord, hear us.

May sinners find a home in the Church where they meet with the mercy of Jesus who welcomed sinners and gave them hope.
Lord, hear us.

In our own lives, may the admission of our faults open the door for God's mercy to come in.
Lord, hear us

   (Add prayers for any local, personal or topical intention)

God of mercy and compassion, hear the prayers we offer in the name of Jesus Christ, the Lord. Amen.

WEDNESDAY

MATTHEW 13:44-46

1. In today's Gospel, Jesus continues to talk about the Kingdom of Heaven in our lives. What is this kingdom? In the Gospels, the Kingdom of Heaven has several different shades of meaning. In today's parables it refers to the hidden treasure in the heart. "The Kingdom of God is within you." It is the realisation that God is not only up there but is also in here, in here in my heart and soul. That is what Pope Francis called the joy of the Gospel, the joy of a personal relationship with Jesus. To quote from his letter on *the Joy of the Gospel*: "The joy of the Gospel fills the hearts and lives of all who encounter Jesus. Those who accept his offer of salvation are set free from sin, sorrow, inner emptiness and loneliness." Emptiness is no longer a lonely place: rather, it is space for enjoying the nearness of God.

2. The treasure discovered in a field represents a totally unexpected experience that brings about a sudden conversion, a new awareness of God as present in one's life. It is like a new birth. For others, the experience is a precious pearl they were searching for. There are people who spent time searching. They read, they studied, tried out various philosophies of life, until eventually they found Jesus and all that he means. Whether it comes in a sudden conversion experience, or as the result of much study and searching, hold on to this treasure at any cost. The cost of discipleship usually involves repentance in the sense of a conversion of thought, values and behaviour.

PRAYERS

Treasuring the teaching of Jesus, we pray.

May the Church shine with the light of Christ drawing people to the treasure of a personal relationship with him.
Lord, hear us.

For people who are searching for meaning to life: may they receive the grace of finding in Christ the answer to their questions.
Lord, hear us.

Buying the treasure might be costly. May we be willing to pay the price of giving up various pleasures and pursuits in order to have more time for our personal relationship with God.
Lord, hear us.

May the witness of our lives be an inspiration to others.
Lord, hear us.

(Add prayers for any local, personal or topical intention)

Almighty God, graciously hear the prayers we offer in the name of Jesus Christ, your Son, our Lord. Amen

THURSDAY

MATTHEW 13:47-53

1. The parable of the dragnet is the last of seven parables describing the Kingdom of Heaven on Earth as a mixture of divine inspiration and human endeavour. The dragnet pulls in a haul of all kinds of fish. This refers to the catholic dimension of the Kingdom since the word *catholic* means all-embracing. There is room for all sorts: for those who want to conserve the past beside those who are impatient for change; people who are attracted to shrines and apparitions alongside others who are dubious about apparitions; people who withdraw from the world and people who are immersed in the world of politics, business, science or sport. Catholic means there is room for all sorts and the more variety of gifts and interests, the richer the community. The dragnet pulling in a haul of all kinds of fish is a good image of the Church.

2. "Every scribe who becomes a disciple of the Kingdom of Heaven is like a householder who brings out of his storeroom things both new and old." Many scholars think that this is a short self-portrait of the author of Matthew's Gospel, a Jewish scribe who had become a Christian. Conflict with the scribes features very prominently in this Gospel. The evangelist is appealing to them to see in Jesus the fulfilment of the Old Testament texts. He is enriched by the wisdom of the old and the new. Nowadays, there is a healthy sharing between Christian and Jewish scholars. This gives us greater insights into our spiritual ancestors so that we can draw from both old and new. A better acquaintance with Jewish culture, local history and daily life increases our understanding of the Gospels. Saint Augustine wrote that in the Old Testament the New Testament is hidden, while in the New Testament, the Old Testament is revealed. A Church that is truly catholic draws from the wisdom of many traditions, like the dragnet filled with many sorts of fish.

PRAYERS

The Kingdom is like a dragnet containing many different kinds of fish: so we pray.

That the Church be truly catholic, embracing all sorts, with respectful dialogue and listening between different parties.
Lord, hear us.

That we may have the discernment to be both conservative as well as progressive, drawing from our storeroom things both old and new.
Lord, hear us.

May we be more tolerant of the different opinions of other people.
Lord, hear us.

Let us pray for our ancestors in faith, the Jewish people. May they never again suffer persecution because of their race or religion.
Lord, hear us.

(Add prayers for any local, personal or topical intention)

O God, you created us with a rich variety of talents and personalities. Help us to get on well together in enriching the world. Through Christ, our Lord. Amen.

FRIDAY

MATTHEW 13:54-58

1. "A prophet is only despised in his own country and in his own house." When Jesus went back to his own town, Nazareth, at first people were astonished when they heard him speak. But the mood very swiftly changed to rejecting him. If he had come back as an Olympic medallist or a famous film-star, he would have had a mighty reception. Local boy makes good! Local star conquers the world! But coming back as a prophet! That was different. A prophet is somebody who challenges us, who wakes us up from our slumbers, who disturbs our complacency. A prophet is somebody who turns the world upside down. The people of Nazareth might have taken up the challenge from an outsider, but not from one of their own. So they would not accept Jesus, one of their own.

2. Jesus did not work many miracles in Nazareth because of their lack of faith. It seems that he did work some miracles there, but very few. But even these miracles did not convince people, just as miracles still do not convince people who do not want to believe. Faith is the key that opens up our acceptance of what the God of love wants to give us. God wants to give to us, but our hands have to be open to take what he gives. Faith is the key to receiving God's gifts.

PRAYERS

As we reflect on the way Jesus was a prophet who was rejected, we pray.

May the Church be a prophetic voice challenging the world to change from war to peace, from exploitation to justice.
Lord, hear us.

Free our hearts, Lord, from small-minded prejudice which prevents us from seeing goodness in others.
Lord, hear us.

May we refrain from putting labels on people, which block us from being surprised at what they can say or do.
Lord, hear us.

Prophets who challenge our complacency will always be criticised. Grant them the courage to continue their good work.
Lord, hear us.

(Add prayers for any local, personal or topical intention)

O gracious God, hear the prayers we offer in the name of Jesus Christ, the prophet from Nazareth. Amen.

SATURDAY

MATTHEW 14:1-12

1. John the Baptist's mission was to go before the Lord, to prepare the way for him. Not only did he prepare the way for the mission of Jesus, he also went before him in death. He was fearless in the defence of morality. He was well aware that by publicly condemning Herod on his illegitimate marriage, he was putting his life in danger. But standing up for God's law meant more to him than protecting his own life. There are times when all of us need courage to stand up for our Christian principles. For Evil to triumph, it is only necessary for good people to do nothing.

2. Herod was a very mixed-up character. When he heard what Jesus was doing, he was convinced that it was John the Baptist coming back from the dead to haunt him. This was partly due to the fact that Herod was seriously paranoid. He had great power at his command, yet he was haunted by fears. It is known that he had some of his own family murdered. He was curious about religious affairs but his religiosity never became a religious commitment. One of the reasons why he carried out the gruesome request for the murder of John was his fear of breaking the oath he had sworn. It often happens that people who do not make a commitment to any particular religion remain full of superstitious fears, such as walking under a ladder, counting magpies, the number thirteen, or some particular colour. Those who do not believe in something end up believing in anything.

PRAYERS

Blessed are those who are persecuted in the cause of right, for theirs is the Kingdom of Heaven.

John the Baptist is an inspirational model in standing up for moral values. May the Church always be a challenging voice upholding the sacredness of life.
Lord, hear us.

May all of us have the courage to stand up for the defence of moral values in the face of opposition and ridicule.
Lord, hear us.

We pray for the conversion of those who are caught up in the spiral of violence and sinfulness.
Lord, hear us.

For people who are victims of violence at home: may the violence cease and may these homes be places of peace.
Lord, hear us.

(Add prayers for any local, personal or topical intention)

God, our Father, graciously hear the prayers we offer in the name of Jesus Christ, your Son, our Lord. Amen

MONDAY

MATTHEW 14:13-21

1. It is interesting that the apostles did not say to Jesus that this is a hungry place but that this is a lonely place. They had touched on the inner hunger of the heart, loneliness. A popular novel years ago was called *The Heart is a Lonely Hunter*. Saint Mother Teresa of Calcutta was shocked when her Sisters went to work in a poor area of New York. In Calcutta, the Sisters had ministered to the dying and fed hundreds of hungry people every day. But in New York, she was confronted by the hunger of loneliness. She described it. "The worst disease is not leprosy; it is being unwanted, being left out, being forgotten. The greatest scourge is to forget the next person, to be so suffocated with the things we have that we have no time for the lonely Jesus – even a person in our own family who needs us." This is a lonely place, a lonely world. Jesus said, "Give them something to eat yourselves". The apostles had very little to give, but they gave all they had. And then, God did the multiplying. We might not have much to give. Give it anyway and let God do the multiplying.

2. One form of loneliness is the grief experienced after the death of a loved one. After the death of his cousin John the Baptist, Jesus withdrew to a lonely place to attend to his grief. The person who is grieving needs time and space. Different people deal with grief in different ways. Pray for the discernment to know when to accompany the person grieving and when to let the person have time alone. In the weeks after the funeral, the person grieving will be very tired. They may not have the emotional energy to pray. It is important to let them know that you are praying for them.

PRAYERS

Inspired by the actions and words of Jesus, we pray.

May the Church continue its long history of inspiring us to care
for people who are poor, destitute or lonely.
Lord, hear us.

May the rich nations and wealthy individuals open their eyes and
hearts to help the millions who are starving today.
Lord, hear us.

Open our eyes to the loneliness of people who may be very near
us. And show us some way that we can help them.
Lord, hear us.

May the God of all consolation comfort and support all who are
grieving the loss of a loved one.
Lord, hear us.

(Add prayers for any local, personal or topical intention)

O God, we thank you for all that you have given us. Inspire us to
be generous to people in any kind of need. Through Christ, our
Lord. Amen.

TUESDAY

MATTHEW 14:22-36

1. The picture of the boat tossed about in a storm is frequently applied to the plight of the Church today. Persecution and killing of Christians is happening in some countries. The uncovering of scandals has shocked people. Numbers are falling and there are very few studying for priesthood. Are we close to sinking? Jesus had gone up the hills to pray. This perhaps refers to the time after his Ascension when he is no longer physically visible in our boat. But fear not. Jesus has not deserted us. As the song says, "God is watching us, from a distance". In God's own time, he comes. "Courage, it is I. Do not be afraid." One of the Seven Gifts of the Holy Spirit is fortitude. Fortitude is the sort of courage that enables us to retain hope even when we are scared stiff. The Holy Spirit will not allow the Church to sink.

2. Peter is the spokesperson for the apostles just as his successor, the Pope, is regarded as the spokesperson for the Church. Peter trusts in the Lord's invitation. He steps overboard into the heaving sea. As long as he remains focused on Jesus, he walks on the water. But once he looks at the breaking waves, he begins to sink. The Letter to the Hebrews says: "Let us fix our eyes on Jesus, who leads us in our faith and brings it to perfection". If we only see the problems, if we let the bad news take possession of our minds, we begin to sink. But focus on Jesus, absorb the Good News, and the hand of the Lord holds us up.

PRAYERS

Let us fix our eyes on Jesus our Saviour as we pray.

May Christ strengthen the faith of Pope *(Name)* who is the successor of Saint Peter to lead us and guide us through the storms of today.
Lord, hear us.

For Christians who are suffering persecution: may they keep Jesus before their eyes as a source of courage and strength.
Lord, hear us.

May we never despair because of the bad news. Open our eyes to see what is good in the world, in our neighbours and in ourselves.
Lord, hear us.

For people who are lonely, depressed and despairing: may they experience the hand of Jesus reaching out to help them.
Lord, hear us.

(Add prayers for any local, personal or topical intention)

God, our Father in Heaven, you watch over us at all times. Carry us safely through all the storms of life, through Christ, our Lord. Amen.

WEDNESDAY

MATTHEW 15:21-28

1. A troubled mother pleaded with Jesus to cure her disturbed daughter. We are surprised to read that he answered her not a word. It's so unlike Jesus. But he knew what he was doing. He was drawing out deeper depths of her faith. A passage from the Old Testament explains why God allowed the Israelites to experience such hardships during their forty years in the wilderness. It was "to humble you, to test you, to know your inmost heart. God was training you as a parent trains a child" (Deut. 8:15). Jesus was drawing out the inner depths of the woman's faith. An immediate answer to her request might not have been fully appreciated. Her persistence developed a deeper faith. Now he could say to her, "Woman, great is your faith. Let your wish be granted." She is a model of persevering in prayer.

2. The prophet Jeremiah has a beautiful saying about God's love. "I have loved you with an everlasting love, so I am constant in my love for you". But how does one survive when God is silent, just as Jesus initially did not answer a word to the Canaanite woman? She was a woman of great faith. Many of the mystical saints, people of great faith, experienced long periods of darkness and spiritual dryness. Saint Teresa of Calcutta lived for forty years without any consolations in prayer. She lived in union with the thirst experienced by Jesus on Calvary. One brave prisoner in a concentration camp scratched these lines on the wall of his cell. "I believe in the sun even when I do not see it shining. I believe in love even when I feel it not. I believe in God even when he is silent".

PRAYERS

Sometimes the answer of God to our prayer is easily seen, but sometimes it is not.

We pray for the grace of perseverance in prayer when it seems that God does not hear us.
Lord, hear us.

The woman who approached Jesus was of a different race and religion. Let us learn to respect people of every race and religion.
Lord, hear us.

May God grant healing and peace to children who are very disturbed.
Lord, hear us.

May God help parents in training their children, sometimes saying "Yes" to what they want, and sometimes saying "No".
Lord, hear us.

(Add prayers for any local, personal or topical intention)

O God, we trust in your wisdom and compassion as we pray in the name of Jesus Christ, your Son, our Lord. Amen.

THURSDAY

MATTHEW 16:13-23

1. This is a story of new names. In the Bible a new name meant a new mission. First of all Jesus asked the disciples what name they were calling him. Names of former heroes were recalled. "But who do you say I am?" Simon Peter spoke up. "You are the Christ, the Son of the living God." This was the first time that Jesus was given the name, Christ. It is a name meaning the Anointed One. To the Jews this meant the promised Messiah. Our naming day was at our Baptism. In addition to our name, immediately after Baptism with water we were anointed with chrism to signify our union with Christ as our prophet, priest and king. In a word, we were Christened, that is Christ-ened.

2. After Simon, son of Jonah, identified Jesus with the new name of Christ, Jesus gave Simon his new name. Jesus recognised the very special faith Simon had received. "It was not flesh and blood that revealed this to you, but my Father in Heaven. So now I say to you: You are Peter, and on this rock I will build my Church". Peter means a rock. At the end of the Sermon on the Mount Jesus had spoken of building a house on solid rock. The first foundation rock of the house of the Church would be Peter. He is promised the keys of the Kingdom. After the resurrection the Risen Lord returned to appoint Peter as the new shepherd of the flock. Then Jesus looked to the future. "The powers of Evil will never conquer this Church." What a wonderful promise!

PRAYERS

Enlightened and encouraged by the light of the Gospel, we pray.

For Pope *(Name)*, the successor of Saint Peter as the Bishop of Rome: as Peter was blessed in his faith, so may his successor guide the Church with divine wisdom.
Lord, hear us.

Lord, protect your Church and never allow the forces of evil to infiltrate the community of believers.
Lord, hear us.

The names Jesus and Christ are sacred names. May we never use these names irreverently.
Lord, hear us.

Peter received the grace of a deep faith in Jesus. May we also grow in our personal relationship with God.
Lord, hear us.

(Add prayers for any local, personal or topical intention)

God our Father, graciously listen to the prayers we offer in the name of Jesus Christ, your Son, our Lord. Amen.

FRIDAY

MATTHEW 16:24-28

1. As we advance in our daily readings from Matthew's Gospel, Jesus leaves Galilee and heads south towards Jerusalem. He tries to make it clear to his disciples that Jerusalem would mean his rejection, death on the cross and rising on the third day. To be a genuine follower of Jesus, one must go through a process of taking up the crosses of life and dying to selfishness. "Anyone who wants to save his life will lose it; but anyone who loses his life for my sake will find it." Pope Francis, in his booklet, *The Joy of the Gospel* wrote: "Only the person who feels happiness in seeking the good of others, in desiring their happiness, can be a missionary. This openness of the heart is a source of joy, since it is more blessed to give than to receive. We do not live better when we flee, hide, refuse to share, stop giving and lock ourselves up in our own comforts. Such a life is nothing more than slow suicide." What does it profit a person to win the whole world and ruin his life? It is like climbing to the top of the ladder of success only to find one had climbed the wrong wall.

2. How could a loving, merciful Father permit the cruelty of the cross. The answer is in compassion. Compassion means suffering with. Jesus would be with us in our suffering. His way of saving was not at a safe distance, aloof from the messy side of life. On the cross, he is nailed beside all human pain and distress. How much poorer would be our knowledge of God's love if Jesus had saved us in a painless way! There are depths in the human heart which are not discovered until one shares in the cross of Jesus Christ. "Anyone who loses his life for my sake will find it."

PRAYERS

The compassion of God was revealed to us in the cross of Jesus Christ: so we pray.

May we grow in our understanding of God's compassion, as we contemplate the cross of Our Lord Jesus Christ.
Lord, hear us.

May people who are suffering in any way recognise that Jesus is very close to them.
Lord, hear us.

May we do all we can to alleviate suffering and to bring comfort to people.
Lord, hear us.

May we never try to gain worldly success or wealth and ruin our souls in the process.
Lord, hear us.

(Add prayers for any local, personal or topical intention)

God of mercy and compassion, hear the prayers we offer in the name of Jesus Christ, our Lord and Saviour. Amen.

SATURDAY

MATTHEW 17:14-20

1. "Faith can move mountains." What does that mean? Obviously it does not refer to mountains of rock. The context is lack of faith on the part of the disciples. The mountains to be moved are the accumulations of questions, doubts and problems. We have a saying that seeing is believing, but that is not entirely correct. Faith goes beyond the physical proof that seeing brings. As the Letter to the Hebrews states, only faith can guarantee the blessings that we hope for, and prove the existence of realities that are not seen. Our ability to know is too small to comprehend the full mystery of God. God is not a problem to solved but a mystery to be enjoyed. What seeing brings is not faith but knowledge, knowledge of facts. When it comes to faith, the popular saying must be reversed. Instead of first seeing and then believing, we should say that if we believe then we shall see. Saint Anselm expressed it in this way: I believe in order that I might understand. It is faith that moves the mountains of questions, doubts and problems.

2. Carlo Carretto was a popular spiritual writer some years ago. A friend of his, a doctor, used to pester him with questions, doubts, objections and problems. Carretto answered as best as he could, but his friend would be back next week with more questions. Carretto decided to reverse roles and he gave the doctor a prescription which he called his Sun-Cure. Put your doubts aside and spend an hour in adoration before the Blessed Sacrament, and your doubts will disappear within a year. If fact it took less than a month. As he gazed in silence before the Blessed Sacrament, his relationship with Jesus developed. He began to trust and his doubts evaporated. Like Peter walking on the water, when he focused on Jesus and took him at his word, he did the impossible. Faith can move mountains. Absolute trust in God removes the accumulation of doubts and questions.

PRAYERS

Faith can move mountains, so we have the confidence to pray with the response: *Lord, increase our faith.*

May the teaching of the Church inspire in us a deep, personal trust in God's love.
Lord, increase our faith.

The demented boy in the story suffered from fits and convulsions. We pray for people with similar problems, and for those who care for them.
Lord, increase our faith.

For family members or acquaintances who say they cannot believe: grant them the grace of a personal relationship in prayer where all the objections dissolve.
Lord, increase our faith.

When our prayer reaches dryness and darkness, help us to persevere.
Lord, increase our faith.

(Add prayers for any local, personal or topical intention)

God of love and compassion, graciously hear the prayers we offer in the name of Jesus Christ, your Son, our Lord. Amen.

MONDAY

MATTHEW 17:22-27

1. This is the second prediction of the death and resurrection of Jesus. A great sadness came over the minds of the disciples. It seems that they were so overcome with sadness that they did not take in the message of rising from the dead. After the death of Jesus on Good Friday, the disciples were totally unprepared for the news of his resurrection. It is very important not to be so overwhelmed by the bad news that we can no longer hear the good news. We need to focus more on the blessings of life. A very helpful exercise is to reflect at the end of the day and recall the blessings of the day. A blessing does not have to be anything huge or extraordinary. A moment of nice music; the scent of a flower; a kind word; a friend; the postman who delivers mail. There are dozens of little blessings every day that we take for granted. If you keep a diary, take note of just one blessing each day. Over a period of time, you will become far more sensitive to the blessings of life. The exercise can transform your life.

2. The half-shekel tax was also known as the temple tax. It was for the support of the religious authorities in the Temple, the very people who were plotting the death of Jesus. Peter assured the fussy official that Jesus did pay the required tax. Then Jesus told Peter that while he could argue the obligation to pay, he would not make an issue out of it with the official. There are several lessons for us here. Don't make a major crisis out of something that could be easily solved. Peter, an experienced fisherman, could catch a fish to cover the payment. A second lesson is to be willing to lose an argument for the sake of peace, which is much more important. A third lesson, never let the wrongdoing of others dictate the agenda in your mind. Jesus was prepared to pay tax to the very people who were plotting his death.

PRAYERS

Let us take the example of Jesus to heart as we pray.

Let us learn from Jesus not to let the wrongdoing of another person poison our minds with bitterness.
Lord, hear us.

May we be ready to lose an argument for the sake of preserving peace.
Lord, hear us.

May we never make a big deal out of some issue that can be easily resolved.
Lord, hear us.

The disciples were so overcome with sadness that they did not hear the promise of his resurrection. May the sadness of bereavement always be accompanied with the glorious hope of Heaven.
Lord, hear us.

(Add prayers for any local, personal or topical intention)

God, our heavenly Father, may your Holy Spirit help us to grow in the likeness of Christ in all we do or say. Through Christ, our Lord. Amen.

TUESDAY

MATTHEW 18:1-5. 10. 12-14

1. "Unless you change and become like little children, you will never enter the Kingdom of Heaven". The disciples had been arguing about who was the greatest among them. It shows how far removed they were from all that Jesus stood for. So he took a little child and set the child in front of them. "You must change your way of thinking. You must move away from the power-seeking, dominating mentality. You must relearn the virtues of the child." An American lady, Ann Voskamp, wrote a very inspiring book about a task she undertook to draw up a list of one thousand gifts in her life. One day she let her little daughter take her camera around the house. Snap here, snap there, great fun. Then they looked at the pictures together. The mother was amazed at what the little child saw. The underside of a table, a doorknob, a bookshelf. Looking up at life is so different to looking down. Looking up is towards Heaven. Looking down is the way of pride and domination.

2. The virtues of childhood include absolute trust, playfulness, imagination, enjoying life, freedom to express emotions. Of course we have to retain adult responsibility. But it is marvellous to rediscover the vision of the child. It is unlikely that anybody could have faith without something of the child's capacity for wonder. "Unless you change and become like little children, you will never enter the Kingdom of Heaven."

PRAYERS

Taking the lessons of Jesus to heart, we pray.

That children will be warmly welcomed into this world, accepted, loved and cared for.
Lord, hear us.

That no child will ever be abused, exploited or suffer violence.
Lord, hear us.

We pray for children who never get enough food or adequate medical care. May the adult world change mentality and share the resources of the world in a just way.
Lord, hear us.

May all of us relearn the child's sense of wonder, trust and playfulness.
Lord, hear us.

   (Add prayers for any local, personal or topical intention)

God our Father, hear the prayers of your children, offered in the name of Jesus Christ, your Son, our Lord. Amen.

WEDNESDAY

MATTHEW 18:15-20

1. Yesterday's Gospel was about the virtues of children: trust, innocence, playfulness, wonder, looking up at life. Today we hear some of the responsibilities of adults. Genuine love includes the difficult task of confronting and correcting. Not to confront a person may be condoning wrong behaviour. Alcoholics are sometimes surrounded by enablers who cover up, make excuses, and passively condone the condition and behaviour. Similarly, democratic government needs an active opposition party to keep the ruling body more responsible. The liberal atmosphere of today makes it very difficult to correct anybody. Teachers are at a loss regarding the imposition of discipline. Parents who fail to set standards or correct their children are doing them no favour. It happens that when children are starved of ideals, they rebel in a perverse cry for attention. Confrontation is probably the most difficult aspect of love.

2. We often hear the words of Jesus, "Where two or three gather together in my name, I shall be there with them". Usually we refer that text to a group of people gathered together to pray, which is all very well. But the original context of the statement is when two or three people get together in a spirit of responsibility to confront or correct somebody who is going off the rails. God is with that group who gather in loving concern. The Lord is the Good Shepherd anxious to welcome back the straying sheep. The group who gather in loving concern are the search party available to the shepherd.

PRAYERS

"Where two or three gather in my name, I shall be there with them."

May the Church be the voice of Christ correcting the sins of the world and inspiring us to live in justice, harmony and peace.
Lord, hear us.

Whenever we gather together in prayer and charity, may we recognise the presence of Christ in our community.
Lord, hear us.

May the Holy Spirit guide us with wisdom and courage when we have to offer correction to somebody.
Lord, hear us.

May those who are offered correction take it in a spirit of charity.
Lord, hear us.

   (Add prayers for any local, personal or topical intention)

O God, hear the prayers of your people gathered here in the name of Jesus Christ, your Son, our Lord. Amen.

THURSDAY

MATTHEW 18:21 – 19:1

1. When somebody has suffered a big injustice or hurt, forgiveness is very difficult. In fact, human nature on its own cannot find full forgiveness. But with the help of the Holy Spirit, a new way of looking at the injustice emerges. Today's parable is about a man who received the cancellation of a huge debt from his master, but he failed to pass on forgiveness to somebody who owed him a little sum. True forgiveness begins in understanding God's idea of justice. Human justice seeks a penalty to fit the crime. It is about punishing, compensation or getting revenge. Fortunately for us, God's idea of justice is not directed towards revenge or punishment. God's justice seeks the healing of the person who did wrong. Any punishment involved is there as a corrective measure to bring about the healing of the person. Saint Paul summed it up beautifully. "Since God loves you, you should be clothed in sincere compassion and understanding, in kindness and humility. Bear with one another, forgive each other as soon as a quarrel begins. The Lord has forgiven you; now you must do the same" (Col. 3:12-13).

2. Human nature on its own cannot reach the full height of forgiveness. The Catechism of the Catholic Church recommends handing over the problem of forgiveness to the Holy Spirit. Quoting the Catechism: "It is not in our power not to feel or to forget an offence; but the heart that offers itself to the Holy Spirit turns injury into compassion and purifies the memory in transforming the hurt into intercession". The Spirit comes like a helicopter to take us up to where we can see with a much wider vision. On the natural road of life, when we look back, we cannot see beyond the last corner. When we look forward, we cannot see beyond the next corner. The Holy Spirit lifts us up to where we can see the bigger picture. We begin to understand where the person who wronged us has come from. We see the moral sickness of the wrongdoer and develop compassion for this sick mind. We then pray for the healing of that person's moral sickness.

PRAYERS

As we reflect on God's loving forgiveness, we pray with the Response: *The Lord is compassion and love*

May we grow in our appreciation of the depths of God's mercy towards us.
The Lord is compassion and love

For people who have been deeply hurt: may the uplifting of the Holy Spirit enable them to view the past with greater compassion.
The Lord is compassion and love

Let us pray for those who have hurt us or wronged us: may they be converted and turn away from wrongdoing.
The Lord is compassion and love

Let us pray for prisoners who are doing time for their crimes: may they seek to change their ways and grow in goodness.
The Lord is compassion and love

(Add prayers for any local, personal or topical intention)

O God of mercy and compassion, thank you for your mercy and enable us to show mercy to others. Through Christ, our Lord. Amen.

FRIDAY

MATTHEW 19:3-12

1. "What God has united, no person must divide." There is a very important line in the Old Testament which we rarely hear quoted. "A cord of three strings is not quickly torn apart." A cord of two strings is easily unravelled. The third string helps to bind the other two. In a marriage, God is the third string. For Catholics, marriage is a sacrament. A sacrament is a celebration of God in our lives at very special moments - at infancy and death, in the forgiveness of sins, in the Bread of life. It was at a wedding at Cana in Galilee that Jesus performed his first miracle. He let his glory be seen and his disciples believed in him. The Sacrament of Matrimony celebrates the presence of Jesus Christ as the third string who strengthens the union of husband and wife.

2. It is sad to see so many marriages unravelling, coming apart. There is an old saying that a wedding is for a day and a marriage is for life. Nowadays, a wedding usually lasts a weekend, or even longer if you count the stag and hen parties. Isn't it ironic that while weddings are of a longer duration, marriages are often for a shorter duration. The third cord in the string is vital... the God-string... the recognition of the place of God in the marriage. The slogan of Father Peyton needs to be heard again: the family that prays together stays together. Little things mean a lot in marriages. Little religious expressions recognise the presence of God as the third string: a religious picture or statue in the house; holy water; grace before meals; night prayer with the children; going to Mass together. "What God has united, no person must divide." A cord of three strings is not quickly torn apart.

PRAYERS

In the light of the teaching of Christ, we pray.

That the teaching of Jesus Christ about the sacredness of marriage may be heard through the voice of the Church.
Lord, hear us

For all married couples: that their faith will recognise the presence and strength of God as the third string in their relationship.
Lord, hear us.

For couples preparing for marriage: that the sacredness of the Sacrament may not be obscured by other matters.
Lord, hear us.

For people who had unhappy experiences in marriage: may God bring them new peace and happiness.
Lord, hear us.

(Add prayers for any local, personal or topical intention)

God of love, united in the Trinity of Father, Son and Holy Spirit, hear our prayers offered in the name of Jesus Christ, our Lord and Saviour. Amen.

SATURDAY

MATTHEW 19:13-15

1. People brought little children to Jesus for him to lay hands on them and say a prayer. Yesterday's Gospel was about the sacredness of marriage. Today we move on to the fruit of marriage, the little children. The disciples meant well when they were pushing back the mothers who wanted to have their children blessed by Jesus. They did not want anybody to interrupt the teaching of Jesus. But, seeing what was happening, Jesus wanted the children to be allowed. Welcoming the little children would say far more than a thousand words. Children are innocent, humble, trusting and vulnerable. They deserve the utmost love and care.

2. Stable, loving family life is the backbone of society. When family life breaks up, massive social problems inevitably follow. Unhappy people make for an unhappy society. The family is the basic cell of the Church. The family is the most important place in handing on values and faith to the next generation. It is said that faith is not so much taught as caught. Teaching is good, but the example of family life is far more powerful. Night prayers with the children are wonderful; explaining the crib and the cross; going to Mass together on Sunday. Nowadays it often falls on the grandparents to do what the parents fail to do. Every child has the right to know of God's love; to hear the story of Jesus; to learn how to pray. Jesus welcomed the little children. He laid his hands on them and blessed them.

PRAYERS

We come to God as children coming to a loving parent.

May every child conceived be allowed the right to life: may every child be welcomed into this world with love and warmth.
Lord, hear us.

May family life be strong: may each home be a place where the practices of faith and prayer are passed on to the next generation.
Lord, hear us.

May children who do not get faith at home find teachers who bring faith and prayer into their lives.
Lord, hear us.

May every child receive food, education and adequate medical care.
Lord, hear us.

(Add prayers for any local, personal or topical intention)

O God, we are told to call you Our Father. Bless all our families as we pray in the name of Jesus Christ, your Son, our Lord. Amen.

MONDAY

MATTHEW 19:16-22

1. The rich young man asked Jesus, "Master, what good deed must I do to possess eternal life?" The key word to this man's mentality is possess... to possess eternal life. He was a very wealthy man. Possessions were important to him. Eternal life would be the ultimate possession. In his life, everything had a price. He speculated that the price for eternal life must be some good deed. Jesus challenged his bondage to possessions. "Go and sell what you own and give the money to the poor, and you will have treasure in Heaven; and then come, follow me." At this, the young man turned away. He went away sad, for he was a man of great wealth. His problem was that he did not own his possessions but his possessions owned him.

2. All the popes of the past century have stressed the obligation of sharing with the poor. Saint Paul reflected on the poverty of Jesus Christ. "Jesus Christ, although he was rich, became poor for your sake, so that you should become rich through his poverty" (2 Cor. 8:9). Jesus was poor in his simple lifestyle, in his dependence on others, in the poverty of undergoing an unjust trial, and finally in the poverty of death. Pope Francis came to Rome from familiarity with the shanty regions of Buenos Aires. He wrote of his ideal Church. "I want a Church which is poor and for the poor. They have much to teach us. They have a deep sense of faith. In their difficulties, they know the suffering Christ. We need to be evangelised by the poor and to embrace the mysterious wisdom which God wishes to share with us through them." The rich young man of the Gospel walked away from that challenge. (Pope Francis: *The Joy of the Gospel,* 198)

PRAYERS

As we reflect on the teaching of Jesus, we pray.

May the Church, by word and example, inspire the leaders of world finance to ensure a fair sharing of the world's resources with the poorer nations.
Lord, hear us.

May the rich nations and wealthy millionaires discover the joy of sharing with others.
Lord, hear us.

May all of us learn to distinguish between what we need and what we want.
Lord, hear us.

May the deep faith shown by many poor people enrich the spiritual lives of all of us.
Lord, hear us.

(Add prayers for any local, personal or topical intention)

O God, the Father of all, inspire us to work for a world of justice, compassion and peace, through Christ, our Lord. Amen.

TUESDAY

MATTHEW 19:23-30

1. "It will be hard for a rich man to enter the Kingdom of Heaven". This was the comment of Jesus after a rich young man walked away when he was challenged to sell his possessions and give the money to the poor. How do I get into the Kingdom of Heaven? The answer is in reversing the question. How do I let the Kingdom and its ideals into me? To enter into the Kingdom is to enter into the mind of Christ and to share his ideals for the world. Material wealth can be a big obstacle. Jesus once called money "that tainted thing" . And he advised people to use it in such a way as to gain friends who will get one into Heaven. It is not Saint Peter who operates the gates of Heaven. It's the poor who let in those who have shared with them and those who did not share.

2. The Bible tells us clearly of God's special love for the poor. Jesus proclaimed his mission in these words: "The Spirit of the Lord is upon me, because he has anointed me to preach the Good News to the poor". The first of the Beatitudes is, "Blessed are you poor, yours is the Kingdom of God". Jesus identified with the poor when he said, "Whatsoever you did to the least of my brothers and sisters, that you did unto me". If you want to give anything to God, give it in charity to those who need it. Mother Teresa of Calcutta gave people a five-finger exercise... five words: you did it to me. Jesus identified himself with the poor.

PRAYERS

To belong to the Kingdom of God we must allow the ideals of the Kingdom to get into us. So, we pray.

May the teaching and example of the Church inspire the world to be converted to the ideals of Christ.
Lord, hear us.

May those who are wealthy resist the temptations of wealth and use what they have for the benefit of those who need it.
Lord, hear us.

May God bless and reward the people who give their time to caring for the poor in any way.
Lord, hear us.

The apostles left everything to follow Jesus. May there be many young men and women who follow in their footsteps in our own days.
Lord, hear us.

(Add prayers for any local, personal or topical intention)

O God, you have a special care for people who are lacking food and shelter. Open up our minds and hearts to care for them. Through Christ, our Lord. Amen.

WEEK 20 OF THE YEAR:

WEDNESDAY

MATTHEW 20:1-16

1. "Why be envious because I am generous?" The parable of the workers in the vineyard is not about paying a fair wage. Every worker got the agreed payment. The parable is about envy. The horrible aspect of envy is that it is a negative reaction to some goodness or success that another person enjoys. It is a poisonous growth that draws its energy out of something that is good and beautiful. The generosity of the landowner should have been admired rather than becoming the subject of grumbling. Envy is one of the seven deadly sins. These are vices that spread out poisonous offshoots. The Catechism of the Catholic Church reads: "From envy are born hatred, detraction, calumny, joy caused by the misfortune of a neighbour, and displeasure caused by his prosperity". Envy is a root that poisons the mind.

2. One cure for envy is to appreciate what we have received and to accept that the good fortune of another person is my good fortune too, since we are all brothers and sisters in God's family. Another help to counteract envy is to replace boredom with a sense of wonder. Open your eyes and ears to the wonders of God's generosity. The American writer, John Shea, said that the best preparation for Heaven is the capacity for surprise. Whoever belongs to the Kingdom of God has eyes open to goodness and ears that are deaf to grumbling; is constantly amazed and never bored; is full of wonder and praise. "His goodness shall follow me always, to the end of my days."

PRAYERS

The thoughts of God are as high above our thoughts as the Heavens are above the Earth. So, let us pray.

Open our eyes, Lord, to the wonders and beauty you have given to the world around us.
Lord, hear us.

Expand our hearts with the ability to rejoice with the good fortune or success of others.
Lord, hear us.

Remove the poison in us that causes us to speak about others in an unchristian way.
Lord, hear us.

We pray for people who are seeking employment. May the door of opportunity open up for them.
Lord, hear us.

(Add prayers for any local, personal or topical intention)

O God, the giver of every good gift, we thank you for all that your generosity has given us. Through Christ, our Lord. Amen.

THURSDAY

MATTHEW 20:1-14

1. When Jesus told the parable of people rejecting the invitation to the royal wedding, it was a pointed reference to the people who were plotting to get rid of him. We can apply the parable to another royal wedding banquet. The Eucharist is known also as the Supper of the Lamb. Sadly, many Catholics are no longer interested in coming to the table of the Lord. Those who did not take up their invitation to the royal wedding banquet had what they considered good excuses. Did you ever hear people say they had a bad excuse! The Irish word for an excuse is *leathsceal*, meaning a half-story. In the parable, the other half of the story is that they were not interested. That seems to be the situation today. People are not sufficiently interested to accept the Lord's invitation. Other interests have taken over. But these excuses are not even half the truth. "Blessed are those who are called to the Supper of the Lamb."

2. At the end of the parable is the puzzling bit about the man who was not wearing the proper wedding garment. We can apply this to people who are not spiritually ready to receive Holy Communion. There might be some serious sin that should first be confessed and forgiven. One might first need to be reconciled with somebody who has been hurt or offended. An invitation to a royal wedding is something people would boast about for the rest of their days. But it is very trivial when compared to the invitation of Jesus to receive him as the Bread of Life. Blessed are those who are called to the Supper of the Lamb.

PRAYERS

Blessed are those who are invited to the Supper of the Lamb.

May we have a deep appreciation of the Lord's invitation to come and receive him as the Bread of Life come down from Heaven.
Lord, hear us.

We pray for people who no longer come to Mass. May they recognise the divine invitation that they are rejecting.
Lord, hear us.

May our faith in the presence of Jesus in the Eucharist inspire us to serve him in the people we meet, especially in the poor and suffering.
Lord, hear us.

Let us pray for vocations to the priesthood so that people might not be deprived of Mass because of the lack of priests.
Lord, hear us.

(Add prayers for any local, personal or topical intention)

God, our Father, hear the prayers of your people gathered here in the name of Jesus Christ, your Son, our Lord. Amen.

FRIDAY.

MATTHEW 22:34-40

1. It was in an attempt to start an argument with Jesus that one of the Pharisees asked his opinion on the greatest commandment. Jesus cut through all their theories and commentaries with a simple and challenging answer. Religious laws are nothing if they are not pointers to total love of God and loving one's neighbour as oneself. That in a nutshell is the meaning of all the commandments. The first three commandments cover the duties of reverence for and worship of God. First, worship of one God only, then God's sacred name and God's day. The next five commandments are practical guidelines regarding family life, the protection of life, marriage, stealing and truthfulness. The final two commandments are about self-control. Taken together, the Ten Commandments are practical pointers to loving God and neighbour.

2. Love your neighbour as yourself. Too many people cannot begin that programme because they have very low self-esteem. People with low self-esteem will be negative towards others too. True self-love is not a preoccupation with self but in respecting one's own unique dignity in God's eyes. God the Father loved me into life. God the Son came down from Heaven to save me. The Holy Spirit is the source of wisdom and sanctification within me. Not to love myself is an insult to God! Saint Paul told the people of Ephesus, "You are God's work of art".

PRAYERS

Inspired by the words of the Gospel, we pray.

That the Church will avoid a web of legalism which obscures the joy and love of true religion.
Lord, hear us.

That the Church of today will resemble the early Christian community when pagan writers remarked how these Christian love one another.
Lord, hear us.

May our appreciation of God's love for us inspire us to treat others as God would ask of us.
Lord, hear us.

May we never start arguments just to upset people or catch them out.
Lord, hear us.

(Add prayers for any local, personal or topical intention)

O God, our loving Father, we thank you for creating us in love. May it be our joy to pass on your love to others. Through Christ, our Lord. Amen.

SATURDAY

MATTHEW 23:1-12

1. "Anyone who exalts himself will be humbled, and anyone who humbles himself will be exalted." Jesus was very merciful regarding sins of weakness but he could not stand religious hypocrisy. He specifically highlighted three temptations likely to affect religious leaders. They do not practise what they preach. They tie up heavy burdens and lay them on people's shoulders but exempt themselves. And they love attention... in the way they dress, mixing with the important people, always in the front line of the photograph and very touchy about their titles. They make a career out of religion. Jesus wants his disciples to show a different sort of leadership. He wants humble service. The greatest among you must be your servant. Anyone who exalts himself will be humbled, and anyone who humbles himself will be exalted.

2. True religion is based on love of God and love of our neighbour. Hypocritical religion makes use of religion for one's own importance. Satan, the master deceiver, will do anything to bring down the Church. Satan will probe a person's character for any little chink of weakness which will allow entrance into that person's life. It may be the greed and dishonesty of Judas, the political fear of Pilate. It may be lust, ambition or vanity. There is a short saying in Latin, *corruptio optimi pessima,* corruption of the best is worst of all. Shakespeare expressed it well in one of his sonnets: "Lilies that fester small far worse than weeds". Jesus showed great mercy towards the weeds of life but he detested the stench of religious flowers which had become corrupt.

PRAYERS

"Anyone who exalts himself will be humbled, and anyone who humbles himself will be exalted." So, we pray.

That those who are appointed leaders in the Church may be motivated by the ideal of humble service.
Lord, hear us.

That we may not consider ourselves superior to others: may we regard others as our brothers and sisters in the family of God.
Lord, hear us.

May we never demand high standards of others while we make excuses for ourselves.
Lord, hear us.

May it be our joy as Christians to be humble servants of God and our neighbour.
Lord, hear us.

(Add prayers for any local, personal or topical intention)

God, our Father, bind us together in your great universal family. We offer our prayer in the name of Jesus Christ, our Lord and Master. Amen.

MONDAY

MATTHEW 23:13-22

1. There is far more criticism of the scribes and Pharisees in Matthew's Gospel than in the other three. The context of Matthew's writing helps us to understand why. At the beginning of the Church, all Christians were Jews. Soon Gentile Christians outnumbered those from Jewish background. Tensions arose about which Jewish regulations should be retained. About fifty years later, the Council of Jewish leaders declared that the followers of the Nazarene should be regarded as heretics and outsiders. Families were split. It is likely that the writer of Matthew's Gospel was a Jewish scribe who had become a Christian. He wrote to explain to his fellow scribes that Jesus did not do away with their core beliefs but brought them to completion. The words ascribed to Jesus in this Gospel are full of anger. A modern Jewish scholar, Edward Kessler, points out that this is an argument or polemic between two groups of Jews. The angry tone of voice and depth of invective are part of in-house argument. As we know, we can say things in the family that we would never say to outsiders. Rather than criticise the scribes and Pharisees, the consciences we should examine are our own.

2. Pope Francis always fostered good relationships with other religions. The Chief Rabbi of Jews in Rome suggested that he should be very sensitive when talking about the Pharisees lest he increase anti-Jewish prejudice. Pope Francis took the point and said that he could personally relate to it. "I am a Jesuit, and the word 'Jesuit' also has a bad effect on people." When we put labels on people, we are self-righteous, acting as if we have the right to criticise them. Instead of criticising the scribes and Pharisees, we should examine ourselves to see if we have the faults they had. For instance, how might I be a blind guide leading others astray? Am I shutting up the doors of the Kingdom of God by the witness of my life... my attitudes... my talk?

PRAYERS

As we apply the criticism of the scribes and Pharisees to ourselves, we pray.

That the Church may be the humble servant of God's Kingdom, cooperating with every institution which promotes justice, good living and peace.
Lord, hear us.

Open our minds to recognise the hand of God at work in other religions and practices.
Lord, hear us.

Take out of our hearts all self-righteousness which makes us judge and condemn others.
Lord, hear us.

May the witness of our lives not turn people off religion: rather, may we be a light of goodness attracting people to God.
Lord, hear us.

(Add prayers for any local, personal or topical intention)

O God, you wish that all people be saved and brought to the knowledge of the truth. Graciously hear our prayers offered in the name of Jesus Christ, our Lord. Amen

TUESDAY

MATTHEW 23:23-26

1. "You neglect the weightier matters of the Law, justice, mercy and faith." The faults that Jesus criticised in the Pharisees continue to be the source of temptation for religious people today. One temptation may be to feel very smug because we are faithful to small details of religious practice.

   We might be strong in matters of devotions or days of fasting while neglecting the social side of religion. As the saying goes, we can be so heavenly minded that we are no earthly good. How can we love the God whom we have never seen, if we do not love the people whom we do see?

2. It is a temptation to want to hold on to customs and regulations which were very meaningful in their time but send out the wrong message today. Time moves on, culture changes and to refuse to change is to die out. Saint John the Twenty-Third was very strong on the idea of reading the signs of the times. The temptation of the Pharisees was to have great external observance while inside the heart there is bitterness, harsh judgement of others, and no mercy. By their fruits you shall know them. The authenticity of spirituality is seen in a life of honesty, concern for others, willingness to help and joy in the Lord. Do not be a sourpuss Christian. If you believe you are saved, pass the message up to your face!

PRAYERS

As we reflect on the temptations of religion, we pray.

May the light of the Church's social teaching inspire us to be committed to matters of justice, mercy and faith.
Lord, hear us.

May our relationship with God in prayer inspire us to serve God in practical works of charity.
Lord, hear us.

May we be open to what we need to change in order to express the Gospel message in ways more relevant to people today.
Lord, hear us.

May the joy of the Gospel be clear for all to see in the way that we live.
Lord, hear us.

(Add prayers for any local, personal or topical intention)

O God, mercifully hear our prayers offered in the name of Jesus Christ, our Lord. Amen.

WEDNESDAY

MATTHEW 23:27-32

1. Jesus was critical of the religious leadership at his time. But are we, members of the Church of Christ, any better today? When Jesus called the first four apostles, two of them were casting nets and two were mending nets. Casting nets represents mission, mending nets represents maintenance. We can be so caught up in maintaining the past that we are neglecting mission. Then we lack enthusiasm for evangelisation. In the words of Pope Francis: "If anything should disturb us and trouble our consciences, it is the fact that many of our brothers and sisters are living without the strength, light and consolation born of friendship with Jesus Christ, without a community of faith to support them, without meaning and a goal in life. We can be shut up within structures which give a false sense of security, within rules that make us harsh judges, within habits which make us feel safe, while at our door people are starving. Jesus does not tire of saying to us: 'Give them something to eat'." (*The Joy of the Gospel*, 49)

2. We may be tempted to maintain a museum full of lifeless fossils of the past, instead of missionary zeal to bring the joy of the Gospel to others. Nowadays, mission is not about travelling abroad, mission starts at home, in our local parish, our schools and above all, in our homes. The most effective way of mission is in witness of life. In the words attributed to Saint Francis of Assisi, preach at all times, sometimes using words.

PRAYERS

Enlightened and challenged by the Gospel, we pray.

May the Church never lose its missionary enthusiasm to bring the light of the Gospel to all people.
Lord, hear us.

May all of us be bearers of the light of Christ, beginning at home.
Lord, hear us.

For those who have no faith to guide them: may the light of Christ penetrate their darkness.
Lord, hear us.

We pray for people who were deeply hurt by the harsh application of rules: may they receive inner healing that enables them to move forward in life.
Lord, hear us.

   (Add prayers for any local, personal or topical intention)

God, our Father, send your Holy Spirit upon us to fill us with enthusiasm to share our faith with others, through Christ, our Lord. Amen.

THURSDAY

MATTHEW 24:42-51

1. "Stay awake, because you do not know the day when your Master is coming". God comes to us every day. God shares life and light and love with us every day. Prayerfulness is the art of being alert to God's presence in our lives. For some, prayer is like a crutch they take up when they need it. But for others, prayer is as much part of life as the leg is part of the body. Their faith is always awake. The old Celtic prayers showed great awareness of God in every action of the day. There were blessings at the lighting of the fire, milking the cow, in times of sickness... prayers for everything. Christ on my right, Christ on my left, Christ above me, Christ below me, Christ in my rising, Christ in my sitting, Christ all around me. What a pity that we have neglected the richness of the Celtic spirituality of constant alertness to God's presence.

2. "Stay awake, because you do not know the day when your Master is coming." The great coming of God refers to the day of our dying. One little story from the wisdom of the East goes like this. A student approaches the Master with a question.
"Master, what does it mean to be enlightened."
"It means knowing I am going to die."
"But, Master, everybody knows they are going to die."
"Ah, yes, but not everybody lives with the knowledge."

   A recent study claims that people today do not mature until after thirty-five. Living as if there is no tomorrow... much less any thought of final judgement and eternity. Maturity involves facing the facts of life, and the fact of death.

PRAYERS

Having reflected on the wisdom of the Gospel, we pray.

May we have our affairs in order at all times so that we are ever ready for the Lord's final coming.
Lord, hear us.

May our faith be a constant light which makes us aware of your presence every day.
Lord, hear us.

For family members or acquaintances who say they no longer believe: may the light of Christ penetrate their darkness.
Lord, hear us.

When our faith is dark, send us a little surprise to wake us up again.
Lord, hear us.

(Add prayers for any local, personal or topical intention)

O God, you are always with us but we are not always with you. Waken up our faith to be more aware of your presence. Through Christ, our Lord. Amen.

FRIDAY

MATTHEW 25:1-13

1. Some people get a bit sore about this parable of the sensible and foolish bridesmaids. They feel it was very selfish of the ones who had oil in their lamps not to share it with others. But that is to miss a very important part of the lesson. There is a light that cannot be borrowed. There are some tasks you have to do for yourself. Nobody can do your believing for you. By all means one can pray for another person. But ultimately one must make the personal decision to believe in God. Jesus saw the faith of the friends who carried the crippled man to him. But it was the cripple himself who had to obey the command of Jesus to stand up and walk. There is a light that cannot be borrowed.

2. Saint Paul said that there are three things that last: faith, hope and love. We call these the theological virtues because they express aspects of our relationship with God. Faith, by which we know God in a personal way; hope, through which we draw strength from God; and love, through which we are inflamed by God's love. Faith, hope and love are three flames in the lamp of light we received in the grace of Baptism. This lamp needs oil. What provides the oil is the three-in-one mixture of prayer, study of our religion and practical action. Prayer, study and action form the tripod of the Christian life.

PRAYERS

As we take the parable of Jesus to heart, we pray.

That the Church will always be a community of believers united in love to welcome Christ, the Bridegroom of the soul.
Lord, hear us.

O God, you sent your Beloved Son to embrace us in the arms of divine love. May we always be ready to open door of our hearts to him.
Lord, hear us.

For people who do not believe: in prayer we carry them to God that they might receive the grace to be able to stand up in their own faith.
Lord, hear us.

May we live in a Christlike way that will attract people to the light of faith.
Lord, hear us.

   (Add prayers for any local, personal or topical intention)

God, our Father, graciously hear the prayers we offer in the name of Jesus Christ, our Lord. Amen

SATURDAY

MATTHEW 25:14-30

1. Well done good and faithful servants. Well done, all of you who keep on praying and helping others. The parable of the talents is a contrast between the productive life and the unproductive life. The productive person is faithful in the little things of everyday life... keeps on going... doesn't look for notice... doesn't wait around for the big event to get going. Artists know that perfection is composed of trifles, but perfection itself is no trifle. Jesus said that the productive life is good and faithful.

2. The unproductive servant in the story is described as good for nothing. He dug a hole in the ground and hid his talent. See how negative and cynical he has become. He does not blame himself. He offloads blame to what others are saying and to the master's severe reputation. It's always some other person's fault, never mine. A buried talent digs a cesspool of cynicism. Just like a healthy lake needs a steady inflow and outflow. Otherwise it becomes stagnant. A healthy mind needs steady stimulation and productive expression. Otherwise stagnation and cynicism take over. And cynicism is good for nothing. Faithfulness in little things is what keeps the flow fresh. In God's eyes no good action is small. A candle is a small light, but if everybody lit a candle, what a bright world it would be. Well done, good and faithful servants!

PRAYERS

As we reflect on the parable of the talents, we pray.

May the Church and our local parish encourage us to use our talents to make life better for others.
Lord, hear us.

May we recognise the talents God has given us and never be reluctant to use them.
Lord, hear us.

Protects us from the temptation to be negative and cynical.
Lord, hear us.

May we take to heart the message of Saint Teresa of Calcutta, to do the little thing with a lot of love.
Lord, hear us.

(Add prayers for any local, personal or topical intention)

O God, the giver of every good gift, we thank you for what you have given us, and pray that we might use our talents for your greater glory. Through Christ, our Lord. Amen.

MONDAY

LUKE 4:16-30

1. Today we commence thirteen weeks when the daily Gospel reading is from Saint Luke. We can get an insight into the purpose of each evangelist by paying attention to the first words of Jesus that each writer records. Luke's opening statement from the adult Jesus is a quotation from Isaiah. "The spirit of the Lord has been given to me for he has anointed me." Luke is the evangelist of the Holy Spirit and of prayer. He tells us of the action of the Holy Spirit in the life of Jesus, and also in Mary, Elizabeth, Zechariah, Simeon and John the Baptist. Luke tells us of the gracious, merciful actions of God and the prayerful reactions of people. Luke was also the writer of the Acts of the Apostles. Luke's Gospel might well be called the Acts of the Holy Spirit in the mission of Jesus: and his second book might then be called the Acts of the Holy Spirit in the life of the early Church.

2. "This text is being fulfilled today even as you listen". Jesus then rolled up the scroll and handed it back to the assistant. He moved from the past to the present, from the Book to life. Scripture is not just the story of the past but it is the God-news, the Good News for every day. By constant reflection on the Scriptures, we become familiar with what God did and said in the past so that we can recognise what God is saying and doing today. We too move from the past to the present, from the Book to life.

PRAYERS

Inspired by the Good News of Jesus, we pray.

May the Church, under the leadership of Pope *(Name),* be the voice of the Holy Spirit bringing the teaching of Jesus to the world of today.
Lord, hear us.

With the inspiration of the Holy Spirit, may the wisdom of Sacred Scripture be the light of our lives.
Lord, hear us.

Jesus brought good news to the poor. May the Gospel inspire the wealthy nations to share in justice with the nations who are short of food.
Lord, hear us.

Jesus brought liberation to captives. May the Holy Spirit help all who suffer from an addiction to be liberated from their problem.
Lord, hear us.

(Add prayers for any local, personal or topical intention)

O God, graciously hear the prayers we offer in the name of Jesus Christ, your Son, our Lord. Amen.

TUESDAY

LUKE 4:31-37

1. Jesus made a deep impression on people because he spoke with authority. He was able to back up his words with action. Sermonising about God is very hollow if it is not backed up by witness of life. As Pope Paul VI said, people today listen more willingly to listeners than to teachers, and if they do listen to teachers, it is because first they are witnesses. There is a saying that what you are thunders so loudly that I cannot hear what you are saying.

2. In the exorcism story there is a huge contrast between the noise of the Devil and the quietness of Jesus. The Devil's presence is marked with loud shouting, frenzy and convulsions. What Jesus says is "Be quiet! Come out of him". The modern world is filled with noise. Electronic amplification has changed music. Thumping noise invades the mind. Tranquillity is a foreign language to people who have fed their minds on noise. Some people would be on the edge of a nervous breakdown if they had to spend a day without their phone or some other gadget. Long ago, the Prophet Isaiah, told the people, "Your salvation lay in conversion and tranquillity, your strength in tranquillity and trust, and you would have none of it." Another lovely line is "Be still and know that I am God".

PRAYERS

After reflecting on the example and words of Jesus, we pray.

Jesus showed his authority in acts of mercy and healing. May the authority of the Church be seen in the power of love rather than in the love of power.
Lord, hear us.

We pray for people who struggle with evil habits and inner demons. May the healing power of Jesus bring them freedom and peace.
Lord, hear us.

May we learn how to be still and quiet so as to give space in our minds to God.
Lord, hear us.

For all who suffer from mental stress and anxiety, may the Lord grant them tranquillity and trust.
Lord, hear us.

(Add prayers for any local, personal or topical intention)

O gracious God, hear the prayers we offer in the name of Jesus Christ, your Son, our Lord. Amen.

WEDNESDAY

LUKE 4:38-44

1. People brought the sick to Jesus and asked him to do something for them. We are encouraged to bring the needs of the sick and suffering to God in prayer. When many people join in prayer, it is especially effective. When one afflicted woman touched the hem of the garment of Jesus, power came out of him. How much more power is released when people are united in a tsunami of prayer! As the poet Tennyson wrote, "More things are wrought by prayer than this world dreams of".

2. Work in the caring service can be very draining. After giving of himself to the needs of people for long hours, even Jesus felt the need to withdraw to a quiet place. People in the health service have a poor record in looking after their own needs. It is important to recognise that it is better to come apart rather than to be torn apart. There are two ways of being alone: loneliness and solitude. Loneliness is a form of emptiness; solitude is a space for fullness. Loneliness is empty of friendship and happiness; solitude is full of joy in having time for reflection, time for God. Be still and know that I am God.

PRAYERS

Encouraged by the works of Jesus, we bring our needs in prayer.

People brought their sick relations and friends to Jesus for healing. Let us pause for a while to mention quietly the names of those who are sick and suffering.
Lord, hear us.

Jesus sought to balance works of healing with time for quiet prayer. May we recognise that the busier we are the more we need to reconnect with God in quiet prayer.
Lord, hear us.

Jesus rebuked the evil spirits. We pray for people who suffer from any addiction: may they find release when they hand their problems over to the higher power of God.
Lord, hear us.

May we discover the joy of solitude in having special time in the presence of God.
Lord, hear us,

  (Add prayers for any local, personal or topical intention)

O God of love and compassion, hear the prayers we offer in the name of Jesus Christ, out Lord. Amen.

THURSDAY

Luke 5:1-11

1. Simon Peter recognised his sinfulness when he glimpsed something of the Lord's majesty in the miraculous catch of fish. Where there is little awareness of God, there is no sense of sin. One of the psalms gives an insight into the mind of the sinner: "Sin speaks to the sinner in the depth of his heart. There is no fear of God before his eyes. He so flatters himself in his mind, that he knows not his guilt". If you want to know about sin, do not ask the sinner, because he knows not his guilt. If you want to know about sin, ask the saint. It is only someone who is close to God who knows the tragedy of offending God. Only those who are aware of God's love know how half-hearted our efforts are. Only those who know the fire of God's love recognise how lukewarm we are. Peter recognised his sinfulness when he glimpsed the majesty of Jesus. "Leave me Lord, for I am a sinful man."

2. "From now on, it is people you will catch." The catch of fish prefigured the mission of the Church. Labouring all night in the dark, the fishermen caught nothing. Once they were directed by the Word of the Lord, see what happened. The mission of the Church is a combination of God's Word and human effort. Peter and his companions left everything to follow Jesus.

PRAYERS

Inspired by the words of the Gospel, we pray.

May the mission of the Church always be directed by the Word of God.
Lord, hear us.

Lord, we humbly ask that we might receive a glimpse of your love for us which will make us more aware of our sinfulness.
Lord, hear us.

The apostles were called to follow Jesus. We pray that many young men and women will hear the call of Jesus and give themselves wholeheartedly to his service.
Lord, hear us.

The apostles pulled in empty nets all night. We pray for all who have experienced failure in life. May the Lord direct them towards a more successful future.
Lord, hear us.

(Add prayers for any local, personal or topical intention)

O God, kindly listen to the prayers of your people, in the name of Jesus Christ, our Lord. Amen.

FRIDAY

LUKE 5:33-39

1. While it is very important to conserve the wisdom of the past, it also important to see that by staying rigidly with the past, one may be resisting the call of the Holy Spirit to adapt to changing circumstances. It can happen to us as individuals, or as a community. Even the Church must always be open to reform. Reading the signs of the times, one recognises cultural changes. There are divine truths that cannot be changed. But there may be regulations and customs which were very helpful in the past but may be counter-productive today. For instance, there was a time when it was important to treat bishops like princes living in palaces and that the local priest should have a big house. In these more democratic times, such customs send out the wrong message. What served well in the past may not be helpful today. Then, to resist change is to stagnate.

2. There is a time for fasting and a time for feasting. Beware of the person of the one book! The one novena. The one liturgical season. A healthy spirituality has the right balance, a time for the penance of Lent and then for the Alleluia of Easter. Wisdom has been described as a virtue that can balance the opposites. The cycle of the liturgical seasons is a school of great wisdom. There are even different colours for the different seasons: purple for penance; white for celebration; red for the fires of the Holy Spirit and the blood of martyrs; while the green of nature is like the default colour for when there is no particular season or feast.

PRAYERS

In the light of Christ's teaching, we pray.

That the Church may always keep its windows open to the breathing of the Holy Spirit, blowing the cobwebs away.
Lord, hear us.

For people who find it hard to accept any change. May they understand that an old garment reaches a state when it can no longer take a patch. Something new is needed.
Lord, hear us.

For people who are in a dark valley at the moment: may the light of the Holy Spirit give them new hope and joy.
Lord, hear us.

May the example of our lives portray the joy of believing to the world.
Lord, hear us.

(Add prayers for any local, personal or topical intention)

God our Father, graciously hear the prayers we offer in the name of Jesus Christ, our Lord. Amen.

SATURDAY

LUKE 6:1-5

1. The Sabbath is God's gift to a busy world. In the bible, the first thing to be declared holy is the seventh day of creation. Sabbath means holy restfulness. The bible's story of Creation was never intended to be a scientific account. But it is a story of wonderful wisdom and it nurtures a psychology fit for all times. God rested from work on the seventh day. God blessed the seventh day and made it holy. Work is not complete until one can stand back and admire it. Imagine, the Creator changed from his dungarees, freshened up and rubbed his hands in satisfaction. "It is good, very good." This is the art of holy restfulness. We live in a world of speed, noise and stress. For many people, recreation is called a workout. Yet one good walk attentive to the wonders of nature would be of more benefit to the whole person, body, mind and spirit, than hours of treadmill and press-ups. The Sabbath's holy restfulness is God's gift to a busy world.

2. The great religions of the world recognise the need for a special day of holy restfulness. Muslims hold it on Friday, Jews on Saturday and Christians on Sunday. A hymn in the Breviary celebrates Sunday as the first day of Creation, the day of Christ's Resurrection and the day of Pentecost.

> O Day of light and life and grace,
> From earthly toil a resting place!
> The hallowed hours, best gift of love
> Give we again to God above.

Show me what you do on a Sunday and you will reveal where God is in your life.

Has the shopping mall become the new temple? Saint Augustine wrote about Sunday. "We shall rest and we shall see; we shall see and we shall love; we shall love and we shall praise." Sunday is soul-day, family-day and God's-day.

PRAYERS

The Third Commandment reads: Remember and keep holy the Sabbath Day.

We thank God for the holy day of rest every week. May we remember to keep God at the centre of that day.
Lord, hear us.

May our Sunday be a time for greater family togetherness.
Lord, hear us.

May our Sunday be a time for prayer and spiritual growth.
Lord, hear us.

Let us thank God for the Jewish people and the rich faith they have passed on to us. May they never again suffer from anti-Semitism.
Lord, hear us.

(Add prayers for any local, personal or topical intention)

O God, who declared the Sabbath a holy day, hear the prayers we offer in the name of Jesus Christ, our Lord. Amen.

MONDAY

Luke 6:6-11

1. It was on the holy day, the Sabbath. It was in the holy place, the synagogue. In this place stood a man with a withered hand. The man's withered hand was a symbol of a withering atmosphere. There were withering looks watching for something to use against Jesus. Withering discussion about how to get rid of this man who was healing people. Excessive legalism had squeezed the joy out of the beautiful Sabbath. The luscious, juicy plum had withered into a wrinkled prune. Unfortunately, there is a false piety which has all the virtues except charity. Withering attitudes, withering looks, withering judgements, withering tongues. Sourpuss religion turns people away.

2. Jesus knew that there is a hierarchy of moral laws. Some duties are more important than others. Saving life is always more important than allowing it to be destroyed. Caring for somebody on a Sunday may be far more important than going to Mass. Wherever works of compassion are performed, God is there. A question or two to ponder. Has my religion made me severely judgemental? Or is the world, even a tiny part of it, a better place because I am here?

PRAYERS

Inspired by the example of Jesus, we pray.

That our religion might be an inspiration to imitate Jesus in improving the quality of life for people.
Lord, hear us.

We pray for people who are blinded by prejudice: may their eyes be open to see with more understanding and compassion.
Lord, hear us.

For people who do good but, like Jesus, they are mocked and persecuted. May they know that God is on their side.
Lord, hear us.

When we have to choose one obligation instead of another one, may we discern which one is more important in God's eyes.
Lord, hear us.

(Add prayers for any local, personal or topical intention)

O God of love and compassion, hear the prayers we offer in the name of Jesus Christ, your Son, our Lord. Amen.

TUESDAY

LUKE 6:12-19

1. Even Jesus needed to pray. Before important decisions, he prayed – before selecting the apostles, before teaching the Our Father, before his Passion. We are told that he went up the hills to pray. A traditional definition of prayer is the elevation of the mind and heart to God, to praise him, to thank him and to ask him for what we need. In raising our minds we strive to rise above the many preoccupations that distract our attentiveness to God. In raising our hearts, we are inviting the Holy Spirit to direct us. Even Jesus felt the need to pray. How much more do we need to raise our minds and hearts to God.

2. Twelve apostles were chosen for special training. Their mission would be to extend the mission of Jesus to far off places. What a motley bunch they were! Peter was impetuous and drew a sword which injured a man. Thomas was a sceptical man who refused to believe the others regarding the resurrection of Jesus. Matthew and Simon the Zealot were from opposite sides of the political fence. Simon belonged to a rebel band dedicated to getting rid of the Romans while Matthew collected taxes for the Romans. The brothers, James and John, were ambitious and had the nickname, Boanerges, meaning the Sons of Thunder. You know about Judas. After going up the hill to pray, Jesus came down and stopped at a level piece of ground where he spoke to the people. He certainly came down to our level with the very ordinary human beings he chose as the foundations of his Church. There is room for us in that sort of Church.

PRAYERS

Following the example of Jesus, we gather our thoughts in prayer.

For those who are chosen like the apostles for leadership in the Church: may the Holy Spirit always inspire and encourage them. *Lord, hear us.*

May all of us be willing to offer our services in our local community. *Lord, hear us.*

We pray for vocations to the priesthood and religious life. *Lord, hear us*

Power came out of Jesus, curing people, when they touched him. We reach out to touch him in the name of our friends and acquaintances who are sick and suffering. *Lord, hear us.*

(Add prayers for any local, personal or topical intention)

O God, the giver of every good gift, hear our prayers as we raise our hearts in the name of Jesus Christ, our Lord. Amen.

WEDNESDAY

LUKE 6:20-26

1. The word *blessed* gives a much clearer understanding of the Beatitudes than the word *happy*. Happy is a description of feeling or well-being. Blessed is a statement of one's standing before God. At the time of Jesus, people were of the opinion that God's blessing could be seen in the four P-words: prosperity, power, prestige and popularity. But what about people who were poor, powerless, persecuted or handicapped in any way? They were regarded as being punished by God for their own sins or for the sins of their ancestors. Jesus turned the whole idea of God's blessings upside down. His whole lifestyle as well as his words showed the special love of God for the poor, the outcast, lepers, sinners, those who were sick or handicapped. "Blessed are you who are poor: yours is the Kingdom of God."

2. Jesus found that the poor and handicapped were far more responsive to the ideals of the Kingdom than people who had it all going for them in this life. Pope Francis wrote that the poor have much to teach us. Often they have an amazing depth of faith. In their sufferings, they can identify with the suffering Christ. "We are called to be evangelised by them." Pope Francis encourages us to embrace the mysterious wisdom which God wishes to share with us through them. In contrast to the poor who are very close to God, Jesus used the word *alas* for the state of those who have all that material prosperity can buy. We may have material prosperity but have we more contentment and peace of heart? Alas, what we do have is the increased number of broken relationships, depression, suicides, and dependence on drugs or alcohol for social life. "Blessed are you who are poor: yours is the Kingdom of God."

PRAYERS

Taking the teaching of Jesus to heart, we pray.

May the Church follow the example of Jesus who made himself poor so that we might become rich. As Pope Francis called it, a Church of the poor for the poor.
Lord, hear us.

That the rich nations and wealthy millionaires have a conscience about sharing in justice with the poor nations.
Lord, hear us.

People are still being persecuted for their religious beliefs. May they experience God's blessing in the depth of their faith.
Lord, hear us.

For all who are caught up in material pursuits: may they give more time to spiritual riches.
Lord, hear us.

(Add prayers for any local, personal or topical intention)

O God, the Father of all, graciously hear our prayers offered to you in the name of Jesus Christ, our Lord. Amen.

THURSDAY

LUKE 6:27-38

1. Today's Gospel is one of the most important passages of religious literature. It sets before us the ideals of a truly Christian life: what the world would be like if we all took the ideals of Jesus seriously. He showed how true love and compassion can overcome all hatred and injustice. Ugly things happen: violence, bullying, cheating, injustice, name-calling. Reacting in hatred only adds to the evil of the world. Responding like Jesus is the only way to heal the world. Jesus set the ideals that goodness is greater than evil, that gentleness is more powerful than violence, that forgiveness is greater than revenge.

2. Back in 1999, the Jewish Rabbi, Jonathan Sacks, visited Kosovo, at a time when the civil war had reached an uneasy truce. Standing amid the wreckage and rubble of war, he came to the conclusion that there is only one word that can change the course of the world. That word is *forgiveness*. Whether it is international conflict, family divisions or interpersonal hatred, it takes the power of forgiveness to move on from the past. According to Rabbi Sacks, the most compelling testimony to human freedom is the ability to live with the past without being captive of it. We cannot turn off memory like a tap. Memory will remember the past. Our option is about how we remember. We have the choice of allowing the hatred to fester or to remember with the decision to move forward with an attitude that is bigger than the wrong. This is where human freedom is important. Somebody has to take the first step to move beyond conflict. "Treat others as you would wish them to treat you. Love your enemies and do good. Be compassionate as your Father is compassionate." The ability to forgive is compelling proof of the nobility of human freedom.

PRAYERS

Inspired by the ideals of Jesus, we pray.

That all nations will recognise the harm and devastation brought about by war: may every effort be made to resolve differences by peaceful means.
Lord, hear us.

Where families are divided, may the desire to move forward in harmony be stronger than the temptation to remain captive to bitterness.
Lord, hear us.

We pray for people who are knotted up in bitterness and revenge. May they accept the grace of the Holy Spirit to be healed in mind and heart.
Lord, hear us.

Blessed are the peacemakers: they shall be called the children of God. Bless and reward all who work for peace.
Lord, hear us.

   (Add prayers for any local, personal or topical intention)

God of mercy and compassion, hear the prayers we offer in the name of Jesus Christ, your Son, our Lord. Amen.

FRIDAY

LUKE 6:39-42

1. The parable of the blind leading the blind questions us regarding whose ideals we follow. Are we true followers of the ideals and morals of Christ? As the Shepherd Psalm says: "He guides me along the right path, he is true to his name." He is the way, the truth and the life. But if we stray from his way, we are likely to follow blind guides. Sadly, the light of Christ has gone from the lives of many people today. Without his teaching, his ideals, his morality and his hope, where will we end up? It is a time of rapid change. People find it hard to make a definite commitment to anything. Footballers change clubs. People change jobs, addresses, partners. Is there any stability? Yes, our God is an everlasting rock. The house that is built on the rock of the teaching of Jesus has weathered many storms in the past and will withstand the flood of changes in society today. Regarding opinion polls or a referendum, always remember that by popular opinion, Jesus was condemned to death while a brigand was released. Morality is far too important to be left to popular choice.

2. People sometimes ask is there any humour in the Bible. Scholars who have studied ancient Jewish texts tell us that humour was often used by Jewish teachers as a way of imparting serious messages. The parable of the splinter and the plank is such a ridiculous exaggeration that it has to be regarded as humorous. Try to picture a plank of wood in somebody's eye! People would remember the joke and with any luck, the serious message should be remembered too. The message here is to see your own faults before you see the faults of someone else. The only conscience you have to answer for is your own.

PRAYERS

In the light of the Gospel, we pray.

That the Church, under the guidance of Pope *(Name)*, will always be a light to the nations, guiding them along the right path of ideals and morals.
Lord, hear us

That the people who make our laws will be faithful to the law of God.
Lord, hear us

For all who are without direction or stability in life, may they have the grace to follow Jesus as the way, the truth and the life.
Lord, hear us.

That we might stop judging others instead of putting our own lives in order.
Lord, hear us.

   (Add prayers for any local, personal or topical intention)

O God, you are the rock of ages, unchanging, everlasting, hear the prayers we offer in the name of Jesus Christ, your Son, our Lord. Amen.

SATURDAY

LUKE 6:43-49

1. In a simple parable, Jesus reminds us that our outward actions are the fruit of our inner life. Our inner life is represented as our heart. We sometimes describe a footballer as having no heart or having a mighty heart, describing the player's inner ability to find extra energy at critical moments. A heart full of goodness will be seen in a life of compassion and caring. But an unhappy heart, a sick inner life, will produce the fruits of hatred, sarcasm, malice, violence and other nasty habits. By their fruits you shall know them. One of the psalms has this lovely prayer: "A pure heart create for me, O God, put a steadfast spirit within me".

2. Three things Jesus asks us to do: come to me; listen to my words; act on them. We must continually come back to Jesus as our guide. What would he ask of me? What is he saying to me? His teaching must be constantly absorbed into our thinking, our values and our actions. Only then will we be Christlike. Saint Paul wrote that what matters most is the faith that is expressed in deeds. In the famous words of Saint James, "Faith without good works is dead". This is where Christian contemplation differs from systems of meditation that come from Eastern philosophies of life. It is said of these that five thousand years of meditation haven't ploughed a single field. Mother Teresa of Calcutta is an example of Christian meditation. Christian meditation inspires Christian action in responding to the needs of the poor and hungry. In Christian meditation, one comes to Christ, listens to his words and acts on them. "By their fruits you shall know them."

PRAYERS

In the light of the teaching of Christ, we pray.

That the Church will always inspire people to come to Jesus, to listen to his words, and to bear fruit in acts of caring and compassion.
Lord, hear us.

May our lives be built on the rock-solid foundation of the teaching of Jesus Christ.
Lord, hear us.

May we grow in inner goodness of heart and produce the fruits of kindness in thought, word and action.
Lord, hear us.

Today we ask God to bless and reward all the people who volunteer their time and talents in charitable organisations.
Lord, hear us.

(Add prayers for any local, personal or topical intention)

O God, the source and foundation of our lives, graciously hear the prayers we offer in the name of Jesus Christ, your Son, our Lord. Amen.

MONDAY

LUKE 7:1-10

1. CYCLE A

   The centurion whose servant was sick was not a Jew, so he asked his Jewish friends to intercede with Jesus on his behalf. We ask our friends to pray on our behalf and we in turn pray for their needs. We also ask the Blessed Mother of Jesus and favourite saints to intercede on our behalf. In today's First Reading, Saint Paul tells us to offer petitions, intercession and thanksgiving for everyone. Then he says that there is only one mediator between God and mankind, namely Jesus Christ. This line is often taken out of context by people who attack the Catholic practice of praying to Mary and the saints. A mediator is a go-between. The literal meaning of intercede is to stand between, exactly the same as to mediate. Nobody can go to the Father except through Jesus. In Christian prayer, we go to the Father through him, with him, and in him. Our prayer for others, or the intercession of the saints, is not a contradiction of the role of Jesus as the mediator but an extension of it. When the Jewish friends of the Roman centurion interceded with Jesus, they were mediators. So too are Mary and the saints, mediators through Jesus, with him and in him.

2. CYCLE B

   In today's First Reading, we have Saint Paul's wonderful words about the Blessed Eucharist. "The blessing-cup that we bless is a communion with the blood of Christ and the bread that we break is a communion with the body of Christ." Receiving the Lord in Holy Communion is an awesome privilege. We take the humble words of the Roman centurion as our prayer of preparation: "Lord, I am not worthy that you should enter under my roof, but only say the word, and my soul shall be healed". Nobody, even the holiest saint, is worthy of this awesome privilege of receiving Jesus. He invites us to come, not because of our merits but because we need this food of divine life.

PRAYERS

In the light of the Word of God, we gather in prayer.

"Lord, I am not worthy that you should enter under my roof." We pray for a deep understanding of the awesome privilege of receiving Jesus in Holy Communion.
Lord, hear us.

For those who no longer come to Mass: may they recognise what they are missing.
Lord, hear us.

The Roman centurion asked people to intercede with Jesus for his servant. We bring to him the needs of our relations and friends who are sick in mind or body.
Lord, hear us.

For peace throughout the world and an end to all warfare and persecution of people.
Lord, hear us.

(Add prayers for any local, personal or topical intention)

God of love and compassion, hear the prayers we offer in the name of Jesus Christ, our Saviour and Mediator. Amen.

TUESDAY

LUKE 7:11-17

1. By raising the young man from the dead, Jesus is revealed as the Lord of life and death. Everyone was filled with awe and praised God. This miracle prepared people for the most wonderful mystery of the resurrection of Jesus. As followers of Jesus Christ, we believe in life after death, in a sharing of the Lord's resurrection. Saint Paul said that through the grace of Baptism, we become children of God and heirs of the Kingdom of God. Our Christian belief is so much more noble than theories of reincarnation.

2. The key moment in the story of the raising of the widow's son at Naim is when Jesus felt sorry for the grieving mother. Philosophers referred to God as the unmoved mover, meaning that some source must have already existed to start the energies of the universe in motion. The First Mover was called the Unmoved Mover. A great Jewish scholar, rather tongue-in-cheek, took issue with this name for God and said that God is the most moved mover. Jesus was moved at the sad funeral in Naim. He felt sorry for the grieving mother. Pope Francis referred to Jesus as the face of mercy. The heart of God is moved in compassion and mercy. If you want to know what God is like, then see what Jesus was like. Jesus is God made known to us in a language we can understand, the language of human life. "The Word was made flesh and dwelt among us."

PRAYERS

Encouraged by our reflection on the power and compassion of Jesus, we pray.

Lord Jesus, in dying you destroyed our death, and in rising you restored our life. May the memory of your resurrection fill our minds with meaning and our hearts with hope.
Lord, hear us.

May people who are in deep sorrow over the loss of a loved one find consolation in their faith.
Lord, hear us.

As Jesus was moved in pity for the grieving mother, may we be moved in compassion for people who are suffering in any way.
Lord, hear us.

Saint Luke wrote that everyone was filled with awe and praised God. Open our eyes to see the wonders all around us and raise our hearts in praise.
Lord, hear us.

(Add prayers for any local, personal or topical intention)

O God, the Lord of life and death, hear the prayers we offer in the name of Jesus Christ, our Lord. Amen.

WEDNESDAY

LUKE 7:31-35

1. Today's Gospel can be summed up like this: there are some people that you couldn't please. They are like surly children at play. Do you want to dance around in a happy game? No! So, let's play funerals then. No! John the Baptist was too strict. Jesus was too liberal. You couldn't please them. But there were others who were moved. The approach of John the Baptist had no frills attached and this is what some people needed to hear. The more merciful approach of Jesus drew others to conversion. Wisdom was proved right in each case.

2. Jesus was the friend of people who struggled with their weaknesses. Most religious leaders at the time kept far away from sinners. Sinners were left with no hope. But Jesus was different. He sat with sinners. He ate and drank with them. In the eyes of his critics, Jesus was a glutton and a drunkard. But he turned the accepted values upside down. He started a revolution. Pope Francis called it a revolution of tenderness. "The Son of God, by becoming flesh, summoned us to the revolution of tenderness." He spoke of the Church as an oasis of mercy in the desert of the world.

PRAYERS

Inspired with the message of the mercy of Jesus, we pray.

Jesus sat with sinners and gave them hope. May the Church always be a hospital of mercy for all who have been wounded in the battlefield of life.
Lord, hear us.

May the grace of the Holy Spirit help us to stop judging and condemning people.
Lord, hear us.

Spare us, Lord, from being so grumpy that nothing pleases us.
Lord, hear us.

We pray for those who are so burdened by their sins that they think there is no hope for them. May they come to know the merciful Lord who is waiting to lift them up.
Lord, hear us.

(Add prayers for any local, personal or topical intention)

God of mercy and compassion, hear the prayers we offer in the name of Jesus Christ, our Lord and Saviour. Amen.

THURSDAY

LUKE 7:36-50

1. Here is a marvellous story which shows how the experience of the Lord's mercy changed a sinner into a saint. "Your sins are forgiven." Your past is blotted out. You have a wonderful future if you accept the mercy of God. Mercy is so important that the Church has elevated it to the level of a sacrament. Saint Paul told the Corinthians that Christ died for our sins. The words of sacramental absolution celebrate the merits of his death and resurrection. "God, the Father of mercy, has reconciled the world to himself through the death and resurrection of his Son. He has sent the Holy Spirit for the forgiveness of sins". Confession of sins opens up a person's life to receiving the life-giving mercy of God. Jesus told the sinful woman: "Your faith has saved you; go in peace".

2. The Pharisee who had invited Jesus to a meal looked down disdainfully at the woman who was washing the feet of Jesus. "Doesn't he know that she has a bad name?" Who gave her the bad name? It must have been those who regarded themselves as good people. Gossip is poisonous.

   Gossip is highly contagious. It spreads like an epidemic. Saint Paul told his young friend Timothy, "Be an example to all believers in the way you speak and act". We have to ask ourselves if our talk is harmful to anybody's good name. Never say anything about another person that you would not like to be said about yourself, even if it is true.

PRAYERS

In the light of today's Gospel, we thank the Lord for his mercy to sinners.

May your Church on Earth continue your mission of mercy, bringing forgiveness and mercy to sinners.
Lord, hear us.

We pray for people who feel powerless in dealing with an addiction or bad habits of behaviour. May the loving kindness of God touch their hearts. May they experience forgiveness and renewal of life.
Lord, hear us.

For people who have been given a bad name by gossiping tongues: may they know that in God's eyes, no creature of his has a bad name. May the love of Christ give people new hope and dignity.
Lord, hear us.

That our tongues may be cleansed of any trace of character assassination.
Lord, hear us.

   (Add prayers for any local, personal or topical intention)

God of mercy and compassion, graciously hear the prayers we offer in the name of Jesus Christ, our merciful Lord and Saviour. Amen.

FRIDAY

LUKE 8:1-3

1. "Jesus made his way through towns and villages, preaching, and proclaiming the Good News of the Kingdom of God." *Proclaiming* is a strong word. Proclaiming is a way of announcing that something has been decreed by the higher authority. What is the Kingdom of God that Jesus was proclaiming? It was the purpose of his mission on Earth, that the rule of God would be totally accepted. Then the world would be free from war, injustice, hatred, selfishness and so on. It would be a world of truth, justice, peace, sharing of resources and care for one another. That is what we pray for in the prayer that Jesus taught us: "Thy Kingdom come, thy will be done on Earth as it is in Heaven".

2. There are several places in Saint Luke's writings where he mentions the important role played by women in the ministry of Jesus and in the early Church. The acceptance of man-woman equality is far advanced today from the culture of the time of Jesus. Saint Paul told the Galatians that all who are baptised are clothed in Christ. "There can be no distinction between Jew and Greek, between slave and free, between male and female." The equality of Jew and Gentile was solved in the 1st Century. It took nineteen hundred years to finally give freedom and equality to slaves. There still remains much work to be done in the Church regarding the distinction between male and female.

PRAYERS

After reflecting on the ministry and preaching of Jesus, we pray.

Jesus proclaimed the Good News of the Kingdom of God. May the Church inspire people to live in harmony and peace, in compassion and caring.
Lord, hear us.

Jesus found a place for several women among his close disciples. May the Church welcome the voice of women and support the expression of their talents.
Lord, hear us.

May God touch the hearts of many men and women to give their lives to the proclamation of the Kingdom of God.
Lord, hear us

Jesus cured many people of their ailments. We bring to him the needs of our sick relations and acquaintances.
Lord, hear us.

   (Add prayers for any local, personal or topical intention)

God, our Father, you sent your Beloved Son to proclaim your reign on Earth. Hear the prayers we offer in this name, Jesus, the Lord. Amen.

SATURDAY

LUKE 8:4-15

(There are reflections on this parable on
Wednesday, Thursday and Friday of Week 16)

1. "The mysteries of the Kingdom of God are revealed to you; for the rest, there are only parables so that they may see but not perceive, listen but not understand." Scripture has been compared to a great swimming pool in which the infant can paddle and the elephant can swim. Most parables were about everyday life so that anybody could understand on one level. But the revelation of God and God's actions takes one into the deep waters of mystery. A person can spend a lifetime with Scripture and never exhaust it. The Word of God is ever new. You can draw some inspiration from a passage today. Maybe next year you read the same passage and a very different image or word is your source of inspiration. One of the joys of a group reflecting on Scripture is in hearing what other people receive from a passage.

2. Study of the Bible is about what happened in the past... "at that time". Praying with the Bible is about what is happening now... "at this time". As Jesus said in Nazareth, "This text is being fulfilled today even when you are listening". Scriptural prayer moves from then to now. After reading a text carefully, spend time pondering on it and ask a few questions. What is this text saying about God (or Jesus, or the Holy Spirit)? What does it say about the Church, or society, today? What is it saying to me today? Study and prayer go together. Study helps us to understand what God said and did in the past. In the light of the past, we are better able to hear what God is saying and doing in the present.

PRAYERS

Enlightened and inspired by the sacred Word of God, we pray.

For all who teach or preach the Word of God: may they always be guided by the Holy Spirit in the path of truth.
Lord, hear us.

Lord, deepen our ability to listen to your Word. Break through all our distractions and preoccupations so that the seed of your Word may take root in our lives.
Lord, hear us.

May our spiritual lives develop in the light of your Word, so that we bring forth the fruits of genuine charity, patience, kindness and goodness.
Lord, hear us.

For people who have been misled by false prophets into wrong interpretations of Scripture: may they listen to the wisdom of the Church which is the pillar and the ground of truth.
Lord, hear us.

(Add prayers for any local, personal or topical intention)

O God, your Word is a lamp for our steps and a light for our lives. Hear the prayers we offer in the name of Jesus Christ your Son, our Lord. Amen.

MONDAY

Luke 8:16-18

1. "No one lights a lamp to cover it with a bowl or put it under a bed". Isn't it amazing what simple language Jesus used in his teaching! We received the candle of Christ's light at Baptism. We are called to be the light of the world and the salt of the earth. The next time you prepare for confession, examine yourself on how you shine the light of Christ or how much you cover it up. Do I bring the light of Christ to others? Am I a witness to the joy of the Gospel by the way I live? Am I an agent of light or of darkness? Jesus also said, "Take care how you hear". Saint Paul said that faith comes through hearing. Are my ears itching more for scandal than for good news about people? Do I pass on malicious gossip? If you were on trial for being a Christian, would there be enough evidence to convict you?

2. "For anyone who has will be given more; from anyone who has not, even what he thinks he has will be taken away." In the Fellowship of Alcoholics Anonymous, there is a saying that sobriety is kept by giving it away. The same is true about believing. Personal faith comes alive when we share our faith with others. Any muscle that is not exercised wastes away. An isolated Christian is a paralysed Christian. It is in giving that we receive.

PRAYERS

In the light of the teaching of Christ, we pray.

May the Church be the light of the nations, leading people to the knowledge of God and to the ideals of justice, peace and care for one another.
Lord, hear us.

We pray for a deep appreciation of the light of faith. May we never hide this light through fear or embarrassment.
Lord, hear us.

For people who are forced to leave their homes because of their religion: may they receive a Christian welcome in their new homes.
Lord, hear us.

For people who are in a dark valley through depression, grief or anxiety: may the light of Christ shine into their lives.
Lord, hear us.

(Add prayers for any local, personal or topical intention)

O God, the Father of light and love, graciously hear the prayers we offer in the name of Jesus Christ, your Son, our Lord. Amen.

TUESDAY

LUKE 8:19-21

1. It might seem at first sight that Jesus was neglecting his mother and relations. He wasn't neglecting his family but extending it. "Who is my mother?," he asked. She was the greatest disciple he ever had. She is the one who said, "Let it be done to me according to thy Word". Jesus was extending his family by welcoming in all those who strive to do the will of the Father in Heaven. Mary is the perfect model of the obedience of faith.

2. All of us who gather at Mass belong to the extended family of Jesus. Our relationship with God is never just a private affair – me in my box with God, you in your box. There is a false piety which never shows any concern for others. So heavenly minded but no earthly good. The motto for the Eucharistic Congress in Dublin read, Communion with Christ, Communion with one another. Think of the model of prayer that Jesus taught us. The first personal singular is missing from the Our Father. It says Our Father, not My Father. Give us, forgive us, lead us, deliver us. It is always in the plural, members of the one family of Christ. God is addressed as Our Father. If we take those two words seriously, there is no basis for exploitation of others, discrimination, racism or prejudice. If we are members of the extended family of Jesus, then others are our brothers and sisters, and should be treated as such. Furthermore, Mary, the mother of Jesus is our mother too. Brothers, Sisters, we are one!

PRAYERS

We gather together at Mass as the extended family of Jesus.

May the Church be a community of disciples who will be recognised as people who care for each other as brothers and sisters.
Lord, hear us.

We ask God's blessing on our families, for our health, unity and support for one another.
Lord, hear us.

We pray for families who are going through a difficult time. May they see the solution to their problems with the help of God.
Lord, hear us.

As we remember the departed members of our families, we pray that we will all be reunited in the family of God in Heaven.
Lord, hear us.

(Add prayers for any local, personal or topical intention)

God, our Father, hear the prayers of your family united in the name of Jesus Christ, your Son, our Lord. Amen.

WEDNESDAY

LUKE 9:1-6

Reflections and prayers today may be taken from Tuesday of Week 16 when Mathew's text is virtually identical with today's reading from Luke.

1. Today's Gospel is about Jesus sending out the apostles to share in his mission of proclaiming the Kingdom of God and healing. The name *apostle* means somebody sent on a mission. There are more than two hundred references in the New Testament to people being sent or told to go. Clearly, Jesus did not intend that his followers would settle for a private God-and-me religion. Pope Francis wrote that our Christian mission is not just a part of life but our attitude should be that I am a mission on this Earth. Our Christian mission has its source in Baptism, its development in the power of the Holy Spirit at Confirmation and its sustenance in the Eucharist. Mass ends with the mission to go out and serve the Lord.

2. The apostles were sent out by Jesus. The Gospel does not tell us what they were to say, but we are told about their lifestyle. Saint Francis of Assisi told the brothers to preach at all times, sometimes using words. Witness of life is far more effective than talk. What is most remarkable about the instruction of Jesus is the emphasis he put on trust: trust in God's providence and trust in the goodness of people. A generous benefactor of Mother Teresa of Calcutta sold his business and told Mother Teresa that he was setting up a foundation to secure the future of her mission. Mother Teresa promptly asked him not to do so as it went against the Gospel principle of trusting in God's providence rather than in a bank account. Saints are exceptional people. But there is the challenge to all of us to trust in God rather than what the Old Testament writer called vanity of vanities.

PRAYERS

Let us take the instruction of Jesus to heart as we pray.

That the Church, founded on the apostles, will be faithful to its mission in humble service of the Kingdom of God on Earth.
Lord, hear us.

The apostles were instructed to trust in God's providence shown in the generous people who would support them. May we too have the grace of total trust in God and people.
Lord, hear us.

The apostles, like Jesus, brought healing to people. We bring to God the needs of all who are sick or facing medical procedures.
Lord, hear us.

May God bless and reward all those who look after the needs of others.
Lord, hear us.

(Add prayers for any local, personal or topical intention)

O God, you wish that all people would be saved: hear the prayers we offer in the name of Jesus Christ, your Son, our Lord. Amen.

THURSDAY

LUKE 9:7-9

1. Herod was anxious to see Jesus. It is unlikely that it was a desire to receive religious or moral instruction from Jesus. His anxiousness was more of an anxiety. Herod was a complex character. He was a seriously paranoid man who had family members murdered, and he built five massive fortresses for his own protection. Obviously, he heard about Jesus. There were rumours that Jesus was John the Baptist come back to life. Herod had killed John. Was this his ghost now come back to haunt him? Herod sensed danger. He needed to see Jesus to check him out. When tyrants get going, murders never stop at one. It is the same today in the world of drugs.

2. Herod is an example of the difference between religiosity and religion. Religiosity is an interest in religious matters without making a commitment of life. Nowadays, one meets people who say "I am very spiritual but not very religious". Or, "I believe but I do not belong". They are probably saying they do not belong to any church. Herod recognised John as a good man and he liked to talk to him, but that did not stop him from ordering John's killing. On one occasion, when some Pharisees told Jesus that Herod wanted to kill him, Jesus called him, "that fox". Later, when Jesus was on trial before Herod, he refused to answer him. Mediocrity was something Jesus despised. The Book of Revelation says of religious mediocrity: "Since you are neither hot nor cold, but only lukewarm, I will spit you out of my mouth."

PRAYERS

In the light of the Gospel, we pray.

That the Church, under the guidance of Pope *(Name)*, will proclaim the teaching and ideals of Christ to the world.
Lord, hear us.

That people who have an interest in spiritual affairs will make the commitment to follow Jesus who is the way, the truth and the life.
Lord, hear us.

For people who are being persecuted by the tyrants of today: may God bless them with great courage and may all persecution cease.
Lord, hear us.

May people who are caught up in lives of violence give up their evil ways.
Lord, hear us.

(Add prayers for any local, personal or topical intention)

O God of love and peace, hear our prayers in the name of Jesus Christ, your Son, our Lord. Amen.

FRIDAY

LUKE 9:18-22

1. Jesus was praying... alone... in the presence of his disciples. His prayer was in touch with three worlds at once... with the Father, with his own feelings, and with the thoughts of others. Being at prayer he was in communion with his Father in Heaven. In Luke's Gospel, prayer is a constant theme. Jesus had withdrawn from outside pressure to have time with his inner feelings. The premonition of his suffering and rejection was beginning to stir within him. Prayer was a space where he could tend to his inner feelings. Although he was alone with his feelings, he was still in the presence of his disciples. And through them, he was in touch with the wider community and with what they were saying. Christian mindfulness is not the pursuit of emptiness. Rather, it nurtures attentiveness to God with time for God alone, time to attend to inner feelings, and time for the concerns and needs of others.

2. The Catechism of the Catholic Church contains beautiful teaching on prayer. It quotes the classical definition of prayer: "Prayer is the raising of the mind and heart to God or the requesting of good things from God". Then it calls to mind the picture of the Samaritan woman coming to the well seeking water. She has had six men in her life. Jesus will be the seventh, the divine number in John's Gospel. Quoting the Catechism: "It is he who first seeks us and asks us for a drink. Jesus thirsts; his asking arises from the depths of God's thirst for us. Whether we realise it or not, prayer is the encounter of God's thirst with ours. God thirsts that we might thirst for him". God is waiting for us every day. "Who do you say I am?" How much time, how much space, do you give to God each day?

PRAYERS

Let us pray in the light of the example of Jesus Christ.

May your Holy Spirit raise us up in mind and heart to the great reality of God, beyond our earthly thoughts and desires.
Lord, hear us.

When we reflect on our own inner feelings, may we know that we are never on our own as you are always with us and within us.
Lord, hear us.

May our prayer open up our hearts to the needs and concerns of other people.
Lord, hear us.

May people who have lost the habit of prayer recognise that Jesus is waiting for them to satisfy the thirst of their souls.
Lord, hear us.

(Add prayers for any local, personal or topical intention)

God our Father, we raise up our minds and hearts to you, united with the prayer of Jesus Christ, your Son, our Lord. Amen

SATURDAY

LUKE 9:43-45

1. People were full of admiration for Jesus, but he knew that there were some who were plotting to get rid of him. He warned the apostles that there was trouble ahead. It was something they could not comprehend in the euphoria of the moment. It was only after the resurrection that they would understand that Jesus was to be the sacrificial Lamb of God for the redemption of the people. It was necessary that the Christ should suffer and so enter into glory. Through Jesus, the tree for a criminal's execution became the tree of life.

2. Jesus told the apostles to keep what he was saying about his passion constantly in their minds. But they did not understand him. We might desire a world of no suffering, but such a wish is a denial of reality. Sadly, there are wars, accidents, betrayals, injustices, sickness and many forms of suffering. By accepting the cross, Jesus entered into solidarity with all who suffer. When suffering is understood as sharing in his cross, it takes on a new meaning. Our crosses become a school of learning where we learn to be more humble, we grow in compassion with others and offer up our sufferings in union with Jesus for the redemption of the world. Any version of Christianity without the cross is fake news.

PRAYERS

Let us pray for the needs of the Church and the world.

As Jesus was the victim of prejudice and hatred, many people today are being persecuted for their religious beliefs. May they remember that blessed are they who suffer for justice sake, for theirs is the Kingdom of Heaven.
Lord, hear us.

May those who hate the Church open their eyes in fairness to see the immense amount of holiness and works of charity in the Church.
Lord, hear us.

May people who are carrying a heavy cross at the moment recognise that Jesus walks with them as their companion.
Lord, hear us.

Let us ask God's blessing on those who are sick in mind or body.
Lord, hear us.

(Add prayers for any local, personal or topical intention)

God of mercy and compassion, graciously hear the prayers we offer in the name of Jesus Christ, your Son, our Lord. Amen.

MONDAY

LUKE 9:46-50

1. The apostles were arguing about which of them was the greatest. This sort of ambition was totally against the mind of Jesus. At the start of his ministry he had rejected the temptation to gain power over many kingdoms by compromising with Satan. Pride and the desire to be number one are at the root of many troubles. We live in a very competitive world. In sport, there is too much of winner takes all. Everyone else is regarded as a loser. The fun has gone out of it when it is no longer recreation but a warfare. Careerism, distrust and jealousy are wrecking peace of mind. Saint John Paul II called for a spirituality of communion. Recognise that we are all parts of the one body. Then one sees that the good fortune or talent of another person is also a gift for me because the entire body benefits from the well-being of any one part.

2. The Apostle John tried to stop a man using the name of Jesus to cast out devils, because "he is not one of us". Jesus had no problem letting this outsider continue his good work. Many people are being warned not to go near any system of meditation, mindfulness, muscular relaxation or breath control unless it is specifically Christian. In these exercises people are finding peace, inner demons of anxiety and compulsions are mastered, and the quality of life is greatly improved. God's healing work is not confined to any one Church.

PRAYERS

Let us pray in the light of the example and teaching of Jesus.

That all who exercise power and authority in the Church or in politics may do so in a spirit of humble service.
Lord, hear us.

"Anyone who welcomes this little child in my name welcomes me."
May all children receive a loving welcome into this world.
Lord, hear us.

Help us to recognise and celebrate the good fortune and talents of other people as gifts from God.
Lord, hear us.

Remove from our hearts any religious bigotry which prevents us from seeing the presence of God wherever good is being done.
Lord, hear us.

(Add prayers for any local, personal or topical intention)

O God, the giver of every good gift, graciously hear the prayers we offer in the name of Jesus Christ, our Lord. Amen.

TUESDAY

LUKE 9:51-56

1. Jesus was on a journey. In reality, he was on a twofold journey. There were the daily journeys from town to town, from village to village, each day a part of his journey towards Jerusalem. Jerusalem was more than a geographical city. It was the city of God, the true direction of the journey of life. When the disciples on the road to Emmaus turned their backs on Jerusalem, it indicated their loss of direction on life's pilgrimage. We too are on a twofold journey. We go from place to place, from day to day, directed by our jobs and personal circumstances. But we must never forget the ultimate direction of the pilgrimage of life. This gives us a bigger picture of life. In today's fast moving world many have lost sight of the ultimate direction of life. Life is then reduced to a succession of unconnected happenings. Then when something goes wrong, perhaps the break-up of a relationship, everything collapses because there is no bigger picture to hold the parts together.

2. When a certain Samaritan village would not accept Jesus, the brothers, James and John, asked Jesus would they call down fire from Heaven to burn the village. They did not ask Jesus would he call down fire. No, but would they do the calling. It shows how much they were out of touch with the ideals of Jesus. He rebuked them and turned away from the inhospitable village. Thoughts of hatred and vengeance were far from the mind of Jesus. The fire of God did come down later, at Pentecost, not to punish people, but as tongues of fire proclaiming the Good News of mercy and salvation.

PRAYERS

Let us pray in the light of the example of Jesus.

That the Church might serve the world by reminding us that we have here no lasting city but seek one that is to come.
Lord, hear us.

May there be peace in the world; peace between nations; peace between neighbours and relatives. Remove all thoughts of revenge from our hearts.
Lord, hear us.

May the victims of persecution who are forced to emigrate find welcome and hospitality.
Lord, hear us.

As the brothers, James and John, converted from thoughts of vengeance to become great saints, we pray for the conversion of violent criminals and misguided nationalists.
Lord, hear us.

(Add prayers for any local, personal or topical intention)

O God, the Father of all nations, hear the prayers we offer in the name of Jesus Christ, your Son, our Lord. Amen.

WEDNESDAY

LUKE 9:57-62

1. Jesus had set his face resolutely towards Jerusalem. Three men expressed an interest in becoming followers. He explained to them that it would not be easy. To the first he explained the insecurity of the itinerant preacher, not knowing where the next meal would come from or where he would sleep for the night. The second applicant said that he would follow after the death of his father. Jesus replied that the call to go and spread the Good News of the Kingdom of God should take priority even over family duty. The third man promised to follow Jesus but first he would like to say good-bye to his people at home. Jesus explained to him that the good ploughman does not look back but keeps his eyes fixed firmly forward. To all three applicants, Jesus was explaining the cost of discipleship. We have no idea whether any of the three followed Jesus or not.

2. Saint Paul was one who was totally committed as a follower of Jesus. He explained his commitment in his Letter to the Philippians. "All I want is to know Jesus Christ and the power of his resurrection, and to share his sufferings by reproducing the pattern of his death." For Paul, the following of Jesus meant sharing the joys of the Resurrection as well as experiencing times of hardship and persecution. He explained how the water of Baptism expressed both dying and rising with Christ. Whether his lot was hardship or consolation, it was all the same to Paul. It was all part of following the footsteps of Christ.

PRAYERS

After reflecting on the cost of discipleship, we pray.

The harvest is vast and the labourers are getting older. We pray that the call of God will touch the hearts of many people who will dedicate their lives to the service of the Kingdom of God.
Lord, hear us.

May all who are called Christians be true followers, not only in name, but in fact.
Lord, hear us.

We thank God for all who have given long years of service in the Church. May God grant them the grace of perseverance.
Lord, hear us.

May all who suffer persecution or mockery because they are followers of Christ, know that the Lord is with them.
Lord, hear us.

(Add prayers for any local, personal or topical intention)

Heavenly Father, we offer our prayers in the name of Jesus Christ, your Son, our Lord. Amen.

THURSDAY

LUKE 10:1-12

1. When the Lord sent out the seventy-two disciples in pairs, his instruction was not so much about what to say as much as how to live. The emphasis was on the witness of how they lived. Pope Paul VI wrote about evangelisation. "The first means of evangelisation is the witness of an authentically Christian life. People today listen more willingly to witnesses than to teachers, and if they do listen to teachers, it is because they are witnesses." The message must be lived before it can convince the listener. One must walk the walk before talking the talk. The seventy-two disciples would witness to charity through mutual sharing and caring, and in the ability to work in pairs. Belief in God's care would be shown by trust in providence and in the kindness of people. Their gentleness would prepare the way for reconciliation and peace.

2. On entering a house, the first greeting of the disciples would be, "Peace to this house!" What destroys peace at home? Drink, late hours, financial worries, insensitivity, bickering, arguments, lack of appreciation, no time for communication, no prayer. Being a slave to the social media is now recognised as seriously harmful to family life. Family celebrations can be very helpful in bonding families. "Blessed are the peacemakers for they shall be called the children of God."

PRAYERS

As we take the message of Jesus to heart, we pray.

May the Church, by word and example, inspire the world to end all wars and to live in harmony and peace.
Lord, hear us.

The harvest is vast and the labourers are getting older. May the invitation of God touch the hearts of many people to dedicate their lives to the service of the Kingdom of God.
Lord, hear us.

May divided families patch up their differences and live in God's peace.
Lord, hear us.

May all of us in little ways be instruments of peace, bringing joy, compassion and love to all we meet.
Lord, hear us.

(Add prayers for any local, personal or topical intention)

O God, the Father of all, may your children on Earth live in harmony and peace, through Christ, our Lord. Amen.

FRIDAY

LUKE 10:13-16

1. "Alas" is always a word of sadness. There was sadness in the heart of Jesus when people were rejecting his call to conversion, even after the miracles they had seen. "Those who reject me reject the one who sent me." It is one thing not to know the signs and the message of Jesus. It is more serious to know his message, at least in broad outline, and then to reject it. There are many people today who have drifted away from religious practice without actually rejecting Jesus. They still classify themselves as Christian. But, like the wheat plant choked by thorns, they are too preoccupied by other matters. Sorry, God, house full, already occupied! Continue to pray for them that they will recognise their need of God, the Higher Power. God has not been rejected, just neglected.

2. "Alas"... that sadness which Jesus experienced is also felt by many parents today when their children drift away from religious practice. Good parents ask, "What did we do wrong?"

   Good parents should not load blame onto themselves. The forces of secularisation are very hard to resist. The best policy to pursue is the witness of good Christian living accompanied by prayer. The odd hint or invitation can be helpful but open confrontation usually leads to an argument. Angry words deepen the divide whereas goodness attracts.

PRAYERS

After listening to the teaching of Jesus, we are moved to pray.

That the Church may be a living witness to the warm, loving, life-giving message of Jesus.
Lord, hear us.

For the people who have drifted away from religious practice: may they experience God's call and return to a daily, personal relationship with him.
Lord, hear us.

We pray for parents who are worried about their children. May the Holy Spirit guide them in the best course of action.
Lord, hear us.

For those who are in a dark valley of depression and for people struggling with an addiction: may the healing hand of God lift them up.
Lord, hear us.

(Add prayers for any local, personal or topical intention)

O God, you wish that all people will be saved and come to know the truth. Hear the prayers we offer in the name of Jesus Christ, your Son, our Lord. Amen.

SATURDAY

LUKE 10:17-24

1. When the seventy-two disciples returned after their mission, they were in great form. Jesus reminded them that whatever good they had done was due to the grace of God. Getting swelled heads about it would be the start of their downfall. Pride goes before a fall. As one of the psalms puts it: "Not to us, Lord, not to us, but to your name be the glory". Instead of feeling proud of our achievements, we should go down on our knees to thank God, the giver of every good gift. Saint Paul wrote a beautiful prayer of thanksgiving in his Letter to the Ephesians: "Glory be to him, whose power working in us, can do infinitely more than we can ask or imagine; glory be to him from generation to generation in the Church and in Christ Jesus for ever and ever".

2. Jesus rejoiced at the way the simple, childlike people were very receptive to his message. Saint Paul thanked God for the way that the poor and uneducated people found great meaning and consolation in the message of a crucified Christ, while the sophisticated class rejected a crucified messiah as nonsense. Pope Francis spent much of his time as bishop among the poor. He saw their deep faith and how intimately they could identify with the suffering Christ. He wrote of the mysterious wisdom which God wishes to share with us through them. "I thank you, Father, Lord of Heaven and Earth, for hiding these things from the learned and clever and revealing them to mere children."

PRAYERS

As children of God, we pray with confidence.

As the seventy-two disciples were granted great graces by the Holy Spirit, so may the Church in our time be wonderfully guided by the same Spirit.
Lord, hear us.

Let us pray for all who are given positions of power and influence. Protect them from the temptation of pride. May they use their power in a spirit of humble service.
Lord, hear us.

Jesus was filled with joy by the Holy Spirit. May all who live in sadness and darkness receive this gift of joy, one of the fruits of the Spirit.
Lord, hear us.

May the poor of this world receive great richness of faith in recognising God's special love for the poor.
Lord, hear us.

(Add prayers for any local, personal or topical intention)

Father of all, the giver of every good gift, hear the prayers we offer in the name of Jesus Christ, your Son, our Lord. Amen.

MONDAY

LUKE 10:25-37

1. The Good Samaritan is the model of practical charity. He saw, he felt and he acted. He saw the need; he felt pity; and he did something to remedy the situation. The first step in love is to notice people, to pay attention to them. By attentiveness we recognise the existence and needs of a person beyond the limitations of selfishness. The next step is to allow ourselves to feel with the person. The priest and the Levite saw the man in distress but passed by on the other side of the road. The Samaritan was moved with compassion towards the victim. Feeling opens up the heart to allow the needs of the other person to enter our lives. But feeling alone is not sufficient unless we are prepared to allow our feeling to inspire us to practical action. The Samaritan acted so generously that he has ever since been associated with practical charity.

2. It was a Jewish expert in law who asked Jesus "Who is my neighbour?" Jesus dropped a bombshell in choosing a Samaritan, a despised outsider, as the one who fulfilled God's law of charity more than the priest and the Levite, the churchy people of the time. In their defence one might suggest they had a good excuse because contact with blood would have barred them from working in the temple until they were purified. It is amazing how many excuses we can find to avoid helping somebody in need. But really, there is no excuse for failing in charity to assist somebody in a case of life or death. Jesus made the Samaritan outsider the model of God's law while the two churchy people put small rubrics before the law of charity. As Saint Augustine said, there are many in the Kingdom who are not in the Church, and many in the Church who are not in the Kingdom.

PRAYERS

Let us thank the Lord that the Church has always been very active in practical works of charity.

Continue to inspire people to be like the Good Samaritan in seeing the needs of people and in reaching out with practical help.
Lord, hear us.

Today we pray especially for the organisation known as the Samaritans. Bless their apostolate of being available to people who reach out for a listening ear.
Lord, hear us.

May people who are in a desperate situation find people like the Samaritans who are willing to help them.
Lord, hear us.

May we never look for an excuse to walk on the other side of the road when somebody needs our assistance.
Lord, hear us.

   (Add prayers for any local, personal or topical intention)

May God, our loving Father, hear the prayers we offer in the name of Jesus Christ, our Lord and Saviour. Amen.

TUESDAY

LUKE 10:38-42

1. The sisters, Martha and Mary, represent two ways of serving the Lord. Martha represents the active life, cooking the meal, helping, doing good for others. Mary represents the contemplative life, giving priority to listening to the Word of the Lord. On that particular occasion, Mary chose the better part. But there were other times when Martha's contribution was more important. For instance, when their brother Lazarus died, Martha seems to have coped much better than Mary. There is a time for giving and a time for receiving. The contribution of each one finds a place in the liturgy of Mass. Like Mary, we sit and listen to the Word of the Lord. Like Martha, we offer the fruit of the earth and the work of human hands. Both of them are celebrated as saints.

2. "You worry and fret about so many things, yet few are needed. Mary has chosen the better part." What Jesus said to Martha might be said to many of us. For many people the development of their prayer has to begin with quietening the mind, making space for God in our time and attention. Often, our fears and anxieties are about things which are not all that important. We cannot see the forest because of the trees. Learn how to be quiet and still. Learn how to trust, how to let go and let God. "Be still and know that I am God."

PRAYERS

In the light of today's Gospel, we pray that the Church, under the guidance of Pope *(Name)* and all our Christian leaders will feed our minds with the wisdom of God's Word.
Lord, hear us.

Help us to see that many of the things we fear and fret about are not all that important. Help us to focus on what really matters.
Lord, hear us.

That people who suffer from constant anxiety or fear may receive the graces of confidence and peace.
Lord, hear us.

We thank you, Lord, for the people who prepare our meals and serve us every day. Bless them and reward them.
Lord, hear us.

(Add prayers for any local, personal or topical intention)

O God of peace, hear the prayers we offer in the name of Jesus Christ, your Son, our Lord. Amen.

WEDNESDAY

LUKE 11:1-4

1. "Lord, teach us to pray as John taught his disciples." To have seen the countenance of Jesus at prayer must have been a sight the apostles would never forget. They wanted to be part of the experience, so they asked him to teach them about prayer. A Jewish teacher was expected to introduce his students to a prayer which would summarise his teaching. John the Baptist must have done so. That is why, from the earliest times, the Lord's Prayer has been recognised as a summary of the Gospels. The celebration of the Eucharist may be regarded as the prayer of Christian memory. The Our Father is the prayer of Christian identity. It expresses who we are in our new relationship with God since Jesus instituted the new covenant between God and people. United with Jesus, we become children of God and heirs of the Kingdom of Heaven.

2. The two keywords in the Lord's Prayer are Father and Kingdom. The recognition of God as our Father is where the New Testament is an advance on the Old Testament in the revelation of God's relationship with us. In the new covenant, ratified in the blood of Jesus, we are offered the Spirit of adoption as children of God. In the Gospel of John we read, "To all who did accept him, he gave the power to become the children of God." Hence God is our Father in a way never previously recognised. If the name Father expresses the new revelation of God, the second keyword, *kingdom*, summarises the mission of Jesus, which was to establish the Kingdom of God on Earth. He began his mission with the proclamation: "Repent, for the Kingdom of Heaven is at hand" (Mt. 4:17)
(See Tuesday of Week 1 of Lent for further reflections on the Our Father)

PRAYERS

Let us pray in the light of the lesson of Jesus on prayer.

Heavenly Father, may your sacred name be held in such reverence that the very mention of your name will make us aware of your relationship with us.
Lord, hear us.

May your Kingdom come in a world where justice, truth and peace reign supreme in every country.
Lord, hear us.

Provide for us each day the daily bread for all our needs. May the wealthy nations learn to share generously with people who lack food and homes.
Lord, hear us.

Father, forgive us our sins, and may your Holy Spirit inspire us to share this forgiveness with all who have offended us.
Lord, hear us.

(Add prayers for any local, personal or topical intention)

God, our Father in Heaven, hear the prayers of your children united in the name of Jesus Christ, your Son, our Lord. Amen.

THURSDAY

Luke 11:5-13

1. "Ask, and it will be given to you; search, and you will find; knock, and the door will be opened to you." Yet all of us have had the experience of praying earnestly for something but we did not get what we wanted. God answers our petitions in three ways. First, God says "Yes" and we see our prayer answered. The second way God answers is, "Yes, but not for a while." God's delay is an opportunity to persevere in prayer. If we get what we want at first time of asking, we might not fully appreciate the gift. Perseverance in prayer helps to deepen our faith. The third way that God answers us is "No, but I will give you something else". It is like the parent who will not give anything harmful to a child but gives something safer. Every prayer is answered although we might not recognise it.

2. If God already knows our needs, why do we have to ask? Are we trying to twist the arm of an unwilling God? The purpose of asking is not to change God but to change us. Having to persevere can help us to grow in awareness of our dependence on God. Or we might realise that we should back up the words of prayer with charitable action, or with some moral improvement in our living. Remember the instruction of Jesus to seek reconciliation with somebody before bringing one's gift to the altar. When prayer is backed up by fasting or charitable action, it is much stronger.

PRAYERS

Inspired by the words of Jesus, we pray with renewed confidence in God's love.

That the Church on Earth will continue to inspire people to trust in God's loving care.
Lord, hear us.

We pray for family and friends whose problems we carry in our hearts.
Lord, hear us.

We unite our prayers with those who are earnestly asking God for a very special intention.
Lord, hear us.

We pray for people who are searching for meaning and direction in life. May the light of Christ lead them to the way, the truth and the life.
Lord, hear us.

(Add prayers for any local, personal or topical intention)

God our Father, the giver of every good gift, hear the prayers we offer in the name of your Beloved Son, Jesus Christ, our Lord. Amen.

FRIDAY

LUKE 11:15-26

1. Many people today do not believe in the existence of the devil. They say it is a relic of times before modern psychology developed greater understanding of mental illness. Yet, people still speak of their inner demons when they struggle to control inner energies and compulsions. It may be an addiction, violent rage, uncontrolled lust or vengeance. Cold, calculated evil in people cannot be explained without reference to evil spirits. Jesus believed in the existence of evil spirits. In John's Gospel, he called the devil the father of lies and a murderer from the beginning. The presence of the devil is seen in confusion of the truth and in anti-life policies. The exorcisms performed by Jesus show his total victory over Satan. So great is the victory of Jesus that even the finger of God is stronger than the devil. The last petition of the Our Father is a powerful prayer for every day: deliver us from Evil.

2. While it is important to recognise the power of evil spirits, one should not exaggerate their power. Unfortunately, there are self-appointed exorcists who claim to find the devil in various illnesses or accidents. Instead of helping people, they are upsetting them and causing deep distress. The First Letter of Peter describes the devil on the prowl like a roaring lion, looking for someone to devour. The writer then advises: "Stand up to him, strong in faith..." faith in Jesus who has complete power over any evil spirit. Keep in mind the parting words of Jesus at the end of the Last Supper: "I have told you all this so that you may have peace in me. In the world you will have hardship, but be brave for I have overcome the world."

PRAYERS

Jesus showed complete power over evil spirits, so it is with confidence that we pray.

That the voice of the Church will inspire the world to turn away from the evils of war and violence.
Lord, hear us.

For people who are filled with fear and anxiety, may they find confidence and peace in handing their problems over to Jesus.
Lord, hear us.

For all who struggle with the inner demons of addiction, may they come to a new life of peace through a strong personal relationship with God every single day.
Lord, hear us.

That all people will respect the sacredness of life from the womb to the tomb.
Lord hear us.

(Add prayers for any local, personal or topical intention)

O God, the source of all life and goodness, hear the prayers we offer in the name of Jesus Christ, your Son, our Lord. Amen.

SATURDAY

LUKE 11:27-28

1. Sometimes we might fancy that it would be great if there was some sort of time machine that could take us back over the centuries to spend an hour as a witness to some historic event. Wouldn't it be great to get back to Galilee and see Jesus and listen to him speak! So much for imagination. The reality is that many people who did see him and hear him through the physical senses did not come to believe in him. A spiritual relationship with Jesus in faith is far more important than a relationship built on the physical senses. Mary, as the mother of Jesus, had a unique physical relationship with him, having carried him in the womb and suckled him. Yet, greater than this physical relationship was her spiritual relationship with him. As the Risen Lord said to Thomas: "You believe because you can see me. Blessed are those who have not seen and yet believe."

2. Saint Luke portrays Mary as a model of discipleship. She heard the Word of God and pondered on it in her heart. She is the one who said, "Let it be done unto me according to your Word." Being a disciple means hearing the Word of God and putting it into practice. "Still happier are those who hear the Word of God and put it into practice." In recent times, Mary has been called the Mother and Model of the Church. In her lifetime on Earth, she was the model of hearing the Word of God and putting it into practice. In her Assumption into Heaven, she is the model of hope. Where she has been taken, we hope to follow.

PRAYERS

In the light of the Word of God, we pray.

Mary is the Mother and Model of the Church. May her example inspire the Church to carry the Word of God to all nations.
Lord, hear us.

"Let it be done unto me according to your Word." In these words, Mary was saying "Yes" to what God was asking of her. May we too have the grace to say "Yes" to whatever God is asking of us.
Lord, hear us.

We call on Mary's motherly intercession as we pray for those who are sick or going through a hard time at the moment.
Lord, hear us.

For people who find it hard to believe: may the faith of Mary inspire them.
Lord, hear us.

(Add prayers for any local, personal or topical intention)

God, our Father, you sent your Son, born of the Virgin Mary, to be our Saviour. Hear the prayers we offer in his name, Jesus Christ, our Lord. Amen.

MONDAY

Luke 11:29-32

1. The people kept on looking for more and more signs from Jesus. Jesus recalled stories about two people from their past, Jonah and the Queen of the South. The fable of Jonah was that he was three days in the belly of a whale before he preached repentance to the people of Nineveh. This story anticipated the three days Jesus spent in the belly of the Earth before his resurrection. The Resurrection is by far the greatest sign given by Jesus. Saint Paul told the people of Corinth that if the Resurrection did not happen, then all our preaching is without foundation and all your believing is useless. The Resurrection is not just a story of a past event. It is about a present reality: Christ is risen and is with us.

2. The second story that Jesus recalled was about the Queen of the South who travelled a great distance to hear the wisdom of Solomon. Jesus told them that there is somebody greater than Solomon here. That somebody was Jesus himself. The Good News for us is that his wisdom is here for us today at Mass, inviting us to a deep, personal relationship. At the beginning of the readings at Mass, we are told that this is a reading from the letter of Saint Paul or Saint Luke or some Old Testament Book. This introduction announces the human writer. But then at the end of the reading, we are told that this is the Word of the Lord, or the Gospel of the Lord. At Mass, our spiritual life is fed at two tables: the table of the Word and the table of the Eucharist. Solomon was noted for his wisdom but the very Lord of wisdom is here today.

PRAYERS

The fame of Solomon's wisdom attracted people from far and near. May the Church continue to bring the light of Christ to all nations.
Lord, hear us.

We pray for people who are struggling with problems of faith. May they receive the grace of a personal relationship with God which will make all their questions dissolve.
Lord, hear us.

The Resurrection is the foundation of our belief. May our faith bring us a great awareness of the presence of the Risen Lord in our lives.
Lord, hear us.

For our families and friends, and for all who are going through a hard time: may they experience signs of God's presence and support.
Lord, hear us.

(Add prayers for any local, personal or topical intention)

O God, the source of all wisdom, hear the prayers we offer in the name of Jesus Christ, our Lord. Amen.

TUESDAY

LUKE 11:37-41

1. There is an old saying that cleanliness is next to godliness. Surely what is meant is inner cleanliness. Saint Francis of Assisi was fond of saying that what you are in the sight of God is what really matters. God is not one bit impressed by expensive jewellery, the latest fashion or cosmetic makeover. These are important for our self-image and confidence. But the beauty of a person in God's eyes means inner qualities, inner virtues. Washing the outside of the cup is less important than washing the inside. As an example of inner cleanliness Jesus said: "Give alms from what you have and then indeed everything will be clean for you." Charity covers a multitude. Above all, what needs to be cleansed is any form of selfishness that puts a limit on our generosity and service. Saint John of the Cross reminds us that, in the end, what we shall be judged on is love.

2. The Pharisee in today's Gospel invited Jesus to his house for a meal. Supposing Jesus was coming to my house for a meal, how would I feel about it? How would I prepare? Would I be unnerved by the prospect? Would I be so concerned with putting on a good show that I would miss the chance to listen to him? Maybe I would be better off if I stopped asking myself what would I do, and concentrated more on what Jesus would want from me.

PRAYERS

In the light of today's Gospel, may we realise that inner beauty of character is far more important than outer, cosmetic beauty.
Lord, hear us.

O God, you know my innermost thoughts: all my ways lie open to you. May we always be aware that we cannot deceive you.
Lord, hear us.

We pray that all who preach the Gospel may not be hypocrites who do not practice what they preach.
Lord, hear us.

One of the Pharisees invited Jesus to a meal in his house. May our faith recognise that Holy Communion is the privilege of joining Jesus at his table.
Lord, hear us.

(Add prayers for any local, personal or topical intention).

Heavenly Father, graciously listen to the prayers we offer in the name of Jesus Christ, your Son, our Lord. Amen

WEDNESDAY

LUKE 11:42-46

1. Jesus had friends and admirers among the Pharisees. Some of them invited him to a meal. He felt sorry for them because they were driven to scrupulosity by the multiplication of rules and regulations. "Alas," he said, an expression of sympathy. The law of tithes prescribed that one-tenth of produce should be paid to the Temple. But some of them applied this to even the tiniest herb. They had become so obsessed with tiny regulations that they lost focus on matters of justice and love of God. There was a time not too long ago when moral theologians counted more than twenty mortal sins a priest could commit during the celebration of Mass. Some claimed that the omission of two saints' names was a mortal sin. It was painful to see good priests driven to scrupulosity. The love and joy of a relationship with God was squeezed out of their lives.

2. Saint Paul was once a devout and zealous Pharisee. He was the sort of person who did not do things by halves. He sought salvation through the perfect observance of the law. His understanding was that death came into this world as a result of sin. Since Jesus had died, it meant that sin had power over him, so he could not have been the Messiah. Paul thought that growth in the veneration of Jesus was a very dangerous error. But everything changed when he encountered the Risen Christ on the road to Damascus. The resurrection showed that instead of being defeated by death, Jesus had conquered it. His Letter to the Philippians shows what a relief this was for him. Everything from the past paled into insignificance with the supreme advantage of knowing Jesus Christ in his death and resurrection. Ask yourself, what does Jesus mean to you? What advantage is it to know Jesus Christ and his teaching? Do you thank him? Do you want to share Jesus with others?

PRAYERS

As we see our lives in the light of the Gospel, we pray.

May the Church be free from any sort of strict legalism or harsh rules which obscure the love and compassion of God.
Lord, hear us.

Let us pray for people who suffer from scrupulosity. May they be freed from this condition. May they go forward with great joy in their relationship with God.
Lord, hear us.

Jesus taught us to set our hearts on the Kingdom of God, manifested in justice for all people and inspired by love of God. May we never lose sight of these great ideals.
Lord, hear us.

Let us pray for people who were hurt by harsh authority or rigid legalism. Enable them to let go of the hurt and to move forward in light and joy.
Lord, hear us.

(Add prayers for any local, personal or topical intention)

God of love and compassion, hear the prayers we offer in the name of Jesus Christ, your Son, our Lord, Amen.

THURSDAY

LUKE 11:47-54

1. When Jesus was brought to the Temple at the age of twelve, he was disillusioned by all that he saw there. He told his parents that one day he would be busy with the affairs in his Father's house. They did not understand what he was getting at. Year later, the time came to challenge the system. It had become excessively legalistic, with so many petty regulations that they had lost their focus on matters at the heart of religion, such as love of God, mercy and justice. Religion had lost its beauty, joy and attractiveness. The system had no place for sinners, or for those who were struggling with human weakness. Jesus said, "You have taken away the key of knowledge." He was a scandal to the religious leaders by the way he sat with sinners and ate with them. He gave them hope.

2. The first important document of Pope Francis was on the Proclamation of the Gospel in Today's World. He called it *The Joy of the Gospel*. He spoke of sourpuss religion which would put anybody off. He recalled with sadness how the confession box was often a torture chamber. Was that what Jesus wanted? There were customs and regulations which were meaningful at one time and in a different culture, but sent out the wrong message today. A stubborn refusal to change would turn the Church into a museum of dead fossils rather than a living community of love, mercy, hope and justice. What was the reaction of the legalists to Jesus? They were furious. They set questions to trap him. Eventually they plotted the death of Jesus.

PRAYERS

We have listened to Jesus criticising the religious leaders of his time. Let us pray that the Church today may not make the same mistakes.

May our religious leaders think and act as Jesus did.
Lord, hear us.

May the Church show to the world the true beauty of a community of love and compassion, of hope and of justice.
Lord, hear us.

May the joy of the Gospel fill our lives with meaning and direction as followers of Christ.
Lord, hear us.

Let us pray for people who find any change difficult. May they have the grace to accept the signs of the times and that one cannot put new wine into old wineskins.
Lord, hear us.

(Add prayers for any personal, local or topical intentions)

God our Father, you sent your Beloved Son to reform the world. Graciously hear the prayers we offer in his name, Jesus Christ, the Lord. Amen.

FRIDAY

LUKE 12:1-7

1. The singer Nanci Griffith popularised a song with a great message. God is watching... from a distance. It might seem that God has forgotten us. The song reassures us that God is watching, though it may be from a distance. Jesus tells us of two ways that God is watching. Firstly, the eye of God can see through hypocrisy. Any abuse or injustice done can be seen by God. God does not need to set up expensive tribunals. Everything that is now covered will be uncovered, and everything now hidden will be made clear. We might fool others, but we cannot pull the wool over the eye of God. Everybody will have to face the light of judgement.

2. The second way that God is watching is more consoling for people who have been victims of abuse or injustice. "To you my friends I say: do not be afraid of those who kill the body but after that can do no more. Fear him who has the power to cast into hell." God is watching. Justice will be done, but it may be at a distance in time. We are asked to take a long-distance view and to trust. "Blessed are those who are persecuted in the cause of right for theirs is the Kingdom of Heaven." Not one little sparrow is forgotten in God's sight, and you are worth more than hundreds of sparrows. God is watching over us.

PRAYERS

After reflecting on the Gospel of the day, we pray.

Lord, may we never forget that everything we think or do is visible to your eye. May this inspire us to think and act as you would wish us to do.
Lord, hear us.

For people who have been wrongly treated in any way. May they understand that God is on their side and that justice will eventually prevail.
Lord, hear us.

That the tribunals and journalists who seek to uncover the truth will be successful in their efforts.
Lord, hear us.

The Bible constantly reminds us, do not be afraid. Help us to take this message to heart.
Lord, hear us.

(Add prayers for any personal, local or topical intentions)

O God, you watch over us at all times and you listen to the prayers we offer in the name of Jesus Christ, your Son, our Lord. Amen.

SATURDAY

LUKE 12:8-12

1. CYCLE A

   The awesome responsibility of human freedom is that we can reject or accept God. God invites us to life and light and love. But to reject the ways of life, light and love is to opt for evil and darkness. And to choose the way of darkness is to reject the Holy Spirit. God offers pardon to every sin, but God's mercy has to be accepted in genuine sorrow and the intention to turn away from sin. The only sin that cannot be forgiven is the final refusal to accept God's love, mercy and forgiveness. This final rejection is blasphemy against the Holy Spirit. God offers forgiveness, but we have to accept it in genuine sorrow for sin and purpose of amendment.

2. CYCLE B

   Saint Paul, in his Letter to the Ephesians, composed a beautiful prayer that they would grow in their appreciation of what God offers us. "May the God of our Lord Jesus Christ, the Father of glory, give you a spirit of wisdom and perception of what is revealed, to bring you to full knowledge of him. May he enlighten the eyes of your mind so that you can see what hope his call holds for you, what rich glories he has promised the saints will inherit and how infinitely great is the power he has exercised for us believers". God offers us life, light and love. At the end of each day, thank God for the blessings of life, the light of faith and the moments of love you received that day.

PRAYERS

As we reflect on the wisdom of God's Word, we pray.

May the Church be the light of the nations, showing forth what hope God's call hold for us, and what rich glories God has promised.
Lord, hear us.

May we never lack the courage to declare openly, by word or behaviour, our allegiance to Jesus Christ.
Lord, hear us.

Let us pray for those who live in moral darkness: that they will accept the offer of God's forgiveness and be converted to the ways of goodness.
Lord, hear us.

May all who die today accept the grace of the Holy Spirit on their final journey to God.
Lord, hear us.

(Add prayers for any personal, local or topical intentions)

God of mercy and compassion, hear the prayers we offer in the name of Jesus Christ, your Son, our Lord. Amen.

MONDAY

LUKE 12:13-21

1. Two brothers fell out over an inheritance, which is not an uncommon happening. Jesus was asked to arbitrate in the case. "That is none of my business," he replied, "but watch, be on your guard against avarice... materialism, consumerism. Your life will not be made more secure by what you own, even if you have more than you will ever need". There is a difference between what we want and what we need. We need enough to pay the bills, have food on the table, a roof over our head and sensible provision for the future. But many of the things we want go far beyond what we need. It often happens that once we get what we have wanted, another want takes over. Many of the wealthiest people in the world are very insecure and always want more, while many who have simple, uncomplicated lives enjoy great peace and serenity. Be on your guard against any kind of avarice.

2. The parable of the rich farmer who had the bumper harvest is unique among the parables of Jesus. It is the only parable in which God speaks. And what is the first word God says? "Fool!" In the Bible, to be a fool meant more than plain stupidity. A fool is somebody who denies the place of God in our lives. "The fool has said in his heart, there is no God above." To be rich in the sight of people is not the same as being rich in the sight of God.

PRAYERS

In the light of the teaching of Jesus, we pray.

That the social teaching of the Church will inspire wealthy individuals and nations towards a just sharing of the resources of the Earth with the poor.
Lord, hear us.

That all of us will have the wisdom to distinguish between what we need and what we want.
Lord, hear us.

That nobody in our country will be deprived of the essential needs of food, housing, education or health care.
Lord, hear us.

Saint Paul wrote that we are God's work of art, created in Christ Jesus, to live the good life as God intended. May we be filled with gratitude for all that we are and all that we have.
Lord, hear us.

(Add prayers for any personal, local or topical intentions)

God, the giver of life, we thank you for all that we have received from you. May we never worship the gifts and forget the giver. Through Christ, our Lord. Amen.

TUESDAY

LUKE 12:35-38

1. Why did God create us? Saint Thomas Aquinas gave this answer to the question: love did not permit God to remain alone. God reaches out to us as the giver of life, of light and of love. God is life: every breath I breathe, or even the energy to lift my little finger, is a gift of life from God. God is light, the source of physical light as well as the spiritual light of faith. God is love, desiring, yearning for us to open the door of our hearts to let him in. Jesus tells us to be always ready for God's visitation. Have the lamp of faith lit, be ready to open the door when he knocks. And when we open up to God, God comes in, makes us sit down, and puts on an apron to serve us. What an amazing picture of God! We can feel at home with a God who puts on an apron.

2. "Have your lamps lit, ready to open the door when he knocks." All around us are the airwaves of dozens of Radio Stations. We do not hear them without a radio receiver. We switch on and tune in to a selected station. God is a mighty radio broadcasting to us twenty-four hours, seven days a week. But we do not hear unless we are switched on and tuned in. There are many stations where we can tune in to God. Prayerfulness grows when we develop the art of listening. We meet God in familiar prayers: the beauty of creation; remembering our blessings; pondering on Scripture; adoration; Mass; prayerful repetition of a favourite aspiration or line of a psalm. Have your lamps lit to welcome the God who loves us and comes to us.

PRAYERS

Encouraged by the teaching of Jesus, we pray.

Lord, increase our faith. May we have a lively faith that makes us more attentive to your presence in our lives every day.
Lord, hear us.

May the light of the Church gather us together to pray as a community of faith.
Lord, hear us.

May our minds and hearts be always open when God comes and knocks.
Lord, hear us.

For friends and family members who have drifted away from prayer: may they hear God's invitation and open up their lives to God.
Lord, hear us.

(Add prayers for any personal, local or topical intentions)

O God of life and light and love, graciously hear the prayers we offer in the name of Jesus Christ, your Son, our Lord. Amen

WEDNESDAY

LUKE 12:39-48

1. Here is a parable about taking precautions to keep a burglar out of the house. The house can represent the inner soul where we want to be at home with God. The burglar is the devil. Satan does not want us to be at home in God's presence so he will probe for any way to break into the house. There are chinks of character weakness that Satan will probe, what we used to call our predominant passions. Nowadays a very common addiction is pornography, easily accessible via the internet. With any addiction, one loses freedom by becoming enslaved. Through pornography one loses respect for the dignity of the human body. Another chink in the wall is addiction to gossip which harms somebody's good name. Other areas that Satan will use are the tendency to be judgemental, overly critical, or being self-centred and mean. These and other temptations are ways that Satan tries to break into your inner house and destroy your relationship with God. The advice of Jesus is, "Stand ready". Treasure your relationship with God. Never do or say anything you know to be wrong in the eyes of God.

2. Speaking on behalf of the disciples, Peter asked if the parable of the burglar applied to them or to others. It applies to everybody but especially to the apostles and to their successors today. Satan knows the truth of the Latin saying that corruption of the best is worst of all. One of Shakespeare's sonnets ends with the line, "Lilies that fester smell far worse than weeds". As Jesus said, "When a man has had a great deal given to him on trust, even more will be expected of him." We must pray every day for those who exercise leadership in the Church. That is why there is always a special mention of the Pope, Bishop and clergy in the Eucharistic prayer. They need our prayers because they are the target of Satan's assault.

PRAYERS

The Church is the Bride of Christ. Satan's greatest desire is to corrupt the Church. Let us pray for the holiness and fidelity of the Pope, bishops and all Church leaders.
Lord, hear us.

May we treasure our relationship with God and strongly resist any temptation to do wrong.
Lord, hear us.

For people who have become addicted to any behaviour that is harmful: may they be liberated from their slavery.
Lord, hear us.

For all who have suffered because of the sinful behaviour of others: may they be healed in spirit and mind.
Lord, hear us.

(Add prayers for any personal, local or topical intentions)

O God, our protector from Evil, hear the prayers we offer in the name of Jesus Christ, our Saviour and Lord. Amen.

THURSDAY

LUKE 12:49-53

1. Jesus spoke about fire and water. These represented his two passions. Fire represents his passion to set the world ablaze with the power of God's Kingdom on Earth. "I have come to bring fire to the Earth, and how I wish it were blazing already!" This fire would be seen at Pentecost when the Holy Spirit descended on the apostles in the form of tongues of fire. In cooking, fire transforms the ingredients. The apostles were transformed by the fire of the Spirit. The community of faith, known to us as the Church, was born at Pentecost. Our popular prayer to the Holy Spirit is a desire for fire. "Come, Holy Spirit, fill the hearts of the faithful and enkindle within them the fire of your love." Jesus came to bring fire to the Earth. At our Baptism, we received the fire of Christ's light in our baptismal candle. Let your light shine. But, as Pope Francis wrote in *The Joy of the Gospel*, a person who is not convinced, enthusiastic, certain and in love, will convince nobody. Come, fire of Pentecost, enkindle within us the fire of your love.

2. The other passion of Jesus was represented by the water of Baptism. He admitted to his distress when he foresaw how he would have to plunge into the stormy water of his suffering on the cross. "There is a Baptism I must still receive, and how great is my distress till it is over!" On several occasions he foretold that his followers would be persecuted just as he was. Fifty years later, when the evangelists were writing the Gospels, they saw the painful divisions in families over belief in him. He came to bring peace, but in some families, those who believed in him were cast out. Sometimes it takes courage to be a Christian. But fear not, the Spirit of Pentecost transformed the fearful apostles with extraordinary courage.

PRAYERS

"I have come to bring fire to the Earth, and how I wish it were blazing already!"

Lord Jesus, may the fire of the Holy Spirit fill us with passion and enthusiasm in our believing.
Lord hear us.

"There is a Baptism I must still receive, and how great is my distress till it is over." Lord, we pray for people who are distressed through fear and anxiety about the future.
Lord, hear us.

For families who are divided: may they overcome their difficulties and be reconciled in God's love.
Lord, hear us.

May the Church be constantly renewed in the fire of Pentecost.
Lord, hear us.

(Add prayers for any personal, local or topical intentions)

God our Father, you sent your Beloved Son to teach us and your Holy Spirit to transform us: hear the prayers we offer in the name of Jesus Christ, our Lord. Amen.

FRIDAY

LUKE 12: 54-59

1. CYCLE A

Jesus said that we are great at observing the signs of change in the weather, but not so good in reading the signs of the times. Saint Pope John XXIII set a task for the Second Vatican Council to read the signs of the times, to see where the Church would need to adapt to keep in touch with the changes in the world. A key document from that Council was called *The Church in the Modern World*. The Church entered into dialogue with international organisations, advances in science, psychology and so on. Time moves on and the culture of thinking and behaving is ever evolving. There is a Latin expression, *ecclesia reformanda*, which means the Church must be ever reforming. In the past, the Church evolved from the simplicity of apostolic times to become a worldwide organisation taking on much of the style of the Roman Empire. Pope Francis pointed to the need to re-examine various rules and precepts which were effective in their time, but no longer have the same usefulness for directing and shaping people's lives. There are fundamental beliefs and morals which cannot be changed, but the manner of preserving them may have to be adapted to a changed culture. Stubborn refusal to read the signs of the times is the road to disaster.

1. CYCLE B

Saint Paul made a heartfelt appeal to the community at Ephesus to be united in complete selflessness, gentleness and patience. In the lines that follow, he used the word "all" six times and the word "one" seven times. The one church community is for all but is composed of individuals. God is Father of all, over all, through all and within all. There is one Body, one Spirit, one Lord, one faith, one Baptism and one God. The one revelation of God is the source of the fundamental beliefs that cannot be changed. But there is diversity of gifts among the individuals who form the community. The presentation of the faith and the celebration of the liturgy have to respect change and diversity. Jesus asked, how is it that you do not know how to interpret these times?

PRAYERS

May the Holy Spirit guide the Church to interpret correctly the times we live in, and have the courage to make the appropriate changes.
Lord, hear us.

For people who find change difficult to accept: may they see that refusing to adapt to change is the road to stagnation.
Lord, hear us.

For people who have a fall-out with family or neighbours: may they have the grace to do all they can to reach reconciliation before matters gets worse.
Lord, hear us.

Where there is conflict between nations, may they seek a peaceful solution rather than resorting to violence and warfare.
Lord, hear us.

(Add prayers for any personal, local or topical intentions)

Heavenly Father, may the wisdom of the Holy Spirit guide us in the way of truth at all times. Through Christ, our Lord. Amen.

SATURDAY

LUKE 13:1-9

1. After two recent tragedies, people were saying that the victims must have been sinners and that God was punishing them. But Jesus told them to examine their own consciences first. "Unless you repent, you will all perish." On several occasions, Jesus tried to make it clear to them that God's business is not about punishing but healing. Jesus came like a doctor to those who were morally sick. The fact is that sin carries its own in-built punishment. The ways of sin are destructive: disrupting our harmony with God; destroying relationships with others by fostering anger, distrust, hatred, bitterness and prejudice; alienating oneself from one's true potential and dignity. There is no need for God to punish because sin bears the seeds of self-destruction and unhappiness.

2. After words of warning about the need to repent, Jesus followed with words of encouragement. In the parable of the gardener, God is the one who always offers another chance. "He came looking for fruit but found none". Are the fruits of the Holy Spirit to be found in my life? Love, joy, peace, patience and so on? Is there any particular poisonous weed I should eradicate? Is there any virtue or fruit I ought to nurture with God's grace? Digging around the roots is a good picture of examination of conscience. Confessing sin is humiliating, but it is good, for it is the truth that sets us free. The Good News is that God is the gardener who will give the sinner one more chance... and again, one more chance. His love has no end.

PRAYERS

After reflecting on the teaching of Jesus, we pray.

Let us pray that the Church will always proclaim the need to repent and to accept God's offer of mercy.
Lord, hear us.

Save us from passing critical judgement on others, especially if they have suffered misfortune or accidents.
Lord, hear us.

The unexamined life is not worth living. May we be very honest with ourselves and avail of the grace of confession.
Lord, hear us.

We pray for those who feel it is not possible for them to be forgiven. May they come to know Jesus as the friend of sinners, and as the gardener who will always give one more chance to the fruit tree.
Lord, hear us.

(Add prayers for any personal, local or topical intentions)

God of mercy and compassion, graciously hear the prayers we offer in the name of Jesus Christ, our merciful Saviour. Amen.

MONDAY

LUKE 13:10-17

1. The healing of the woman who had a painful curvature of the spine for eighteen years was an act of untying the bonds that restricted her. By contrast, the synagogue official would have preferred to leave her in her infirmity rather than see her healed on the Sabbath. He was seriously knotted up in cold, unfeeling legalism. When Father Jorge Bergoglio, the future Pope Francis, was fifty years old, his life was in deep turmoil. He had been through very difficult years as Provincial of the Jesuits in Argentina. He was advised to take a study break in Germany. He found great consolation in a little church which had a painting called Mary, Untier of Knots. She was unravelling a long white ribbon which represented marriage at one time. Father Bergoglio felt his own knots unravelling as he gazed at the picture. Mary was the Untier of Knots, because at a marriage in Cana, she brought the embarrassing problem of a newly married couple to the attention of Jesus. And, at her request, he let his glory be seen.

2. We can be tied up in knots of many kinds. Like the synagogue official – in knots of legalism, scruples, anxiety. Knots of guilt, of hurt, of unforgiving. Knots of stubbornness, rigidity or inability to adapt. "Woman, you are rid of your infirmity." Jesus laid hands on her and she was released. The onlookers were overjoyed at all the wonders he worked. May Jesus and Mary open up the knots that tie us down. "This God of ours is a God who saves."

PRAYERS

A synagogue official put unfeeling legalism above the healing of an infirm woman.

May the laws of the Church be expressions of reverence, charity and compassion.
Lord, hear us.

May the Spirit of the Lord untie the knots of fear and anxiety that can restrict us; may the Spirit open us up to the freedom of the children of God.
Lord, hear us.

The woman who was cured by Jesus had suffered for eighteen years. For those who have long-term illness, may they be strengthened by the Lord in body, mind and spirit.
Lord, hear us.

May the Lord bless and reward those who care for patients with long-term infirmity of mind or body.
Lord, hear us.

(Add prayers for any personal, local or topical intentions)

O God, the giver of every good gift, hear the prayers we offer in the name of Jesus Christ, the Lord. Amen.

TUESDAY

LUKE 13:18-21

1. The parables of the tiny mustard seed and the little spoon of yeast are very inspiring. A mustard seed looks like a tiny, yellow grain of dust, but it is full of life and possibilities. An artist knows the importance of tiny details. Perfection is composed of trifles, but perfection itself is no trifle. Mother Teresa of Calcutta took that message to heart. She often met with idealistic people who talked about changing the world, but they never went beyond their talk. Where do we start? Mother Teresa's advice was, do the little action but do it with a lot of love.

2. The seed of Mother Teresa's example attracted others, and the Missionaries of Charity were founded. One night there was a loud pounding at the door of one of their convents. A drunken man was there, very aggressive, demanding food. The Sister at the door did not tell him it was too late or anything like that. She prepared a bag of food and placed a chocolate bar at the bottom. The man took the bag away, devoured the food and then discovered the chocolate bar. It shocked him back to sobriety. He returned to the door and knocked gently. When the Sister opened the door, all he said to her was: "Sister, tell me about your Jesus". The presence of the Kingdom of God is like a tiny mustard seed, or a pinch of yeast or a chocolate bar. Don't be waiting around for the big deal. Just do the little thing today with a lot of love.

PRAYERS

Inspired by the parables of Jesus, we pray.

Because the mustard seed is so small, it is blown a great distance and the plant spreads rapidly. May the little acts of charity performed by many people spread the Good News and make people want to know more about Jesus.
Lord, hear us.

A little yeast raises up the stodgy dough to produce beautiful bread. So may the witness of our lives raise up light and joy in all we meet this day.
Lord, hear us.

May we never spend our days waiting for the big mission to come our way. Let us do a little act of kindness to someone this day.
Lord, hear us.

May those who are struggling with human weakness learn that a little step they make is more pleasing to God than the virtuous life of someone who never had such struggles.
Lord, hear us.

(Add prayers for any personal, local or topical intentions)

O God of the little things, hear our prayers in the name of Jesus Christ, your Son, our Lord. Amen.

WEDNESDAY

LUKE 13:22-30

1. "Try to enter by the narrow door." Jesus was focused on the way to Jerusalem and on what would happen to him there. The narrow door does not mean being narrow-minded. It means being focused: having a clear idea of where you want to go and how you plan to get there. Be like the archer or the golfer who has to focus on the target. The archer shuts one eye in order to eliminate distractions. When a man asked Jesus would there be only a few saved, he answered that many will try to enter but will not succeed. If you don't aim to go somewhere, you will end up going anywhere, and there is no guarantee that this will be a good place.

2. The permissive culture of today resents being subjected to rules and dogmas. Don't put in on my freedom. It is my right to choose. As a result of permissiveness, people have taken their focus off the target of salvation. Life has become a succession of disconnected moments with no big picture to frame them all together. There is no backbone to life, and all hope can collapse in the face of a single crisis. It is significant that in this permissive age, we hear of boredom, inertia, depression, chemical dependence and suicide. One moment of crisis and everything collapses. Faith gives us the big picture of where we have come from, where we are going, and how to get there. We have come from God our Creator and life is a journey of returning to God. Jesus once called himself the door. Focus on his way and enter by the narrow door.

PRAYERS

Jesus once said, "I am the door. Anyone who enters through me will be safe."

We pray that people will listen to the voice of the Church directing people on the way to salvation.
Lord, hear us.

May people who have lost the big picture of life discover in Christ the way, the truth and the life.
Lord, hear us.

May we resist the temptations of permissiveness and humbly accept the wisdom of the laws of God.
Lord, hear us.

May our focus be on Jesus Christ: on what he said, what he did and on what he would ask us to do.
Lord, hear us.

(Add prayers for any personal, local or topical intentions)

Merciful Father, you desire that all people would come to the truth and be saved. Hear the prayers we offer in the name of Jesus Christ, your Son, our Lord. Amen.

THURSDAY

LUKE 13:31-35

1. Anybody who has kept hens knows that the greatest predator is the fox. Today's Gospel is about a fox and a hen. Jesus compared himself to a mother hen gathering her chicks. But he called Herod a fox. A fox is a very sly, silent predator. Herod was interested in spiritual matters but his first interest was protecting his own career. After arresting John the Baptist, he enjoyed listening to him. He was convinced that John was a good man, but this did not stop him from having John beheaded. Some Pharisees tipped off Jesus that Herod intended to kill him too. It was then that Jesus called him "that fox". Later, at the trial of Jesus, he refused to answer Herod. When we find that there is somebody whose behaviour absolutely turns us off, it is consoling to remember that even Jesus could not relate to Herod.

2. The image of Jesus as the mother hen is very attractive. "How often have I longed to gather your children as a hen gathers her brood under her wings, but you refused." What does that say to you? God loves you. God wants you to come to him. God wants to protect you. God wants to nourish you in the Eucharist. God wants you to grow in a loving, personal relationship. Saint Paul urged the Ephesians to grow strong in the Lord in time of temptation. In Paul's Letter to the Romans he wrote, "With God on our side, who can be against us? Since God did not spare his own Son, but gave him up for the benefit of us all, we may be certain, after such a gift, that he will not refuse anything he can give." Do not refuse the gifts of God.

PRAYERS

Let us pray for Christians whose lives are in danger from the hands of tyrannical authorities, as were the lives of John the Baptist and Jesus.
Lord, hear us.

May all political leaders and lawmakers be guided by the principles of justice and compassion.
Lord, hear us.

As we reflect on Jesus as the mother hen, let our trust in God's protection grow ever stronger.
Lord, hear us.

We pray for people who feel unloved. May they have the grace to experience the personal love that God has for each one of us.
Lord, hear us.

(Add prayers for any personal, local or topical intentions)

Loving God, nothing can come between us and the love you have for us. Hear our prayers offered in the name of your Beloved Son, Jesus Christ, the Lord. Amen

FRIDAY

LUKE 14:1-6

1. Meals are very important in Luke's Gospel. There are ten meals and each one has a special significance. Today's reading introduces us to a meal where Jesus was invited to the house of one of the leading Pharisees. It shows that all his contacts with the Pharisees weren't confrontational. Some Pharisees were more moderate than others. Table fellowship, that is, the people with whom you share food, was very significant. To share food meant sharing life and values with somebody. This was especially true of a meal on the Sabbath. There was a sick man there in need of healing. A Sabbath regulation forbade healing on the Sabbath. Jesus asked his Pharisee friends if it was against the law to heal this man. They remained silent. At least, they did not tell him not to do it. He healed the man and sent him away. Then he reminded them that they too did necessary life-saving work on the Sabbath. The law in the Statute Book said one thing, but the law of common sense said something else.

2. Pope Francis, in his booklet *The Joy of the Gospel*, reminds us that all rules do not have the same degree of importance. When you are in a dilemma between two obligations, which one should you choose? Should you go to Mass on a Sunday or should you stay at home to look after somebody in need of care? Ask yourself what would God want you to do? What would Jesus have done? The example of Jesus shows us that works of compassion and caring are to get priority. If you miss Mass because you were helping somebody, or you were sick, or it wasn't really possible to get to Mass, obviously it wasn't a sin. And if it wasn't a sin, there is no need to say it in confession. God does not expect the impossible.

PRAYERS

In the light of the Gospel, let us pray.

That the rules of the Church may be guidelines directing us to greater love of God and people.
Lord, hear us.

That we will never hide behind the letter of the law as an excuse for not helping somebody in need.
Lord, hear us.

May we never develop a legalistic mentality that would make us harsh judges of others.
Lord, hear us.

Jesus healed the man with dropsy on a Sabbath. We bring to him our friends and neighbours who are sick, that he might lay his healing hand upon them.
Lord, hear us.

(Add prayers for any personal, local or topical intentions)

May the God of compassion hear our prayers in the name of Jesus Christ, our Lord. Amen.

SATURDAY

LUKE 14:1. 7-11

1. In Luke's Gospel, Jesus is never far away from a table. Much of his teaching is given at meals. A light-hearted exchange can reach into areas that formal instruction could not touch. Table-talk comes in a different tone to the sermon voice. In the merriment of a good meal, one can expect humour and caricatures of various poses. One can detect humour in his tone of voice when Jesus paints a caricature of people blatantly vying for positions of importance. You know the sort of person who always gets to the centre of the group photograph. And then there is the embarrassment when one is moved aside because somebody more important has to be accommodated. The caricature is light-hearted but the message is important. We are invited to look at ourselves. Am I touchy about being honoured or admired? Am I jealous when someone else is honoured? How do I fell when I am overlooked?

2. In the light-hearted tones of table-talk, Jesus poked fun at petty pomp and its little vanities. Gentle humour can be an effective way of getting a point across. But real pride is ugly and no laughing matter. It is arrogant, stubborn and uncooperative. It rebels against divine authority and will not serve. It despises others and puts self at the centre of everything. Little wonder that pride is first in the list of capital sins, those seven evil tendencies which are at the heart of sinful behaviour. "Everyone who exalts himself will be humbled, and the one who humbles himself will be exalted."

PRAYERS

Taking the teaching of Jesus to heart, we pray.

We pray for those who are appointed to positions of leadership in the Church. May they be inspired by the example of Jesus who came, not to be served, but to serve.
Lord, hear us.

Deliver us from small-minded jealousy when we see other people being honoured.
Lord, hear us.

Deliver us from the sort of pride which would make us regard ourselves as superior to others.
Lord, hear us.

As we think of Jesus invited to a meal, we pray for people who will have no meal today. May the resources of the world be more fairly distributed.
Lord, hear us.

(Add prayers for any personal, local or topical intentions)

O God, the giver of every good gift, hear our prayers offered in the name of Jesus Christ, our Lord. Amen.

MONDAY

LUKE 14:12-14

1. CYCLE A

Writing to the Romans, Saint Paul spoke of the depths of God's wisdom and knowledge and how impossible it is to penetrate his motives or understand his methods. The humorous tone of Jesus at the Pharisee's table should prepare us for the surprises at the final messianic banquet. The last shall be first, the humble exalted, the blind will have the beatific vision, while the cripples dance for joy. A God who puts on an apron to serve at table must be full of surprises. And a God who insists on a day of holy rest after six days working cannot be regarded with po-faced seriousness all the time. The God of surprises has a sense of humour.

1. CYCLE B

Sitting at the table of a rich Pharisee, Jesus continued in the light-hearted tone of table-talk. "When you give a lunch or a dinner, do not ask your friends, brothers or sick neighbours, for fear they repay your courtesy by inviting you in return". This is rather tongue-in-cheek. Pity the perplexed host compiling a list of guests, double-checking that nobody gets through who might possibly return the compliment. The serious message comes in the list that Jesus suggests: the poor, the crippled, the lame, the blind. Their handicaps were regarded as a sort of curse and they would have no place at the final messianic banquet at the end of life. Jesus turned the prevailing ideas upside down in the Beatitudes. "Blessed are the poor." Saint Paul, writing to the Philippians, captured the ideals of Jesus. "Let there be no competition among you, no conceit. Always consider the other person to be better than yourself."

PRAYERS

Having listened to the words of Jesus about inviting the poor and handicapped, we pray.

That those who are poor, starving or homeless might get their just rights through a fair distribution of the world's resources.
Lord, hear us.

That the people who have great wealth will not waste it on vain luxuries: may they learn that it is more blessed to give than to receive.
Lord, hear us.

May those who have special needs discover how special they are in God's love.
Lord, hear us.

May God bless and reward all the volunteers who work for charitable organisations.
Lord, hear us.

(Add prayers for any personal, local or topical intentions)

O God, the giver of every good gift, graciously hear the prayers we offer in the name of Jesus Christ, your Son, our Lord. Amen.

TUESDAY

Luke 14:15-24

1. Today's Gospel is about God's invitation and our excuses. God does not force us: he invites us. God respects our freedom because without free will, we could not love. "Blessed are those who are called to the Supper of the Lamb." Pope Francis repeated the invitation of Jesus Christ to all. "I invite all Christians everywhere to a renewed encounter with Jesus Christ, or at least an openness to letting him encounter them. I ask you all to do this unfailingly every day. No one should think that this invitation is not for him or her, since no one is excluded from the joy brought by the Lord." Jesus did not die for some of the people: he died for all. His mercy is not confined to some people: it is available to everybody. There are no good excuses for refusing the Lord's invitation. Jesus is waiting for us beside the well. All he asks from us is to give him our empty bucket. He wants to give us the answer to every thirst.

2. In the Gospel parable, some people came up with excuses for not accepting their invitation to the royal wedding. "I have bought a piece of land I must see." "I have just bought new ploughing teams, and I am on my way to try them out." "I have just got married." All good excuses. But did you ever hear anybody say "I have a poor excuse"? The Irish word for an excuse is brilliant. Leathsceal. Half a story! It is never the full story. A very successful sports coach never allows his team to find an excuse – the weather, hard luck, the referee. No excuses are allowed. Any defeat is treated as a challenge to eliminate mistakes and to do better. "Blessed are those who are called to the Supper of the Lamb." The Lord invites us to a banquet greater than any royal wedding.

PRAYERS

"Blessed are those who will be at the feast in the Kingdom of God!"

We pray that the whole world will hear the voice of the Church inviting all people to a personal relationship with God.
Lord, hear us.

That we might stop making excuses and do all we can to respond to the Lord's invitations.
Lord, hear us.

May all who are looking for spiritual nourishment realise that Holy Communion is the greatest source of medicine for the soul.
Lord, hear us.

For people who have drifted away from prayer: may they recognise what they are missing and come back to God who is waiting for them with open arms.
Lord, hear us.

(Add prayers for any personal, local or topical intentions)

Heavenly Father, King of Heaven and Earth, hear the prayers we offer in the name of Jesus Christ, our Lord. Amen.

WEDNESDAY

LUKE 14:25-33

1. Great crowds were flocking to Jesus. They came out of curiosity, or to seek help, to use him for political leadership, or to trap him. The time had come for Jesus to spell out the cost of discipleship. Would they follow him to the cross? For some, it would mean leaving the family circle. Others would be called to share totally with the poor. For every disciple, it would mean taking up the cross at some time or other. Take the cross out of Christianity and what have you got? A pick and choose approach which takes what one likes from religion but rejects what does not appeal. As Chesterton put it, when Jones says he is following his conscience, then Jones is following Jones... which may not be the same as following Jesus. Without the cross, there is no backbone in time of suffering: God is used as a personal feel-good factor.

2. Jesus said "Carry your cross and follow me". One of Mother Teresa's Sisters was heading out one morning to serve among the poor, but her face was dark in sadness. Mother Teresa gently called her aside and asked her: "What did Jesus say, go in front of me or follow me?" The Sister replied, "Follow me," and she began to smile. The Good News is that when suffering comes our way, when we have a cross to carry, Jesus is there in front of us, leading us, showing us, accompanying us. Make sure there is a crucifix in your home. Saint Francis used to call the crucifix a book. When you look at Jesus on the cross, you can read the story of Christ's total self-giving out of love for us. "How much do you love me, Lord?" Then he opened his arms on the cross. "That's how much I love you."

PRAYERS

Gathered together as a community of disciples of Jesus, we pray that we will be true disciples.

May the Church be faithful to Jesus in teaching, not only the consolations of faith, but also the cost of being a disciple.
Lord, hear us.

That we will take the ideals of Jesus wholeheartedly, even when it costs us.
Lord, hear us.

When we look at the crucifix, may we see the total love of Jesus as he entered into solidarity with every kind of suffering.
Lord, hear us.

For all who have a heavy cross at the moment, through illness, or darkness, or injustice: may their faith be a source of strength to carry them through.
Lord, hear us.

(Add prayers for any personal, local or topical intentions)

Heavenly Father, your sent your Beloved Son as the shepherd to lead us. Hear the prayers we offer in his name, Jesus Christ, the Lord. Amen.

THURSDAY

Luke 15:1-10

1. The Pharisees came to prominence about two hundred years before the time of Jesus. The Jews were being forced to take up pagan practices imposed on them by their Greek rulers. The name Pharisee means the Separate Ones, people who keep away from pagan contamination. Even after the defeat of the Greeks, keeping apart from any form of contamination became the main focus of their religion. This included keeping apart from people whose behaviour or occupation classified them as sinners. Jesus was a scandal in the eyes of the Separate Ones, the way that he mixed with these sinners. Worse again, he ate and drank with them. Jesus wanted to bring joy back to their religion, so he told them three parables about joyful celebrations when something lost was found... a lost sheep, a lost coin and a lost son. Jesus came to seek out those who were lost and to give them hope.

2. Although there are billions of people alive today, yet each one is important in the eyes of God the Father, our Creator. One lost sheep is sought. One lost coin. One prodigal son. On Calvary, paradise is promised to one, a man with a criminal background. One is important to God. That means that you are important to God. If you were the only sinner in the world, Jesus would have died for you. Many people are shy of intimacy with God: respect God but at a respectful distance. No! God loves you. God wants to hear the sound of your prayers, the beat of your heart. Imagine, God wants me! It follows that what I receive from God, I must pass on to others. There is such a thing as long distance charity, full of concern about faraway problems but insensitive to people around us. Charity begins at home. Is there one to whom I owe an apology? Is there one I won't talk to? Remember, that one person is precious in God's eyes.

PRAYERS

Inspired by the example of Jesus, we are moved to pray.

May the Church faithfully follow the example of Jesus as a hospital of mercy and hope for all who are morally and spiritually lost in the turmoil of life.
Lord, hear us.

That sinners might realise that in God's eyes they are never lost: may they experience the joy of repentance.
Lord, hear us.

That each one of us might realise how much we are loved by God, how important we are in his eyes.
Lord, hear us.

That we might respect every other individual as somebody precious in the eyes of God.
Lord, hear us.

(Add prayers for any personal, local or topical intentions)

O God, Creator of all, you have carved us on the palm of your hand. Hear the prayers we offer in the name of Jesus Christ, your Son, our Lord. Amen.

FRIDAY

LUKE 16:1-8

1. Today's Gospel is the story of the crafty steward who prepared for his dismissal. He knew he was about to be dismissed because he was denounced as a waster, so he cooked the books to make his landing after dismissal as soft as possible. His boss, a wealthy business man who knew a trick or two, admired cuteness when he saw it. The punchline of the story is that the children of this world are more astute in dealing with their kind than the children of light. The moral lesson to be drawn from the parable is to prepare thoroughly for the next life.

2. Saint Paul said that for us our homeland is in Heaven. From Heaven comes the Saviour we are waiting for, the Lord, Jesus Christ. He will transform our mortal bodies into copies of his glorious body. Our faith tells us that we have a glorious future on offer to us. We are called to live as children of the light, that is, to be faithful to the teaching of Jesus Christ. No eye has seen, no ear has heard, it is beyond our imagination all that God has prepared for those who love him. Today's parable encourages us to prepare for Heaven with the same effort that successful business people or athletes put into their careers.

PRAYERS

Let us take the lessons of the Gospel to heart as we pray.

May the teaching of the Church be a beacon of light guiding people on the road to eternal salvation.
Lord, hear us.

May we live as children of the light and reflect the light and love of God to others.
Lord, hear us.

May no material concerns distract us from the eternal wonders of our ultimate homeland in Heaven.
Lord, hear us.

May the glorious future that God offers us remove all fear of dying from our minds.
Lord, hear us.

(Add prayers for any personal, local or topical intentions)

O God, you have prepared a home for us in Heaven. May nothing divert us from that glorious destiny. Through Christ, our Lord. Amen.

SATURDAY

LUKE 16:9-15

1. We hear Jesus talking about money. He says three things about it. Use it; it is tainted; and don't be a slave to it. First of all, he says to use it. Forget all those jokes about Saint Peter operating the gate of Heaven. It's the poor who examine your credentials. How we treat the poor is how we treat God. "Whatsoever you do to the least of my brothers, that you do unto me." If you want to give to God, give to the poor. To waste money on unnecessary luxuries or to waste food is to rob the poor. Money has temporal value but no eternal value. Have a conscience about money and use it in such a way as to win friends who will welcome you, on behalf of Christ, into the homes of eternity.

2. Secondly, Jesus said that money is tainted. It is a carrier of temptation. Saint Paul wrote, "The love of money is the root of all evils and there are some who, pursuing it, have wandered away from the faith and so given their souls any number of fatal wounds" (1 Tim 6:10). Even one of the apostles succumbed to the temptation to steal from the common fund. Eventually, he betrayed Jesus for thirty silver pieces. There have been very costly tribunals attempting to uncover tax evasion and graft, which is the misappropriation of public money. Jesus also used the word *slave* in connection with money. One becomes a slave to money when it preoccupies the mind, sets values, colours behaviour and deadens one's conscience. Saint Paul showed a marvellous freedom in the way it never bothered him whether he had money or not. Money is a talent with the opportunity to do great good for others. But it is tainted with temptation and burdened with responsibilities. You cannot be the slave of God and of money.

PRAYERS

In the light of the Lord's teaching, we pray.

May people who are wealthy share generously to alleviate the needs of those who are lacking food, education and healthcare.
Lord, hear us.

May all governments set the alleviation of poverty as a priority in their planning.
Lord, hear us.

May we never become slaves to material things. May we recognise that it is more blessed to give than to receive.
Lord, hear us.

That we might cut down on the waste of food, and stop buying what we really do not need.
Lord, hear us.

(Add prayers for any personal, local or topical intentions)

O God, the giver of every good gift, may we use what we have received for the service of your people. Through Christ, our Lord. Amen.

MONDAY

LUKE 17:1-6

1. Jesus was usually very gentle with human failures. But in the matter of harm done to children, he was very angry. "Better for him to be thrown into the sea with a millstone put round his neck than that he should lead astray one of these little ones. Watch yourselves." It is only in recent times that there has been any understanding of the depth of harm done to the lives of those who were abused physically, emotionally or sexually in childhood. Most abuse occurred in the family circle. Schools and sporting clubs were also places of abuse. But the fact that some of this abuse was done by church personnel has become a huge obstacle to faith for many people. As Shakespeare said, "Lilies that fester smell far worse than weeds." A great deal has been done for the safeguarding of children, but the state of high alert has to be maintained. As Jesus said: "Watch yourselves".

2. Forgiveness, the grace to move beyond the injustices of the past, is one of the essential teachings of Jesus. The standard that was accepted in his time allowed for equal retribution, an eye for an eye and a tooth for a tooth. But in the Kingdom of God that Jesus preached, a higher standard was introduced. Let there be no revenge. Christianity is about a love that refuses to be poisoned by the wrongdoing of another. "Be compassionate as your Heavenly Father is compassionate." The motto for the Year of Mercy was "Merciful as the Father". How often must I forgive? Once, twice, seven times? And even more if necessary? Human nature on its own cannot reach that standard. The only way is super-human, or super-natural. That is where the Holy Spirit comes in. The Holy Spirit can lift us up to see things more through the eyes of God, and the eyes of God are full of compassion for the moral sickness of the person who does wrong. With the apostles we ask God, "Increase our faith".

PRAYERS

Guided by the teaching of Jesus, we pray.

May those who were abused as children find the grace to be healed within and to move on into a new life.
Lord, hear us.

We pray for those who abused children: may they recognise the harm they did, may they truly repent and be converted.
Lord, hear us.

Lord, increase our faith in the power of the Holy Spirit to enable us to see those who wronged us with eyes of compassion.
Lord, hear us.

May the love in our hearts be so strong and pure that it refuses to be poisoned by the wrongdoing of others.
Lord, hear us

   (Add prayers for any personal, local or topical intentions)

God of mercy and forgiveness, heal all hatred in our hearts by the power of the Holy Spirit. Through Christ, our Lord. Amen.

TUESDAY

LUKE 17:7-10

1. The background to the parable of the faithful servant is the request of the apostles, "Increase our faith." How did Jesus answer? He did not give them lessons in theology, or visions, or charismatic experiences. His answer is in the parable of the servant who is faithful to his daily chores. The increase of faith that Jesus wants is faithfulness. One of the seven gifts of the Holy Spirit is piety. The real meaning of piety is faithfulness to one's duties. To believe is more than mental acceptance of doctrines. The Latin word for *I believe* is *credo*, which literally means "I give my heart". We give our hearts to God when we commit our energy to his service. "We are merely servants: we have done no more than our duty."

2. The faithful performance of daily duties is a sign of faithfulness in any job. But some people are quickly bored by repeated religious exercises. Mass is boring! The Rosary is so repetitive! I'm always making the same confession. Yet the most important acts in life are repetitive… your heartbeat, breathing, eating, sleeping, and so on. Do we ever call these repeated actions boring? Daily fidelity is what keeps the body functioning in a healthy way. It is the same with the spiritual life. "When you have done all that you were told to do, say 'We are merely servants: we have done no more than our duty'."

PRAYERS

Inspired by the example and teaching of Jesus, we are moved to pray.

As Jesus came not to be served but to serve, so may his Church be noted as the humble servant of God and of mankind.
Lord, hear us.

The members of the Church are often called the faithful: may we be faithful not only in name but also in fact.
Lord, hear us.

May we appreciate the value of being faithful in the performance of our religious duties.
Lord, hear us.

May we show our appreciation and gratitude to all those who serve us each day in the ordinary course of duty... cooking the meals, driving the bus, delivering the mail, sweeping the street, and so on.
Lord, hear us.

(Add prayers for any personal, local or topical intentions)

Heavenly Father, graciously hear our prayers in the name of Jesus Christ, your Son, our Lord. Amen.

WEDNESDAY

LUKE 17:11-19

1. David Steindl-Rast wrote a very fine book called *Gratefulness the Heart of Prayer*. He also suggests that happiness is born of gratitude. The story of the cure of the lepers is about gratitude. Once the Samaritan leper found himself cured, he turned back, praising God at the top of his voice. He threw himself at the feet of Jesus and thanked him. Praise is more about the giver and thanks is more about the gift. How can we ever give proper thanks to God? Our own words are great but nothing is as powerful as the Eucharist. The word *Eucharist* is Greek for praise and thanks. Do you want to offer worthy thanks to God? Jesus invites us, "Come join with me in my journey through death and resurrection, returning to the Father. Do this in memory of me". In the Eucharistic Prayer, we lift up our hearts to give praise and thanks to God. Through Jesus as our mediator with the Father; with him as our brother in human flesh; and in him as parts of the Body of which he is the head.

2. Luke's Gospel tells of the gracious actions of God and the reactions of people. Notice how he describes the reactions of the Samaritan leper to his healing. "Finding himself cured". Then he turned back, praising God and thanking Jesus. Luke did not simply say that the man was cured. He found himself cured. Gratitude begins when we find our gifts, when we become aware of what God has given us. It's a lovely practice at the end of the day to reflect on the blessings of the day: inspirations, helpful people, music, a flower, fresh air, birdsong. Pick out just one item or blessing, turn back to God in praise and thanks. Just one blessing per day. Maybe note it in a diary. Over time, this practice will make you much more aware of God's blessings. It will train you to find your blessings. Gratitude is the heart of prayer.

PRAYERS

Inspired by the Samaritan leper, let us turn to God in praise and gratitude.
The Response is: *We praise and thank you, Lord.*

For the gift of the Eucharist, in which we return thanks to God, through Jesus, with him and in him.
We praise and thank you, Lord.

That we might find our blessings each day.
We praise and thank you, Lord.

That we might be more grateful to the people who help us each day.
We praise and thank you, Lord.

For all the wonders and beauty of your creation.
We praise and thank you, Lord.

(Add prayers for any personal, local or topical intentions)

O God, the giver of every good gift, we praise you through your Son, Jesus Christ the Lord. Amen

THURSDAY

LUKE 17:20-25

1. One of the Pharisees asked Jesus when the Kingdom of God was to come. The name Pharisee meant the Separated Ones. They sought perfection by keeping themselves separate from pagan influences and from contamination by sin or anything unclean. They believed that the Messiah would inaugurate the absolutely perfect state. When was it going to come? The answer of Jesus was that it is already among you. The power of God is already working in an imperfect world. Like seeds in different types of soil; like wheat in the midst of weeds; like a tiny mustard seed or a pinch of yeast; like a net taking in all sorts of fish. Don't be waiting for the perfect world, like the man who was looking for the perfect wife only to find that she was looking for the perfect husband. A great golf instructor has a motto that golf is not a game of perfect. Jesus asks us to bloom where we are planted. Thank God for an imperfect Church because there is room for us in it.

2. Every so often a new guru gains popularity. Or there is a new course, a new diet, a new exercise that will solve everything. At the beginning of the new millennium, Pope John Paul II wrote about the expectation among people that there would be some new magic formula to answer the problems and questions of our times. His answer was that there is no need for a new programme. The programme already exists in the Gospel and in the living tradition handed on by the Church. We are not saved by a formula but by a person, Jesus Christ. "Look there! Look here!," people cry. But Jesus said, "Do not move". The Kingdom of God is among us. The Church community is the task force for implementing this kingdom of love, truth, justice, peace and mercy. That is our mission.

PRAYERS

Jesus came to inaugurate the reign of God on Earth.
Let us pray with the response: *Thy Kingdom come.*

That the Church may be true to its calling to be a community of people dedicated to the ideals of God's reign on Earth.
Thy Kingdom come.

May each one of us try to make our little corner of the world a place of justice, peace, caring and compassion.
Thy Kingdom come.

May we never be depressed by the bad news. May we be people of hope who see the many seeds of goodness in the world.
Thy Kingdom come.

Let us pray for people who are persecuted or mocked because of their dedication to justice, peace truth and compassion.
Thy Kingdom come.

(Add prayers for any personal, local or topical intentions)

Father in Heaven, may the world be converted to your kingdom of justice, peace and joy, through Christ, our Lord. Amen.

FRIDAY

Luke 17:26-37

1. Cycle A

   Life can be changed in the twinkling of an eye. An accident; an unwelcome medical diagnosis; a bereavement; a financial crisis; a scandal that shakes us to the roots. The vultures of doom are waiting for our collapse. Life is radically changed by the crisis, but life is not ended. God is here and God is greater than any crisis, although it may be hard to believe. Shakespeare wrote: "There's a divinity that shapes our ends, rough-hew them how we will." We cannot control what has happened. But maybe we can do something to control how we deal with it. Begin by being grateful for the treasured memories of the past. But do not stay in the past. Trust in God and move on. Let go and let God. Go forward in hope, believing that God is with us, even in the darkness. "If I should walk in the valley of darkness, no evil would I fear. You are there with your crook and your staff: with these you will bring me comfort."

2. Cycle B

   The Book of Wisdom makes this observation: "Naturally stupid are all men who have not known God, and who, from the good things that are seen, have not been able to discover Him-who-is." Somebody who did make the journey from creation to the Creator was Saint Augustine. He left us a wonderful description in his Confessions. "Late have I loved you, beauty so old and so new: late have I loved you. And see, you were within and I was in the external world and sought you there, and in my unlovely state I plunged into these lovely creatures which you made. You were with me and I was not with you. These lovely things kept me from you, though if they had not their existence in you, they had no existence at all." The biographer of Saint Francis described how he moved from the art to the artist. Praying with the wonders and beauty of the universe, we admire the beauty but we worship God the Maker. To quote from a Psalm: "The skies proclaim the glory of God, the firmament shows forth the work of his hands." (Saint Augustine: *Confessions*, trans. Chadwick)

PRAYERS

May the Church always be a beacon of light and hope in a world where bad news dominates the headlines.
Lord, hear us.

We pray for people whose lives have been shattered by some happening or crisis. May the Lord reveal his closeness to them.
Lord, hear us.

For the victims of war and persecution who are forced to leave home and country: may they receive a Christian welcome wherever they go.
Lord, hear us.

For those who are struggling with an addiction: may God, their Higher Power, help them to get safely through this day.
Lord, hear us.

(Add prayers for any personal, local or topical intentions)

God our Maker, hear the prayers we offer in the name of Jesus Christ, your Son, our Lord. Amen.

SATURDAY

LUKE: 18:1-8

1. Today's parable about the persistent widow has a very clear message: don't give up, continue praying, persevere. Perseverance isn't always easy because there are times when God is delaying the answer. "Will not God see justice done to his children who cry to him day and night even when he delays to help them?" Why would God delay in answering our petition? There is a line in the Old Testament which says that it was to humble you, to test you and to know your inmost heart. If we got an instant answer to every prayer, we might not appreciate it. We might think that it is due to the power of our own prayer, not God's doing. When God delays an answer, it humbles us. A child with no toys appreciates a gift far more than the rich child who takes gifts almost as his right. We need to be humbled to appreciate the depths of our dependence on God.

2. God might be testing us in order to stretch and expand our faith. In daylight, we can see all the objects near us, but it is only in the darkness of night that our vision stretches to see the distant stars. God wants to stretch our vision and to extend our faith. Sometimes a team trainer pushes the team through the pain barrier to test their commitment. Our commitment is tested if we see the necessity of backing up our words with action. Back up the words of prayer with an act of penance, or better again, an act of generosity. Don't give up: continue to trust. God knows what is best for you.

PRAYERS

Encouraged by the teaching of Jesus, we pray.

For the grace of perseverance in prayer even when we feel that God does not hear us.
Lord, hear us.

For the humility to accept that God's will might not always be what we want.
Lord, hear us.

That times of darkness may become opportunities to deepen our faith and stretch our vision.
Lord, hear us.

We pray for people who have given up on prayer and religion. May the light of Christ penetrate their darkness.
Lord, hear us.

(Add prayers for any personal, local or topical intentions)

God our Father, confident that you always hear us, we offer these prayers in the name of Jesus Christ, your Son, our Lord. Amen.

MONDAY

LUKE 18:35-43

1. "Jesus, Son of David, have pity on me." The prayer of the blind man at Jericho is a model of how to keep a prayer simple. It is the inspiration of what is called the Jesus Prayer. The more we complicate prayer, the more we are letting ourselves, with our worries and anxiety, become the centre of prayer. The simple prayer of the blind man has three steps: the name, the title and the petition. The name identifies the One to whom the prayer is addressed. This prayer is addressed to Jesus. The sacred name calls up the person and the power. The title here is Son of David. For the blind man, this title expressed his belief that Jesus was the Messiah. We might prefer some other title such as Jesus Saviour, Lord Jesus or Jesus Friend. Keep it short and simple. The third step is petition: have pity on me. There is no need to complicate it as Jesus already knows what you mean.

2. Sit or kneel in a comfortable position. Relax your breathing and any tension in your muscles. Let the name of Jesus bring you into his presence and power. He is already present but we are not attentive to it. Gently breathing his name makes us aware that he is with us. Jesus Lord; Jesus Saviour; Jesus Friend; or any title you prefer. Then add what you want to express. There are five basic movements of prayer: asking, loving, thanking, adoring, and repenting. Their first letters spell the word ALTAR. "Jesus, Son of David, have pity on me." The man's sight returned. The name of Jesus opens the eyes of faith to his presence.

PRAYERS

Lord Jesus, may the Holy Spirit teach us how to pray with the simplicity and confidence of the blind man at Jericho.
Lord, hear us.

May the sacred names of God or Jesus be a constant source of contact between us and God.
Lord, hear us.

May those who abuse the sacred name of Jesus recognise their disrespect for our Lord and Saviour.
Lord, hear us.

Lord Jesus, have pity on our friends who are suffering. Today we pray especially for those who are blind.
Lord, hear us.

(Add prayers for any personal, local or topical intentions)

O God, graciously hear the prayers of your people who cry out to you in the name of Jesus Christ, the Lord. Amen.

TUESDAY

LUKE 19:1-10

1. The meeting of Zacchaeus and Jesus is a story of up and down. Zacchaeus was a small man but he had climbed up a sycamore tree. He had also climbed up to top of the financial ladder. He was a wealthy man. But it is a major disappointment to have climbed to the top of the ladder only to find it was up the wrong wall. He was financially rich but he was spiritually poor. Money had not brought him inner contentment. So, he was anxious to see what kind of man Jesus was. If Zacchaeus was the man who climbed up, Jesus was the one who came down. He came down from Heaven to stand with us on the ground-level of life. From ground-level, he looked up at Zacchaeus and invited him to come down. He did not say to Zacchaeus, "Come up to my superior position." No, he said, "Come down to my level." This is the level of the Beatitudes. Blessed are the poor, blessed are the gentle, those who work for justice, those who are pure in heart. As Saint Paul put it: "Although he was rich, he became poor for your sake, so that you should become rich through his poverty."

2. Zacchaeus did come down. He came down from his false superiority to the ideals of Jesus. He there and then resolved to give half his wealth to the poor and to make fourfold restitution to the people he had cheated. He might not have much money left, but he would have the happiness and contentment that money could not buy. The Son of Man came down to seek and save those who were lost.

PRAYERS

Although he was rich, Jesus made himself poor for our sake so that we might become rich. Let us pray.

May the Church be like Jesus Christ, a Church of the poor and for the poor.
Lord, hear us.

May the financial agencies and governments who dictate policies and laws be guided in conscience towards a more just distribution of wealth.
Lord, hear us.

May those who have great wealth come down like Zacchaeus to see the needs of others and then discover the joy of sharing.
Lord, hear us.

Jesus said the Zacchaeus, "I want to stay in your house today." We invite him to stay in our houses today and every day.
Lord, hear us.

   (Add prayers for any personal, local or topical intentions)

God, the Father of all, rich and poor, hear the prayers we offer in the name of Jesus Christ, your Son, our Lord. Amen.

WEDNESDAY

LUKE 19:11-28

1. At the end of a Cursillo weekend, the participants are presented with a little cross inscribed with the message: Christ is counting on you. Blessed John Henry Newman wrote a prayer about using our talents. "God has created me to do some definitive service. He has committed some work to me that he has not committed to another. I have my mission. I may not know it in this life, but I shall be told it in the next. I am a link in a chain, a bond of communication between persons. He has not created me for naught." Christ is counting on you. There is somebody that you can reach whom no other person can reach. There are situations where you can bring light into somebody's darkness. You might mistakenly think that you have nothing to offer. Remember – when Jesus entered Jerusalem in triumph on Palm Sunday, it was on the back of a donkey. There is a job for every donkey in God's Kingdom. Christ is counting on you.

2. The man who did not use his talent wrapped it up in a linen cloth. In Matthew's version of the parable, there is a powerful image. The servant dug a hole and buried the talent. A wasted talent digs a cesspool of negativity and cynicism. This servant tried to offload the blame to the others, to what people were saying about the Master's reputation. Pope Francis described unproductive servants like this: "When we flee, hide, refuse to share, stop giving and lock ourselves up in our own comforts – this is slow suicide." The wasted talent is a waste of life.

PRAYERS

As we reflect on the talents that God has bestowed on the community of the Church, we pray.

May Pope *(Name)* and all those who have the responsibility of authority in the Church be guided by the example of Jesus and the light of the Holy Spirit.
Lord, hear us.

That each of us might recognise the talents and opportunities that God has given us and that we will not be afraid to use them.
Lord, hear us.

For those who think they have nothing to offer. May they recognise the importance of giving even a tiny bit of attention and compassion to somebody in need.
Lord, hear us.

May those who have buried their talents in negativity, change their ways, open up their doors, and learn the joy of sharing life with others.
Lord, hear us.

(Add prayers for any personal, local or topical intentions)

O God, the giver of every good gift, we thank you for all that you have given us. Through Jesus Christ, your Son, our Lord.

THURSDAY

LUKE 19:41-44

1. As Jesus drew near to Jerusalem and came in sight of the city, he shed tears over it. There is a little chapel on the site called Dominus Flevit, meaning "the Lord wept". It was designed in the shape of a teardrop. The name Jerusalem is rooted in Shalom, meaning peace. Sadly, it is a city that has known constant conflicts. Eighteen times in the course of history, it has been flattened to the ground. Some of the walls are pockmarked with bullet holes of modern warfare. Jesus wept because he was offering the path to justice and peace but he was rejected. The history of Jerusalem is the story of the world in microcosm. "If only you had understood the way to peace, but, alas, it is hidden from you." What hides the path to peace? Pride, domination, racial hatred, and rich nations selling weapons to kill. As the song put it, when will they ever learn?

2. The path to peace is clearly expressed in the popular Peace Prayer associated with Saint Francis of Assisi. Make me an instrument of your peace. It calls us to replace hatred with love; injury with pardon; doubt with faith; despair with hope; darkness with light and sadness with joy. We then ask for the grace to be less self-centred: not to be seeking consolation, understanding and love for ourselves, rather than passing these blessings on to others. It is important to learn that it is in giving that we receive, that it is in pardoning that we are pardoned. And finally, the fullness of peace comes when in dying we are born to eternal life.

PRAYERS

Jesus set out the path to peace. Let us pray.

For peace in the world, and especially in Jerusalem and the surrounding countries: may all people turn away from the ways of hatred and violence.
Lord, hear us.

For all the people who have been forced to leave their homes and countries: may the restoration of peace give these people the chance to return home.
Lord, hear us.

For peace in family life: may divided families be reconciled.
Lord, hear us.

For all whose lives are filled with fear, anxiety and worry: may they enjoy deep peace of mind.
Lord, hear us.

(Add prayers for any personal, local or topical intentions)

God, the Father of all, may all your children throughout the world be united in harmony and peace, through Christ our Lord. Amen.

FRIDAY

LUKE 19:45-48

1. When Jesus as a boy of twelve visited the Temple in Jerusalem, he was very disappointed with what he saw. He resolved there and then to do something about it when he grew up. Twenty years later, he was back there. This Temple designed by Herod was not yet complete even after forty-six years. The whole project was massive, taking up thirty acres. The Temple itself was covered with plates of gold to reflect the sun. In the surrounding courtyards, foreign currency was changed and lambs were bought and sacrificed. One ancient writer said that as many as two hundred thousand animals were sacrificed for Passover, although one must allow that this number was greatly exaggerated. Imagine the stench, the noise, the hustle and bustle. Everything was there except the atmosphere of prayer. It was more a monument to Herod's brilliance as a builder than to God's glory. The pilgrims who came from near and far were exploited, so much so that Jesus called the place a robbers' den. This did not go down well with the Temple people who had become very wealthy out of the transactions. So they sought to get rid of Jesus, but they could not carry out their plan because the ordinary people were so impressed with Jesus.

2. Trying to get rid of Jesus. Doesn't this sound familiar? Take religion out of the schools. Get rid of religious statues or saints' names in hospital wards. Get rid of Christian ideals in the protection of the life of the unborn. For Evil to triumph, all that is needed is for good people to do nothing. Doing something begins in holding onto the words of Jesus, his ideals and his example. We need to be educated in matters of faith. And we need courage to stand up for Christ.

PRAYERS

In the light of the Gospel, we pray.

That the Church will always proclaim the ideals of Jesus Christ as the foundation of a just and caring society.
Lord, hear us.

That our Government and lawmakers might always recognise and respect the wonderful human values in our Christian tradition.
Lord, hear us.

That our homes might be temples of faith and family prayer.
Lord, hear us.

That all of us will have the courage to stand up for our Christian ideals.
Lord, hear us.

(Add prayers for any personal, local or topical intentions)

Heavenly Father, hear the prayers we offer in the name of Jesus Christ, your Son, our Lord. Amen.

SATURDAY

LUKE 20:27-40

1. Is there life after death? Jesus was very clear that there is. Not just life as we know it, but so much greater. Life is changed, not ended. Just as the tree or flower or vegetable is greater than the seed which died in the earth. Nowadays there are many theories about life after death. Some say there is nothing, that death is the end of everything. Some believe in reincarnation, that we come back again in another form of body. Some say that we lose our personal identity and we are absorbed into one great cosmic spirit. No theory comes anywhere near the nobility of the teaching of Jesus. Such hope, such glory, such dignity. "They are the same as angels, and being children of the Resurrection, they are sons and daughters of God."

2. One line in today's Gospel might puzzle some people. "In the resurrection of the dead, they do not marry because they can no longer die." We can look at marriage from two angles. The question about the Resurrection and Marriage which the Sadducees raised looked at marriage as necessary for the procreation of life, for the survival of the species. But if those in Heaven do not die, then the survival of the species will no longer require marriage. However, a second purpose of marriage is the union of two people in love. Surely, the love of people in this life will continue more gloriously in Heaven. In the celebration of the Sacrament of Marriage, there is a prayer that the couple will have long and happy days together and be united forever in the Kingdom of Glory. It is something to look forward to, being united once more with family, and with the previous generations.

PRAYERS

The resurrection of Jesus Christ was the greatest moment of human history. So let us pray.

Risen Lord Jesus, may your resurrection be the foundation of our faith and the inspiration of our hope.
Lord, hear us.

Risen Lord Jesus, you invite us to share in your resurrection. Grant that we might never stray away from you by serious sin.
Lord, hear us.

May those who have strayed away from Christian beliefs come to recognise all that Jesus offers us.
Lord, hear us.

Risen Lord, grant consolation and hope to all who grieve at the loss of a loved one.
Lord, hear us.

   (Add prayers for any personal, local or topical intentions)

O God, the beginning and the end, hear the prayers we offer in the name of Jesus Christ, your Son, our Lord. Amen.

MONDAY

LUKE 21:1-4

1. Jesus observed the rich people putting their offerings into the alms box. I'm sure Jesus admired them for doing so, but he made the comment that they were giving from what they had over. The poverty-stricken widow put in two small coins but this was all she had to live on. Pope Benedict XVI wrote of the distinction between what is given in justice and what is given in charity. Whatever we have in surplus really belongs to the poor, because they have a human right to share in the world's resources. So, giving from what is surplus is a matter of justice. It is giving back to the poor what is really their right. Charity builds on justice and goes beyond it. Justice gives to the poor what is theirs by right: charity gives what is mine. The poor widow gave all she had, showing an extraordinary trust in divine providence.

2. Saint Paul made the famous statement that even if I give all I possess to the poor, but without love, then it profits me nothing. Pope Francis suggested that when we give some money to a beggar, add a little personal touch. Hand the coins rather than throw them down. Share a look, a word, a smile. The personal contact might mean more than the money. In his booklet *The Joy of the Gospel*, he declared his desire for a Church of the poor which is for the poor. They have much to teach us. They have a deep sense of faith, like the poor widow. They are close to the suffering Christ. "We need to let ourselves be evangelised by them. We need to embrace the mysterious wisdom which God wishes to share with us through them." The poverty-stricken widow, who gave all she had, was greatly admired by Jesus.

PRAYERS

Taking the teaching of Jesus to heart, we pray.

May the social teaching of the Church inspire wealthy nations to stop exploiting the poor and to give back to the poor what they have a right to in human justice.
Lord, hear us.

May we be inspired by the trust in divine providence shown by the poor widow and by many of the poor today.
Lord, hear us.

May we all have a conscience about spending money on unnecessary luxuries instead of giving to a worthy cause.
Lord, hear us.

Money is not the only way of giving. May we be generous in giving time to people, paying attention to them, really listening to them.
Lord, hear us.

(Add prayers for any personal, local or topical intentions)

O God, from whom all good gifts come, listen to our prayers in the name of Jesus Christ, your Son, our Lord. Amen.

TUESDAY

LUKE 21:5-11

1. This is the last week of the liturgical year and the readings touch on the end of life. When Luke was writing his Gospel, the magnificent Temple in Jerusalem had been razed to the ground. It was an awesome structure. A portion of the Western Wall survives. Many of the massive stones were more than two metres in length and one metre in height. Each stone was carefully sculpted and embossed in a style that was Herod's trademark. It took eighty years to build, but a mere five years later it was utterly destroyed by the savage Roman general, Titus. The unimaginable had happened. It was the same with the Titanic, struck by an iceberg on its maiden voyage. We know not the day nor the hour. A young monk asked the wise man what does it mean to be enlightened. "I know that I am going to die". The young man said, "but doesn't everybody know that they are going to die". The wise man replied, "Yes, but not everybody lives with the knowledge".

2. On September 11th, 2001, the Twin Towers in New York were destroyed. On one of the high-jacked planes, many of the doomed passengers sent messages to family and friends. Virtually all the messages were about love, affection or apology. A moment of crisis can bring startling clarity to life. People suddenly see that personal relationships matter far more than other occupations or interests. Is there anything that can last? Saint Paul said there are three things that last: faith, hope and love. We hear a lot about faith and charity. Hope does not get mentioned often enough. Faith might have to struggle through a time of darkness. Love might meet with rejection and become cold. Then it is hope which keeps us going, through the darkness and the coldness. Jesus said that your perseverance will win you your lives.

PRAYERS

In the light of the teaching of Jesus, we pray.

May we never forget that we have here no lasting city but seek one that is to come.
Lord, hear us

Grant us all the anchor of hope which will enable us to remain calm and faithful in times of storm.
Lord, hear us.

We pray for people who are being persecuted because of their religious beliefs. May their hope and courage sustain them.
Lord, hear us.

Enable us, Lord, to lift up those who are feeling down, and to bring light to those in darkness.
Lord, hear us.

(Add prayers for any personal, local or topical intentions)

God of all hopefulness, hear the prayers of your people gathered in the name of Jesus Christ, your Son, our Lord. Amen.

WEDNESDAY

LUKE 21:12-19

1. One of the seven Gifts of the Holy Spirit is fortitude. Fortitude is extraordinary courage in the face of adversity. It is a courage that goes beyond natural courage: it is supernatural. A person might be shaking with fear but still have courage. Jesus warned people who followed him that it would not always be pleasant. When Luke was writing his Gospel, Christians had first-hand experience of persecution and family rejection. In our own time, people are being persecuted because of their faith. Churches and schools are being destroyed. People are being forced to migrate from home and country. Closer to home you will see hatred in very biased media: open hatred of the Church, imbalanced discussion panels, and headlines of scandals while oblivious to all the good that faithful Christian organisations are doing. According to Jesus, that will be your opportunity to bear witness. The Holy Spirit will give the gift of fortitude, the courage to persevere in the belief that with God, all things are possible.

2. Back in the 14th Century, Dame Julian of Norwich lived in very depressing times. Her health was suffering. The world was in the grip of the Black Death, a recurring plague which devastated the population. The Church was in a mess of political intrigue and scandal. But God was with her, and she persevered with a lovely simple prayer. God is my maker, my lover and my keeper. Your endurance will win you your lives. God is my maker, my lover and my keeper.

PRAYERS

As Jesus was rejected and crucified by powerful enemies, the Church of his followers also suffered persecution.

Let us pray for Christians who are being attacked and forced to leave home and country. May the Holy Spirit strengthen them with great fortitude. May they receive a Christian welcome in their new home.
Lord, hear us.

May the Holy Spirit sustain all who have serious health problems.
Lord, hear us.

For people who are going through a family break-up, or the collapse of a business, may they receive the gift of fortitude to carry them through and beyond the crisis.
Lord, hear us.

May there be justice and peace in every land.
Lord, hear us.

(Add prayers for any personal, local or topical intentions)

O God, our maker, our lover and our keeper, graciously listen to the prayers we offer in the name of Jesus Christ, our Lord. Amen.

THURSDAY

LUKE 21:20-28

1. By the time Luke was writing, Jerusalem and the Temple had been laid waste by the Roman army, just as Jesus had predicted. When he drove the money changers out of the Temple, he was asked for a sign of his authority to do this. He said, "Destroy this Temple and in three days I will raise it up." He was speaking of the temple of his body and the three days referred to his resurrection. The Temple was intended to be the most important place for sacrifice and worship. Jesus replaced this temple of stones and identified himself as the centre of true worship. Later, Saint Paul told the Corinthians, "You are the temple of God with the Spirit of God living in you. God's temple is holy and you are that temple." The temple of stones has been replaced by the temple of people. Saint Peter called Christians living stones: "Living stones making a spiritual house as a holy priesthood to offer spiritual sacrifices made acceptable to God through Jesus Christ." We no longer have to sacrifice lambs. Jesus is known as the Lamb of God, and the celebration of the Eucharist is the Supper of the Lamb. When we gather to celebrate the Eucharist, we are the new temple in Christ.

2. "Stand erect, hold your heads high, your liberation is near at hand." Because of the war in Jerusalem, Christians in the city fled to other places. As a result, the Christian message was brought to many other people. What was originally a great tragedy turned out to be a great liberation. The same can happen in our lives. A problem becomes a possibility. We can be in a rut without realising it. We might need to be liberated from being self-centred, or from clinging too rigidly to the past, or from holding on to old grudges. You cannot put new wine into old wineskins. Sometimes God has to shock us into removing the cataracts so that we can see with new eyes. It seems a tragedy at the time, but in hindsight we will recognise it as a liberation. So, stand erect, hold your head high, your liberation is at hand.

PRAYERS

Encouraged by the words of Jesus, we pray.

That Church members might be open to liberation from holding on too rigidly to regulations and customs which were meaningful once, but have now become an obstacle rather than a help.
Lord, hear us.

For Christians who have seen their churches and homes destroyed and are forced to flee to other lands. Like the early Christians, may they become ambassadors for Christ.
Lord, hear us.

When disaster happens, may we see some good eventually coming out of the situation.
Lord hear us.

Lord grant us the faith and courage to stand erect at all times with heads held high.
Lord, hear us.

(Add prayers for any personal, local or topical intentions)

O God, hear the prayers of your priestly people, gathered here in the temple of Jesus Christ, the Lord. Amen.

FRIDAY

LUKE 21:29-33

1. "Heaven and Earth will pass away, but my words will never pass away." Sometimes people are puzzled by this statement. Will Heaven pass away? Jesus was not referring to the eternal home of God, but to the skies above us, part of the physical universe. Jesus was emphasising that his words will be relevant to all times. His message is as valid today as it was two thousand years ago, and will still be true in the future. At the end of the Sermon on the Mount, he described his words as a solid rock which gives a firm foundation to life. Time moves on. Fashions change. New inventions change the way we travel or communicate. New medications benefit our health. But the truth, ideals and values of Jesus Christ remain forever.

2. It is interesting to read Saint Justin's account of what Christians did on a Sunday morning around the year 150. On the day named after the sun, they gathered in prayer and listened to readings from the prophets and apostles. The one presiding delivered a homily connecting the readings with life. This was followed by prayers. Bread and wine mixed with water were brought up. The one presiding took the gifts and gave praise and thanks (in Greek, *eucharisian*) to God. At the end of this thanksgiving *(eucharistic)* prayer, all present gave voice to the acclamation, *Amen.* Then followed the distribution of the bread and wine over which the prayers had been said. The deacons brought portions to the sick and housebound. There was even a collection for the welfare of the poor. That was in the year 150, essentially the same as we do today. Fashions come and go, but the eternal truths and exercises of our religion go on forever. Jesus Christ yesterday, today and the same forever.

PRAYERS

The teaching of Jesus Christ is for all time. It is the mission of the Church to proclaim his message in every age.

We pray for Pope *(Name)* and all our Christian leaders. May the Holy Spirit always guide them in proclaiming the Gospel.
Lord, hear us.

We live in a time of rapid change. May our faith remain as an unshakeable source of what to believe in and what to hope for.
Lord, hear us.

For those who are searching for meaning in life: may they discover the joy of believing in Jesus Christ as the way, the truth and the life.
Lord, hear us.

May the good example of Christians be a shining light drawing the world to Christ.
Lord, hear us.

(Add prayers for any personal, local or topical intentions)

O God, the Rock of Ages, we send up our prayers to you in the name of Jesus Christ, your Son, our Lord. Amen.

SATURDAY

LUKE 21:34-36

Today is the last day of the liturgical year. Advent will commence after sunset this afternoon. Time and tide wait for nobody. The liturgical year has gone full circle. As the poet T.S. Eliot wrote, "In the end is my beginning." The line of a circle ends where it began. From God our Creator we return, hopefully, to God our ultimate destiny. We, like the year, go full circle. We know not the day nor the hour. Recall the song made famous by Frank Sinatra. "And now, the end is near, and I must face the final curtain". The song goes on to the main message, "I did it my way." The problem is that my way may not always be the right way. My way might be completely in the wrong direction. Today's Gospel mentions three wrong directions: debauchery, drunkenness and materialistic preoccupations. The Lord tells us to stay awake, praying at all times for the strength to survive all that is going to happen and to stand in confidence before the Son of Man. Don't be thinking of the final judgement as some day in a distant future. Treat each day as the day of judgement. Live each day in the presence of God. Pray that my way may be perfectly in tune with Christ's way.

PRAYERS

As we come to the end of the liturgical year, we thank God for all his blessings. And we pray for God's guidance during the coming year.

May the Church be greatly blessed by God through the liturgical celebrations of the coming year.
Lord, hear us.

May we live each day aware of God's presence in all places and at all times.
Lord, hear us

For those who have gone down the wrong road of life: may they convert their lives and return to Christ's way.
Lord, hear us.

For those who are addicted to alcohol, drugs, gambling, or pornography. May they experience God's support as they hand over their lives to God's higher power each day.
Lord, hear us.

(Add prayers for any personal, local or topical intentions)

O God, the beginning and the end of life, help us to keep our minds always focused on the right way. Through Christ our Lord. Amen.

Epilogue

. . . .

Dear Reader,

We have travelled together in the light of the daily Gospel readings. Thank you for trusting me. If you have received any insights, inspiration or challenge, thank God for it. If I have misled you in any way, please forgive me and pray for my future guidance. May the living Word of God be a lamp for your steps and a light for your eyes.

Silvester O'Flynn OFM Cap